The Chinese Cultural Revolution

A HISTORY

Paul Clark

The University of Auckland, New Zealand

CAMBRIDGE
UNIVERSITY PRESS

CAMBRIDGE UNIVERSITY PRESS
Cambridge, New York, Melbourne, Madrid, Cape Town, Singapore, São Paulo, Delhi

Cambridge University Press
32 Avenue of the Americas, New York, NY 10013-2473, USA

www.cambridge.org
Information on this title: www.cambridge.org/9780521697866

First published 2008

Printed in the United States of America

A catalog record for this publication is available from the British Library.

Library of Congress Cataloging in Publication Data
Clark, Paul
The Chinese Cultural Revolution : a history / Paul Clark.
p.   cm.
Includes bibliographical references.
ISBN 978-0-521-87515-8 (hardback) – ISBN 978-0-521-69786-6 (pbk.)
1. China – History – Cultural Revolution, 1966–1976.   2. Arts, Chinese – 20th
century.   I. Title.
DS778.7.C53   2008
951.05′6–dc22   2007037913

ISBN   978-0-521-87515-8 hardback
ISBN   978-0-521-69786-6 paperback

Contents

Figures   *page* vii

Acknowledgments   ix

Chronology of Cultural and Political Developments,
1949–1980s   xi

Introduction: A Revolution in Culture 1

1. Modelling a New Culture 10
    1. *Modernizing Chinese Opera*   11
    2. *The Start of the Cultural Revolution*   18
    3. *The First Five Model Operas*   26
    4. *The Art of the Model Operas*   43

2. Spreading the New Models 55
    1. *Proclaiming the Model Performances*   56
    2. *Other Model Operas*   62
    3. *Transplanting the Models*   73
    4. *The Importance of the Model Performances*   88
    5. *Reorganizing the Ranks*   92

3. Fixing Culture on Film 109
    1. *Films Besieged*   112
    2. *Cleansing the Ranks*   116
    3. *Fixing the Model Performances on Film*   123
    4. *New-Style Feature Films*   134
    5. *Growing the Industry, Pleasing Audiences*   145

4. Elaborating Culture: Dance, Music, Stage,
    and Fine Arts 157
    1. *Dancing for the Revolution*   158
    2. *Scoring the Revolution: Music*   175
    3. *Staging Culture: Spoken Drama,* Quyi,
        and Other Performance Forms   192
    4. *Visualizing the Modern: Fine Arts
        and Architecture*   202

5. Writing Wrongs: Public and Private Fictions
    and Resistance 217
    1. *Models on the Page: Official Literature*   218
    2. *Hidden Pleasures: Unofficial, Underground
        Literature*   226
    3. *Model Assertions: Criticizing Works*   231
    4. *Screening Resistance: Films under Attack*   240

6. Conclusion: Forcing Modernity 249

Notes   263
Bibliography   325
Index   339

Figures

1.1 Guo Jianguang and New Fourth Army men in the model opera *Shajiabang*. *page* 34

1.2 The 'three prominences' from modern operas in a comic book illustration from the Criticize Lin Biao and Confucius campaign. 47

1.3 Fang Haizhen, the all-knowing Party secretary of the model opera *On the Docks*. 51

2.1 Li Tiemei, heroine of *The Red Lantern*, as inspiration for a young militia woman. 58

2.2 Performers and Jiang Qing: 'The red lantern of the revolution lights the stage.' 60

2.3 The actor Li Guang and comrades in the modern Peking opera *Fighting on the Plain*. 69

3.1 The dockworkers and Fang Haizhen in *On the Docks*. 127

3.2 The 1930s boy hero Pan Dongzi from the 1974 film *Sparkling Red Star* as an inspiration to contemporary children. 143

3.3 A mobile projectionist shows *The Red Lantern*. 153

4.1 Qinghua, the heroine of *The Red Detachment of Women*, leaps in defiance of her landlord captors. 167

4.2 A piano accordionist entertains waiting passengers. 181

4.3 Model peasant art gallery visitors admire *The Old Party Secretary*. 210

4.4 A local farmer and a sent-down youth meet in the fields. 214

4.5 Reed Cliff Reception Room (*Ludiyan jiedaishi*), Guilin. 215

5.1 Jiang Qing as revolutionary leader of cultural activities. 242

Acknowledgments

This book has sprung from two experiences: living as a student in Beijing in 1974–1976 and writing about films in the Cultural Revolution and by a generation that those years shaped. Over the course of the research, I have been helped by many people and institutions. The people include Peter Averi, Elizabeth Caffin, Chen Xin, James Kember, Richard King, Wayne Lawrence, Ian Lilly, Pearl Picardo, and Paul Yee. Bonnie McDougall gave encouragement and concrete advice on the manuscript. Geremie Barmé commented thoughtfully on the book proposal. Chinese scholars and artists, some of whom are identified in footnotes, have given generously of their time and tried to correct my understanding. Research grants from the University of Auckland Research Committee and from its Faculty of Arts helped support several of my visits to China. A New Zealand Ministry of Foreign Affairs and Trade Historical Research Grant enabled me to use archives of a 1975 orchestra tour to China. The East-West Center in Honolulu provided space for two months of early writing. Four libraries have been keys to this project. The holdings of the Universities Service Centre for China Studies at The Chinese University of Hong Kong are a treasure trove. The Peking University Library in Beijing is a pleasure to work in, as are the National Library in Beijing and the Shanghai Library. My colleagues and students at The University of Auckland have tolerated my distraction over many years. Eric Crahan and Lewis Bateman at Cambridge in New York and Mary Paden and Andre Barnett at Aptara Inc. have made concluding the project an enjoyable experience. Jeff Lau has given more support than he realizes. All these people and places have generously tried to make this a better book, and I thank them warmly. The shortcomings are mine alone.

Chronology of Cultural and Political Developments, 1949–1980s

1949	Establishment of the People's Republic of China
1951	Mao initiates criticism of the film *The Life of Wu Xun*
1956	Hundred Flowers call for criticism of Communist Party practices
	Rural cooperatives formed, later becoming communes
1957	Anti-Rightist campaign against critics of the Party
1958	Great Leap Forward uses mass mobilization to increase production
1959–61	Famine, death of more than 30 million people
1963–64	Socialist Education Movement aims to restore support in the countryside
1964	Beijing convention of modern-subject Peking opera performances
	Criticism of films in national newspapers
1966	Conference on PLA literature and artwork, convened by Lin Biao and Jiang Qing
	By late spring, literary and other journals stop publication
	From summer, Mao reviews Red Guards in Tian'anmen Square
1967	Eight 'model performances' (*yangbanxi*) officially promulgated
1968	Mass transfer of educated young people to the countryside, military, and large enterprises begins
1969	PLA helps restore order in cities; revolutionary committees formed in enterprises, educational institutions, and local government bodies
1970	First film adaptations of the 'model performances' released
1971	Lin Biao, Mao's named successor, dies after allegedly attempting to assassinate his leader

1972   Expansion of literary and artistic activities includes new periodicals

1973   Campaign to criticize Lin Biao and Confucius begins

1974   First new Chinese feature films (other than *yangbanxi* adaptations) since the mid-1960s released

1975   Factional disputes reflected in disputes over new films
Regional and national conventions of dance, opera, and music held

1976   Premier Zhou Enlai dies (January)
5 April demonstrations in memory of Zhou
Tangshan earthquake (July)
Death of Mao (September)
Arrest of the Gang of Four (October) marks end of Cultural Revolution decade

1978   Deng Xiaoping returns to power and charts a new course for economic development

1978–84 Cultural Revolution memories recalled in 'scar literature' and films

1980s   New-style literature, art, and films represent a 'search for roots' and response to Deng's opening up to international influences

THE CHINESE CULTURAL REVOLUTION

A Revolution in Culture

The Great Proletarian Cultural Revolution was the biggest non-wartime, concentrated social upheaval in world history. Conventionally dated from 1966 to 1976, the event saw a nation of 800 million people apparently respond to the whims of one man. Mao Zedong called on Chinese, particularly the young, to renew his revolution in order that China might avoid the perils of revisionism and complacency he observed in the Soviet Union. Only through perpetual efforts could the achievements of his Chinese Communist Party be secured for future generations. But the Cultural Revolution ended shortly after the death of its instigator. China since 1978 has been transformed by economic policies that are the antithesis of Mao's. Economic reform and opening up, rather than Mao's "continuous revolution," have made China stronger and increasingly influential in the modern world.

In 2006, to mark the fortieth anniversary of the start of the Cultural Revolution and the thirtieth of its end, a major new history of these events was published in the United States. In *Mao's Last Revolution*, Roderick MacFarquhar and Michael Schoenhals argue: 'To understand the "why" of China today, one has to understand the "what" of the Cultural Revolution.'[1] In almost 700 pages, they chronicle with magisterial insight events behind this vast political and social upheaval. Using a range of materials, including publications of that decade and memoirs and other records published since, MacFarquhar and Schoenhals offer forensic analysis of the factional politics at the highest levels that propelled the majority of Chinese to be caught up in Mao's last great gesture. Most of the narrative focuses on the very top of Chinese politics, on the leadership compound in Zhongnanhai, beside the Forbidden City in the heart of Beijing.

Missing from this important study is the cultural dimension of the Cultural Revolution. Indeed MacFarquhar and Schoenhals never explain directly why Mao's movement was labelled this way. They merely suggest that Mao saw that continuing his revolution required a cultural transformation, not just a political commitment. Cultural production and consumption hardly appear in the volume at all. The occasional reference to a Peking opera, film, or ballet is always in the context of top-level political disputation.[2] Rarely do these two authors venture beyond Communist Party politics to touch on what these years meant for the ordinary citizen, obliged to perform ritual loyalty to a Beijing leadership that kept dropping people.

This present work has three purposes: to offer a history of culture during the Cultural Revolution; to provide more insight into life beyond the political or social elites during these years; and to place this decade more firmly into its twentieth-century Chinese context. A focus on culture can offer more for these latter two aims than a concentration on life at the highest echelons of politics.

A comprehensive cultural history of the Cultural Revolution has not been attempted before. Studies in Chinese and Western languages of opera, literature, art, and music have offered considerable insight into these particular activities between 1966 and 1976, although most frequently in the broader context of post-1949 or twentieth-century developments. The usual approach is to regard these ten years as a period of limited and distorted activity. Many Chinese, when asked about culture in these years, will suggest only half facetiously that there was no culture. The old joke: 'Eight-hundred million people watching eight shows' (*Bayi ren kan ba ge xi*) is frequently cited as adequately summing up culture during this decade. The following pages, drawing upon contemporary materials, recollections, and scholarly studies produced in the thirty years since Mao's death, and taking an approach that attempts to respect the professionalism and skills of many of the artists involved, will try to show how misleading that old joke is. The madness of Maoist politics can explain the stupidity and emptiness of much of cultural practice in these years. We will see how political leaders constantly worried about their control of cultural production and consumption. But there was more going on, with more lasting impacts, than a concentration on the political dimension can begin to grasp.

An approach that brings together a wide range of cultural practices, from opera and dance to writing, reading, fine arts, and even architecture, shows the interconnectedness of cultural production and consumption in these years. A model Peking opera hero had a life beyond the opera theatre, in posters, newly created folk dance, story-telling, comic books, and even on everyday household utensils. This repetitive presence illustrates the ambition of the cultural authorities to invent a new mass culture. The ubiquity of such heroes also alerts us to audience responses to these new cultural products. As we shall see, two responses are evident: an internalization of such heroics and the rhetoric surrounding it, or a counter-discourse of underground satire or elaboration of such heroics in more satisfyingly emotional and personal terms.

Coverage of everyday life in the Cultural Revolution has tended in recent decades to be the domain of the memoirist. Books in the vein of *Wild Swans* have dominated the market in Western languages, competing to present tales of suffering, persecution, and determined survival.[3] Western readers cannot help but be moved by these stories, though few such readers are able to assess the interests behind many of these tellers of family tales. Most of these memoirs have been the work of Chinese whose positions of relative social and political influence were challenged by Red Guards, Mao's youthful shock-troops in his last revolution. The writing and publication of these memoirs have often been part of a re-assertion of social status and what the authors see as political propriety, even if unacknowledged by the writers.

An account of cultural practice in the Cultural Revolution offers another way to understand what life was like for most Chinese in these ten years. The production of operas, dances, films, and fine art can take us beyond political elites to encounter a range of specialists trying to survive in challenging circumstances. Cultural consumption, in the world of Chinese audiences, can provide a glimpse into the kinds of entertainment and worldviews of ordinary Chinese subjected to much more than eight 'model performances'. Culture can help round out our picture of the Cultural Revolution, for it was at its heart.

Understanding audience responses to cultural production during the Cultural Revolution presents a challenge. Published discussion of officially approved works makes heroic assumptions about mass audience appreciation of the efforts of proper-thinking artists and their managers. Richard Kraus, in his excellent *The Party and the Arty*, alerts us to the possibilities of autonomy for audiences.[4] From his focus on the commercial commodification of art and literature since the 1980s, he argues that audiences and readers were able to establish their own relationships with works of art and literature. The following chapters share this view of Chinese audiences, applying it even to a period when the Party was making its strongest claims to control the consumption as well as the production of culture. The evidence for this audience autonomy is largely anecdotal, based on my own observations as a resident of Beijing in the last two years of the Cultural Revolution. Even published accounts, however, sometimes contain implications about actual audience responses to works. Fulmination against backwards local opera troupes presenting "black" shows, for example, indicate that some artists saw an unfulfilled demand for old-style works. Generally, the more shrill the rhetoric in praise of a new work, the more uncertain were the cultural authorities that audiences would respond in the appropriate ways. A third source of information about audiences lies in the ways in which Chinese responded after 1978 in a new cultural marketplace. I would argue that we can read responses, expectations, and interests from the 1980s, discussed by Kraus, back into the 1960s and 1970s, despite very different political circumstances. Indeed, the commercial commodification of culture that has characterized Chinese artistic life in the last quarter-century was made possible by the ideological commodification of culture in the Cultural Revolution. Constant and repeated re-working of model works in those ten years included what we might now identify as cross-genre product tie-ins. A hero of a model opera would appear in posters, songs, comic books, even on pencil cases and enamel mugs. This commodification made the rise of the cultural marketplace in the 1980s and 1990s seem less of a break with the past than has generally been assumed.

An approach through culture offers a potentially productive way to understand the power of the Cultural Revolution experience, its nature, and its repercussions. Stills from the filmed versions of the 'model performance' operas and ballets are part of the collective visual memory of the era for Chinese and for others who take an interest in the period. A study of cultural activities during these years can help our understanding of the Cultural Revolution in two ways that counter the usual interpretations of the period. First, the innovation and experimentation in the field of culture in these ten years contrasts with the orthodox emphasis on destruction and failure. Second, a cultural perspective can encourage a greater sense of the continuities between the period before and after the Cultural Revolution. Instead of simply a period of madness, the Cultural Revolution was also a time of considerable creative energy, official and unofficial, that built on earlier developments and made possible a reorientation in Chinese cultural discourse since the 1980s.

The third, general aim of this study is to show how the Cultural Revolution is best understood in its broader twentieth-century context. Those who play up the artistic excesses and limitations of these years and memoirists intent on righting wrongs both tend to emphasize the disconnection between the Cultural Revolution and the periods before and since. The madness of Mao's last revolution indeed showed the bankruptcy of his politics and made easier the task of making changes after his passing, as MacFarquhar and Schoenhals show.

Instead of being seen as an aberration, these years are better approached in the context of certain tendencies in Chinese cultural and social developments in the twentieth century. Cultural practice between 1966 and 1976 had deep roots in the Chinese experience not simply after 1949 but since China's nineteenth-century encounter with Western power and culture. A profound ambiguity pervaded Chinese responses to the new political and cultural environment created by the interruption of Chinese paramountcy in East Asia, with the rise of Western countries joined by Japan. An urge to make China again wealthy and strong was entwined with an uncertainty about the value of the Chinese cultural inheritance. By the last decades of imperial rule, social reformers, inspired in part by apparent Japanese success in facing these dilemmas of modernization, had begun to produce new ideas, media, and even institutions to strengthen the nation.[5] The Qing dynasty made a belated run in introducing new-style education and other ideas, but it was too late and imperial China came to an end in 1911.

In the second decade of the century, as Chinese power-holders tried to work out effective political structures for the new republic, Chinese intellectuals were engaged with new ideas about the way forward. The ambivalence towards the Chinese cultural heritage continued, though the complete rejection of the past was a major theme of the May Fourth movement. On 4 May 1919 students and other nationalists had demonstrated in cities across China against post–World War I concessions the warlord government was offering to Japan. The date of the demonstrations gave a name to the current efforts to make China 'wealthy and strong'. The more radical May Fourthers called for the complete abandonment of Chinese values, personified for many by Confucianism, and their replacement by foreign morality and ways of organizing society. From among the exponents of radical change came the men involved with founding the Chinese Communist Party in 1921. A Western ideology, Marxism, in its Leninist iteration, would provide a way forward for stagnant Chinese society.

The May Fourth era in the first half of the twentieth century was a period of literary and artistic innovation. A new literature, written in a new-style language that resembled everyday speech, had a strong commitment to social reform, which even more popular writing also espoused. A reformist urge was also behind efforts to modernize Chinese musical theatre, with opera artists attempting to match the newly introduced spoken drama in contemporary relevance. Film, particularly in Shanghai, China's most modern city, was largely in the hands of socially progressive artists who saw the mass audience potential of the medium to effect change.

Just as war with Japan in 1895 had been a catalyst for dynastic reform and ultimate collapse, so war with Japan from the 1930s until 1945 also had huge repercussions. The Nationalist (Guomindang) regime that had brought a degree of national unity after 1928 was revealed as weak and corrupt during the years of the Pacific War. Meanwhile the Communist Party in its wartime headquarters in Yan'an was able to experiment with new ways of mobilizing rural populations for nationalist resistance to invasion and for the transformation of social power in the countryside and towns. Leninist ideas on mobilization were combined with Chinese notions (whether imagined or real) of collectivist cooperation. Mao Zedong and party ideologues produced writings laying down policy for the return to the cities.

These policies included recasting traditional ideas about the social functions of literature and art to enlighten, uplift, and unite popular understanding of the world. In this field, as in others, imported concepts were combined with local traditions to produce a new hybrid to serve China's (and the Communist Party's) own purposes. Westernized writers and artists from such places as Beijing and Shanghai were obliged to explore ways to use popular or folk cultural traditions for new, revolutionary purposes. Such policies were put into effect, first in Yan'an and the Communist base areas, then across the nation after 1949.

The delineation of eras according to key events (for example, the 1911 fall of the Qing dynasty, the 1937 Japanese invasion of China proper, and the establishment of the People's Republic in 1949) has been the norm in thinking and writing about China in the twentieth century. A cultural perspective, however, calls into question the importance of these dates. The kinds of changes in literary style typical of the May Fourth writers publishing in *New Youth* after 1915 had origins in the new-style novels on modern subjects that emerged in the 1890s and before the fall of the dynasty. More important for art and literature in mid-century was not the Japanese occupation of much of China but the enunciation of policies on cultural practice by Mao in Yan'an in the spring of 1942. Bonnie McDougall and Kam Louie, in their comprehensive 1997 overview of Chinese writing in the twentieth century, outline a more useful periodization that acknowledges deeper changes than simply the political. They suggest three major periods: 1900–1937 'Towards a New Culture', 1938–1965 'Return to Tradition', and 1966–1989 'The Reassertion of Modernity'.[6] As the titles of each period indicate, the 1949 political divide shrinks from significance and Mao's efforts to connect with popular and elite Chinese traditions take centre stage. Xiaobing Tang, writing in 2000, offers a similar backward glance at the preceding century, identifying the coherence and totality of its literature and art.[7]

An unprecedented step in not using the standard ten-year periodization of the Cultural Revolution appeared in 2005 in a 600-page chronology of dance in China since 1949. Mao Hui and the rest of the editorial team make their breaks in 1965 and, remarkably for a Chinese publication, in 1975. For a Chinese book the step is so bold that the editors chose not to explain their decision. But the content of the chronology reinforces the view that change in this area of cultural practice was not dependent upon political chronologies.[8] The following chapters will illustrate three broad phases into which cultural activities and politics during the ten years after 1966 can be divided. An initial period (1966–1968) was typified by urban social unrest, Red Guard activism, and a cultish focus on Mao. The second period can be identified with the People's Liberation Army, which helped restore order in 1969 and lost its commander-in-chief in 1971 when Lin Biao, Mao's chosen successor, fell from power (and from the skies over Mongolia, while fleeing after an alleged attempt on Mao's life). During this second phase, millions of ex–Red Guards and other young people were 'sent down' to the countryside. From the early 1970s, a degree of routinism returned to Chinese cultural and even political life. Cultural activities, including the publication of literary journals, new feature films, and a broadening of performing and literary genres, saw a marked expansion.

The following pages will show how in the realms of cultural production and consumption the activities in the ten years after 1966 drew upon efforts since even before Yan'an days to combine Western and Chinese traditions and elements in new cultural practice. It is no coincidence that the eight so-called model performances of the Cultural Revolution consisted of modernized musical theatre with deep roots in Chinese popular culture, two ballets which reworked a Western classical genre, and a symphonic music piece based on one of the modern-style operas. I will try to show how the whole range of cultural activity in 1966–1976 continued, deepened, or distorted the modern inheritance of cultural responses to China's changing global condition. Making China's culture modern, I argue, was as much an obsession of artists and leaders in the Cultural Revolution as it had been for their counterparts during the previous eighty and more years.

In examining cultural continuities in the twentieth century, Miriam Hansen's concept of 'vernacular modernism' has particular relevance. Hansen's writings on American and other films have been applied by

Zhang Zhen to Chinese film culture from its beginnings in 'shadow plays' in the 1890s until the 1930s.[9] Zhang makes clear the popular (or vernacular) responses to the modern that film-going reflected and enhanced among urban Chinese, especially in Shanghai. 'Vernacular modernism' offers an alternative, or counter, discourse to the elitist ambitions of political and social leaders. Neither Hansen nor Zhang have applied this concept to post-1949 Chinese cultural history. The Cultural Revolution experiment can be seen in the light of their writings as a doomed attempt to combine the vernacular and the elitist in a modern project. Mao and his supporters could be no more successful than social and political leaders had been in the first half of the century in directing popular cultural discourse.

The popular initiative in making Cultural Revolution culture their own, as outlined in the following chapters, fits well with the experience of vernacular modernism before 1937. These tensions between elitist and educated ambition and popular response and resistance underline the following chapters. They alert us to the issue of three realms of audience and artist: the truly popular, the educated, and a middle field in which learned writers borrowed from and contributed to the elaboration of what were essentially vernacular forms. As Patrick Hanan and others have shown in popular fiction and theatre before the twentieth century, elite writers could enjoy and even produce works that revealed strong roots in vernacular, popular traditions.[10] These three kinds of audiences differ from the readership topography suggested by Bonnie McDougall in her stimulating essay collection, *Fictional Authors, Imaginary Audiences*.[11] Intent on demolishing the fiction of a unitary audience for Chinese fiction from the 1950s to the 1980s, McDougall identifies four broad groups. The primary readership consists of educated young people. A secondary audience is made up of literary intellectuals and cultural bureaucrats, who are joined by two additional audiences outside China (Sinologists and Overseas Chinese, and general readers). An examination of audiences for literature, performing arts, and fine arts during the Cultural Revolution confirms the importance of the first two audiences outlined by McDougall. During these ten years, the secondary audience was at its most powerful and ambitious in seeking to shape cultural practice. They sought, with some success it would seem, to expand the primary audience to include people from a wider range of educational and generational backgrounds. Cultural Revolution art and literature attempted to embrace and promote the popular, the educated, and the modern.

Instead of being a sidetrack on China's road to modern wealth and influence, the Cultural Revolution is best understood as firmly part of the process. The powerful themes of the Cultural Revolution, including mass mobilization and the renewed push to combine Western and Chinese elements in a new-style mass culture, fit well with the previous decades' obsessions. Suffering subjected on some Chinese between 1966 and 1976 should not obscure these long-term continuities with the preceding and following decades. Instead of being perceived simply as a period of destruction or as an arena of factional political conflict, the Cultural Revolution can be seen also as an era of modern innovation and efforts at real change in China's cultural inheritance. Failed or half-hearted attempts to update cultural forms stuck in conventions for artists and audiences gave way to an all-out shift to modern subject matter, forms, and values. The ultimate failure of these efforts or rejection of their absurd politics does not detract from the astonishing innovation and commitment they represented. The participants in these upheavals went on to grasp the opportunities provided with economic changes after the 1970s. The ambition of Cultural Revolution culture continued to reverberate even in the art and writing in the 1980s onwards that seemed to reject utterly Maoist culture.

The first chapter starts with the origins of Cultural Revolution innovation in the modernized Peking opera. It will show how these new operas were the product of decades of experimentation by a range of modern specialists working with performers. Chapter Two examines the ways in which these new operas and ballets became models for a new mass culture, including the so-called transplanting of the operas into other regional musical theatres. Films are the focus of Chapter Three, for it was in film that the models and their innovation became most familiar to Chinese audiences. Chapter Four discusses the expansion of official and unofficial cultural production in the 1970s, including attempts to popularize and modernize dance, music, other stage works, fine arts, and architecture. Writing and reading are examined in Chapter Five, in which the reaction of audiences, artists, and some politicians against excessive political interference is also discussed. The conclusion suggests some of the ways in which Cultural Revolution modernity enabled the further experimentation of the 1980s and after.

CHAPTER ONE

Modelling a New Culture

On the night of 28 August 1977, Yu Huiyong, the former Minister of Culture, was rushed to hospital. Earlier that day, after more than ten months' detention at the State Council's No. 4 Guesthouse, he had written a last testament and then drunk a bottle of sulphuric acid, used as lavatory disinfectant. For three days Yu lay in agony, conscious for most of the time while the acid ate away at his throat and stomach, until he died on the last day of August. It was a terrible end for one of the artists most responsible for the key cultural artefacts of the Cultural Revolution.

Yu Huiyong had been involved in the creation of several of the model operas and other works of the new culture of the 1966–1976 repertoire. Born in 1925, Yu had joined a Communist performance troupe as a teenager during the War of Resistance. Assigned after 1949 to work at Shanghai's music conservatory, he helped transform the institution from a somewhat Western-oriented, middle-class school into a training ground for a musical corps for Mao's China. By the start of the Cultural Revolution in 1966, Yu Huiyong headed the theory department at the Shanghai Conservatory. He had also become head of the Drama Reform and Creative Group, directing Chinese opera modernization in the city. By the early 1970s Yu had become Minister of Culture in Beijing. It was a long way from a peasant background in Shandong province.[1]

Opera modernization, which Yu Huiyong helped lead, was at the heart of the cultural innovation of the Cultural Revolution. Five of the eight 'model performances' that were initially presented as touchstones of artistic creativity were modernized Peking operas devised by people like Yu. An examination of the origins of modernized Chinese opera reveals that the cultural developments of 1966–1976 began before 1949. These model works grew out of the efforts of a wide range of artists, professionals, and specialists that had begun even before 1949. This chapter will trace the modernizing of opera before the mid-1960s before outlining the central place of culture in the start of the Cultural Revolution. The innovations of the five model operas are our central concerns.

We begin with an overview of the project to make Chinese opera more relevant to contemporary experience. This modernization work became entangled with the determination of some Chinese leaders to strengthen the political thrust of cultural production. A modernized opera with a dynastic setting offered a touchstone for rhetoric about cultural purposes, at what became the start of the Cultural Revolution. The third section here examines the creation of the first five-model, modernized Peking operas. The chapter ends with some observations about the world of these new-style operas.

I. MODERNIZING CHINESE OPERA

Chinese opera was at the core of Cultural Revolution efforts at modernization. Opera had presented perhaps the biggest challenge to Chinese cultural modernizers throughout the twentieth century. The Communists after 1949 continued this work. A relatively young artistic form (having only several centuries of history) and one distinct from the high culture of scholar-officials, Chinese musical theatre was an actor-centred art. Its transmission of stories, music, and singing styles from the past was by old style master student training. All these features made opera seem the most resistant to modernizing of all forms in the Chinese cultural heritage. Waves of modernizers, from the reformist or iconoclastic intellectuals of the May Fourth era in the second through fourth decades of the twentieth century through the Communist revolutionaries with equally totalistic rejections of the past, all denounced the 'feudal' thinking that opera purveyed.[2]

Like the established classical operas of Western musical theatre, audiences knew the story in advance. The interest was in the skill of the performers in presenting the characters in song, recitative, and to a lesser extent movement. Its traditional formalism of role, musical type, and story made Chinese opera vulnerable in a modernizing world and an obvious target for reform. The usual response to the challenge of remaining relevant in the first half of the twentieth century was to adapt the subject matter of operas to tell contemporary tales using the old performance forms. In this area, the influence of spoken drama (*huaju*), a stage art introduced only in the first decade of the century, can be identified. Perhaps as important in encouraging opera to simplify and to dramatize its stories and subjects was the cinema. Even in silence, the stories, emotions, and drama of Hollywood and Shanghai-made films had made a big impression on viewers. Opera reformers tried to replicate that effect by emulating the new art forms. The reformed operas were shortened and became more focused. They had more deliberate arrangement towards a climax and denouement, in the manner of Western drama or film. The musical motifs were drawn from a narrower range and differentiated more clearly to enhance the concentration on plot development.

Urban and educated audiences seem to have appreciated the effort towards modernization that these adjustments to the old forms represented. Political reformers (and even underground revolutionaries associated with the Chinese Communist Party) saw also the potential of such a well-rooted popular art to spread progressive messages to a wide audience.[3] Broader, non-urban, and less-educated audiences had fewer opportunities to see the reformed, modernized operas. When they were seen, a natural conservatism seems to have ruled out much popularity.

When the Chinese Communist Party established its national regime after 1949, these efforts at reform of old opera tales continued, on a larger and centralized scale. Like film, reformed opera was seen as having a great part to play in the modernization of popular culture and the dissemination of new, approved ideas. On 2 October 1949, one day after the proclamation of the People's Republic, the National Opera Reform Committee (*Zhonghua quanguo xiqu gaige weiyuanhui*) was established.[4] Through this and subsequent bodies, opera personnel were subject to political training, the troupes were re-organized and, those approved, put on a sounder financial footing, and harmful plays were banned.

The trial performance convention (*xiqu guanmo yanchu dahui*) became a standard device to promote and regularize opera modernization. The Cultural Revolution 'model operas' were also tested and refined at such gatherings. Actors, musicians, writers, and managers from opera troupes would gather together to watch trial performances, hear statements of official policy, and exchange opinions on the works seen. At the first of these conventions in 1952, only eight out of eighty-two performances had been on contemporary subject matter.[5] Clearly, the re-working of traditional opera presented major problems. Audiences had a long history of opera appreciation with which to compare the new-style plays. Artists had generations of conventions in all aspects of performance which might or might not be changed in the name of reform.[6] Both performers and audiences chafed as reform-minded leaders and writers, such as the musicologist and composer Yu Huiyong, took up the challenge of opera modernization.

The Great Leap Forward in 1958 was Mao Zedong's way of jumping over the expected stages of industrial development to achieve international levels of prosperity and modernization through human effort on a massive scale. The Great Leap reflected efforts to find Chinese ways to modernization, ones less dependent until then on Soviet Union models and advice. In art and literature, the emphasis on 'socialist realism' was replaced by a new coinage by Chairman Mao: 'the combination of revolutionary realism and revolutionary romanticism' (*geming xianshizhuyi yu geming langmanzhuyi xiang jiehe*). Under this new rubric, more acknowledgement could be made of Chinese traditional aesthetic practices.[7] Here Chinese opera could also find a new relevance to the modernizing program. In a cultural enterprise which valued the social and transformative functions of art and literature more highly than any other feature, modern subject matter could help save Chinese opera from threatened eventual marginalization. The post-1949 centralized system of opera management made such efforts more effective: Troupes were now state run or local-government supervised, in a hierarchy which attached more prestige to companies identified with central, provincial, or major municipal cultural bureaus. The new organization proffered more stability, with regular salaries, subsidies for performances, and guaranteed access to performance spaces. The price was a greater degree of intervention by the new paymasters. This intervention took many guises, as the three reforms (of repertoire, personnel, and system) were carried out at all levels.

The central place of roles in opera proved the greatest challenge. Modern subject matter threatened to make redundant these roles-types. Advocates of the modern subjects expected opera to present stories similar to those promulgated in the new films, spoken plays, and fiction. Workers, peasants, and soldiers (*gong-nong-bing*) were the central characters in the new art and literature. There was no ready match with the customary role types in Peking opera and other regional forms. The noble general of old-style opera could not be easily transformed into the self-sacrificing ordinary soldier of the new canon. A beautiful maiden, usually accompanied by a mischievous maid or harridan elderly chaperone, could not be switched into the role of self-confident, public-spirited young peasant woman leading communization in the countryside. Blushing young scholars, much given to being smitten by lovely, almost unattainable young women, could not instantly become determined workers exposing class enemies in the factory.

The national tenth anniversary celebrations in October 1959 included sustained performances of several newly revised traditional operas in major cities. They reportedly aroused hearty audience enthusiasm and specialists' endorsement. In contrast, modern-subject operas were hard to find in the commemorations.[8] The real push for the creation of operas on modern subjects emerged after 1963 in close association with a number of related developments in Chinese politics. An old-fashioned but still immensely popular art form like Chinese opera became an obvious target for the attention of those who wanted to transform Chinese culture. The eminence of major opera actors, true stars on China's stages, could disrupt these plans. The complete modernization of Chinese opera, particularly what had become the 'national genre', Peking opera, had immense symbolic value to the cultural radicals. If this essential art could be transformed, then the rest of China's literature and art would follow. For those engaged in this endeavour, the pressure to succeed was enormous.

Two first skirmishes in this push came in 1963: the call to 'write about the 13 years' and the debate on 'ghost plays'. At New Year 1963 the mayor of Shanghai, Ke Qingshi, who, like many Chinese political leaders, took a keen interest in cultural policy, enunciated the idea of 'writing about the [past] 13 years' (xie shisan nian).[9] He meant, of course, the thirteen years since 1949. Calling for a renewed emphasis on writing and art about the New China (as it was known) was a way to shift the focus on a number of artistic and literary fronts, including slowing reform of traditional-style operas and filming the classic works of early twentieth-century May Fourth literature.[10] This new slogan gave impetus to work on creating Peking and other operas on new-style, modern subjects.

'Ghost plays' had been a contentious issue for some time in opera circles and for the cultural leadership. Other performing arts and contemporary fiction generally excluded this supernatural element, so the inclusion of ghosts in operas made them more welcome for many viewers.[11] Although the Ministry of Culture in a March 1963 report noted a positive element in some ghost plays that presented, through ghostly interventions, the spirit of resistance among oppressed people, ghost plays were effectively banned after these debates.[12]

History plays (lishiju) next proved a ground for contention on directions in China's new cultural project. For the Communist Party China's socialist future was pre-determined; it was the past that needed proper sorting out, for it provided scope to other users of history. Mao Zedong sanctioned the old notion of 'using the past for present purposes' (guweijinyong). It was not surprising that others took up the idea but for purposes of which Mao would not necessarily approve.

Most such plays were somewhat interminable retellings of history, lacking in drama, pace, and interest expected by most operagoers. They were, after all, a hybrid form with a mix of regular dialogue, recitative, and sung arias. The Beijing deputy mayor and historian Wu Han, a specialist on the Ming dynasty (1368–1644), saw history plays as a means for professionals

like himself to reach beyond their classrooms and spread popular understanding of the past.[13] Wu Han had something of a vested interest in this
issue, as in 1959 he had written a history play titled *Hai Rui Dismissed
from Office* (*Hai Rui ba guan*). This had been produced on stage in Beijing,
though only briefly, apparently because of audience indifference.[14]

Even this relatively new form of opera could not provide a way out
of the problem of the modernization of Chinese musical theatre. The
issue was more pressing by the early 1960s, as the dissonance become
more conspicuous between a resolutely contemporary focus in fiction,
films, poetry, spoken drama, and the visual arts and the glaringly antique
concentration on traditional costumes, make-up, and plots of the opera
stage. Audiences may still have enjoyed the skills and familiarity of these
old sung dramas, but the gap was obvious to many viewers.

True reform could only come with the creation of Chinese operas about
non-traditional, preferably contemporary topics. Efforts to bring such
works to audiences had been fitfully made throughout the 1950s, though
with only limited success from an artistic or audience point of view. As
political radicals gathered support in competition with more conservative
leaders, opera modernization became an arena for engagement by both
sides in the political debate. The first signs of the Cultural Revolution
were seen in the opera theatres and in the pages of specialist journals.[15]

By 1964 these considerations of how traditional opera might be modernized and how operas could present modern-day subject matter and
characters came to a head. Most emphasis was put on using Peking opera,
with up to 100 Peking opera companies nationwide engaged by the spring
of 1964 in performing or rehearsing modern plays. One immediate result
of these endeavours with modern subjects was an apparent expansion
of opera audiences. The Beijing Peking Opera Company's performance of
Sparks amid the Reeds (*Lu dang huozhong*), itself an adaptation of a modern Shanghai opera (*Huju*), reportedly attracted an audience of 'worker,
peasant, and soldier' masses and young students who were not accus-
tomed to watching Peking opera. Some opera troupes were more active
than others. The Changchun City Peking Opera Company had presented
860 performances of modern operas over the previous seven years. The
word needed to be spread. Between February and April 1964, the Shanghai branch of the China Opera Artists Association held three symposia on
modern-subject Peking opera, discussing the challenges of presenting the
new stories.[16] The main national drama periodical *Xiju bao* produced a
summary of discussions on modern subjects in Peking opera in May 1964.
Audience responses were an underlying issue in these specialist debates.[17]
Relying purely on traditional skills in modern-style operas was wrong.

New tools and methods were needed to present modern life, building on rather than being confined by operatic traditions.[18]

One of the most effective ways to tackle the problems of modernizing opera and presenting modern subjects was to actually produce such new-style works and seek feedback from specialists and audiences on what worked and what did not. In the summer of 1964, the most significant of these conventions, and one of the few such national-level gatherings, was held in Beijing. Cultural Revolution leaders subsequently invested this convention with enormous importance, citing it as the launching pad for the model operas of those years and as the place where Jiang Qing's stamp was firmly placed on the opera modernization enterprise.

Even without this retrospective gloss, the 1964 Beijing modern Peking opera trial performance convention (*Jingju xiandaixi guanmo yanchu da hui*) was indeed significant. It lasted five weeks (from 5 June until 12 July) and presented close to 200 performances involving more than 2,000 members of twenty-nine opera companies as well as more than 300 members of special trial troupes. They mounted thirty-five different operas to live audiences totalling 200,000. A further 460,000 viewers watched courtesy of Beijing Television, which broadcast the convention over twenty-three nights.[19] The whole event took on something of a victory celebration for the new-style operas on modern subjects.

Mao's wife, Jiang Qing, was later credited with the success of the 1964 national opera convention. In a contemporary report, however, she does not appear in the photograph of the national leadership on the dais at the closing ceremony. Premier Zhou Enlai, Beijing mayor Peng Zhen, and Luo Ruiqing take pride of place in the photo, though prominent playwright and film scenarist Xia Yan is also featured, having positioned himself in the row behind the premier. Xia was to become a major target of condemnation of literary and artistic hegemons in 1966. Jiang Qing, however, was among five major speakers at the convention whose speeches the participants are reported as sincerely studying and discussing. The other speakers were Premier Zhou, Mayor Peng, and alternate Politburo members Lu Dingyi and Kang Sheng.[20]

More than fifty speciality discussions were held during the five weeks of the convention. Among the resolutions was a call for greater unity within and between opera companies, which hinted at competition and jealousy in the efforts to produce new-style operas. Also reported were calls to strengthen progressively the system of using directors. Using specialist theatre directors was a new element, closely associated with the effectiveness of the new modern operas presented that summer in Beijing.

Major figures from sister arts (spoken drama, modern musicals, and film) attended the discussions, as did personages from the musical world. The new music of the modern operas was singled out for particular praise in the way it broke down old narrowness. Also attending were actors and writers from other sung theatre genres: Hebei *bangzi* (clapper opera), Sichuan opera, Cantonese opera, and Shaoxing opera, among others. These artists reportedly agreed that the new-style Peking opera indicated the way forward for other opera forms, being models (*bangyang*) for the other operas. Cited in reports are the names of younger actors who identified themselves as revolutionary successors to the opera heritage.

Many of the convention's works were drawn from plays (*huaju*), feature films, and modern musicals, in the kind of cross-pollination that specialists had advocated as a means of updating Peking opera. Of the thirty-five works presented (including nine short operas), all but two were not adaptations of film scripts, spoken plays, novels, or earlier published works.[21] The Beijing Peking Opera No. 2 Company's *Red Guards of Lake Hong* (*Honghu chiweidui*), for example, was based on the modern musical from the late 1950s that had been turned into a highly popular movie in 1961. The Nanchang City Peking Opera Company from Jiangxi province had adapted into a short opera the popular 1962 film *Li Shuangshuang*, itself an adaptation of a novel about domestic strife between a peasant couple during the formation of communes in the 1950s countryside. The Tianjin City Peking Opera Company's *Gate No. 6* (*Liu hao men*) told a story of waterfront worker organization in the early 1950s. It had also been a spoken drama and one of the early works of the newly nationalized film industry.

A long-term assessment of the achievements of the 1964 Peking opera convention rates it highly, despite the subsequent gloss put on the event by Cultural Revolution radicals. Writers in 1999 noted the watchability (*kekanxing*) of a lot of the operas, with their lively plots and reflection of the richness and diversity of modern life. Real progress in dealing with the problems of modernizing Peking opera was evident. This helped account for the reported attraction of new kinds of audience members to the opera theatres during the 1964 convention, particularly young people for whom the old-style opera was a semi-incomprehensible bore enjoyed only by parents and grandparents.[22]

The national convention in the summer of 1964 gave a major impetus to a number of developments, among them the involvement of figures like Jiang Qing in the opera modernization project. As the first rumblings of what became the Cultural Revolution began to sound, it was clear that Peking opera would have a central role in further cultural developments.

Versions of four of the five modern Peking operas in the eight Cultural
Revolution model performances had been presented at the Beijing convention in 1964. Audiences, some of whom had earlier been guinea pigs
for the fitful efforts to find new ways to present new subject matter, could
only wait and see what would evolve.

2. THE START OF THE CULTURAL REVOLUTION

By the mid-1960s, audiences in opera and spoken drama theatres and in
cinemas had begun to notice changes in what they could watch and listen
to. As new-style, modern-subject Peking opera and other opera forms
became more available, the old, historical opera of painted faces and
handsome scholars became harder to find on China's stages. Film buffs
observed a similar narrowing of choice, as more and more of the new films
from the studios presented celluloid versions of contemporary life: 'boy
meets tractor', as the old joke described these resolutely revolutionary
works. More nuanced productions, based on fiction of the May Fourth
era, for example, were no longer made, and such films from the early 1960s
came under sustained criticism in the media from 1964. In spoken drama
theatres, the plays performed took on a plainness, as writers concentrated
on stories set in post-1949 times, finding the necessary conflict to propel
the drama in class enemies, spies, and recalcitrant elements in society. The
performing arts in general were becoming more uniform, more obvious,
and more contemporary.

Historians of the Cultural Revolution usually date the start of the 'ten
years of catastrophe' to 16 May 1966, when the Chinese Communist
Central Committee Politburo issued a central document (Zhongfa) about
the ideological errors of the People's Liberation Army chief of staff, which
spoke of a 'Great Cultural Revolution'. Politics clearly entered a new, more
challenging phase, particularly for those who held power. From a cultural
standpoint, dating the start of the Cultural Revolution is a much less
clear-cut proposition. Cultural challenges to existing holders of influence
in the literary and artistic realms had been mounting for at least two
years before that date. This was not surprising, as culture was the arena
in which rivalries were indirectly aired and advanced before being openly
expressed in the political media.

Different areas of cultural life, especially in the performing arts in the
period from 1964 to 1966, saw rising tensions as cultural and political
insurgents asserted their views against those of more established figures.
Modern-subject operas was one such area in which relative newcomers
made rapid advances. History plays were another arena of dispute, in

this case over the appropriate use of historical allegory to make commentary on the present day. Filmmaking was a third realm of conflict, being vulnerable to attack from puritanical adherents of narrower views of politics.

Indeed, this religious metaphor (Puritans versus the established church, perhaps, or even the Salem witch trials) may be a productive way to think about the start of the Cultural Revolution and the difficulty of assigning roles and responsibilities to different players. As in a religious conflict, moral superiority was assumed by all sides, with no clear means of assessing who, in fact, was innocent of charges, if anyone was. The commitment of different players to their views had in itself a religious, in some cases fanatical, quality that could seem inexplicable to agnostic or secular observers. As could happen in ecclesiastical disputes, arguments tended to rapidly reach a point in which absolutist terms were used, making even more opaque the actual reasons for the initial conflict.

A knowledge of what happened to many of the establishment figures who were the targets of the insurgents in the mid-1960s further complicates our understanding of the start of the Cultural Revolution. Broken bodies and shattered limbs that emerged from the shadows in the 1970s served as an indictment of the evils of Cultural Revolution excess. This suffering cannot be ignored or explained away as a marginal, unsanctioned accident. But the obvious damage also clouds assessments of the insurgents' purposes by lending a nobility to their targets of criticism. Sympathy for suffering by pre–Cultural Revolution cultural establishment figures may obscure proper judgements of these persons' actions and attitudes when in positions of power for the seventeen years after 1949. In such conflicts, a monopoly of innocence on one side or in one group's hands is a rarity. Retrospective innocence is even more suspect.

One strand that helped form the start of the Cultural Revolution involved film. In 1964 several films became objects of criticism in the pages of *People's Daily* and hence newspapers across the nation. They included *Jiangnan in the North (Bei guo jiangnan)*, *Early Spring in February (Zao chun eryue)*, *The Lin Family Shop (Lin jia puzi)*, and *Stage Sisters (Wutai jiemei)*. *Early Spring in February* and *The Lin Family Shop* shared origins in short stories written in the 1930s. Criticism of these films could accordingly be interpreted as an attack on the May Fourth, reformist heritage. These kinds of writers and artists represented a pluralistic alternative to the certainties and somewhat narrower, plainer possibilities enunciated as cultural policy after Mao's Yan'an *Talks* in 1942.[23]

History plays were the immediate objects of criticism at the start of the Cultural Revolution. History caught up with the historian Wu Han when in September 1964 Mao Zedong directed that a collection of thirty-nine literary documents be distributed nationwide down to cadres at the county level, for study and criticism. Among them was Wu Han's 1961 script of *Hai Rui Dismissed from Office*, which apparently had been performed over a four-year period.[24] Over a year later, in November 1965, Shanghai's main daily newspaper, *Wenhui bao*, published a lengthy criticism of *Hai Rui Dismissed from Office*. Twenty days later the same piece was published, with a substantial editor's preface, by *People's Daily* in Beijing. The article's author was Yao Wenyuan, an ambitious writer mostly on Marxist political theory, who was based in Shanghai. He had allegedly spent ten months writing and polishing the article, with assistance from political allies.[25] The thrust of Yao's argument was that Hai Rui could not be regarded as some sort of proto-revolutionary and defender of the common people against the abuses of the dynastic state. While Wu Han was still referred to as a 'comrade', his play was identified by 'many articles' as a 'poisonous weed' (*du cao*). This label was to be extensively used in the next several months, as the Cultural Revolution got under way in earnest.

Mao Zedong was more direct on why Wu Han and his Hai Rui play were condemned. Speaking in December 1965 in Hangzhou, where he had a habit of escaping the dry cold of Beijing each winter, Mao reportedly remarked: 'The crucial point about the play is "dismissed from office" (*ba guan*). The Jiaqing emperor dismissed Hai Rui from his office. In 1959 we dismissed Peng Dehuai from his office.'[26] Marshall Peng had been one of the heroes of the civil war in the 1940s and had led the Chinese troops sent to aid North Korea in the early 1950s. At a 1959 Party plenum at the resort of Lushan, Jiangxi province, Peng Dehuai had led criticism of Mao's Great Leap Forward excesses, pointing out the neglect of basic agricultural production and irrigation in the mad rush to report wildly successful results. For his troubles, Peng Dehuai was dismissed from all government positions and expelled from the Communist Party. It was not a big leap to see parallels, as Mao did, between the Ming scholar-official Hai Rui and Mao's former comrade-in-arms.[27] By late 1965 Mao was back in a strong enough position to condemn publicly this allegorical attack.

On 27 December 1965, the day after Mao's seventy-second birthday and four weeks since the *People's Daily* publicized Yao Wenyuan's criticism, the *Beijing Daily* published Wu Han's 'self-criticism' (*ziwo piping*). Wu acknowledged the limitations of Hai Rui as a figure from the 'feudal' past and offered an historian's explanation of some of the Ming dynasty land policies referred to in his play. Zhang Chunqiao, a cultural leader in

Shanghai and ally of Jiang Qing, was reportedly furious that Wu Han had not made a sufficiently abject confession of wrongdoing. But clearly the historian was in deep political trouble. So too were other newly written operas. *Hai Rui Memorializes the Emperor, Xie Yaohuan*, a play about China's only female emperor, Wu Zetian (624–705 AD), and a ghost play, *Li Huiniang*, also came under fire.[28]

The modern-subject opera strand that helped form the start of the Cultural Revolution was the positive contribution to this saga. Criticism of films and of history plays allegedly showed what was wrong with cultural policy and with what audiences had been watching. In a sense, modernized opera could show audiences what was right. The attention given the summer 1964 convention in Beijing sent a message to all parties involved. The kind of ritual performance when national leaders paraded onto a stage and sat at covered tables listening to or giving speeches could send powerful signals, even if we ignore what the speeches said. The performance itself was sufficient.

The momentum was clearly in the modern operas' favor. An indication of this came in an unprecedented 'message to readers' from the editors of *Xiju bao*, the pre-eminent theatre journal published by the China Theatre Artists Association. The two-page statement at the very end of the October 1964 issue was an example of the self-criticism that was standard practice in Communist China as a confession of sins and promise of improvement. The foremost area in which mistakes had been made, the editors noted, was in their lack of support and coverage of modern-subject opera, to which they had held an indifferent, nitpicking attitude.[29]

Work at creating, refining, and performing new modern operas and other drama continued apace in 1965, inspired by the success of the summer 1964 convention in Beijing. During 1965 six major regions held eight conventions for trial performances of new stage works.[30] The persistent regionalism is noteworthy. The East China modern opera convention in early 1965 included Shaoxing opera (*Yueju*), Shandong opera (*Lüju*), Wuxi opera (*Xiju*), *Huangmeixi* from Anhui province, and thirteen other kinds of local opera, but not a single Peking opera.[31] Opera companies tried, as political and other conditions allowed, to create performances that would appeal to their actual and potential local audiences. Peking opera may have been the 'national' opera form, but it was a status enjoyed by default, deriving from the nation's capital being in Beijing. Given a choice, audiences appear to have continued to prefer their own, local versions of musical drama. The subject matter, stories, and characters on the stage may have been novel in these new-fangled operas, but at least the language and much of the music were nicely familiar. On the opera stage, localism persisted as late as the eve of the Cultural Revolution. Other performing arts, including film, in some senses the most modern, took on a national role. For Peking opera to assume its national role would not necessarily be easy, at least among many opera professionals and among operagoers with their strong local ties.

Other performing arts were also under pressure to respond to the increasing political demands being placed on the arts. The Socialist Education Movement (*Shehuizhuyi jiaoyu yundong*) had begun in 1963 and was ongoing. It formed another thread in the lead up to the start of the Cultural Revolution. This movement served several, somewhat disparate purposes for both the recipients of the 'socialist education' and for the supposed providers. Mao Zedong launched the campaign in part in response to the crisis in the countryside brought on by widespread famine and death because of the excesses of the Great Leap Forward.[32] The Party needed to address the loss of faith that lay behind peasant indifference and even unrest. The movement amounted to a major infusion of urban talent and organizational skills into the countryside. Peasants in the 1940s civil war had provided Mao with the means to surround the cities and win victory against his enemies. In the early 1960s, peasants could again assist the chairman to assert himself against his more moderate rivals in the Party leadership.

The parallel function of the Socialist Education Movement was its effects on the thousands of urban intellectuals who participated in it by being sent to the countryside. Starvation in 1959–1961 had not been confined to rural areas, despite government efforts at least in the capital to disguise the extent of the problem. The movement was a means to assert discipline and control over disgruntled segments of urban populations, obliging them to rethink their positions and attitudes. Learning from the peasants had been placed firmly in the Party's canon in Yan'an days.

Included in the stream of urban dwellers to the countryside during this political campaign were artists and performers, as well as writers and other cultural professionals. Performances by opera companies, normally based in the cities and not known for travelling shows, were a way to raise peasant morale. They were also opportunities for the opera professionals to mount two kinds of productions. Traditional, old-style performances by then were frowned upon by the cultural authorities and almost impossible to present in urban theatres without risk of condemnation by politicians. In the countryside, controls, as always, were somewhat looser, even in the midst of a campaign to reassert Party influence. While generally not reported in the media at the time (for fear of encouraging backsliders), later Cultural Revolution denunciations of individual opera company members showed that some companies did indeed present the traditional plays. Audiences starved of live performances and nostalgic for the old, familiar operas presumably appreciated these rare opportunities to indulge memories. For performers, this 'going deep into life' (*shenru shenghuo*) could have practical benefits in exposing artists to the ways the people they portrayed in the modern-subject plays actually lived and moved.

On the eve of the Cultural Revolution, the military gave further impetus to these efforts at creating a new style of popular culture. In February 1966 the People's Liberation Army General Political Department held a nineteen-day conference in Shanghai on army literary and art work. Ten years later this was identified as a key moment in the alleged conspiracy between Lin Biao, the army head, and Jiang Qing, Mao's wife. At the meeting, held in Shanghai supposedly to be beyond immediate interference from opponents in Beijing, lavish praise was heaped upon the rather simplistic spoken dramas and other morality plays that had come out of the Socialist Education Movement. Various targets were attacked, including Wu Han and his Hai Rui obsession. In early April Mao Zedong is reported to have made three revisions of the minutes of the conference, then ordered them distributed for internal Party study nationwide.[33] The military element in much of the model works of the Cultural Revolution will become clear later in this study.

Indeed, it was in a military medium that the first shots of the Cultural Revolution were fired. On 18 April 1966, the *Liberation Army Daily* (*Jiefangjun bao*) published an editorial under the headline 'Raise High the Glorious Red Flag of Mao Zedong Thought, Actively Participate in a Socialist Cultural Revolution' (*jiji canjia shehuizhuyi wenhua da geming*). For the first time in such a widely distributed medium, the term 'counter-revolutionary revisionist black line in art and literature' was used.

The minutes (*jiyao*), identified in some contexts as 'Minutes of the Conference on Army Literature and Art Work called by Comrade Lin Biao on behalf of Comrade Jiang Qing', consisted of ten parts. In the first, the 'theory of the dictatorship of the black line' (*heixian zhuanzheng lun*) was expounded through an analysis of art and literature during the seventeen years since Liberation. The 'black line' was the work of the established leaders of the cultural apparatus, including the cultural commissar Zhou Yang, the playwright and film writer Xia Yan, and the Vice-Minister of Culture, Lin Mohan. Men such as these could cite revolutionary credentials back to the underground urban Communist movement of the early 1930s as well as, in some cases, activism in Yan'an during the war against Japan. The cultural insurgents behind the preceding two years' attacks on films and other works were a generally younger group who saw advantages in association with the hitherto politically inactive wife of Mao Zedong. The power of the black line was such that since 1949 very few works which were truly socialist and genuinely served worker, peasant, and soldier audiences had been able to find readers and audiences.

Army literary and art work offered a way forward, by offering a 'cultural revolution [that] both destroys and creates. The leaders must personally take charge and bring forth good models (*yangban*)'. Praise was heaped on the best of the plays at the 1964 Peking opera convention. These dramas were worthy of study and emulation. Here were the beginnings of the notion of model works or prototypes that was to dominate cultural activity for the next ten years. The minutes endorsed the 'combination of revolutionary realism and revolutionary romanticism'. Furthermore, literary heroes could not have shortcomings and love stories were condemned. These and other strictures help account for the peculiarities of leading characters in the model works of the Cultural Revolution.

The documents from the February 1966 army conference on literature and art called for the re-education of cadres in charge of cultural work and for a re-organizing of the cultural ranks. Newly insurgent leaders like Jiang Qing and her allies saw the weakness of their positions versus the influence of establishment figures in the field. In retrospect, the ridiculing of Wu Han and his Hai Rui fixation, the criticism of playwrights like Tian Han and filmmakers like Shen Fu, and the May 1966 attacks on intellectual and cultural figures Deng Tuo, Liao Mosha, and Wu Han for their *Evening Chats at Yanshan* (*Yanshan yehua*) and *Notes from Three Villages* (*San jia cun zhaji*) were all part of undermining established cultural leaders. A revolution always needs new blood in its ranks and can best succeed when the other side crumbles from within.

As the rhetoric became more shrill, the praise of Mao Zedong and his wisdom more inflated, and reports on mass enthusiasm more hollow, China was clearly heading for a period of considerable upheaval and uncertainty. By early 1966 it was obvious that this movement was more than just another campaign, with targets identified for attack, quotas drawn up for enemies to be found in work units and elsewhere, and ritual acknowledgement made of the leaders who had the wisdom to save society from such evil.

One new feature of the mounting rhetoric was hinting that the targets might be at the highest levels in the Party and state apparatus. Open attacks in the media were still not possible, but the choice of lesser targets suggested patterns that pointed higher. Past campaigns had always had this element, adding frisson for observers and terror for those directly

involved. By 1966, different factions among the leadership were manoeu-
vring, forming special groups to promote their views. Thus, in February
Peng Zhen, the mayor of Beijing and member of the Politburo, convened
a meeting in his city of the five-person Cultural Revolution Group, comprising Kang Sheng, Zhou Yang, Lu Dingyi, the historian and opera writer
Wu Han, and himself.[34]

A sense of drama was growing. That the eventual movement should be
a 'great proletarian cultural revolution', not the 'socialist cultural revolution' of several documents from early 1966, indicates a special quality
to this campaign. Throughout Chinese history, emperors have been convinced that the broad population warmly supported them. It was only
the stubborn, powerful, and venal bureaucrats who stood in the way of a
great harmony between ruler and subjects. Chairman Mao's call for young
people to mobilize into army-style Red Guards and lead the criticism of
his chosen targets was a typical imperial gesture. Jiang Qing's appearance
at her husband's side or on the stage in the company of cultural authorities at opera conventions catered also to a leader's sense of the dramatic.
A sweep of the hand or, in Jiang Qing's case, her greatcoat or cape would
send a paroxysm of excitement and worshipful fervour through the adoring masses who only awaited a signal to rise up in righteous support for
their noble leaders.

Ritualized displays of loyalty had dominated popular political activity
since the spring of 1966. Since 1949 all Chinese from school age onwards
had been obliged to enact publicly their commitment to the Party and
its government. These performances had been somewhat in the vein of
the Confucian emphasis on rites (li) and the public ceremonies led by
local government and social leaders that had given public expression of
the order in Chinese society for most of two millennia. Weekly political
study meetings on the factory floor or in the neighbourhood committee
rooms required a great deal of patience and bladders of steel. Selected
participants took turns in speaking the phrases and slogans of the regime,
enlivened perhaps by new expressions coined in yesterday's People's Daily
editorial.

Soon, however, the ritualistic display of loyalty broke down. When
the leadership at the top of the political structure was clearly divided,
it was difficult to maintain facades of local orderliness and propriety.
Factions at the top fought verbally, presenting their arguments obliquely
in newspaper articles penned by pseudonymous hands. Educated Chinese
were skilled in reading between the lines in the news media, for there
was little actual news directly reported. Factions at the top helped give
rise to factions further down in the apparatus of the state and in society.

In the heightened atmosphere, where loyalty to Chairman Mao was the ultimate measure of human worth, young people in particular took on the tasks of determining who was loyal and who was not. Red Guards, mostly university and other tertiary students, seized the opportunity for more forceful displays of their commitment. Others, including employees in factories, government offices, and even film studios, also saw advantage in trumpeting their revolutionary virtue.

Attack was the best form of defence in these circumstances. Many of the early Red Guards were from established, influential homes. Having parents in official positions gave access to more information, including restricted (*neibu*, internal) documents, on factional divisions at the top of the nation. Soon, however, rival groups emerged to denounce the privilege and alleged hypocrisy of the first groups. This second wave of activists claimed to be the true spokespersons for the 'masses', a political audience never really defined but available for appeals to their supposed sacred status as heirs of the Communist revolution. Factional divisions in many parts of China turned to armed fighting, when some activists gained access to the weapons of the People's Liberation Army. The latter were brought in to restore order in urban centres in 1969, when the bloodshed in some places could not be tolerated.

Ten years later the victors in another factional conflict in October 1976 accused the survivors of what was now identified as the Gang of Four of plotting in 1966 to seize control of the Communist Party and thus the nation. If this was true, they had chosen an unusual means of seeking control. Culture was the weapon of choice. The reasons for this choice involve reference to ancient Chinese reverence for learning and a modern Maoist conviction that ideas could change the world. In Marxist terms, the ideological and cultural superstructure could transform the economic base, a reversal of the orthodox explanation of change. Political tensions mounted in the spring of 1966. Mao Zedong prepared to launch youthful storm troopers at his enemies, and on the opera stage, a marvellous set of new operas emerged.

3. THE FIRST FIVE MODEL OPERAS

The old saw that during the Cultural Revolution '800 million people [were] watching eight shows' refers to the eight 'model performances' (*yangbanxi*) at the heart of culture in those years. These eight were formally promulgated in May 1967, one year into the Cultural Revolution. Five of the eight models were modernized Peking opera. The joke about the perceived narrowness of choice should not obscure the innovation and creativity that the five model operas represented. Each had been through an intensive period of gestation before 1966, drawing on the kinds of debates and experimentation outlined earlier in this chapter. A whole range of the best and brightest in China's opera and theatrical worlds continued to work on the operas until they were fixed on celluloid in the early 1970s.

The five 'model operas' identified in 1967 as *yangbanxi* were *The Red Lantern (Hongdeng ji)*, *Taking Tiger Mountain by Strategy (Zhiqu Weihushan)*, *Shajiabang*, *Raid on the White-Tiger Regiment (Qixi Baihutuan)*, and *On the Docks (Haigang)*. The first three were all set in the two decades before 1949. *Raid on the White-Tiger Regiment* had a Korean War setting. Only *On the Docks* was a contemporary story.

Taking Tiger Mountain by Strategy was one of two model operas with the longest pedigree. At the heart of the opera was one of the most widely recognized and enduring heroes in modern Chinese drama, Yang Zirong. Yang had first appeared in a novel by Qu Bo published in 1958. *Tracks in the Snowy Forest (Linhai xue yuan)* proved a major publishing success, running rapidly into several printings totalling in the millions. In a field which mostly offered a rather drab diet of supposedly uplifting stories of worthy socialist heroes, Yang Zirong and his comrades stood out. In the civil war period in the late 1940s in a remote area in the Northeast, Yang Zirong is a resourceful member of a Red Army brigade in a location under the evil sway of a bandit gang with close links with the Guomindang (Nationalist) Army.

A master of disguise as well as a brave soldier, Yang Zirong succeeds in lulling the bandits into a false sense of trust before his comrades spring their raid. This episode in particular captured the novel's use of traditional Chinese picaresque tales of derring-do. The tradition of a brave band of brothers devoted to each other and to a notion of social justice had attracted Chinese readers, old and young, high and low, for centuries. Qu Bo's novel tapped into this heritage highly effectively.

Several drama companies saw potential in this episode from such a popular novel.[35] In 1958 the Shanghai Peking Opera Theatre No. 1 Company created the first opera with this title. The script was the work of five writers, among them the actor who played Yang Zirong. The opera was so well received locally that a booklet of the script was published in the following year. The Shanghai company added the new opera to its repertoire, performing it frequently between 1958 and 1963.[36]

In 1963, in anticipation of the forthcoming national Peking opera convention planned for the summer of 1964 in Beijing, the Shanghai Peking Opera Theatre, with support from the city's Culture Bureau, set about preparing a suitably impressive range of new operas to represent Shanghai on Beijing's stages. Jiang Qing, in the city for convalescence, asked to see *Tiger Mountain* and agreed that it provided a good basis for further revisions.[37] Ying Yunei, a director at the Shanghai Film Studio, was brought in to remodel the performance and lead rehearsals.

At the June 1964 convention in Beijing, an ersatz 'Shanghai Performance Troupe' (*Shanghai yanchutuan*) performed the opera. It proved a hit and was watched by Mao, Premier Zhou Enlai, and others. It was held over for performances in the city in August and published in script form in *Juben* (*Play Script*). The next year a book version from the Shanghai Culture Publishing House was printed in more than 40,000 copies. In spring 1965 the newly established Shanghai Peking Opera Party Committee (*Shanghai Jingju dangwei*) helped reduce the original twenty-four scenes to twelve (and subsequently to ten). In the summer of 1965, music extracts of this opera and others, including *The Red Lantern*, were published in Shanghai to accompany gramophone records of selected arias.[38]

Tong Xiangling twenty-eight years later gave an oral account of how he created his version of Yang Zirong.[39] Fundamental for Tong was 'setting out from life' (*cong shenghuo chufa*), a phrase much used in the 1960s and 1970s, but which still had relevance for the actor in the 1990s, when there was no strong political requirement to use such words. What Tong meant was that without a basis in real life the character could not be made convincing. The challenge in reworking Yang Zirong's part in *Tiger Mountain* was how to use and build upon the traditions of Peking opera while creating something new and modern. 'We ... break down the old, traditional patterns of Peking opera, adhere to artistic laws, and through destruction and building embody continuity and development. Transformation in content requires transformation in form.'[40] Actor Tong found it was not easy to overcome his traditional training to transform the character. The solution was a halfway kind of delivery that was neither modern speech nor the sounds of traditional opera. Only then could this Yang Zirong engage his audience.

Movement was a third major means by which a Peking opera actor created a character and gave him presence on the stage. Yang Zirong's cape presented a challenge, for it was not like an old-style costume but also an opportunity for sweeping gestures and striking a pose (*liangxiang*) with it swept from one shoulder. As Tong Xiangling observed almost three decades later, through this effort on *Tiger Mountain* he started to genuinely grasp how continuity and innovation in modernizing Peking opera were interconnected. After a lot of testing, a heroic character emerged to appeal strongly to audiences.

There were plenty of outside opinions offered to assist the *Tiger Mountain* company in its revision of the opera. Marshall He Long, one of the heroes of the civil wars of the 1930s and 1940s, suggested more stage time for Yang Zirong's horse riding. Jiang Qing reportedly visited the company five times. Sometimes, later accounts claim, she represented herself as speaking for Chairman Mao. Post–Cultural Revolution accounts mock her input.[41] The new and much improved *Taking Tiger Mountain by Strategy* was performed in Beijing in 1966 at National Day celebrations. Mao Zedong watched it and expressed support.[42]

These new-style operas had such an important role in the promulgation of a new, allegedly more authentic mass culture that attention from highly skilled writers, actors, directors, and musicians continued to be devoted to their further refinement. This was an uncommon luxury for opera artists used to the pressures of a changing repertoire and a sometimes fickle box office. With the start of the Cultural Revolution, new specialists came in to add their skills. In some cases they were replacing members of the *Tiger Mountain* company who had had to step down after Red Guard or other criticism.[43]

The new cultural apparatus in Shanghai was chaired by Yu Huiyong from the Shanghai Conservatory. Yu expressed general endorsement of the revised musical score of *Tiger Mountain*, though he made a few changes to help tunes and lyrics find a better match and to be easier to sing. It was Yu who added the *East Is Red* melody, theme song of Chairman Mao, to the opera. In May 1967 it was included in the list of model performances.[44]

To cap off the four and half years that *Tiger Mountain* had been revised and polished, an official final version of the script was published on 1969 National Day, 1 October, in *Red Flag*, as well as in *People's Daily* and other newspapers throughout China. The following year the People's Culture Publishing House brought out the script as well as books of the music, dance, and guides for production of *Tiger Mountain*, consolidating its position as *the* model among the model performances.[45] Yang Zirong, splendid in his cape and tiger-skin waistcoat, had become an icon of the Cultural Revolution.

Raid on the White-Tiger Regiment could claim a longer pedigree than *Tiger Mountain* by a year or so, although it never achieved the popularity of its younger model sibling. The first version of the opera, written in 1957, was by three members of the Peking opera company attached to the Chinese People's Volunteer Army (*Zhongguo renmin zhiyuanjun*) still stationed in North Korea since the 1953 armistice.[46] Based on a real-life account, the opera presents how a Chinese scouting platoon leader named Yan Weicai teams up with the Korean People's Army liaison officer Han

Tae-Nyon to lead a joint reconnaissance team into the heart of enemy territory. They successfully sabotage the White-Tiger Regiment command post, sweeping away a barrier to a successful counterattack against the South Korean forces.

The army opera company in North Korea was merged with the Shandong Provincial Peking Opera Company in 1962, as Chinese military involvement in Korea wound down and many cultural organizations were disbanded, rationalized, or combined to save resources after the disastrous financial and human consequences of the Great Leap Forward. Two years later, in early 1964, the Shandong company staged a newly created version of *Raid on the White-Tiger Regiment*. Like what happened in Shanghai with *Tiger Mountain*, the local political leadership, in this case the Shandong Provincial Party Committee, took an interest in the production.[47]

That summer audiences at the Beijing national Peking opera convention responded positively to the excitement and drama of the story. The work was the first in the programme. In August national leaders watched the opera at their annual summer retreat at the seaside resort of Beidaihe and expressed their endorsement. Many in the top Party leadership, including Mao, were big traditional opera fans. Tours to Shanghai, Nanjing, Jinan, Guangzhou, and elsewhere occupied 1965, during which the popular appeal of the opera was confirmed.

The songs and musical accompaniment were a major point of attention. After learning of the death of Aunt Cui (Choi in Korean), the central hero, Yan Weicai, expressed his emotions in an aria that carefully built upon a complex series of traditional meters. As *Tiger Mountain* had incorporated some bars from *The East Is Red*, the start of *White-Tiger* included the tune from socialist anthem the *Internationale* to underscore the internationalist theme. In similar vein the highly familiar 'Battlesong of the People's Volunteer Army' echoed through the score as a central theme tune, a device more usual in a modern musical than in a Peking opera. In the musical accompaniment, Western instruments and some Chinese folk instruments were added to the usual operatic mix of Chinese percussion and strings.[48]

After undergoing further adjustments in Shanghai, where the Shandong company worked alongside the *Tiger Mountain* team under the guidance of Shanghai propaganda chief Zhang Chunqiao for most of 1966, *Raid on the White-Tiger Regiment* was deemed a suitable model of opera modernization in December of that year. Zhang Lihui, writer on *Tiger Mountain*, and Yu Huiyong, musical adviser to the *Tiger Mountain* company, offered assistance in refining this opera.[49] *Red Flag* published the performance script (*yanchuben*) in September 1972 and major newspapers across the nation included the script in a November issue.

Shajiabang, one of the most enduringly popular of the 'model performances', started life not as a Peking opera but under a different name as a Shanghai opera (*Huju*). From January to March 1960, the Shanghai City People's Shanghai Opera Company presented *Emerald Water and Red Flags* (*Bishui hongqi*), based on an episode during the War of Resistance to Japan. In early spring 1963, the company returned to the script and began revisions for a new version of the opera.[50] The new Shanghai opera, now titled *Sparks amid the Reeds* (*Ludang huozhong*), played from March 1963 to an impressive number of viewers, even if many came in groups organized by their workplaces. More than 3,600 such work units enabled their employees to see the opera.[51]

Shajiabang (or *Sparks amid the Reeds*, as it was then titled) was set in the riverine country that stretches hundreds of kilometres west of Shanghai. Sister Aqing (*Aqing sao*), an underground Communist Party member and tea shop proprietor in the village of Shajiabang, helps hide eighteen wounded soldiers from the Communist New Fourth Army, operating underground in the area which was under Japanese occupation but controlled more directly by puppet Chinese troops. Although she wore an embroidered apron rather than a tiger-skin waistcoat, Sister Aqing had the similar qualities audiences admired in Yang Zirong. Like the *Tiger Mountain* hero, Sister Aqing is resourceful, brave, and witty, outfoxing the puppet Chinese officers.[52]

In 1963 Jiang Qing, having watched the Shanghai opera version in the city in May, gained permission of the Ministry of Culture to recommend the *Huju* script to the Beijing Peking Opera Company.[53] This was of course in the respectable tradition of 'transplanting' operas and other stage performances from one regional form to another. The writing group at the Beijing company was led by Wang Zengqi, a respected writer but former Rightist, who brought a literary polish and effectiveness to the language of the script. This contrasted with the usual attitude towards opera texts in traditional plays – that they were simply for the benefit of actors, as something to hang their performance on.[54] The excellence of the lyrics of the model operas is one point which continued to attract praise long after the Cultural Revolution. The opera played at that summer's national convention of modern-subject Peking operas in the capital.

Mao Zedong saw the play there and offered the view that the fighting skills and bravery of the New Fourth Army and the close relationship between the Communist army men and civilians needed to be clearer. Mao also suggested a change in title: 'There's water everywhere in reeds, so how can the sparks of revolution set them alight? Besides, in the war against Japan the revolution was already ablaze!' Mao went on to observe: 'The story takes place in Shajiabang. Lots of plays use place names in their titles. Why not call this opera *Shajiabang*?'[55] To strengthen the military aspects of the opera, much work went into the character of the New Fourth Army political instructor Guo Jianguang. His scenes were greatly increased (at the expense of Sister Aqing's). The New Fourth Army soldiers were also given more stage time, using an updated version of operatic acrobatics.

Writers could produce the lines, but it was the actors who had to make something of them and the whole character on stage. Tan Yuanshou, who acted the new version of Guo Jianguang, reported vividly on the familiar challenge of taking traditional opera acting skills and revising them for the new-style character and situations. Having performed as emperors and ministers for thirty years, the veteran Tan found he naturally slipped into the old style when he first played Guo in *Sparks amid the Reeds*. It was hard to get rid of the baggage (*baofu*) of the old Tan school of opera (*Tan pai*) in which he had been trained and performed for decades. Even with the new additions to the script, Tan found himself still bound by the old styles.[56]

The breakthrough came allegedly after the company conducted an investigation and small-scale rectification (*zhengfeng*) of the inordinate self-satisfaction and pride that had come after the successful launch on stage of *Sparks amid the Reeds*. Such rectification had been a common Party technique to correct unwelcome attitudes and work styles since Yan'an days. As then, study of the writings of Mao Zedong was reportedly the catalyst to changing perceptions. In this case, the company also studied an inspirational speech, 'On How to Play Ping Pong' (*Guanyu ruhe da pingpangqiu*), by China's international champion Xu Yinsheng, which questioned the old framework of seeking personal fame. Another factor in this change of thinking was watching amateur performers from an 'Ulan Muchir' mounted cultural troupe from the grasslands of Inner Mongolia.[57] According to Tan, the Mongols were most impressive. The content of their performance was revolutionary, and they ignored all restrictions and conventions. We might question the somewhat hackneyed attribution of help from the Party, but the reality of theatre people wedded to ways that had brought them personal acclaim can be understood in any society. It clearly took some effort to move performers into more experimental mode.

The Beijing company also watched another modern-subject opera, *The Red Lantern*, which Tan described in his 1965 account as 'the most realistic model' (*yi kuai huoyangban*).[58] Some old schools' techniques could be used with the new-style plays. Tan cited the need in the new operas for clarity in singing the words of the text. Here the Yu school's and Yan school's precision in pronunciation could be adopted with suitable adjustment. The key was to make sure the old schools' techniques were put into the service of the new plays, not vice versa.

Despite the new attention on Guo Jianguang, Sister Aqing was not ignored. The contrast clarified between the coolness and apparent propriety she showed, as host of the teahouse, when she outwitted the puppet troops, and her genuine warmth in her relationships, as an underground Communist Party member, with the other villagers and the New Fourth Army men. Although the reports do not note it, audiences may well have found this contrast had considerable pertinence. On the eve of the Cultural Revolution and throughout those ten years, many Chinese experienced and tried to preserve a kind of double existence. In public contexts, like Sister Aqing at the teahouse when visited by Diao Deyi and his men, people performed according to expectations and the requirements of current policies. In private, like Sister Aqing among her own people, Chinese were more inclined to express real feelings about their lives.[59]

In the old operas, musicians chose from a conventional menu of tunes and rhythms, working with the actors to match music with situation and lyrics. The new operas were such thoroughgoing revisions of tradition that specialist composers, such as Shanghai's Yu Huiyong, and writers were needed to find new ways of presenting the new content. Being too new threatened to leave audiences behind: 'There is only one criterion: the masses' tastes (literally, habits of enjoyment *xinshang xiguan*). We cannot fall behind the masses' tastes nor can we go too far out in front.'[60] Devices and other features imported from outside must be 'domesticated' (*xunhua*) to fit in with Peking opera's true qualities. One new device was the use of music to enhance the atmosphere or as mood music, in the manner of a film score, when the curtain (itself a modern opera innovation) was drawn between scenes. Deeper-toned instruments were added to the orchestra, including some Western instruments because of the feeling that the traditional Chinese instruments were weak in their expressive range, given the new kinds of modern, martial situations and people on the stage.

Military-style acrobatics were a vital and much-loved part of Chinese opera (see Figure 1.1). Audiences delighted in the imposing stage presence of generals striking poses with swords, spears, and pheasant feathers. Their foot soldiers were the more acrobatic, tumbling across the stage, carefully timed to avoid collisions. With modern subjects, these stage movements needed considerable revision. This aspect was the last one tackled in the revisions of *Shajiabang* and amounted to the finishing touches (dotting the eye of the dragon was the phrase used in one report). Directly transferring old-style acrobatics to the new opera looked too

1.1. Guo Jianguang (center) and New Fourth Army men in the model opera *Shajiabang*. Source: *Litterature Chinoise*, 1971, 2 (February), cover. Published by the Foreign Languages Press, Beijing.

old-fashioned, but attempting real-life accuracy in the movement of the stage soldiers lost suitable theatricality. The solution, as in most other aspects of opera modernization, was a critical reworking of the tradition from a departure point of real life. Through trial and error, the necessary effects were achieved. The spears and swords of the traditional opera stage, for example, were replaced by pistols and rifles. Direct replacement did not fit the new style, so new movements were invented. As a theatrical touch, red cloth hung from the handgrips of pistols, enabling audiences to see them more clearly.

One major issue in mapping out stage movements was how to present a memorable image of the mass of New Fourth Army soldiers while, at the same time, giving special stage attention to their heroic leader, Guo Jianguang. The initial acrobatics failed to make much distinction between Guo and the other soldiers: Guo needed to be given prominence (*tuchu*). In the middle of the disciplined, simultaneous movements of the soldiers, Guo would be part of the collective but also have his own, distinctive placement and actions. Centre stage was reserved for officer Guo, particularly when he struck a frozen pose, in best Peking-opera style. Here in mid-1965 were some of the roots of a major guiding principle in all the 'revolutionary model performances', ballet and opera, the theory of the 'three prominences' (*san tuchu*) on presenting heroes.[61]

The result of all this experimentation was an impressive theatrical experience that captured the delights of Peking opera but in fresh and still somewhat unfamiliar ways. Members of the Shanghai People's Shanghai Opera Company, who had first performed *Sparks amid the Reeds*, were invited in the summer of 1965 to see the new-look *Shajiabang*. Their collective report began by noting that both this *Shajiabang* and the China Peking Opera Academy's *The Red Lantern* were 'models' (*yangban*) for the revolutionizing (*geming hua*) of Peking opera. This word 'model' was to become official almost two years later when eight such works were formally identified as model performances.[62] The lesson of the new *Shajiabang* was that 'to transform opera well, first people must be transformed' (*yao gaihao xi, shouxian yao gaihao ren*). It was a lesson soon made unavoidable by the launching of the Cultural Revolution.

Even so, the old *Sparks amid the Reeds* took some time to disappear. In the summer of 1965, several extracts from that opera were among the modern-subject aria music published in Shanghai to accompany the release of recordings of the music.[63] But the Beijing troupe's Shajiabang story triumphed. In late 1966 *Shajiabang* was counted a 'model opera', though work continued on polishing and perfecting. By 1970 a new official script was fixed and published on international Labor Day, 1 May, in *Red Flag, Guangming Daily* (*Guangming ribao*), and elsewhere.

The Red Lantern ranked with *Shajiabang* as one of the major achievements in Peking opera modernization as well as being one of the most well received by Chinese audiences. The Harbin City Peking Opera Company had adapted an opera from a film script published by the Northeast's Changchun Film Studio. The film script and opera were titled: *The Revolution Has Successors* (*Geming ziyou houlairen*). It told the story of a railway worker and his family comprising a daughter and her grandmother during the War of Resistance against Japan. Li Yuhe, the railway man, is a signaller who uses his red lantern also as a device to communicate with underground Communist fighters. Captured and interrogated by the Japanese gendarmerie, Li Yuhe sacrifices his life for the revolution but not before passing the red lantern on to his iron-willed daughter, Li Tiemei. Like *Shajiabang* and *Tiger Mountain*, the story offered opportunity for heroes in tight situations to outwit their enemies and delight their audiences.

The Peking opera from Harbin was transplanted in 1962 into Shanghai opera (*Huju*) formed by the Aihua Shanghai Opera Company.[64] At Spring Festival in early 1963, a traditional time for the presentation of new operatic works, Shanghai audiences responded with enthusiasm to this new-style opera. The run lasted three months, with 'house full' signs in the foyer most nights. The magazine *Theatre Script* (*Juben*), published in Beijing, printed the script in its February 1964 issue.[65]

During this first run in February 1963, Jiang Qing saw the opera in Shanghai and pronounced it 'not bad' (*bucuo*). As she also did that year with *Sparks amid the Reeds* (the future *Shajiabang*), Jiang Qing took the script back to Beijing. She handed it to the deputy head of the Propaganda Department, the playwright Lin Mohan, suggesting it be transplanted to the Peking opera form.[66] Only later in the fall of 1963 did Lin pass the script over to the China Peking Opera Academy, where two of the most accomplished opera writer-directors in the nation were charged with producing a Peking-opera version of the Shanghai play.[67] A Jia and Weng Ouhong had considerable experience and good political connections. A Jia had taught at the Lu Xun Art Academy in Yan'an during the war against Japan and been active in opera reform. After 1949 he was instrumental in introducing the new system of opera director at the opera academy, specialists who had not existed in actor-centred opera companies in the past.[68]

At the time Lin Mohan gave him the Shanghai script, A Jia was busy on two other modern-subject operas: *Fighting the Flood Peak* (*Kang hongfeng*) and *The Red Detachment of Women* (*Hongse niangzijun*), based on the popular 1961 film (also known as *Qionghua*). The film was the basis also for a 'model ballet'. Given these immediate responsibilities, A Jia passed the script on to his academy colleague, Weng Ouhong, who wrote the first draft.[69] Weng produced a very rough draft, which in a later memoir he called a 'non-script' ('*bu shi juben*' *de juben*).[70] A Jia took Weng's draft and, as director, created a second draft. He later said he changed eighty percent of Weng's rough draft. All together eight or nine drafts were produced, all written down by A Jia.

Although the Beijing opera troupe presented *Red Lantern* at the 1964 summer modern-subject opera convention in Beijing, A Jia and others working on the Peking opera visited Shanghai to watch the *Huju* version.[71] Mao saw the new opera in November 1964. Southern viewers were as eager when the Beijing company took the opera south at Spring Festival 1965 to Shenzhen (then a small town, but on the Hong Kong border for day-trippers from the colony), Guangzhou, and Shanghai. In the eighteen months from early 1964, more than 200 articles about the Peking opera were published in newspapers and journals nationwide.[72] Meanwhile the Aihua Shanghai Opera Company kept working on their opera, studying the Peking-opera version for new ideas. They were encouraged by Zhang Chunqiao of the city's Culture Bureau.[73]

Later, during the Cultural Revolution, the indigenous Shanghai opera version was suppressed, and the Aihua Shanghai Opera Company was instructed to transplant the Peking opera directly into the *Huju* form. The Aihua efforts had a tragic end. Yuan Binzhong, the actor who played Li Yuhe, the railway signalman, was arrested and interrogated by 'rebel' (*zaofanpai*) Red Guards, who objected apparently to his version of the opera hero. To show their determination, they smashed Yuan's steel watch. They also smashed his spirit. On 28 December 1967, Yuan Binzhong took a woollen scarf and hung himself. He was thirty-five.[74] The later report of this omitted the irony that a long red scarf was a key part of the costume for the Li Yuhe character, one he used to strike a pose.

The Beijing creative team set out to produce an operatic experience that emphasized the magnificence (*zhuangmei*) of these heroes. This concept represented a kind of toughened, polished beauty (*mei*) that, ironically, had parallels with the post–Cultural Revolution 'New Wave' in Chinese filmmaking announced by *The Yellow Earth* (*Huang tudi*) in 1984.[75] It was a somewhat masculine aesthetic: broad shouldered and determined, unlike the sparkle and wit of a Yang Zirong–type hero (at least before such heroes were all fit into the Cultural Revolution mould created by Li Yuhe).

One issue was to balance the effect of the three characters and make sure that Li Yuhe's status as the main hero of the opera did not undermine the audience's understanding of the role of Li Tiemei, when she picks up the lantern at the end, as revolutionary successor.[76] Li Yuhe and Grandma Li in the original Shanghai opera died in prison. In the new version, they die on an execution ground. This provided more room for the powerful presence of the determined heroes than the cramped prison and placed them in a pine grove, which symbolize eternity.[77]

Central in this heroic creation was the scene in the middle of *The Red Lantern* in which Grandma Li tells Tiemei about the history of their family. She explains that in reality they are not blood relatives. She was surnamed Li, but Li Yuhe was surnamed Zhang and Li Tiemei (literally 'iron plum') was born a Chen. It is a climactic revelation for the girl's understanding of her past and for her future responsibilities as revolutionary successor. All of A Jia's directing skills were brought to bear on the scene, which he felt in the Shanghai version had been too much 'like a movie' (*dianyinghua*).[78] Despite the intimacy of Grandma Li's confession, he decided to start with the two women at a considerable distance apart. The older woman would occupy centre stage throughout the scene, but Li Tiemei would begin downstage, close to the audience. In effect her closeness would encourage audience members to identify with the young woman and be moved, as she so visibly is, by the history Grandma Li recounts. As Grandma tells her story, Li Tiemei moved closer and closer to her, eventually falling into her arms, as a young child might with her mother. Audiences reportedly sniffled their way through this scene, so effective was A Jia's staging and the actors' conveying of their characters' emotions.[79]

With such an emphasis on magnificent heroism, selecting actors who could carry this off without bombast was a challenge. A Jia and the team made some unexpected choices. The part of Grandma Li was given to Gao Yuqian, who was more used to playing young female roles, which used a higher vocal range than old woman characters. But her natural voice fit the part. She also, crucially, could act, engaging audiences in the inner feelings of her characters.[80]

The actor chosen to create the Peking opera version of Li Yuhe had almost achieved a convincing level in the role when he hurt his back. A search was mounted for a new Li Yuhe: A Jia selected Qian Haoliang, for his acting abilities as much as for his singing skills. Qian thus had the glory of creating a seminal figure in the Cultural Revolution pantheon of heroes thrust upon him almost by accident. In an early 1965 article on this role, Qian Haoliang noted how the cast had studied Xu Yinsheng's article on playing ping-pong. Qian recorded how Xu's table tennis experience helped him abandon old notions of individualism and concentration on himself, an occupational hazard for actors, even a Communist Party member like Xu.[81] During the Cultural Revolution, Qian Haoliang became associated closely with the group led by Jiang Qing and turned against many of his former colleagues, including A Jia who had been crucial in his achieving fame.[82]

Other aspects of the creation of *The Red Lantern* also focused on the heroism of the central characters. The musical design, itself a modern notion, reflected an unprecedented concern for consistency in the musical underscoring of the different characters' actions and emotions. Songs, acrobatic movement, and percussion were all carefully designed, adjusted, and revised. The aim was to make sure the sound and movement dimensions of the opera added their own emphasis on the three central heroes.[83] A Jia's directing had the same focus: Each new scene had to have a clear centre, physically and in terms of the audience's understanding of the theme. The heroes consistently occupied centre stage.[84]

One early 1965 article in praise of *The Red Lantern* had long-term significance. Titled 'Opera Music Must Serve the Creation of Heroic Figures', it was written by Yu Huiyong, who two years later was to contribute to the musical redesign of *Taking Tiger Mountain by Strategy* and take charge of Jiang Qing's program of model performances, including *The Red Lantern*. Writing in his capacity as a professor at the Shanghai Conservatory, Yu noted how the new opera made appropriate, though critical, use of the resources of traditional opera music but at points when this approach was unsuitable, it boldly created new music on the basis of the old.[85] As these comments from specialists indicated, *The Red Lantern* was already subject to special attention from the Chinese opera world. It had been first produced under the close attention of Jiang Qing. Now its success was also earning it model status as an example of how Chinese opera could be modernized.[86] Audiences were simply impressed by the emotion conjured by the opera.

Having been formally incorporated into Jiang Qing's model performances by late 1966 (though these were only officially announced in May 1967), *The Red Lantern* grew in status as one of the most important of the new-style Chinese operas. In 1968 it was one of the first of the models to be selected to be filmed. This would fix a version of the opera as standard. Accordingly even more attention was lavished on its further refinement. Qian Haoliang, the actor in the Li Yuhe role, who had now changed his name to Hao Liang (literally 'great and bright'), was in charge of the project.[87] By then A Jia and Weng Ouhong had been sent to Cultural Revolution confinement in so-called cow sheds (*niupeng*), and a new group was charged with rewriting. Zhang Yongmei, a poet with the Guangzhou military district, was brought in to polish the lyrics of the arias. The orchestration was supplemented with the talents of well-known musicians, and stage blocking was revised by three new, respected directors.[88] Drawing nationwide upon the best available operatic talent indicates how important *The Red Lantern* and its role as a model had become by 1968. Weng Ouhong, unable to participate, later lamented in his memoirs how the opera, originally close to a three-hour performance, had been reduced to two hours to fit closer to feature-film length.[89] When the script was published in *Red Flag* in February 1965, Weng Ouhong heard colleagues wonder whether this was an indication that *The Red Lantern* should be regarded as a 'national opera' (*guo ju*), a status never accorded any previous work.[90]

On the Docks, in contrast, was perhaps the least successful of the model performance operas, in terms of artistic accomplishment and audience reception. The history of its creation is a tale of frequent, substantial rewriting from its origins as a Huai opera (*Huaiju*), a form popular in northern Jiangsu province around the Huai River flood zone and in Shanghai, to its transplanting into Peking-opera form. *On the Docks* was the most modern of the Cultural Revolution model performances, which may account in large part for the difficulties its creators and audiences experienced with the play. As opera modernizers had noted since the 1950s, the more distant a modern-subject setting from the present day and the more fantastical the story, the easier it was to create convincing drama and attract enthusiastic viewers. *On the Docks* was too familiar and too similar in setting to the other cultural products being churned out by the literary and art apparatus to find a niche in just about anyone's affections. It was the orphan opera of the Cultural Revolution models. Alone among the first five model operas, a version of it had not been officially presented at the summer 1964 Beijing modern-opera convention.

The opera is set on the waterfront in Shanghai in 1962. Han Xiaoqiang has started work as a loader. A class enemy named Qian Shouwei (literally 'money conservative thinking') sabotages a shipment of wheat bound for export to a Third World ally of China by secreting fibreglass beads from another shipment in some of the wheat sacks. The wily Qian manages to shift the blame to young Han. Party secretary Fang Haizhen (literally 'honest sea treasure') investigates the incident and with help from the dockside workers spends a night turning the warehouse upside down to find the affected sacks of grain. From this incident Han Xiaoqiang learns to heighten his vigilance and Qian Shouwei is exposed.

The Huai opera original was written by Li Xiaomin, a young writer attached to the Shanghai People's Huai Opera Company, responding to the current call to 'write about the 13 years' since Liberation.[91] By December 1963 Li had completed his first draft, with the title *Early Morning on the Docks* (*Haigang de zaochen*). In his writing he was able to draw upon some earlier attempts by the Huai opera company to portray life on the docks, as well upon film scripts with a similar setting.[92] In February 1964, to coincide with Spring Festival, the time-honoured occasion for the release of new Chinese operas, the company premiered Li's work.[93]

Shortly afterwards Jiang Qing saw the Huai opera when visiting Shanghai. At about the same time, she also watched the Shanghai operas *Sparks amid the Reeds* (the future *Shajiabang*) and *The Red Lantern*. After seeing *Early Morning on the Docks*, she reportedly made a visit to the dockland, seeking out the leader of the No. 3 zone. Jiang Qing is said to have asked three questions: What did the dock workers themselves think of the opera? Was the incident of the accidental mixing-up of cargoes a realistic event? Did a mistake with fibreglass beads ever happen? The answers were positive on all three counts. Although the 1990s source of this story does not note it, Jiang Qing's actions suggested she was aware of her own ignorance about workers' lives and wanted to be sure she was endorsing a relatively realistic portrayal of dockers.[94]

The well-known spoken-drama director, Yang Cunbin, was invited to direct the new version. Actors with some experience in playing in modern-subject operas also joined the cast. All the supporting dockworkers were played by specialist acrobatic opera performers. To help the writers concentrate, Li Taicheng, the deputy cultural bureau head in charge of opera work, arranged for them to be relieved of all other duties and to stay at the Jinjiang Hotel, Shanghai's finest. By 20 April they had produced a draft Peking opera: *Early Morning Dockside (Haigang zaochen)*. Director Yang Cunbin drew on his spoken drama experience in creating new ways for the cast to move about on stage. Instead of a traditional V-shaped arrangement of the supporting players, Yang experimented with other ways of grouping them, along the lines, a source states, of two basketball teams on the court before a game starts.[95] *Early Morning Dockside* made it to the 1964 Beijing convention but for 'restricted access' (*neibu*) dress rehearsals only.[96]

What followed for the next three years was a constant round of revisions and adjustments of the opera, in an effort to make it effective and reportedly to satisfy the demands of Jiang Qing. On their return to Shanghai from Beijing, the team went again to experience life on the docks directly, while the writers and composers worked up a new version. In rethinking the staging, Yang tried borrowing the film technique of montage. In the 'chase boat' (*zhui zhou*) scene, successively spotlighting actors on different parts of a darkened stage would give a film editing effect and focus on the individuals, as if in a close-up. By October 1964 a new script was ready and approved by Zhang Chunqiao. In February 1965, a year after the original Huai opera had been premiered, the Peking opera was presented in 'experimental public performance' (*shiyan gongyan*). Jiang Qing finally saw the piece and raised three specific concerns. There was too much prominence given to middling characters (*zhongjian renwu*), like the young dockworker, as opposed to the heroes; the 'chase boat' scene with film-inspired spotlighting had the air of a ghost play about it; and the set looked like a bird's nest.[97]

In March 1965 a new team was organized to take up the challenge, headed by writer He Man. Two new writers were added and a new director, Zhang Qin. Two new composers joined the team: Zhuang Dechun and Yu Huiyong, the Shanghai Conservatory professor who would later work also on *Tiger Mountain* and *Red Lantern*. Li Xiaomin, the amateur Huai opera writer who had created the original's script, joined the group, reportedly tasked in secret by Jiang Qing with ensuring minimal deviation from the Huai opera version. With different writers assigned to different aspects of revising the script, a lack of uniform tone and approach threatened. Each writer had his own strengths and naturally played them up. The Party secretary's arias reportedly sounded like modernist poetry. Those of the docker's team leader took on the flavour of an essay, while another lead sang lyrics that were close to old-style Peking opera. By May 1965 a revised script was ready, and in the heat of the summer months, full-dress rehearsals further refined the performance. Still the opera seemed not right. Further adjustments were introduced. Young Han's close friend relationship with another worker was at first deleted, so that only class solidarity prevailed on stage. Young Han also lost his mother (from the play). The task of conveying stories of pre-Liberation suffering rested entirely with Party secretary Fang, increasing her prominence as the main hero. The title also became the simpler *On the Docks* at this stage.

These revisions were finished in February 1966, on the eve of the Cultural Revolution and a full two years since the idea of transplanting the original Huai opera had been raised. The dress-rehearsal stage was reached in May. Even then Jiang Qing raised further concerns and recommended that the team watch the new, contemporary Peking opera *Song of the Dragon River* (*Longjiang song*) for ideas on how to present their heroes. The team duly did so, but then pointed out (probably through gritted teeth) that their play was about dockworkers led by a woman Party secretary, not about peasants led by a man. As some consolation, *On the Docks* took part in the 1966 National Day celebrations in Beijing.

Even in 1969 and 1970 revisions of *On the Docks* continued. A new writing team took out their pens. They included Li Xiaomin, whose Huai opera script had started it all. Jiang Qing saw the new version in September 1971 and pronounced herself satisfied. The official script of *On the Docks* appeared in a February 1972 issue of *Red Flag*, more than two years after *Tiger Mountain* had been published in the Party's main ideological journal and a full seven years after *Red Lantern* had been published there.[98] At the same time, the script appeared in newspapers nationwide. Meanwhile the original Huai opera, *Early Morning on the Docks*, had long since vanished from Shanghai's stages. Any transplanting to other opera forms would now be done from the Peking opera 'original'. This was, after all, one of the functions of the model operas.

Red Flag in May 1972 contained a long article by the Shanghai Peking Opera Company *On the Docks* group which gave insight into what were considered the strengths of the new version and of the model operas in general.[99] The writers outline the internationalist theme but do not note that by late 1965, when the opera was going through its second of three major reworkings, China's theatre audiences were watching several dramas with a similar message. China's actors and dancers have never had much moral qualms about putting on 'black face'. *Storm over Gambia* (*Gangguo fenglei*) was a spoken drama in six scenes presented by one of the top theatre groups in the nation, the Beijing People's Art Theatre. The story involved Chinese support of the African struggle against Western imperialism.[100] While to twenty-first century sensibilities such productions seem offensive, for Chinese watching an exotic, colourfully clad cast in a setting outside of China had a profound attraction. It was welcome, bright relief from a steady and by now over-familiar diet of worker, peasant, and soldier dramas.[101] At this time, too, the newspapers were full of reports on demonstrations in Chinese cities supporting Cuban and African independence. *On the Docks* fitted nicely into this foreign-policy initiative, as the grain being sent from the Shanghai waterfront was changed to be seed rice sent as aid, a longer-term expression of Chinese worker solidarity with the struggling masses of the Third World.

Part of Chinese opera's attractions to audiences is its combination of aural and physical display. *On the Docks*, in film or on stage, was not strong on stage acrobatics and movement. Unlike the other four initial model operas, it was not set in wartime. A waterside worker can only do so much with a sack of seed rice and an empty stage, no matter how physically adept the actor may be with tumbling and falling. Essentially *On the Docks* proved that fully contemporary settings did not work as well as more distant stories in the new-style opera forms.

4. THE ART OF THE MODEL OPERAS

This overview of the making of the first five model operas suggests how much effort and resources went into their creation. The experience was very different from life for old-style opera troupes before Liberation, which tended to work through a rotating repertoire of audience favourites, familiar to those on the stage and in front of it. In contrast, the operas that became part of the Cultural Revolution pantheon were intensively developed over six years using first-class actors and musicians brought together specifically for the production.[102] In addition, the development process of these new works gave unprecedented status to relatively new players in Chinese opera: writers and directors. In the old days of Chinese opera, actors were centre stage. They worked with musicians on developing plays and finding new ways to present old favourites which could appeal to audiences. There was not much room for writers of opera, though the old repertoire included both borrowings from poets and other writers as well as more complete works from the brushes of educated men with an interest in the stage arts.

The aural dimension of the model operas included both the musical accompaniment and the singing. In both aspects, major innovations achieved considerable success, a fact attested by the continued popularity long after the Cultural Revolution of the arias from *Tiger Mountain*, *Shajiabang*, and *The Red Lantern*. Specialist researchers in the 1990s studied the music of the model performances, treating this dimension of the operas with the seriousness it deserves. One of the most prominent of these researchers was Wang Renyuan, whose *Outline Theory of the Music of the Peking Opera 'Model Performances'*, published in 1999, was the first full-length study of model opera music. As the theatre veteran Zhang Geng suggests in his preface, Wang Renyuan is among the first Chinese scholars to draw a distinction between the art and the politics of the Cultural Revolution works, and take the former seriously.

Wang makes a strong case for the musical dimension of the model operas being their most prominent achievement. He divides the history of the music of the model operas into three phases. In the first, the issue of continuing but developing the tradition dominated musical efforts. The deeper experimentation and creation of new forms was the concern in the middle period. At that time the musical specialists made a major effort to add Western instruments and musical styles to the operas. The last phase in the process of creating the music for the model operas undermined some of the achievements of the earlier stages. Rigidity and a drying up of ideas replaced innovation and borrowing.[103]

The model opera composers worked in a twentieth-century tradition of efforts to amalgamate, in musically convincing ways, Chinese and Western music. Wang Renyuan argues that the use of Western music, including the addition of Western instruments to the opera orchestras, was not something tacked on to the new dramas to reinforce somehow an impression of their newness. The musicologists attempted not to undermine or distort the folk elements in the operatic musical heritage. The Western musical elements were carefully selected and integrated with the more traditional. The results can be considered the first successes in this enterprise since 1949.[104]

The professionalism and modernity of the musical construction of the model operas can be heard in the way the plays are infused with coherent musical themes and in the planned associations with certain characters and themes. This contrasted with the usual way in which Chinese opera music had been created. Put rather crudely, Chinese opera music can be considered like a collection of set pieces, or standard materials. The opera orchestra, together with the lead actors, customarily selected from these standards pieces as seemed appropriate or were sanctioned by long usage to construct the impressions on audiences that they sought. There were rules and conventions but also considerable latitude within boundaries. Different regional and local operas had always borrowed from others, for example, effectively widening the collection of available pieces to make up the architecture of an opera.

Whereas developments until the 1950s had been unconscious and unplanned, Wang suggests that by the time the model-opera work began, times had changed. The depth, breadth, and complexity of approaches to musical challenges that had taxed earlier generations of musicians were new. Three relationships were addressed more profoundly than ever before: Those between the popular and the specialist; between Chinese and Western music; and between the general and the specific, meaning music for broad enjoyment and that designed for narrower purposes.[105]

Despite the contemporary rhetoric about the bankruptcy of traditional music and its capture by landlords in the old society, Wang Renyuan argues that in reality the composers of the model-opera music generally had a profound appreciation of traditional music and an urge to transform it for modern purposes. Wang even suggests that news reports from 1965 about the writers of the (future) model operas studying Mao's theoretical 1937 work *On Contradiction* (*Maodun lun*) offer a clue to the reality of their work at the time. These professionals were grappling, like their predecessors throughout the twentieth century, with the 'contradiction' between continuing the musical tradition and innovating (*gexin*) beyond it. The work on the music of the model operas in effect was part of accumulating a new tradition (*jilei xin chuantong*). The work had begun, without a lot of theoretical baggage, in 1958 when *Taking Tiger Mountain by Strategy* was first scripted. Musical specialists, both modern trained and opera based, created in the model operas a body of work that deserves acknowledgement as part of China's musical heritage.[106]

Musical design helped enhance the stage presence of the model operas. Here again bringing in outside professional composers on a large scale markedly raised the standard of operatic musical innovation. The inclusion of folk and Western music and the efforts to associate the main characters with the equivalent in a modern musical of theme music broke through the limitations of conventional opera. Audiences seem to have taken to this experimentation quite readily, understanding the accumulation of musical devices, old and new, rather than being put off by them. They may have been helped by their growing familiarity with film music. In a similar vein, the language of the modern operas marked a break with tradition, attempting to make the sung and spoken words more readily comprehensible to audiences, while preserving a necessary theatricality. Similarly, the considerable innovation made in the spoken parts (*nian-bai*) of these operas, employing a musicalized version of real-life speech to replace the traditional, highly affected speech exclusive to the opera theatre, was readily received.[107] Of course, the novelty of seeing modern characters in modern dress on stage undoubtedly made modernism in the music more expected and acceptable.

One of the animating principles of the model operas, the theory of the 'three prominences' (*san tuchu*), evolved in the creation of the first five model Peking operas in the early 1960s. The three prominences was given an exceptional status in all performing arts during the Cultural Revolution and was hailed as a major contribution to socialist artistic theory. Other arts, such as fiction, poetry, and painting, were also expected, at various points in these years, to reflect the application of this theory. In its first published form, the theory stated as follows: 'Among all the characters, give prominence to the positive characters; among the positive characters, give prominence to the main heroic characters; and among the heroes give prominence to the central character.'[108]

Yu Huiyong, composer of the music for *Shajiabang* and *Tiger Mountain*, who had recently been appointed preparatory head of the Shanghai City Culture System Revolutionary Committee, first expressed this formulation in a 23 May 1968 article. The three prominences were slightly reworked a year and a half later, in the kinds of adjustments to wording to which politically active Chinese of the time needed to pay close attention to avoid blotting their theoretical copybooks. The November 1969 issue of *Red Flag*, the Communist Party's main theoretical organ, rephrased the last prominence as emphasizing the 'main heroic character' (*zhuyao yingxiong renwu*). The *Red Flag* article was about the creation of the heroes in *Taking Tiger Mountain by Strategy*. No art was safe from this theory, however improbable its application: 'not only dramas, but television, novels, even those arts that do not necessarily include people, such as poetry and painting, all use the three prominences.'[109]

This all-embracing theory did not spring from the head of Yu Huiyong in 1968. As we have seen, reports on the creation of the model operas in the three years before the start of the Cultural Revolution generally mention the efforts of the directors and actors to get right the position given the heroes. In 1965, the continuing work on *The Red Lantern* included trying to give more prominence to the individual roles of each of the three main characters and experimenting with their placement on the stage in various scenes. Likewise in mid-1965, the *Shajiabang* production team wrestled with how to render Sister Aqing as a second-tier hero, so that she would not steal the show.[110]

The principle extended to all aspects of the model operas, including even their language, which helped emphasize the special nature of the central heroes: their politically advanced thinking and their wit. A

孔丘游说几十年，   郑国人民骂得好：
为了 "复辟" 腿不闲。   "活像一条丧家犬!"

1.2. The 'three prominences' from modern operas in a comic book illustration from the Criticize Lin Biao and Confucius campaign. Source: *Tianjin wenyi* (Tianjin Literature and Art), 1974, 3 (May), pp. 40–41.

July 1973 analysis of the language of *Taking Tiger Mountain by Strategy* showed the superiority of Yang Zirong's song lyrics and spoken dialogue and how they changed between the 1967 and 1968 scripts of the opera. This was a significant acknowledgement that the operas had been worked on and polished for years, even if in the second line of his nine-page article Zhong Wenyu quotes 'Comrade Jiang Qing's pointing out (*zhichu*), "script, script, it's all in the script" (*juben, juben, yi ju zhi ben*)'.[111]

Perhaps the biggest advantage of having an alleged theoretical basis like the three prominences was the comfort it gave its practitioners. For Jiang Qing and her self-image as dashing heroine of the revolution, it could excuse immodest occupying of centre stage. More seriously, for the creators of new Peking operas, new regional and local dramas, and even indeed painters and poets (as we shall see), as well as the hapless managers of these people in the cultural apparatus, the three prominences was a useful, relatively objective yardstick by which to measure correctness. At a time of mass study of theory, even the most simple had its uses (Figure 1.2).

The effect in practice of the three prominences was obvious to audiences of the model operas. The art of the new operas concentrated attention on Yang Zirong, Li Yuhe, Guo Jianguang, Fang Haizhen, and their ilk as the central heroes of the dramas. Heroes inevitably occupied centre stage, were well lit, and were deferred to by the grouping of his or her allies. By 1974 it was acknowledged that the proper use of the theory required a balanced approach. The bad characters in operas and other arts should not be so interesting and the heroes so bland and predictable that audiences would naturally prefer to root for the former.[112]

Approaches borrowed from spoken drama were put to use in the service of the new-style operas. There were, as Jiang Qing pointed out to the modern-subject Peking opera convention in Beijing in the summer of 1964, only about ninety spoken-drama companies in the nation, but more than 3,000 opera troupes.[113] From spoken drama came the relative distillation or concentration of elements, including plot and its shaping, and characterization that were often weaker in traditional opera.

The use of skilled stage directors was a new factor in the art of the model operas. The position of director is associated with the establishment of the central opera academies and theatre school in Beijing in the early 1950s. As in other areas of Chinese life, Soviet experts were invited to advise Chinese specialists on ways to train a new corps of stage performers and other specialists. Chinese opera was less directly affected by these imported advisers than, say, spoken drama, modern musicals, dance, and film. But the theatre arts were a broad church, and China's cultural leaders were keen to see Chinese opera also adopt modern, and, of course, more manageable, ways of operating. The directors came from spoken drama and from film. Their production design, including blocking the actors in ways that were previously unknown on the traditional musical stage, brought an initial freshness to the operas. Opera had always been an actor's art. Professional directors took an audience's point of view and worried about rhythm, what needed to be exaggerated for effect, and how each sequence and scene would contribute to the overall effect on audiences.

Using professional directors, often from other stage arts, encouraged actors to step beyond traditional role types and conventions of performance. Actors were urged, in the long process of the reworking these first model operas, to take risks. The vocabulary of movements available to lead and supporting actors was expanded. Yang Zirong's horse riding at the start of *Tiger Mountain* is said to have been a combination of traditional stage practice and Mongolian dance movements. Similarly, the dance movements of Yang's men, including when they ski across the snowy plateau, combined real-life actions with operatic and folk-dance traditions for an overall effect that was both novel and almost familiar to audiences.[114] Some movement was taken directly from traditional operas. Audiences had always enjoyed sequences in which characters fight supposedly in the dark, unable to see each other. This was transferred to a scene in *Shajiabang* where the New Fourth Army men fight against an enemy they cannot see.[115]

Actors adapted to the conditions of the modern subjects. Fang Haizhen, the Party secretary in *On the Docks*, wore a short red scarf draped around her shoulders. She occasionally wiped her brow when she performed physical labour or was under pressure. The kind of stage business that the actress portraying Fang could do with the scarf was the modern equivalent of the actions much loved of actors, and of audiences, once done with handkerchiefs and sleeves. Li Yuhe in *The Red Lantern* had his long red scarf to fling back across a shoulder or hold out in his hands to punctuate a point in an aria. Soldier characters like Yang Zirong and Guo Jianguang could resort to pistols, horsewhips, and other props in similar echo of older devices.

The three prominences rubric, however, could hinder the creation of a desired stage effect. Having to reserve centre stage as much as possible for the central heroes worked against more creative directing and inevitably encouraged exaggeration of these heroes. Audiences reportedly grumbled about the concentration on these monumental characters and the plots that became horribly familiar. Popular sayings put the mocking summaries of the operas into rhyming couplets but the gist can be expressed in English: 'Company commander makes a mistake, Party secretary points out the correct path; the bad egg is revealed, the play's over'. In a similar vein, the prominence given to female heroes was ridiculed: 'a big girl, wearing red clothing, stands at the highest place, and points out the direction we should go'.[116]

Even costuming and stage design in the model operas built on conventional opera expectations rather than rejecting the past. The costumes of People's Liberation Army soldiers may have looked like the real-life uniforms, but the designers took great pains to acknowledge theatrical needs, modifying through simplification and exaggeration. The seventeen-year-old Li Tiemei presented on stage a crystallized notion of what a poor peasant girl in the 1930s looked like. Sister Aqing, in her apron and with frog-fastened crossover neckline, similarly was a distillation of signs from real life and from the theatre. Yang Zirong's splendid and bandit-fooling tiger-skin waistcoat has been mentioned before. The restrained use of stage furniture and of drop cloths and other set devices acknowledged the relative simplicity opera audiences had always expected on stage. The lighting and painted backdrops created a sense of place for the action to unfold. Yet, tensions between the suggestions of real settings and the artificiality of the songs actors delivered from them were probably inevitable.[117]

This artistry was dedicated to bringing to audiences the content and themes in entertaining and educational ways. The content of the first five model operas reveals a good deal about the expectations of their creators, particularly the leaders, including Jiang Qing, who helped drive their creation forward. It is a somewhat curious picture.

Take, for example, the common features of the central heroes in these five works. All have no family. Yang Zirong, Guo Jianguang, Fang Haizhen, and Yan Weicai, fighting the White-Tiger Regiment in Korea, make no reference to a domestic life. Their entire beings seem dedicated to the tasks of the revolution (Figure 1.3). Even Yang Zirong's 'good buddy' relationship with another soldier was eliminated in a later revision of *Tiger Mountain*. The one 'family' presented in the first five model operas is a construction. As Grandma Li explains to Tiemei in the 'telling the family history' scene, the girl was adopted as an orphan and Li Yuhe, Tiemei's 'father', is not related to her, even though they brought up the girl together. The explanation of them coming together has as much to do with dedication to the revolutionary cause as it does to ordinary human feelings identified with real families. This constructed revolutionary 'family' makes it both easier and more impressive for Li Tiemei to take up Li Yuhe's red lantern after his death. She is doing so in memory of Li as a revolutionary martyr and, perhaps secondarily, as the man who treated her as his daughter. Revolutions, in the world of the model operas (and perhaps in the fantasy world of Jiang Qing, as constructed by her victims and critics), required the obliteration of individual emotions not directed at serving the inevitable triumph of the proletariat. Of course, Chinese audiences, imbued in a culture in which families remained of paramount individual concern across the 1949 change of political system, could identify Li Tiemei's actions as in support of her family. This was unavoidable, even if the promoters of the opera hoped that Tiemei's identification with the revolution would come across to a viewer more strongly than any family feelings.

Love stories are a major genre in old-style Chinese opera. The model operas treat this aspect of human existence with the same interest as they show in families. None of the heroes in these operas has a love interest. In *Shajiabang* the wedding of one of the puppet-soldier enemies which was used as a cover for a New Fourth Army attack on the traitors was

1.3. Fang Haizhen, the all-knowing Party secretary of the model opera *On the Docks* (photograph by Shi Shaohua). Source: *Xiandai Jingju: juzhao mingxinpian* (Modern Peking opera: stage-still postcards), Shanghai: Shanghai renmin meishu chubanshe (Shanghai People's Fine Arts Publishing House), 2003.

abandoned in an early reworking of the *Sparks amid the Reeds*. So even the bad characters are denied a love life. People, it seems, are defined by their class stands and their attitudes to the revolution.[118]

The militarization of the first model operas is striking. Four of the five feature armies of the good and the bad. Fighting acrobatics was a much-loved feature of old-style Chinese operas of non-romantic genres. The settings and stories of the four operas offered opportunities for actors to display their skills and audiences to enjoy them. Even *The Red Lantern* includes martial movements, with the guerrillas from the mountains and the Japanese gendarmerie. Likewise, the dockworkers of *On the Docks* engage in acrobatics drawn from soldiers' movement in traditional opera.

But the dominant military elements in four of the first five model operas point to a larger feature of Cultural Revolution political and cultural life. The verbal and visual rhetoric of the Cultural Revolution put great store on the military, in the form of the People's Liberation Army and, by extension, the people's militias, youth corps, and other organized, semi-militarized groups. The language describing the revolution as well as the personal, social, and other transformations that the revolution demanded of citizens was a language of armed struggle, disciplined fighters, and noble, far-sighted commanders. On the eve of the Cultural Revolution proper, Jiang Qing and Lin Biao organized a conference on cultural work in the army. The suggestion was that the army's accomplishments in this area offered a model to civilian society.

The start of the Cultural Revolution saw young people answering Mao Zedong's call to rise up against the establishment (excluding himself) by organizing themselves into Red Guards (*Hongweibing*, literally red guarding soldiers). On the several occasions when he appeared before millions of adoring Red Guards and other young people in Tian'anmen Square, Chairman Mao was often in an army uniform. When different factions of Red Guards fell into armed warfare in major cities, the disciplined, coordinated manoeuvres of the Chinese army in 1969 were crucial in restoring order. Students and older intellectuals went to the countryside in organized bands, 'sent down' to learn from the peasants or to labour at May Seventh cadre schools, a semi-militarized system of camps.[119] The model operas were not alone in placing soldiers and the army centre stage. A great deal of visual art invariably featured images of soldiers, male and female. Almost all the first new feature films made in 1973–1974 were on military themes.

Women had a special place in many of the model operas. The two model ballets that were also part of the eight 'revolutionary model performances' had women at their centre.[120] The only real contemporary opera among this first group of model performances, *On the Docks* was also the only one of the five in which the central hero was female. Fang Haizhen was different from her Shajiabang sister, Aqing, for Fang took centre stage. Sister Aqing became second fiddle to political instructor Guo Jianquang in revisions of *Sparks amid the Reeds*, though audiences reportedly found her a more engaging character than soldier Guo. Fang Haizhen, as Party secretary, guides the Shanghai dockworkers to realize their internationalist duties and to expose the class enemy in their ranks (note the military expression). This dominant position in a Chinese opera represented a real revolution. Traditional operas usually paired major female characters with scholars or other men: Take the various tellings of *White Snake* (*Baishe zhuan*), in which a ghost returns to Earth as a beautiful maiden and falls in love with a handsome young scholar, or the versions of *Farewell to My Concubine*, in which the title character requires a male companion. Even modern re-workings of opera stories such as *Li Huiniang*, attacked in 1964 as a 'ghost play', did not present women as firmly in control as Secretary Fang.

One extraordinary characteristic of the model opera heroes, male and female, was their lack of growth and development. Fiction and drama in most cultures depend on conflict and the responses of the central protagonists to the situations in which they find themselves. Usually these characters change in some way, finding inner resources they may not have realized they had or learning lessons from their experiences and finding new ways of dealing with their circumstances. But there is also a long tradition in most cultures of commanding heroes (often with supernatural connections), who spring full blown into the situation presented and act with god-like certainty in ensuring that the forces they represent triumph. The latter kind of drama, or story, is often called *mythology*.

The heroes of the Chinese model operas most definitely belonged to the world of myth. They started the drama fully in command of the ideological resources and emotional discipline to tackle the challenges presented. They ended the plays having defeated their enemies and proudly secured victory. Li Yuhe, an experienced fighter in the revolutionary cause, knows what he must do with his railwayman's signal lantern to support the struggles of the Communist guerrillas in the mountains against the Japanese occupiers of Chinese soil. He is arrested and interrogated but does not betray the cause, dying a martyr's death in the process. At the end he is no more wise in the needs of the revolutionary fight than he was on his first entry onto the stage. Yang Zirong may be a less stolid character, with his engaging puckishness and ability to dissemble. But he too is not shown to learn from his experiences as he enters the bandits' lair and misleading them into defeat. Yang adjusts his tactics in order to succeed in fooling the bandits but that is the extent of the change associated with his character. His strategy is complete and unchanging from start to finish. Fang Haizhen clearly knows what's what and spends her time making sure her fellow dockworkers benefit from this knowledge. These qualities of determination and idealism were, of course, familiar to Chinese audiences and readers since 1949. They also resonated with the kind of heroism many Chinese readers enjoyed in translated foreign novels.[121]

The conflict in these stories seems to reside elsewhere, in the non-central heroes, the second tier of positive protagonists. They learn, from the main hero, to better distinguish right from wrong. Thus, the young dockworker Han Xiaoqiang comes to fully appreciate the importance of combining revolutionary commitment with work duties. Only in this way can he contribute to the Chinese internationalist project. Li Tiemei is already a girl of revolutionary ambition when she hears the real story of her family's background, but that pivotal episode helps make her more determined to live up to her revolutionary heritage. Even Sister Aqing to a small extent learns from political instructor Guo Jianguang how to better manage her dealings with the puppet troops who are stationed in Shajiabang.

What this second-tier development presents to audiences is the notion of revolutionary succession. There will be suitable successors to Fang Haizhen, Li Yuhe, and the others. Li Tiemei ends *The Red Lantern* holding high the lamp her 'father' had passed on to her. Han Xiaoqiang survives a night in a class education exhibition with the enthusiastic Fang Haizhen and goes on to give his all for the revolution and production. Others around the central heroes come to unequivocal understandings of their appropriate actions in the future. It is an outcome directed firmly at the operas' audiences. They too were expected to leave the theatre with a firmer grasp of their own place in the revolutionary enterprise. Although full of awe and admiration for the central heroes, audiences could identify with the second-tier heroes and receive a similar education through the shared experience. Identification between audience and character on stage was a powerful characteristic of Chinese opera and, indeed, of all traditional drama in other cultures, even with the most fantastical or remote kinds of roles. With the Cultural Revolution model operas, this identification was facilitated by the guidance of the three prominences and the other clear signs for viewers.[122]

The result essentially was a mythology of the Chinese Communist revolution. God-like main heroes came down to often remote earthly situations, showed the way forward for other heroes, and sometimes died in the process. The deep roots that such stories were able to tap into help to account for the power of these model operas. It was not just the mind-boggling repetition of their performance during the Cultural Revolution years, whether on stage or on celluloid or in other versions and extracts, that put these operas at the centre of Chinese culture in those years. There were deeper roots that help explain their impact on Chinese audiences.

CHAPTER TWO

Spreading the New Models

In July 2002 Li Guang sat in a midtown Beijing hotel coffee shop and recalled his experience as a Cultural Revolution stage and screen star. Playing the lead role in the second-tier model Peking opera *Fighting on the Plain* had opened up exciting opportunities for the young actor, whose father had been a performer of old-style operas. The *Fighting* company had been provided with the best of everything: fellow actors, musicians, designers, make-up specialists, and even stagehands. Jiang Qing and other state leaders were frequent visitors or hosts at dinners for the creative team. Mao's wife had even had a hand in arranging his marriage. But between 1976 and his retirement from the stage, Li had found more fans in tours to Japan performing new-style opera with ancient settings than in China.[1]

The artistic and box-office success of the model works ironically had undermined their appeal. So much effort had gone into perfecting them that anything less perfect could not measure up. As models, the operas set such high standards that the expectations placed on artists like Li Guang to produce new works and perform the existing modern operas had been enormous. Audiences responded with their own assessment, thrilled by the artistic perfection but numbed by their politics.

Artists like Li Guang were not the only parties in the cultural enterprise who felt under pressure. The promulgation and expansion of the model works, the 'transplanting' of these into local musical theatre forms, and the sorting out of a somewhat over-staffed performing corps placed stress on all those involved. For artists, the importance of their roles as transmitters of the new, mass culture was tempered by an awareness of the consequences of artistic and political failure. For the managers of artists, including national and regional cultural authorities, the natural ambition to excel in these important new ventures was also balanced by worries about being held responsible for errors. Audiences watched the playing out of continuing tensions between the national and the local, occasionally pleased at attempts to apply the new styles to familiar performing genres. Indeed these tensions between centralization on Beijing and localism animate much of this chapter.

We begin with the formal consolidation of the first eight 'model performances' as exemplars for the new, modern mass culture. The first five operas were soon joined by an additional suite of modern works. The Peking opera experience showed the way for further experimentation in the updating of local operatic forms, with deeper roots in the regions. The fourth section offers an assessment of the actual place of the model performances in cultural life in these years, particularly by taking a local view. The chapter ends with another look at the grass roots, in an analysis of the experiences of performers and organizations under pressure to rationalize their ranks.

I. PROCLAIMING THE MODEL PERFORMANCES

The 'model performances', particularly the five model operas in the initial group of eight presented to Chinese theatrical and political audiences in May 1967, were the centrepieces of Cultural Revolution culture. As insurgents, Jiang Qing and her allies had seized control of the existing cultural apparatus or set up new organizations to express their paramountcy over Chinese cultural life. But they had to produce an alternative cultural product, one untainted by associations with the old, now discredited leadership and old ways of thinking. This put a heavy burden of expectations on the model works themselves. We have seen how some took years to write, rewrite, and eventually get right. The stakes were so high that some prospective operas were abandoned, sometimes after a long period of effort by many specialists. In this sense the model operas carried the seeds of their own destruction as models. As perfected as they may have been, they were presented as so quintessential and definitive that they could not really be matched.

Part of the burden of the model operas was their ubiquity: They could not be avoided during the Cultural Revolution. Audiences enjoyed the operas on a first or even fifth viewing. Seen in organized groups on film screens over and over, or in extracts on communal television screens, or sung in amateur shows and reworked into other performing genres, the model works became too much. The amount of resources and talent that was invested in them cannot be denied. The limited role that Jiang Qing seems to have had in their creation needs also to be noted, despite Cultural Revolution and post-1976 exaggerations. But ultimately the model operas failed because of their very success in filling China's stages and screens.

In May 1967, about a year after the start of Cultural Revolution political upheaval, China marked the twenty-fifth anniversary of Mao Zedong's *Talks at the Yan'an Forum on Art and Literature*, which had laid down the principles for cultural policy since that time. At such a significant historical milestone and in the heightened atmosphere of Mao worship, a special commemoration was required. On 24 May, the day after the *Talks'* anniversary, *People's Daily* led with the promulgation of the model performances (*yangbanxi*), which were all to be publicly performed in Beijing. In addition to the five modernized Peking operas, the group included two full-length ballets (*The White-haired Girl* and *The Red Detachment of Women*) and a symphony based on the model opera *Shajiabang*.[2]

In using models of behaviour and attitude to help shape and control social praxis, China is no different from other cultures. The moral authority achieved by Confucianism and the attractions of Buddhism owed a good deal to their presentation in the form of models of behaviour for all levels of society. Model devotees of both these moral philosophies acted out or performed behaviours intended to express their own commitment and to transform their audiences' attitudes and actions. Model performances likewise were more than just stage shows. They were the ritual enactment of a morality that its audiences and performers needed to internalize. The promulgators of the model operas regarded them as models for behaviour and, more specifically, for art and literature in general.[3]

The terms 'model opera' (*yangban xiju*) and 'model performance' (*yangbanxi*) emerged out of the process of their creation, rather than being inherent in their design from the beginning or suddenly being identified when they had been completed. Creating these Peking operas was an ongoing project without an apparent end point, until about ten out of a larger number of operas were fixed as models in the late 1960s or early 1970s.

The archaeology of the term 'model' (*yangban*) offers insight into this process. The term appears to have emerged out of and been most closely associated with the work on *The Red Lantern* (Figure 2.1). Tan Yuanshou, the Beijing Peking Opera Company actor involved in 1964–1965 in developing the role of Guo Jianguang in *Shajiabang*, referred to *The Red Lantern* in February 1965 as 'a living model' (*yi kuai huo yangban*) for his work on *Shajiabang*.[4] The next month, two *Theatre Journal* articles described *The Red Lantern* as 'an outstanding model' (*chuse de yangban*) of revolutionary modern Peking opera. One reported the China Peking Opera Academy creators of the drama as saying they were prepared to spend ten years work on revising the opera to make it even better.[5] The

2.1. Li Tiemei, heroine of *The Red Lantern*, as inspiration for a young militia woman. The slogans read: 'Be this kind of person' and 'Carry out the revolution to the end'. Painting by Shan Lianxiao. Poster published in 1968 by Renmin meishu chubanshe (People's Fine Arts Publishing House, Beijing). Poster in the author's collection.

second March 1965 article agreed that the revolutionary modern operas (*geming xiandaixi*) 'established models, not only for the local region or the particular type of opera' (*buyou wei ben diqu, ben juzhong shuli qi yangban*).[6] The 22 March issue of the national newspaper *Guangming Daily* included an article by the well-known Shaoxing opera artist Yuan Xuefen on *The Red Lantern* under the headline 'A Model That Keeps Improving' (*jingyiqiujing de yangban*). The work of the China Peking

Opera Academy 'has had the function of providing us with a model' (*wei women qi le yangban de zuoyong*).[7] In July 1965 the Shanghai City People's Shanghai Opera Company wrote in *Theatre Journal* in warm praise of the Peking opera transplanting of *Shajiabang*, which had started out as their opera. The first sentence of their two-page review, which had first appeared in Shanghai's *Liberation Daily*, started:

> *Shajiabang*, performed by the Beijing Peking Opera Company and the China Peking Opera Academy's *The Red Lantern*, are the same: they are both models (*yangban*) of the revolutionizing (*geminghua*) of Peking opera.[8]

As these last three citations indicate, the term *yangban* could just as appropriately be translated as 'example' or 'prototype'.

Jiang Qing, the person most blamed for an excessive focus on the *yangbanxi*, began to use the term 'model' at about the same time. On 27 April 1965, when meeting with some of the key creators of *Taking Tiger Mountain by Strategy*, she spoke of 'last year's three models' (*qunian san kuai yangban*). By this Jiang Qing meant *Tiger Mountain*, *The Red Lantern*, and *Sparks amid the Reeds*.[9] Later published documents from the February 1966 army conference on literature and art, organized in Shanghai by Lin Biao and Jiang Qing, include praise for the modern operas and suggest that 'leaders should personally take charge, and bring forth good models' (*lingdaoren yao qinzi zhua, gaohao de yangban*).[10]

The apparent first official use of the term 'model performances' (*yanbanxi*) is much easier to locate. On 28 November 1966, the Central Cultural Revolution Leadership Group called a 'Capital Literature and Art Circles Proletarian Cultural Revolution Meeting'. There Kang Sheng, the Leadership Group head, formally announced that the five Peking operas *Taking Tiger Mountain by Strategy*, *The Red Lantern*, *On the Docks*, *Shajiabang*, and *Raid on the White-Tiger Regiment*, the ballet dance dramas (*balei wuju*) *The White-Haired Girl* (*Baimaonü*) and *The Red Detachment of Women* (*Hongse niangzijun*), along with the symphonic music *Shajiabang* were 'revolutionary model performances' (*geming yangbanxi*). The troupes or companies that had produced the works, Kang reportedly called 'model troupes' (*yangban tuan*).[11]

Jiang Qing benefited politically from her association with the model performances. The June 1967 issue of *Red Flag* included a version of Jiang Qing's speech almost three years earlier at the summer 1964 modern-subject Peking opera convention. She had not been powerful enough to have it published at the time of its initial delivery. In June 1967 she had to settle for pages 25 to 28, followed by a two-page editorial in praise of the opera revolution, which mentions Jiang Qing's 1964 speech in three of its

2.2. Performers and Jiang Qing: 'The red lantern of the revolution lights the stage' (artist unidentified). Source: *Chinese Literature*, 1967, 8 (August), after page 124.

forty-eight lines and praises her at one point later for helping eliminate old-style opera (Figure 2.2). At the same time, the speech was reprinted in *People's Daily* and *Liberation Army Daily*.[12] Looked at without the baggage of accusations against the Gang of Four, the speech is a serious and even thoughtful commentary on progress in opera modernization to date.

Jiang Qing offered two sets of statistics. First, 3,000 drama troupes existed in China, not including amateur groups and what she called 'black drama troupes' (*hei jutuan*), which apparently still existed in 1964, despite fifteen years of reforms in management and administration. Among the 3,000 were about 90 professional spoken-drama companies, 90 performing arts troupes (*wengongtuan*, which specialized in modern songs and dances), and 2,800 opera and traditional variety troupes. The opera stage was occupied by 'emperors, ministers, scholars and maidens', as well as 'cow ghosts and snake spirits' (*niugui-sheshen*). Likewise, the spoken-drama stage did not necessarily present workers, peasants, and soldiers. Instead, 'big, foreign, and ancient' were the watchwords there too. In the circumstances, these troupes could not protect the nation's economic base and could even damage it.

Jiang went on to suggest that the first task was to create modern-subject operas, particularly about people and events in the last fifteen years. Traditional operas were not totally unwanted. Except for 'ghost plays' and those 'praising capitulation' (*gesong touxiang*) to 'feudal' power-holders, good traditional operas (once corrected) could still be performed. Based on her recent two years of systematic opera attendance, Jiang Qing argued that without revision and improvement, no audiences would want to see traditional operas. But work on them should again not detract from the 'number one task' (*di-yi ge renwu*), modern operas.

Having analyzed the situation, Jiang Qing devoted the second half of her 1964 speech to advice on how to proceed. Scripts were the key: As people said: 'Scripts, scripts, it's all in the scripts.' Writers were few and lacked life experience. Training a new corps of talent would take time, but in three or five years, results could be achieved. Transplanting of operas from one regional form to another was another policy Jiang Qing recommended, although it required careful selection of the work to borrow, including examining its political tendencies and its match with conditions in the adopting troupe. Creating positive characters was not easy. Originally the baddies in Shanghai's *Taking Tiger Mountain by Strategy* had been dominant, a problem compounded by the superior acting abilities of the player of the bandit leader. Revisions ensured prominence (she used the verb *tuchu*) for Yang Zirong and his comrade-in-arms, Shao Jianbo.

As an encouragement to participants at the 1964 convention, Jiang Qing's speech on the surface looks reasonable and affirming. That was certainly the view of the editorial writers of *Red Flag* in the following pages of the June 1967 issue. They first quoted Mao Zedong in a recently released letter he had written in 1944 to an opera troupe in Yan'an urging critical use of tradition and the reform of old-style operas. The next paragraph started with reference to Jiang Qing's 1964 speech. Thus, her remarks were put on a par with Mao's. They even referred to it as her 'talks' (*jianghua*), echoing the title of Mao Zedong's 1942 Yan'an *Talks*. However, there is no mention of any role Jiang Qing may have had in the creation, revision, or promulgation of the five model operas.

This acclaim and massive publicity for the model operas (and other model performances) in 1967 suggested a triumphant progress for the process of Peking opera modernization. The references Jiang Qing and the *Red Flag* editors made to the problems of recalcitrant colleagues, inappropriate topics, and other obstacles tend to be overlooked in a fixation on the typical triumphalism of the editorial and others like it. One example of the many failed attempts in the mid-1960s at creating model operas was the abortive *Red Crag (Hongyan)*, based on a popular 1961 novel about underground Communist intellectuals in the 1940s. The 1965 film adaptation of the novel, starring Zhao Dan and Yu Lan, was released in the midst of work on an opera version and was well received. Reportedly, this did not please Jiang Qing, who wanted an opera version to steal its thunder.[13] Work on *Red Crag* was suddenly abandoned in February 1966 when Jiang Qing explained to the startled writers that she had not realized earlier that the Sichuan Party organization, featured in the story, on the eve of Liberation had been riddled with supporters of Wang Ming, the Party leader who had preceded Mao and had been deposed in early 1940s.[14]

2. OTHER MODEL OPERAS

Other modern-subject operas began life in the early 1960s but were not included among the initial five operas named in the eight model performances. Their turn for model status came later, after further work during the Cultural Revolution. For the three parties involved in the cultural enterprise, the need for more model works became clear by the mid-1960s. Jiang Qing and her allies at the centre and local cultural authorities saw that five models were too limited. An expansion in works would indicate how valuable the original operas as models were for further creative work. For artists, having more new-style operas (and later experimenting with local performance forms) meant more opportunities to engage in the enterprise, earn merit from leaders, and keep busy. Audiences naturally welcomed more choices on opera stages, even if the new works soon became almost as familiar as the original models.

The six second-wave model operas were *Song of the Dragon River*, *Azalea Mountain* (*Dujuanshan*), *The Red Detachment of Women*, *Fighting on the Plain* (*Pingyuan zuozhan*), the reworking of the former in *Guerrillas on the Plain* (*Pingyuan youjidui*), and *Boulder Bay* (*Panshiwan*). Companies in Shanghai and Beijing were responsible for all six because that was where the talent was found or could be relocated and where the projects could be more easily supervised.[15] The creation of these new works was a familiar mix of ambition, innovation, and caution, punctuated by intervention from the authorities.

Like *On the Docks*, *Song of the Dragon River* had a contemporary setting. In the spring of 1963 a village on the southwest coast of China is experiencing a drought. The county committee decides to build an embankment at the Dragon River Production Team to bring in water. The production team Party secretary Jiang Shuiying initiates the undertaking and helps the production team leader, Li Zhitian, to change his political thinking. Through working together, the cadres and masses complete their task of diverting the river, allowing 90,000 *mu* (6,000 hectares) of drought-stricken land to be restored to production.

Song of the Dragon River had begun in Fujian as a spoken play. The Xinhua Peking Opera Company in the southern suburbs of Shanghai transplanted the work to the opera stage.[16] Xinhua was not a top-tier company but had shown strong interest in attempting modern-subject works, perhaps in the hope of raising its professional status. By April 1964 the company began public performances. But such instant transplanting from play to opera was not without problems. Too many places looked simply like the play with songs added. The new opera was not chosen to be presented at the Beijing convention that summer.

In the best tradition of grass-roots research and 'learning from the people', the *Song of the Dragon River* company went south to Fujian in November 1964. For almost four weeks they visited the original setting of the spoken play, met with the local people who had fought the drought, and listened to the views of Chen Hong, the writer of the original spoken drama. In 1965 work continued, drawing in a range of talented directing, composing, and dance professionals, a measure of the commitment the Shanghai cultural leadership had made to this modern opera, despite the relative obscurity of the Xinhua opera company. The Xinhua company proudly presented their new opera at the East China Regional Modern-subject Opera Convention in May–June 1965.

Success for the Xinhua company brought sudden loss when, on Jiang Qing's instructions, *Song of the Dragon River* was taken out of their hands in March 1966. Available sources assume Jiang's decision was motivated by her evil ambitions, but the Xinhua company was a suburban, small-scale opera group, probably without the creative and other resources to engage in the kind of lengthy revision Jiang envisaged. Her other instruction is perhaps more revealing: The Party secretary in the opera should be made a female. In 1968 and 1969, two successive teams of specialists were established to work on revisions, drawing on opera companies, amateur writers, the composer Yu Huiyong, and even the Shanghai modern musicals company.[17] The scale of this venture was another indication of the kind of resources put into these potential model operas and of the importance with which they were invested by the Cultural Revolution leadership.

When she joined Yu Huiyong in inspecting the revised version of the opera in May 1969, Jiang Qing made two main suggestions. The class struggle in Dragon River commune should be given more prominence and the music should use an enlarged, mixed Western and Chinese orchestra, rather than rely simply on the pure, percussive music of Peking opera. A similar change was introduced around this time into the score of *Taking Tiger Mountain by Strategy*, also with help from the ever-ready Yu Huiyong.

In February 1970 Zhang Chunqiao, Jiang Qing's ally in the Shanghai leadership, watched a full dress rehearsal and suggested that the opera be disconnected from its Fujian setting: 'That way we can have more leeway [to perfect the opera].' The opera was subsequently set in an unnamed place. New talented actors were transferred to the company and new dance, design, and music professionals invited to contribute. Even the 1997 report on these events acknowledges that the artistic level of *Song of the Dragon River* was raised by their input. The cult of the amateur took second place in this new group. The six writers, four directors, five musical directors, and three stage designers recruited were all experienced professionals. The composers included the ubiquitous Yu Huiyong. Three actresses helped develop the part of the now female Party secretary, Jiang Shuiying, a practice also used with the first five operas, where more than one person prepared a role, being assigned to an A, B, or C cast.

The whole team made five trips to live in the countryside, taking the entire opera apart and re-building its structure of scenes, the language sung and spoken, and the musical design. It is easy to mock these frequent resorts to the countryside, particularly when timed to take the opera crews from the cold of Shanghai, with heating prohibited in the winter (as the city is south of the Yangzi River), to more salubrious climes in the south. But these trips were designed to be used directly in the creation of the characters on the stage, particularly in a case like *Song of the Dragon River* with its contemporary setting. Fantastical versions of a character like *Tiger Mountain*'s clever hero, Yang Zirong, were easier to create than figures on stage that audiences reckoned they knew better.

The report by the C cast's Jiang Shuiying sheds light on the process of creating a character and adjusting their art to modern life that all Chinese opera actors faced.[18] In her 1972 account, actress Li Bingshu recalled her initial efforts at creating the character:

> I still had the mistaken notion that acting in modern plays would be much easier than in traditional ones. It would be simply a matter of moving and speaking just like in real life. But in fact it was exactly the opposite. At rehearsals for *Song of the Dragon River* as soon as I got on stage, I was surprised: I didn't know where to put my hands, or how to step. I felt everything had gone from my brain and didn't have a clue. Previously, in performing old-style operas, I just followed mechanically the patterns that the master had taught us. No-one could say whether a performance was life-like or not, as no-one had seen what kind of appearance ancient scholars and maidens had.

Now I was to play Jiang Shuiying, and must create her according to real life and the script. What kind of person was Jiang? The broad audience, especially the poor and lower-middle peasants, had in their minds a 'standard'. If you strayed from that 'standard', then you could not make it a success. But that 'standard' in my own mind was like a pot of paste [without form].

In this dilemma Li Bingshu found 'experiencing life' in the countryside of great help. She went with the troupe to the countryside five times in 1969–1970. Her first attempt at playing Jiang Shuiying looked to the local peasants like an intellectual. She needed to make her character simple, warm, painstaking, and generous. The character had to show these qualities in the scenes in which she helps Li Zhitian, the production team leader, with his political thinking: 'I finally realized that in playing a hero like Jiang Shuiying, the simpler the better. There was no need for any fancy business.'

Finding the right voice for a hero was also a challenge for an actress trained in the old operas. Li had previously played virtuous young women. The posture and voice of such characters were always refined and charming. But Jiang Shuiying needed to be forceful and expansive. The maiden's falsetto would not do. Jiang Shuiying's singing needed to combine the falsetto with the natural voice. Her spoken dialogue should also be in her natural voice. This also demanded quite a shift in thinking for the actress. In the beginning Li Bingshu had feared using her natural voice could damage her falsetto, which was her 'capital' in playing those old-style, maidenly roles. But she came to realize that the new role was more important than these somewhat dated and politically backward concerns. The character sang and spoke as she should in such a contemporary setting. Even discounting the political breathlessness about 'poor and lower-middle peasants' and Chairman Mao's guiding her thoughts, Li Bingshu's 1972 description of her struggles to create a modern hero has a ring of authenticity amid the ideological dross.[19]

Seven more drafts were needed before, on 25 November 1970, the State Council Culture Group approved the latest *Song of the Dragon River* script and it and the performance were 'fixed' (*ding ge*). When the company travelled to Beijing in September 1971, a television documentary of their performance was made. Mao Zedong, by now almost seventy-eight years old, watched this version, rather than attend a live show. He endorsed the opera: His wife declared it could be one to which foreign guests of the state could be taken. She was mindful of the imminent arrival of President Nixon and his wife. At New Year 1972 Jiang Qing, Zhang Chunqiao, and Yao Wenyuan (three-quarters of the future Gang of Four)

watched *Song of the Dragon River*. To Jiang's apparent horror Party secretary Jiang Shuiying sang 'gazing at the Big Dipper (*Beidou*) increases my
strength'. Jiang Qing insisted the words be changed to a more politically
correct 'gazing at Beijing'. From then on, Zhang Chunqiao reportedly
decreed, any changes to even a single word in the opera required official
approval. The official version was made available to the public in the
March 1972 issue of *Red Flag* and in the 3 March issue of *Guangming
Daily*. From a start in the southern suburbs of Shanghai to the pages of
Red Flag had taken eight years.

Perhaps the main reason for the exceptional level of political attention
the opera attracted was shared with *On the Docks*, a project also developed initially by a second-tier opera company. Among the model operas
of the first and second tranches, these two were the only ones with contemporary settings in civilian society. Audiences were likely to be more
critical of stories and characters that resembled their own experiences.
Soldiers from the past or in Korea could be treated as the fabulous heroes
they were supposed to be. A Party secretary, dockworker, and poor peasant were more familiar game to critical audiences. Their creation needed
special attention, from the actors and others in the opera company and
from the politicians for whom audiences were larger but could be just as
critical.

Azalea Mountain took even longer to create, despite its less politically
delicate setting in the relatively distant past. In the autumn of 1927, the
Iron Blood regiment of the newly established Red Army at its base on
Azalea Mountain welcomes Ke Xiang from the Communist Soviet base
headquarters in Jinggangshan. In presenting the Red Army's battles with
local landlords' forces, *Azalea Mountain* was an obvious opportunity for
military acrobatics, a popular feature of old-style Peking opera.[20]

Azalea Mountain started out in Shanghai in 1963 as a spoken play. Qiu
Shengrong, an established 'painted face' actor in the Beijing Peking Opera
Company, liked the legendary aspects of the story, a quality it shared with
Taking Tiger Mountain by Strategy. Qiu thought the play had potential for
the Beijing convention of modern-subject operas planned for mid-1964.[21]
A script was written and preparations began. The actress Zhao Yanxia
helped create the part of Ke Xiang, the political commissar, just as she was
also working on Sister Aqing's role for the future *Shajiabang*. Intelligent
and creative opera actors able to work on these modern-subject plays were
obviously not numerous. Qiu Shengrong took the lead, finding it hard to
strike the right balance between his familiar 'painted face' movements
and the relative naturalism of spoken-drama acting. But the songs and
acrobatics the company developed met the support of Beijing mayor Peng

Zhen, who had been no big fan of modern-subject opera. They also proved exceptionally popular with audiences in the city, both at and after the summer modern-subject Peking opera convention in 1964. The opera played more than 200 times to full houses.

But *Azalea Mountain*'s supporters in 1964 and after proved a problem once the Cultural Revolution started. Its links with disgraced mayor Peng Zhen, and with the writer Deng Tuo and others attacked on the eve of the Cultural Revolution, meant the opera was removed from the repertoire as a precautionary measure, despite its proven popularity. The senior actor Qiu Shengrong had also been criticized as a 'reactionary artistic authority' and held under house arrest.[22] But reportedly Jiang Qing's enthusiasm for this opera had never waned. In late 1968 she ordered the Beijing Peking Opera Company to revise the opera but to change its name to *Du Spring Mountain* (*Duquan shan*) to make the point that the opera had been changed.

The Beijing company's creative team of more than thirty persons was given a lot of time and resources to complete the revisions. Part of the effort involved 'experiencing life' in the Jinggangshan base area in southern Jiangxi province. Actor Qiu Shengrong was even released from his 'cow shed' and joined the company going south.[23] More than a year and a half later, Jiang Qing handed responsibility for the completion of *Du Spring Mountain* over to the ever-helpful Yu Huiyong, now deputy head of the State Council Culture Group, the new replacement of the old Ministry of Culture. Yu Huiyong felt empowered to negate much of the previous work on the opera, including the writing, directing, and acting. Qiu Shengrong was dropped from the team.[24] The new writers included Wang Zengqi, who had first worked on the opera script in 1963 and again in 1968. Yu Huiyong, in his overseer capacity, asked that all the lines of dialogue be delivered with a distinctly poetic rhythm. He even supervised the plans for the stage design and acrobatic dance movements, in addition to composing the music for the whole piece.

A 1973 report on the dance and martial acrobatics in *Azalea Mountain* emphasized the innovations made by the opera creators on the basis of traditional stage movement. Some of these new features were designed to give prominence to the central hero, Ke Xiang. Her first entrance, for example, was made particularly striking, with the actress in white clothing for dazzling effect. A major innovation was having Ke, despite her gender, using forms of stage movement usually associated with male roles in traditional opera, such as exaggerated steps and turning of the body to show a man's determination and strength. The martial acrobatics were given a sense of the real, using folk-style weapons, for example. The result, the designers hoped, was the presentation of certain patterns and forms but without being formulaic.[25]

Clearly the stakes had been raised by the full-scale promulgation of the original eight 'model performances' in 1967. Given the importance and expectations placed on the model works during the Cultural Revolution, a major new opera from the hands of creators of the earlier works needed to be really impressive. On International Labor Day 1973, test performances of the revised *Du Spring Mountain* started in the Beijing's Workers' Club theatre. Impressed by the performance, Jiang Qing relented and the title *Azalea Mountain* returned to the marquee. After some further small adjustments, the September 1973 performance script of the opera was published in the October issue of *Red Flag* and in the 10 October editions of *People's Daily*, *Liberation Daily*, and other newspapers around the country.[26] The writing credit on the published script was to 'Wang Shuyuan and others'. Wang had written the spoken play a full ten years earlier. This gave rise to mocking comments after 1976 about 'ten years grinding out one opera' (*shinian mo yi ge xi*). Amid the mockery, there must have been some envy at the time lavished on getting these productions to such levels of required perfection.

The Red Detachment of Women was a ubiquitous presence during the Cultural Revolution through the ballet, named in May 1967 as one of the model performances. That a Peking opera on the same story should be produced speaks to the popularity of the 1961 film of the same title, the relative success of the ballet, and the paucity of subject matter deemed reliable as politics and entertainment during these years. The work on the Peking opera version of *Red Detachment* began in 1972 at the China Peking Opera Theatre (*Zhongguo Jingju yuan*), the same company that had created *The Red Lantern*. They based their opera directly on the model ballet, which provided perhaps a more politically secure basis than exploration of the now-banned feature-film version. Like the ballet, and unlike the original film, the central heroic role was given not to the slave girl Wu Qinghua but to the man who turns her into a disciplined revolutionary, Party representative Hong Changqing. When the latter dies a martyr's death before the landlord has been overthrown, Qinghua takes over as Party representative in the detachment. A 1999 history of modern opera praises the writing, directing, and music of the Peking-opera version, though it curiously omits the names of those responsible. When it was performed and the script published, the credit went to a collective group.[27] Although always overshadowed by its ballet cousin, the opera was filmed in 1972.

2.3. The actor Li Guang and comrades in the modern Peking opera *Fighting on the Plain* (photograph by Chen Juanmei). Source: *Xiandai Jingju: juzhao mingxinpian* (Modern Peking opera: stage-still postcards), Shanghai: Shanghai renmin meishu chubanshe (Shanghai People's Fine Arts Publishing House), 2003.

Fighting on the Plain was also presented as a collective work by the China Peking Opera Theatre, though Zhang Yongmei was credited as the group's amanuensis (*zhi bi*). As the lead actor, Li Guang, recalled some years later, the company was an assemblage of the best talents available from a range of other troupes and academies.[28] The story is set on the north China plain during the war with Japan (Figure 2.3). Zhao Yonggang, the central hero, is commander of an Eighth Route Army company engaged in guerrilla warfare with the help of the local peasants. The latter are represented chiefly by two women, Aunt Zhang and her daughter Xiaoying. Together the army and the people (like fish in water, as the standard Cultural Revolution metaphor had it) achieve a major success against the Japanese. The wartime setting allowed for plenty of acrobatics, including night fighting, in an echo of more ancient opera traditions. The emphasis on the lead hero put a big strain on the stamina of the actor: Li Guang was the centre of attention in six of the eight scenes.[29] The opera was made into a feature film in 1974 at the army's August First Film Studio with the renowned pre–Cultural Revolution directors of traditional opera adaptations, Cui Wei and Chen Huai'ai.[30]

Guerrillas on the Plain, based on a feature film from 1955 of the same name, never made it into the Cultural Revolution group of modern Peking operas, even though the 1955 film was remade in colour, with adjustments to reflect current political emphases, in 1973–1974. The story and setting were similar to *Fighting on the Plain*. Jiang Qing had reportedly in 1965 already identified the black-and-white film as suitable material for Peking-opera adaptation. Weng Ouhong, A Jia, and others were sent to conduct fieldwork in May that year in the region of the story's setting. They worked up a script and rehearsals by the China Peking Opera Theatre started in early 1966. But the writers did not finish revising the second half of the script and were soon diverted to further work on *The Red Lantern*.[31] Dress rehearsals ended fruitlessly in March 1966 and the start of the Cultural Revolution put the project on hold, particularly once A Jia and Weng came under Red Guard attack as representing the 'black line' in cultural practice. The project was only taken up again after 1976.[32]

One of the last of the Cultural Revolution modern Peking operas was set in the 1960s and told of the battles by a people's armed militia on the southern coast against spies sent from Taiwan by the Guomindang government. The story of the making of *Boulder Bay* provides an insight into the kinds of collective and individual ambitions behind the emergence of all of the model operas.[33]

Members of the Shanghai Youth Peking and Kun Opera Company (*Shanghai qingnian Jing-Kun jutuan*) wanted to present a work at the national convention on modern-subject Peking operas held in Beijing in mid-1964. The company had only been formed three or four years earlier, and its reputation and artistic strengths were somewhat undeveloped. In an artistic field like Chinese opera, it was apparently hard to compete with established companies that had roots and famous members from before 1949. Making a modern opera offered a way forward for the ambitious youngsters. At the Beijing convention Jiang Qing had suggested that a Shanghai company adapt the new spoken play, created and performed by an army troupe, *Great Wall in the Southern Seas* (*Nanhai changcheng*). The Shanghai Peking Opera Company had its hands full with *Tiger Moun-tain* and *On the Docks*. The young company leapt at the chance to take on an adaptation that enjoyed such high-level sponsorship: It was a way to raise the standing of the troupe.

A new writing group was needed for which people were brought from outside. Four writers, including He Man, who was also working on *On the Docks*, started work with visits to Guangdong province, where the play was set and had originated. In February 1965, rehearsals began on *Great Wall in the Southern Seas*. About a dozen members of the fighting acrobatics team working on the opera spent several months at military training and 'experiencing life' in the ranks at the Jiangwan military airfield. By the end of March, the teams working on script, music and songs, and directing had finished two major revisions of the opera. In June it participated in the East China modern opera convention.

The level of involvement from people who had other responsibilities is striking, even given the critical purpose of reporting this concern in post–Cultural Revolution accounts. Chen Pixian, Shanghai Party secretary in 1965, for example, found time to phone the company and inform them that he felt the two women protagonists in the opera were not as good-looking as those in the original spoken play. *Great Wall in the Southern Seas* opened for public performances around National Day, 1 October 1965.

Seven months later the Cultural Revolution officially got under way. The 100 or so members of the Shanghai Youth Peking and Kun Opera Company were not immune to the upheavals. Indeed, as a younger group, they may have included members who saw the Cultural Revolution as an opportunity to assert their individual and company interest over the more established and thus more politically vulnerable opera groups in Shanghai. In June 1967 'rebels' (*zaofanpai*) among the Red Guards at the Youth Company pasted up a 'big-character poster' (*dazibao*) with the headline: 'Thoroughly lift the lid on the two-line struggle in the creation and production of *Great Wall in the Southern Seas*.' The poster accused the troupe leadership and, more importantly, the previous city cultural apparatus leaders of seeking to promote the 'black line' in literature and art and trying to prevent the opera from becoming a 'model performance'. The 'rebels' in 1967 were using their accusations mostly to attack Chen Pixian, Li Taicheng, and others among the, by then, disgraced city and cultural leadership.

The second period in the story of the adaptation of the play *Great Wall in the Southern Seas* started in late 1967, six months after the promulgation of the first five model Peking operas. Because many of the original creative team that had worked on *Great Wall* in 1965 had been discredited at the start of the Cultural Revolution, the new company organized a new team. They did the usual, and headed south to 'experience life' on the southeast sea coast, where winters are less severe than in Shanghai, a fact noted in none of the sources on these kinds of 'to the grass roots' episodes. The new group produced a new script, though one based heavily on the 1965 version. It was revised and reworked over a long period, with full dress rehearsals before invited audiences being held in 1970. The amount of time and resources devoted to these efforts would make present-day

Chinese opera company members weep with envy. Throughout these years the opera company and creative teams collected their wages, whether or not there were any operas on Shanghai's stages.

In the spring of 1971, Jiang Qing reportedly ordered Yu Huiyong, composer and now cultural authority, to reorganize yet again the *Great Wall* creative team. Thus began the third stage in the revision of the opera. The team went to spend time on the coast in Shandong province. They added two scenes inspired to a large extent by traditional Peking opera, one on a spy seeking his contact on the bay and one involving fighting in a dark cave. Blind fighting and miming getting onto and off a heaving boat were old standards from Chinese opera known to generations of viewers.

In the spring of 1972 rehearsals started, with new specialists brought in to assist with the singing and art design. More revisions were made, based on this studio work, until full dress rehearsals of the complete opera began in September. This was the third draft and was now titled *Boulder Bay*. After further feedback from politicians, the team in November 1972 headed south to Fujian again to 'experience life'. It is tempting to ascribe to these artists the practice of stretching out tasks to fill as much time as possible, which was the norm in a great many Chinese organizations such as factories and government offices. But these people were under pressure. Their work was liable to political inspection and could bring heavy criticism. The team worked night and day, according to a 1996 report, and finally completed a fully revised script.

On their return to Shanghai, Tao Xiong, who had been an earlier member of the *Tiger Mountain* creative team, joined the group to help render the dialogue into rhyming verse. This was apparently Yu Huiyong's idea. *Azalea Mountain* had pioneered this verse trend. Yu thought it would give *Boulder Bay* a fresh, up-to-date feel. At Yu's suggestion the entire *Boulder Bay* cast and crew, by then numbering more than 100 people, went to southern Fujian in July 1973 to experience living in a fishing village at the height of the summer heat. Dialogue versification continued, with comments from the local folk.

In September 1973 the huge cast and crew, back in Shanghai, worked feverishly to rehearse a rough version of the opera. Yu Huiyong, back from Beijing, was not impressed: 'You've stopped when you're only halfway there.' Four aspects needed serious work: the poetry of the dialogue; the acrobatic and dance movements; the pacing; and the uniformity of the look of the piece. These were serious charges perhaps not surprising, given the chequered history of writing and re-writing.

Boulder Bay was presented in August 1974 at a national modern-opera performance convention in Beijing. Work continued back in Shanghai in the fall and winter. The opera was finally approved in February 1975. Instead of the usual collective writing credit, a pseudonymous A Jian was identified as author. The company started work on filming the opera at the Shanghai Film Studio. The performance was credited to the Shanghai Peking Opera Company. It was over ten years since the first rehearsals of the Peking opera *Great Wall in the Southern Seas.*

After all that effort, *Boulder Bay* went beyond the standard Cultural Revolution operas in several remarkable respects, chiefly related to the presentation of the main heroes. As we have observed, model-opera heroes were all single, widows, or widowers. The absence of family was remarkable. In *Boulder Bay*, however, the central hero and militia leader Lu Changhai has a beloved wife, Qiaolian, who comes from less progressive political stock. Audiences are able to see their frictions, when they disagree and when they make up, even their affection for each other. The 1999 history of modern opera argues that this relatively accurate reflection of real life gave the opera considerable interest.[34] These elements are so unexpected that, when combined with the lively pace, the opera seems almost a parody. The effect is heightened by the final fight-acrobatic sequence, filmed and performed as if underwater.

The considerable emphasis on old-fashioned stage-fighting acrobatics increased the potential for audience enjoyment. The language of the spoken dialogue was also unusual. It was entirely in poetic rhyming phrases, giving it a musicality that contrasted with the relative closeness to real life of other elements in the performance. The early cast included Tong Xiangling in the main role, bringing the dazzle of his Yang Zirong to a somewhat different setting from the snowy highlands of the northeast. He also had no tiger-skin waistcoat. But the opera did have new-style stage effects, modelled somewhat more closely on real life than was usual for most model operas. Paradoxically, as the later opera historians concede, this may account for the distinct lack of enthusiasm from many audiences, who found the almost camp elements hard to take.[35]

3. TRANSPLANTING THE MODELS

The model performances, especially the Peking operas, were models in several senses. At the most basic level, they were models for other Peking operas on modern subjects. A degree of innovation and stretching of the boundaries of model-opera content and style occurred, as seen in the novel features in *Boulder Bay*. These Peking operas were also models for the modernization of regional and local forms of Chinese opera. This was a reverse of the transplanting (*yizhi*) that had occurred in the first creation of the Peking opera models that had started life as Shanghai or Huai operas. Thus, *Taking Tiger Mountain by Strategy*, for example, was transplanted into Sichuan opera. Perhaps the most remote such transplanting was the adaptation of *Shajiabang* into a Uighur-style musical for audiences in Xinjiang in the far northwest. At the same time, in the 1970s, local opera forms appeared with new stories and characters but modelled on the styles and ethos of the model Peking operas. The tensions between the centralizing implied by Peking-opera models and an acknowledgement of the regional were never overcome.

Beyond opera, the model works supposedly provided a template for the creation of works in other performing arts, including dance, variety performances with Chinese instrumental accompaniment (*quyi*), comic dialogues (*xiangsheng*), spoken dramas (both long and short), street theatre, massed slogan chanting, and other, more potty forms of entertainment-cum-education.[36] It also included feature films, which began to emerge from the studios shortly after the first films of the model performance operas and ballets.

Modelling was not confined to the performing arena. Other forms of creative art were also, at one stage or other during the Cultural Revolution years, expected to incorporate the spirit and ethos of the model performances. Fiction writing, for example, gave prominence to central heroes and a single superhero in novels and short stories about the kinds of situations and characters seen on the model-opera stage. Songs and poetry were also expected to be based on these model examples. Painting and sculpture were also arts in which, at least with human subjects, prominence could be given to heroes and debasement visited upon the politically backward.

The ambition of the Cultural Revolution cultural leadership in this respect is striking. The assumption that the whole of modernized Chinese art and culture could in some broad sense be unified, inter-related, and further refined speaks to a remarkable confidence in leadership. Mao Zedong was a god-like figure during the Cultural Revolution years. The cultural ambitions of his most ardent followers were little short of fascist in their assumption of global modelling and control. Chinese audiences – political and cultural – had little choice in the matter, though they could and did avoid much of this work with a quiet determination.

Beyond art, the model works of the Cultural Revolution were also to serve as models of behaviour and correct political views and actions in a pattern Børge Bakken has shown has strong historical roots and continued pertinence in today's China.[37] Audiences may have found it quite a leap from Yang Zirong's tiger-skin waistcoat in the snowy forests of

1940s Jilin to their own somewhat duller existences, but the attitudes and fearlessness of Yang and his fellow heroes were to be copied by lesser mortals. The artistic bombast and inflation of the model works were shared with the rhetorical hyperbole of the media. Judging from these media, the world was a Manichean nightmare of good versus evil in which constant vigilance was necessary to ensure survival. Chinese political and cultural audiences knew better.

The major effort at transplanting the model performances into regional and local forms came rather late in the Cultural Revolution. *People's Daily* in early 1971 published two articles calling for the large-scale popularization of the model performances through their use in other genres.[38] By this time the cultural authorities had relaxed a little in their attempts at tight control over artistic activity. New films, stage performances, and other cultural products emerged after 1972–1973, when Mao Zedong, Zhou Enlai, and other state leaders pointed out the paucity of cultural works available to their audiences. In 1972 Mao had noted to a meeting of literature and art workers that 'at the moment there are very few films, operas and literary and artistic works'.[39]

The big push at model opera transplanting into local forms came after 1972, once the Peking-opera versions of the model operas had been fixed and recorded in standardized form on film. One estimate records several hundred groups established nationwide in the early 1970s to transplant and study the model performances.

Hebei alone had thirty-three such teams (*banzi*). Even remote parts, such as Tibet, got into the act. In 1971 a Tibetan group performed the Peking opera *Shajiabang* and the model ballet *The White-Haired Girl*.[40]

A Hebei province-wide festival in late 1972 included a Hebei *bangzi* version of *Tiger Mountain*, a *pingdiao* (Hebei opera) version of *The Red Detachment of Women*, a *laodiao* (literally 'old tune') production of *Red Lantern*, a Henan opera (*Yuju*) re-working of *Song of the Dragon River*, a 'silk string' (*sixian*) opera version of *Tiger Mountain*, a Shanxi opera (*Jinju*) re-working of *Song of the Dragon River*, a Northern opera (*pingju*) version in the style of Tangshan city (*Tangju*) of the same opera, and a Northern opera version of *Tiger Mountain*. Each troupe was to bring to the festival 200 copies of the scores or at least main melodies and of any summary of their experiences in transplanting the model works.[41]

Transplanting proceeded apace in the distant Xinjiang Uighur Autonomous Region. One of the key model operas, *The Red Lantern*, had been adapted into the local Uighur musical drama (*geju*) form by the Xinjiang Song, Dance and Spoken Drama Company (*Xinjiang gewu huaju yuan*), the all-purpose provincial-level performance organization that had gathered together remnants of other performing troupes that had been disbanded during the years of upheaval (1966–1969).[42] After a full year of writing and rehearsal the Uighur musical version of *The Red Lantern* had its public premiere in Urumqi, the provincial capital, in time for the May 1972 thirtieth anniversary of Mao's Yan'an *Talks*. The so-called Uighur musical drama form was itself a relatively recent invention, without a long heritage to draw upon. Efforts to create such modern-style sung dramas in imitation of the opera forms so popular back east, in China proper, arose in parallel with increased Han Chinese immigration to the far western regions. Han settlers brought their own opera forms: Peking opera from the capital, Shaoxing opera and other forms from Shanghai, the other major source of migrants to Xinjiang in the 1950s and 1960s. Mindful of the sensitivities of the indigenous Uighur ethnic majority, cultural authorities encouraged the invention of a local musical-drama form performed in the Uighur language. The Uighur-language version of *The Red Lantern* was thus a somewhat novel and ersatz musical invention for most inhabitants of Xinjiang. It was as if this new form could place the autonomous region on a more equal artistic footing with the eastern provinces and their associated musical theatres. To confirm this approach, the Xinjiang regional revolutionary committee determined, in December 1972, that the new musical should be put on celluloid, in the same manner as the Peking opera version of *The Red Lantern* had been filmed.

The filming of the Uighur version of *The Red Lantern* in turn had considerable appeal to the central authorities. For Jiang Qing and her allies, increasingly anxious, in the face of audience weariness, to sustain the importance of the model performances in the cultural pantheon, the new-style opera could be brought to all corners of the nation. This would confirm the centrality of model operas like *The Red Lantern*. For other political leaders, distribution of the new film would confirm the enlightened ethnic policies of the central government, in which even the Muslim Uighur people from the far northwest participated enthusiastically in the cultural life of the nation. That the cultural traffic in this case was from the centre or Han majority to the minority people was unremarked upon. Han audiences in the Chinese heartland had long embraced the exotic, Central Asian or Turkic rhythms of Uighur and other songs and dances from Xinjiang. Indeed, such performances were a welcome relief from a steady diet of Han, Peking-opera inspired, or orthodox exhortatory modern songs that were the usual fare in public performance in the Chinese heartland.[43]

In August 1974 *People's Daily* published an endorsement of transplanting that was widely reprinted in provincial literary magazines that had

re-started publication in 1972–1973.[44] The *People's Daily* report coincided with a convention in Beijing of stage performances from around
the nation.[45] From Shanghai came Shanghai opera (*Huju*), Shaoxing
opera (*Yueju*), and Huai opera (*Huaiju*). From the Guangxi Zhuang
Autonomous Region came Zhuang minority opera (*Zhuangju*), Guilin
opera (*Guiju*), and *caidiao* (Guangxi Zhuang) opera. Hunan was represented by flower-drum opera (*huaguxi*) and Hunan opera (*Xiangju*). The
northeast province of Liaoning sent a Northern opera (*pingju*) troupe.[46]
In a desert largely of Peking opera, the variety was a treat. These conventions were similar to the trial performance (*guanmo yanchu*) conventions
ten years earlier from which the model Peking operas on modern subjects
had emerged.

This move amounted to re-engagement with the lively arts of the
provinces and regions and recognition of the variety and diversity of customs and cultures across the nation. It was an acknowledgement that one
regional form (Peking opera), even one with national pretensions before
1949, could not satisfy audiences or adequately serve the expectations
placed on art and literature. These regional performing forms had deep
roots in the localities, despite the efforts at 'reforming' and bowdleriz-
ing that had occurred since the early 1950s. As the *People's Daily* writer
noted: 'Local plays have a close relationship with the life of the people,
their particular languages and their customary tastes'.

But transplanting was not a full acknowledgement of local power. The
aim was still Beijing-centred, serving the political purposes represented
by the Peking operas as much as catering to local preferences and tastes,
which needed channelling in the right directions.

> Transplanting makes it easier for the revolutionary model performances to
> be understood and accepted in each location and among each ethnic group
> (*minzu*)...it enables the heroic figures of the revolutionary model perfor-
> mances to go deeper into people's hearts and will better develop the fighting
> function of the revolutionary model performances to consolidate the dicta-
> torship of the proletariat.

The *People's Daily* cited the example of the shift in Hunan flower drum
plays from those featuring young scholars (*xiaosheng*), young women
(*xiaodan*), and clowns (*xiaochou*) to presenting *Shajiabang*. This was
hardly a generous recognition of the power of local tastes over audiences,
though audiences tended to take whatever opportunities were presented
to endorse the even partial restoration of local performing arts.

Vital to the creation of new local operas through transplanting was a
suitably reformed and skilled corps of personnel. The 'thorough-going

reform of local opera [was] still an arduous task' with a need to get over the fallacy that 'the standards of the model performances are so high that they cannot be transplanted'. Effort at training was needed, judging from the hints at resistance to the models from some quarters. This opposition was not from diehard opponents of the Cultural Revolution, allegedly ever ready to spring back into action and mislead the unwary, but from people described as 'comrades'. An article on the 'three prominences' published in mid-1973 noted that 'some comrades think it is easier to write about middle characters (*zhongjian renwu*) who are lively and have drama (*you 'xi'*)'. In similar vein, 'some comrades' felt that the 'three prominences' could be respected in theatre works and novels in which there were a relatively large number of characters and complex plots. But in smaller-scale, lower-key works, the principle was hard to put into effect. This rare mention of a lack of complete consensus on the part of 'some comrades' was striking, in a context insisting on the correctness and perfection of the model performances as models for artistic and literary creation.[47]

The mid-1974 *People's Daily* article hints at the problems that the recent Beijing convention of local opera forms seems to have revealed. The writer notes that transplanting is 'a process of development . . . it is normal in this development process to go from the immature to the relatively mature' and to have 'neither fish nor fowl [literally, neither donkey nor horse] phenomena'. Among the local operas presented at the convention a lot of the singing and supporting music was 'at an early stage of exploration'. After seven years of model works, this was a striking confession of lack of progress. Such indirect reference to problems, underscored by headlines and textual comments about how promising the whole enterprise was, was typical of the media at the time. Clearly, no matter how perfect were the model Peking operas, their transplanting into local opera forms would be no easier than the original creation of the models. Bell Yung's pioneering study of the transplanting of *Shajiabang* into Cantonese opera (*Yueju*) form shows how the original text of the opera was adopted with only limited adjustment to Cantonese colloquialisms. The tunes for *Sagabong* presented the biggest challenge to the adaptors in Guangdong, especially matching the linguistic tones of the modified Peking opera text and the pitch contour of the melodies.[48]

One of the earliest local opera forms that attempted to transplant the model operas was Sichuan opera (*Chuanju*), a popular element in the cultural life of the Sichuan basin, granary of China and home in the 1970s of over eighty million people. By the end of 1972, after work since the first years of the Cultural Revolution, *Taking Tiger Mountain* by *Strategy*, *The Red Lantern*, and *Shajiabang*, the most popular and accomplished of the first five model operas, had been adapted into Sichuan opera.

The purpose of transplanting was twofold: to bring the model operas in a familiar form to local audiences and to accelerate the reform of Sichuan opera.[49] An early 1973 commentary argued that two tendencies were to be avoided: a mechanical imitation which produced 'neither Peking opera nor Sichuan opera' (*jing bu jing, chuan bu chuan*) and too much of a fresh start (*lingqi luzao*, literally, set up another stove) which created, not opera, but a new-style musical (*geju*). Transplanting, the Sichuan experience showed, was a kind of 're-creation' (*zai chuangzao*). The themes, personalities of the characters, and plot lines of the model operas could not be freely changed, but the transplanting could fully bring into play the specialities of the local opera form. Use of the unique characteristics of Sichuan percussion and the relatively high-pitched singing style (*gaoqiang*) rendered *Tiger Mountain* in Sichuan-opera style. At issue was a proper balance between innovation and continuation, issues not unfamiliar to the creators of the original model Peking operas.

By 1974 a range of new operas had appeared on China's stages. They included the Peking opera set among the Miao people of Guizhou *Tempest on Miao Ridge* (*Miaoling fenglei*), the Shanxi opera (*Jinju*) *Climbing Peach Peak Three Times* (*San shang Taofeng*), the small-scale Hunan opera (*Xiangju*) *Song of the Teachers* (*Yuanding zhi ge*), the short Shaoxing opera from Zhejiang province *Half a Basket of Peanuts* (*Ban lan huasheng*), the short Huai operas from Shanghai *Old but Still Red* (*Ren lao hong xin*) and *Collecting Coal Cinders* (*Jian meizha*), the Peking opera from Inner Mongolia *Sons and Daughters of the Grassland* (*Caoyuan er nü*), and the short Hebei clapper opera (*bangzi*) *The Ferry Crossing* (*Dukou*).[50] Innovations were possible in the process of creating these new works. *Tempest on Miao Ridge*, for example, included folk-style songs ('mountain songs' *shan'ge*) in its score.[51] Several of these works had origins before the Cultural Revolution. The call for new works modelled on the model Peking operas allowed some old scripts to be dusted off and adjusted to fit the new rubrics. Audiences were undoubtedly relieved at the greater number of works available for watching, though not by the repetitive emphasis on heroes and correct thinking that characterized all these stories. *Ferry Crossing*, a children's story about an old ferry man and his young daughter foiling class enemies, had had its premiere in 1973. Before long, more than 100 opera companies were busy transplanting it from Hebei clapper opera into local stage forms.[52] Being a short work may have been part of the attraction to other localities' opera workers:

They could complete an adaptation more quickly and thus indicate their commitment to the transplanting project.

Having appeared to offer some relief to Chinese audiences, several of these works had extended, multi-form lives. *Sons and Daughters of the Grassland*, for example, had started in 1964 as *Heroic Little Sisters of the Grassland* (*Caoyuan yingxiong xiao jiemei*), a work by the Peking opera company of the Inner Mongolia Art Theatre, presented at the national convention on modern-subject Peking operas. In that same year, an animated version of the story came from the Shanghai Animation Film Studio.[53] In the summer of 1972, the story had been turned into another Peking opera by the same company, *Little Sisters of the Grassland* (*Caoyuan xiao jiemei*). By April 1973, the story was in ballet form as *Sons and Daughters of the Grassland*.[54]

Half a Basket of Peanuts had its origins in a Wu opera from Jiangxi in south-central China. It had been adapted as early as December 1970 from the grippingly titled one-act spoken play *Flowers of Philosophy Bloom Everywhere in the Mountain Village* (*Shancun kaibian zhexue hua*). The allegorical potential of a half-basket of peanuts must have been obvious, as in June 1971, the propaganda and cultural authorities of neighbouring Zhejiang set up a 'Zhejiang provincial *Half a Basket of Peanuts* writing group' to create a Shaoxing opera. The new opera appeared on a Hangzhou stage the next month. Chairman Mao watched the opera on videotape in the city and declared: 'This show has drama and the characters are really engaging. It shows that peasants can study philosophy and do it well.' With this kind of endorsement, the opera had a future. Beijing Television broadcast a black-and-white version and in the winter of 1972 the Changchun Film Studio made a colour television version. This was practice for a 1974 colour stage documentary of *Half a Basket of Peanuts* by the same studio. In the same year, the Shaoxing opera script was published by the Zhejiang People's Publishing House.[55] Philosophers across China no doubt rejoiced.

Two keys guided the transplanting of the model performances: the 'three aims' (*san duitou*) and the 'three smashes' (*san dapo*). The former aimed to capture the feelings, characteristics, and sense of the historical period of the original model works. To be smashed were the role types, schools of performing, and formulas of the target opera form into which the model was being transplanted.[56] Despite the claims that such activities were a way of modernizing and strengthening the futures of the local opera forms, the assimilationist aims of the promoters of model performance transplanting cannot be ignored. Several reviewers, for example, remarked on the limitations of roles in Hunan flower-drum operas and the consequent traditional concentration on love stories and soft music that earned it the nickname 'tofu cube' (*doufukuai*) opera. In contrast, the transplanting of the model Peking operas brought fighting and militancy to the flower-drum opera stage for the first time. Quite what was left of the 'flower drum' is unclear. A fixation with the revolutionary and political superiority of the central modernized Peking operas had the potential to obliterate the regional forms into which it was being transplanted.

A major emphasis in reports of the August 1974 performances in Beijing is on the emergence of new performing personnel. If the model performances were to serve as the basis for a new Chinese culture, there needed to be many more artists available to help disseminate the models and apply them to new performance forms. One writer noted the youth of actors who played Jiang Shuiying, heroine in the Northern opera (*Pingju*) transplant of *Song of the Dragon River*, and the actor who played Sister Aqing in the Hunan flower-drum opera version of *Shajiabang*. They were around twenty years old.[57]

The model performances were not just to remain on stages in the hands and throats of professional actors and musicians. The Cultural Revolution from its beginnings had emphasized the efficacy of mass mobilization. In the 1970s, once the first set of model Peking operas had been committed to celluloid and were thus more readily seen by audiences around the nation, renewed efforts were made to encourage mass participation in their dissemination. It would help the spread of the models and was a good thing, simply as a social activity that organized people to act in groups. The models were not just available in film. Radio broadcasts throughout the Cultural Revolution had presented a steady diet of model-opera arias, retelling as stories, and advice on singing Peking opera. Television, still underdeveloped but available in major cities to be viewed collectively in neighbourhood centres, cultural palaces, and similar locations, was another vehicle for dissemination.

An early 1975 report from suburban Tianjin gives an insight into the ways in which the study of the model Peking operas was organized.[58] With the coming of the Cultural Revolution, members of the Xiaojinzhuang Brigade in Baodi County had sold the costumes, props, and other equipment belonging to their amateur Northern opera (*pingju*) troupe (the report does not say to whom) and the money raised used to buy a television set. On this the brigade members could watch the 'revolutionary model performances'. The organized study of the songs started from there. The twenty-six members of the brigade's literature and art propaganda team (*wenyi xuanchuandui*) learned the songs relatively quickly and well. They seized opportunities in rest periods in the fields, at night school, and by going door to door to families to teach the arias to their fellow commune members. The results were impressive. Most brigade members, old or young, male or female, could sing the model-opera arias. The report argued that this knowledge directly benefited morale, commitment to work, and on productivity. Peasants identified with a particular model-opera hero. As Huo Fengling, a member of the women's committee of the brigade, noted: 'When we are in the midst of battling against the force of the old values and customs, as soon as we think of Li Tiemei, Ke Xiang and Fang Haizhen energy fills our bodies and our courage increases.' The female heroes of *The Red Lantern*, *Azalea Mountain*, and *On the Docks* were models for ordinary women. Outsiders remarked on the 'Dragon River style' of the brigade, which enjoyed the patronage of Jiang Qing. But amateur performance of works based on the model operas presented dangers, as so much was invested in the political importance of the works. In Shanghai in 1969–1970, adaptations of episodes from *Tiger Mountain* were criticized as 'against the model performances' (*fan yangbanxi*). The political pressure was so great, some of the amateur artists committed suicide.[59]

A four-page spread in *Revolutionary Successors* (*Geming jiebanren*), a magazine for youngsters, illustrated with line drawings, showed in September 1974 how central the model performances had become in cultural life.[60] 'Now literature, opera (including local operas), films, music, dance, fine arts, variety performances (*quyi*) and other creative arts are all achieving pleasing results.' The line drawings include a cinema with billboards for *Fighting on the Plain* and *Azalea Mountain*, with delighted families heading inside.

A poem by a county mobile film-projection team member in Fujian was another indication of the alleged importance of the 'model performances' to mass audiences. Hu Daxin's five-verse poem was first carried in the Yongding County *Worker, Peasant and Soldier Literature and Art* (*Gongnongbing wenyi*) magazine and included in a collection of popular literary compositions published in September 1974 by the Yongding County Propaganda Station (*xuanchuan zhan*).[61] Hu's title was 'Taking Model Performances to a Mountain Village':

> Crossing streams, ravines, and rows of ridges
> taking model performances to the villages.
> Chairman Mao's *Talks* are engraved in our hearts.
> We show films for the revolution.
>
> In the mountain village, all is astir
> Boys shoulder stools and girls hold up lamps:
> 'Uncle, aunty, let's go quickly,
> Tonight they're showing model performances.'

Study the heroes, express lofty sentiments,
Hearts are red like fire covering sky and earth.
The songs of the heroes transform the spring floods,
The revolution produces great news.

Old poor peasants, awash with hot tears:
In the old society living was hard for us poor.
Today films come to our mountain village.
Chairman Mao's care is as warm as our parents'.

Each word is heavy like a hundredweight
and sweeps, cleansing, through our hearts.
The journey is marked by a red line.
We leap over the green mountains for the people.

The doggerel loses nothing in translation. It indicates, however, the expectations that the model performances were carrying in distilling revolutionary experience and inspiring heroic emulation. They also inspired modest local efforts at writing short modern operas. The Kunming City Commerce Bureau Amateur Literature and Art Propaganda Team, for example, presented the one-act *Red Odd-job Man* (*Hongse qinwuyuan*).[62]

Promulgation of the model performances occurred at all levels, from the mountain villages of Hu Daxin's poem to regional and provincial performance conventions in 1973–1974. Yunnan province's was held in 1974 around Spring Festival, a traditional time for stage entertainment,[63] where there was considerable emphasis on the combination and cooperation of amateur and professional writers and artists. The Cultural Revolution assumption was that the former were more politically reliable but that professionals had more experience and polish.

Five large-scale works were presented and discussed by fellow artists at the Yunnan convention. There were Peking opera, Yunnan opera (*Dianju*), a 'revolutionary spoken drama', *Bonds on the Plateau* (*Gaoyuan niudai*), a Bai minority musical (*Bai ju*), flower-lantern plays and flower-lantern songs and dances, as well as folk songs presented at the convention. A report noted that they showed the falsity of complaints by 'class enemies' at home and abroad that there was not much available on China's stages and that what was there was not as good as in the old days. The report, however, does acknowledge the persistence of complaints about the new arts based on the model works. Moreover, some bad books and old-style performances were still in circulation or being performed in certain localities and backward work units. Such negative developments of course made more necessary heightened vigilance and strengthened Party control. Like projectionist Hu's poem, little was heard subsequently of the transplanted operas tried out in Yunnan in early 1974.

National-level exchanges of experience were a means to spread best practice. In February–March 1975, the Ministry of Culture organized a performance festival (*wenyi diaoyan*) in Beijing for troupes from Xinjiang, Shaanxi, Sichuan, and Heilongjiang.[64] The thirty-five shows in Beijing by Shaanxi artists drew an audience totalling more than 42,000 persons, a testimony perhaps to the capacity of the capital's theatres and the organizational powers of work units in distributing tickets. But the numbers attending may also indicate that audiences welcomed relief from the somewhat steady artistic diet of Peking-opera model works and exhortatory plays, songs, and dances in standard spoken Chinese. At least the Shaanxi players brought the distant, local colors of northern Shaanxi singing styles to the capital. Northwestern artists had always relied on these differences, even before the Cultural Revolution, to attract attention. By the mid-1970s, they were more than welcome. Newspapers, the national radio station, and Beijing television station recorded some of the shows or covered the event. Beijing radio sent a team to the province to record local versions of the model-opera highlights for broadcast and pressing into gramophone discs. There was mutual benefit in these activities: The provincial cultural apparatus and writers and artists received encouragement and national attention. The central cultural authorities in Beijing could likewise cite the lively Shaanxi performances as proof of the continued vitality of the Cultural Revolution model performances and related stage off-shoots.

Performers nationwide regarded participation in the annual late May commemoration in Beijing of Mao's Yan'an 1942 *Talks* as a signal honor. The 1975 anniversary of the *Talks* brought performers from across the nation to the capital. Transplanted versions of the model operas included the Uighur musical adaptation of *The Red Lantern*, the Hubei opera version of *The Red Detachment of Women*, a Cantonese opera adaptation of *Azalea Mountain* and extracts from other model operas done in the styles of Henan opera, ballad opera (*quju*) also popular in Henan, Shaanxi opera (*Qin qiang*), Mei Hu opera (also from Shaanxi), as well as in the *wanwanqiang* style popular in the Weinan region of Shaanxi. But the May 1975 gathering also presented spoken drama, Hubei opera, songs and dances, and folk vocal art forms (*quyi*) from all over the nation.[65] The widening of the repertoire was apparent in the experimental presentation in Beijing in May 1975 of four new 'revolutionary model Peking operas': *Red Cloud Ridge* (*Hong yun gang*), *Investigation of a Chair*, *Fighting the Waves* (*Zhan hailang*), and *The Ferry Crossing* (*Jinjiang du*).[66] In addition, symphonic versions of *Shajiabang* and *Taking Tiger Mountain by Strategy* were performed in the capital, as well as a piano-concerto version of *The Yellow River* (*Huanghe*), which had first appeared in 1970. But the heavy dependence still on the model works or versions derived from them indicates that, at least in the relatively restrictive context of official commemoration in the capital, new styles and themes did not have much space yet allowed to them.

Some of the transplanting worked not from Peking opera to another form of Chinese opera but between genres. In mid-1976 a spoken drama based on the model opera *Azalea Mountain* appeared on Shanghai's stages. The work of the Shanghai Spoken Drama Company, it was thought it could help spur a revolution in spoken drama like that in Peking opera. As we have seen, plays without songs came relatively late to China and never really took hold. The adapted play seems also to have been a means to rehabilitate the spoken drama troupe in Shanghai. The reviews of the spoken drama version of *Azalea Mountain* rather pointedly suggest its potential in promoting the Sinicization of the genre, noting it had a 'national style and national air' (*minzu fengge he minzu qipai*).[67] The actors reportedly rejected the Stanislavskian approach that had been adopted from the Soviet Union by many actors in the 1950s, instead approaching their roles from a 'proletarian stance'.

Despite these claims, scepticism is warranted. Chinese theorists and critics had been using these phrases about 'national style' for more than twenty years. If *Azalea Mountain* had achieved this so well on China's spoken-drama stages, it is surprising that few other attempts were made to transplant the model operas into spoken form. Here again the supposed perfection of the model operas worked against their use in other genres. The inflated expectations invested in the operas could not possibly be matched on a spoken-drama stage or in other performing forms. In effect the model-opera model was too good to work.

The model operas could model other genres as well. Poetry writing was an area in which mass participation could be relatively cheaply encouraged. The model operas, so familiar to all Chinese by the mid-1970s, provided inspiration and examples of how to write lyric poetry in particular. In the mid-1970s, one local effort at a new poetry-writing campaign was at the Xiaojinzhuang Brigade near Tianjin, which had earlier distinguished itself in learning to sing the arias from the model operas. A book of Xiaojinzhuang Brigade poems was published in early 1975 in which the peasant poets had been inspired by the model works' presentation of their central heroes.[68] One reviewer of the book found examples of operatic style 'frozen poses' (*liangxiang*) in some poems. Many of the arias themselves were fine poetry and could serve directly as models for lyrical compositions.

As in the mass poetry campaign in 1958's Great Leap Forward, part of the motivation in promoting this kind of amateur composition was an effort to undermine the influence of established, professional writers. By the early 1970s, some specialist writers had returned to their profession, though in closely watched circumstances. The cult of the amateur, illustrated in a small way by the Xiaojinzhuang poetry campaign, was intended by the cultural leadership as a means to limit a sense of the restoration of the professional. Ironically, the means of promoting this relied on the consummate and vast range of professionalism that had been mobilized in the creation of the model performances.

Painting could also learn from the model performances. The peasant paintings of Hu County in Shaanxi province near Xi'an enjoyed considerable vogue in the period 1973–1976. One of the most widely reproduced Hu County paintings lacked the primitivist aura of most such work but allegedly drew its inspiration from the artist's study of the model performances. It was by Liu Zhide, the Party secretary of the Qinsan Production Brigade of the Qindu commune in Hu County, who was described as an amateur painter. In his painting, titled *The Old Party Secretary* (*Lao shuji*), the greying man sits in a field beside his hoe and hat, lighting his pipe but deep in concentration on a political booklet in his lap. Liu Zhide attributed the success of his painting to following the model-opera creative principle of 'sourcing from life, higher than life' (*yuan yu shenghuo, gao yu shenghuo*).[69] This held that the model operas (and works inspired by them) should spring from real life but at the same time be a heightened version of reality.

Liu Zhide described the process by which he produced *The Old Party Secretary*. It was a process of realizing the need to give full prominence to the heroic old man, along the lines of the model-opera concentration on the central hero. His original concept of the figure in the painting was insufficiently ambitious and not treated as a model or representative (*dianxing*). He had drawn him from life but not gone beyond real life. Through trial and error and a summarizing of the aim of the painting, a more typical character emerged. The painting was reproduced far and wide in 1974, perhaps because of the apparent ordinariness of the old man, in contrast to the tiger-skinned waistcoats of a model performance hero like Yang Zirong. The images of the two men, however, shared similar theoretical roots, if we are to believe Liu Zhide's account.

Even the writing of popular songs could be modelled on the experience of creating the model performances. Members of the Music Writing Team of the Culture Bureau of Liaoning in the northeast were the proud composer and writers of more than twenty songs grouped under the title 'Chairman Mao travels throughout the great homeland' (*Mao zhuxi zoubian zuguo dadi*).[70] The artists ascribed their success to 'studying the creative experience (*chuangzuo jingyan*) of the revolutionary model performances'. By this they did not mean the actual process of the creation of the model operas and ballets. By the early 1970s, these histories had been suppressed. Records of the experimentation and false starts, published to a limited extent before the start of the Cultural Revolution, were no longer available to ordinary Chinese. Libraries were difficult to access and all had closed-stack and even closed-catalogue policies. The various stories of the creation of the model operas had been homogenized into a standardized account of the 'two-line struggle' between goodness and evil (given a Marxist class and theoretical gloss). When artists like the Liaoning songwriters noted their indebtedness to 'the creative experience' of the models, they meant the creative example of these works. The so-called theoretical concepts that the model operas exemplified were to inform all cultural production.

Publishing was another means of spreading the model functions of the 'model performances'. Stills from the film versions in particular were published on important holidays in newspapers and magazines nationwide. Using stills from the film versions ensured a standardized and, increasingly, familiar set of iconic images. The performance scripts of the model operas were also published as monographs, along with the musical scores and comprehensive guidebooks giving details of stage, costume, and properties design to enable standardized live performances of extracts or complete operas. Covers of all these publications were generally a plain deep red colour (with gold lettering), usually reserved for Mao Zedong's writings and other seminal publications, an indication of the importance invested in these works. From 1970 the People's Literature Publishing House (*Renmin wenxue chubanshe*) had a specialist 'revolutionary performances editing office' (*bianjishi*) devoted to publishing these materials and volumes of reviews and discussions of the model works. In addition various local and national publishing houses produced guides on how to sing the arias or play the music from the model operas. Performance of the two model ballets was harder to promote, though this did not stop amateur performances. *Dance* (*Wudao*) magazine resumed publication in early 1976 and included helpful sections on both common dance steps and dance injuries.[71] The last of the model-opera script monographs came from the Shanghai People's Publishing House, when the May 1975 Shanghai Peking Opera Company performance script of *Boulder Bay* hit the nation's bookstores in May 1976.[72]

The insistent promulgation of the model operas ultimately ill-served the considerable artistic achievement in these works. By 1974 even the official media made occasional reference to 'a tiny minority of people' who opposed the promulgation of the model performances.[73] All the rhetoric comparing the rise of the model operas for the proletariat with the capitalists' Renaissance and the Enlightenment could not obscure the over-burdening of these works.[74] They were weighed down with political and artistic significance, and they were over-played to an increasingly indifferent mass audience, obliged to feign public interest in them to avoid trouble. This is not the way great art takes root in popular consciousness. All the transplanting in the world could not hide the limitations of the root stock.

4. THE IMPORTANCE OF THE MODEL PERFORMANCES

Although recollection, nostalgia, and mythology place the eight model performances firmly at centre stage in the Cultural Revolution, the reality was somewhat different. Once identified, the eight model performances were promulgated with the full resources of Chinese state cultural apparatus. Even in the midst of the Cultural Revolution, in supposed chaotic conditions on the streets, the cultural organs continued to function. Insurgent groups at all levels, with factions of Red Guards or similar activists denouncing their colleagues and rivals with great bitterness, do not seem to have disrupted the payment of salaries and the provision of housing, rudimentary health care, and other services to members of these cultural work units. Only in 1969–1970 were a large number of cultural organizations disbanded, but even then at least a proportion of wages appear to have been paid to ex-members or under-employed continuing staff.

Social and political upheaval does not seem to have hindered the presentation of the model works across the nation. The original opera and ballet troupes (and the Central and Shanghai Symphony Orchestras) spent their time performing the works widely. Despite their iconic status, continuous refinement was carried out on all seven theatrical works, with different dated 'performances texts' (*yanchuben*) filling pages of *People's Daily* and the other national and regional newspapers in the late 1960s and early 1970s. Other lesser troupes rehearsed and presented the works locally and had been doing so since before May 1967. By the early 1970s, scores, full libretti, and stage and costume design books had been published for each of the model works, to ease nationwide efforts to duplicate their perfection live on stage. As we have seen, new modern-subject Peking operas were also being created and popularized. Transplanting gave the models further relevance across the nation.

Official media treatment of these eight titles, seen in even the most casual perusal of the pages of *People's Daily* or any provincial newspaper, shows that they certainly were granted great prominence. But the attention was not constant: Sporadic intensive coverage was punctuated with periods in which little was mentioned of the model operas and ballets. The May commemorations of the Yan'an *Talks* and National Day celebrations each year were two of the most sacred times in the Maoist cultural calendar. An examination of May and September–October issues of central and provincial newspapers between 1966 and 1976 suggests the fortunes of the model performances waxed and waned. Contention and disputation ensured that an imagined linear development of the role of the model performances is misplaced. The changes in the attention given the model works indirectly reflected the relative strength of Jiang Qing and the Cultural Revolution radicals from year to year. As in other aspects of cultural activity in these years, strident emphasis on models and Cultural Revolution conventionality was not a sign of strength. More often it was an indicator of the sense of threat this faction felt at that time.[75]

The May 1966 commemorations of Mao's *Talks* were overshadowed by the 16 May Circular of the Central Committee, regarded as the official start of the Cultural Revolution. The first National Day after this was a time of considerable political and social uncertainty. Examination of the cultural performances that October offers the chance to establish something of a baseline for pre-model performance culture, less than eight months before their May 1967 promulgation. *Tianjin Daily* (*Tianjin ribao*), the main newspaper of China's third-largest city, just ninety kilometres from the capital, offers an extensive listing of cultural events around the October 1966 festivities.[76] Covering about one-third of the back page of the issue, the advertisement gives prominence to several documentary films, most starring Mao Zedong.[77] Contrary to a standard claim that all feature films made in China before 1966 were banned from public screening during the Cultural Revolution, National Day that year included several popular films from the 1950s and 1960s.[78] Among a dozen Chinese and foreign features on screen that October was *Others Will Follow Us* (*Ziyou houlairen*, 1963), the same story that was told in the modernized Peking opera *The Red Lantern*. The latter and *Shajiabang* were the only signs of the operas and ballets that would make up the official eight model performances announced almost eight months later. These two modernized Peking operas did not yet enjoy a monopoly in late 1966, almost half a year after the official start of the Cultural Revolution, for other non-model, modern-subject operas were also advertised. Some local opera companies had invented new-style performances of 'praise songs' for Chairman Mao. One such was from the Tianjin Northern Opera Company (*Pingju tuan*), which offered 'A Great Joyous Occasion for the Whole People' (*Quanguo renmin de da xishi*). This is identified in the newspaper advertisement as 'Northern opera' (*Pingju*), at a time when modernized Peking opera was supposedly the only approved opera form.[79]

Other previously well-established performing groups had also adopted a change of repertoire by late 1966. The Tianjin City People's Art Theatre (known in shorthand as *Renyi*) was now the City Worker-Peasant-Soldier Song and Dance Ensemble. Its members were presumably pleased to at least preserve their status and access to resources as a municipal-level artistic group. They were reduced to presenting *Chairman Mao's Red Guards*, the ubiquitous *A Great Happy Occasion for the Whole People*, and *A Fine Son of the People* (*Renmin de hao erzi*). Performances through to 11 October were sold out. Like the opera troupes, other groups also put the old vocal art forms to Cultural Revolution purposes. The Tianjin Acrobatic Troupe had a program of *Acrobatic Art Reflecting Real Life* (*Fanying xianshi shenguo zazhi yishu*) on at the People's Theatre. At one of Tianjin's biggest performance venues, it was sold out through to 12 October.

Apart from questioning the claim that there was no advertising during the Cultural Revolution,[80] this lengthy schedule of National Day performances and films suggests both narrowness and breadth. There was a wider range of entertainment options available to the public in Tianjin than usual statements about the paramountcy of the modernized Peking operas and model ballets acknowledge. At the same time, the triumph of Cultural Revolution praise of Mao Zedong and all his works shows how limited choices had become.[81]

In May 1967, at the same time as the official promulgation of the eight model performances, the models were not alone on stages across the nation. In Kunming the (renamed) provincial East is Red Flower-Drum (*huagu*) Troupe and the provincial East Is Red Peking Opera Troupe joined forces to present what they identified as '*Jingju wudao*' (Peking opera dances) and '*Jingju xiao yanchang*' (Peking opera small-scale songs), such as 'Sayings of Chairman Mao' (*Mao zhuxi yulu*) and a Mao poem. Even in the capital, Beijing audiences were presented with a range of agitprop works unconnected with the model operas, while artists in Guiyang mounted a song-and-dance drama (*gewu ju*) titled *Spring Thunder in the Southwest* (*Xinan chunlei*).[82]

By 1968, the model performances seemed firmly centre stage in Chinese cultural life, at least as reflected in the official media. But we should not forget that they were surrounded by a great deal of other cultural activity: films, spoken plays, variety performances (*quyi*), choral songs, instrumental music, and other programs called vaguely 'revolutionary art and literature' (*geming wenyi*).[83] Perusal of the pages of provincial newspapers in the last two years of the 1960s suggests a decline in official public interest in the model works. The May 1969 commemorations of Mao's Yan'an *Talks* in Ningxia, for example, seem to have been a low-key affair, without the usual articles or stage stills of model operas and ballets.[84] Even at other times of the year, the unrelenting presentation of the model works faded somewhat in 1968 and 1969. For operas that had been in the public eye for half a decade, this was perhaps only natural, if naturalness could be allowed in Chinese public discourse at the time. In the quasi-official Red Guard newspapers of 1967–1968, the absence of much reference to the model performances is also striking.[85]

Even the model performances apparently needed defending. In the September 1969 issue of *Red Flag*, the pseudonymous writer Zhe Ping wrote of threats to their status as models for the new culture. Under the title 'Study the Model Performances, Defend the Model Performances', the article suggested that two kinds of evil persons were actively undermining the models. One group included people who had been expelled from opera troupes when these had been recently purged (*qingxi*). Such critics had pieced together (*pincou*) 'black' opera troupes to perform the old-style 'ghost, pornographic, and traitorous plays'. A second, more insidious kind of class enemy had infiltrated amateur song and dance troupes and ensured that the model performances were presented in ways that damaged them in the eyes of their audiences.[86] Discounting the inflated Cultural Revolution rhetoric, this report indicates that even the model performances could be tampered with, particularly at a local level, far from centralized control.

A new means offered a way to restore the central attention on the model works and establish definitive versions of them. The release of film versions of the operas and ballets, starting in October 1970, was the most significant step in the spread of the model performances. Until then, for most Chinese the operas and ballets were familiar through radio broadcasts of arias and music and through the reproduction of stage stills in newspapers and other mass media. Amateur and local professional performance, which was encouraged in these years, did not necessarily serve the artistic reputation of the model works.[87] Film provided perfected, fixed versions, though the perfection may have served further to discourage

local live presentations. The 1971 commemoration of Mao's *Talks* saw
the models back at centre stage in media coverage, this time as newly completed films or television documentary recording of stage performances.[88]
The attention did not last long. Provincial newspapers in the 1972 and
1973 anniversaries of the *Talks* generally had little on the model performances and their offshoots.[89] The filming of the model performances can
be said to have guaranteed them the kind of immortality in recollections
and reconstructions of the Cultural Revolution. The films, of course, also
took these works to international audiences around the world, reinforcing
the impression of their importance in China.

5. REORGANIZING THE RANKS

Model operas required a reorganization of the opera companies of the
nation. Such an important task as live performance of these works, the
cultural authorities concluded, needed to be in the hands of fully reformed,
fully capable, and trustworthy artists. With such a narrow repertoire
focused firmly on the so-called national opera form, many specialist
regional opera troupes found life difficult. For companies whose core
opera form was further removed from the singing, acrobatic, and musical
styles of Peking opera, transforming themselves into model-opera troupes
was problematical. Furthermore, the Cultural Revolution leadership were
also concerned that the existing companies could not be trusted. The task
of promulgating the model operas was invested with such significance
that a reorganizing of the ranks was required to secure the correctness of
the performances.

The massive increase after 1949 in the number of opera companies and
their members meant that the opera enterprise included a large proportion
of relative newcomers, freshly trained in the opera schools established
in Beijing and at the regional and provincial levels. One set of statistics
published to mark the tenth anniversary of the People's Republic of China
indicated that professional members of opera companies nationwide grew
from more than 50,000 in 1,000 opera companies in 1949 to more than
220,000 in 3,300 companies in 1959.[90] According to these statistics, the
average company grew from about fifty members to closer to seventy
members in those ten years, while the number of companies themselves
tripled. The same statistical summary claims that the number of forms of
opera or, more correctly, dramatic performance with singing (*juzhong*),
also tripled from more than 120 to 469 forms. A note indicates that this
tripling was a product of research and more scientific investigation, not
from the invention of more than 300 new kinds of entertainment.

With this rapid expansion, ensuring the artistic professionalism and the ideological correctness of the opera companies was a challenge. Once the Cultural Revolution got under way in 1966, the cultural radicals were greatly exercised by the potential for opera troupes and other artists to undermine their new efforts at creating a model mass culture. A re-establishment of the ranks (*chongxin jianli duiwu*) was the means to assert greater control over professionals in many areas of cultural life, including opera and other performing arts. Given this concern for control and the narrowing of the repertoire to just several titles in the Peking opera form, many companies closed down or were merged by the late 1960s and early 1970s. Many companies went into a kind of suspended animation, in which company members, including actors, musicians, stagehands, and janitors, continued to collect their wages. Compulsory collective political study helped kill some of the time, as did learning the model works. Some troupes were sent to the countryside again, which had happened to many during the early 1960s in the Socialist Education Movement, to work and perhaps entertain the local peasants with possibly unofficial performances from an older repertoire.

The push to ensure the political loyalty and correctness of the rapidly expanded opera and performing art corps had begun well before the Cultural Revolution. The emergence of the model operas lent this work even more significance, but it drew on earlier experience. A crucial area was the training of the new corps of opera professionals. The conventional approach of learning complete operas meant that students did not have the independent creative skills to take up work on new, modern-subject reper-toire once they joined opera troupes upon graduation.[91] Opera schools tended naturally to teach what was relatively familiar, so without a reso-lute determination to acknowledge the importance of new-style operas at these training establishments, a vicious cycle followed. In the mid-1960s, most senior members of any opera company had been trained and worked for years in old-style companies long before 1949, when the new govern-ment started to reform the opera system.[92]

General accounts of the performing arts during the Cultural Revolution usually make broad comments about the dissolution of opera troupes and the dispersal of company members, implying, where dates are not supplied, that immediately after the 16 May Circular all opera companies somehow and suddenly ceased. The real picture is more complicated.

An 8 August 1966 resolution of the Communist Party Central Com-mittee set the tone for the next several years. Known as the '16 clauses' (*shiliu tiao*), the document outlined the mode of 'struggle, criticism and reform' (*dou, pi, gai*) to be used against bourgeois elements and those taking the capitalist road.[93] Struggle implied a kind of shock treatment, usually involving public humiliation of establishment cultural authorities and leaders. Art and literature, along with education, were to be 'reformed' (gaige). Most performing companies, including opera troupes, had stopped presenting shows, except for the newly minted 'praise songs' and the like. Now, in the summer heat, the so-called revolutionary masses of the companies took to travelling to 'establish ties' (chuanlian) with like-minded members of other performing groups. In a society which in normal times allowed most of its citizens about as much geographical mobility as had medieval European society, these opportunities to see the world were seized with alacrity by young Red Guards and 'rebels' of all descriptions in 1966–1967. Most Peking opera troupes, according to a 1999 history, 'sank into a state of paralysis' (tanhuan).[94]

The future of opera troupes was addressed in a 17 February 1967 set of rules about cultural organizations (wenyi tuanti) approved by the Party Central Committee and its Cultural Revolution group. This had six parts, including a call to root out the influence of men like the former cultural commissar Zhou Yang and the playwright Xia Yan. Another part called for members of cultural groups to stop immediately 'establishing ties' through travelling about and return to their original units. There they should carry on 'struggle, criticism and reform' in their units at the same time as rehearsing and presenting art works, operas, and so on that were modern, revolutionary, and served workers, peasants, and soldiers. Performing arts and other companies could in a planned, systematic way go about 'experiencing life' in factories and on communes in order to transform their members' worldviews.

The 17 February 1967 resolutions also called for 'resolute rectification (zhengdun) and sorting out (qingli) of the literary and artistic work ranks.'[95] As in other work units across the nation, this call to identify and root out bad elements was a recipe for suspicion and mutual recrimination. Performing troupes were diverted by these political requirements. This distraction, together with an absence of items to perform or great caution over what might be acceptable for performance, meant that many troupes simply stopped performing or remained idle, as they had been since 1966. The February 1967 resolution noted this situation:

> If they have difficulties from now on in performing and have no source of income to cover basic living expenses, they can arrange with the local government for some other sort of employment opportunities. These would mostly be settling in the countryside or being assigned to factories or to newly established enterprises to do manual labor.[96]

According to a 1999 history of Peking opera, from the promulgation of this resolution in early 1967, all troupes stopped their professional activities.[97]

Most accounts of the Cultural Revolution period for individual opera companies tend to include vague references to the troupes being 'disbanded' or 'dissolved' (*jiesan*, *sanluo* or *chixiao*) in the late 1960s or early 1970s. Broad statements after 1976 about troupes ceasing to exist encouraged an impression that the model operas of the period were performed by only a relative handful of professional companies which fell under the thrall of evil cultural and political bullies. After 1976, most cultural professionals were eager to assume a mantle of victimhood during the Cultural Revolution.[98]

The reality of opera troupe experiences during the Cultural Revolution was more varied than the impression of general disbandment. Many troupes were reorganized as 'song and dance ensembles' (*wengongtuan*) or as 'Mao Zedong Thought Propaganda Teams' (*Mao Zedong sixiang xuanchuandui*), in which a proportion of the same personnel continued to be members, working up new-style, agitprop performances. Figures on the number of performing troupes in China from 1949 to 1990, for example, reflect some decline during the Cultural Revolution. These figures are for performing companies (*xijutuan*), a term which generally includes both opera companies and spoken drama troupes.[99]

1963	3,428 companies	1972	2,681
1964	3,478	1973	2,731
1965	3,458	1974	2,760
1966	3,374	1975	2,836
1967	3,223	1976	2,906
1968	3,030	1977	2,941
1969	2,683	1978	3,150
1970	2,541	1979	3,482
1971	2,514	1980	3,533

The biggest drop came between 1968 and 1969 and was little more than eleven percent. Between 1957 and 1958, with the coming of the Great Leap Forward, troupe numbers had increased by ten percent. The table indicates the decline between 1966 and the lowest point in the Cultural Revolution period was about one-quarter. Between the start and finish of the ten-year period, the drop was in the order of fourteen percent. These raw, global figures for the entire country belie the image of massive lay-offs and abandonment that accounts of individual opera companies generally convey.

Even if we accept them as accurate, these national figures offer no guidance on what actually happened in individual opera companies. Membership of the ranks of performers may have changed substantially. Nor do these numbers offer any indication of what was performed, how frequently, or with what quality. Local histories of developments in these years offer some corrective to the broad-brushed claims of close-downs and disbandment. One 1995 report on Shanghai uses the expression 'resuscitation' or 'recovery' (*fusu*) to characterize performing arts in 1966: a somewhat ironical expression given the narrowing of the repertoire with the rise of the model performances.[100] In the period from January to July 1966, which spanned the 16 May official start of the Cultural Revolution, 17,619 performances of opera, ballet, and other large-scale works were presented in Shanghai theatres (*juchang*), and 20,781 performances of story-telling accompanied by string or percussion music, comic dialogues, and other smaller-scale shows were mounted, mostly in smaller, less formal venues.

Concrete evidence of the shrinkage of professional activities is provided by the reduction in the number of specialist or professional theatres in Shanghai in the course of 1966. In August the thirty-five theatres were cut to seventeen, and then to just six in November. By December 1966 only one professional theatre venue was still open in the city. Despite the reduction in venues, performances (implicitly of the model operas and ballets) continued at a high level. There were 1,007 such performances between August and December, inclusively. A similar reduction occurred in the venues for smaller-scale story-telling and similar performances. The number halved in August 1966, from sixteen to eight venues. In November this dropped to five, and in December it hit one. In August–December, 531 shows were presented in this decreasing number of venues. Meanwhile much emphasis was put on taking professional performances out of theatres to the work sites of audiences. The absence of repertoire, with the rise of the new model operas and ballets, is indicated by the report that only five shows played in the remaining single venue in the month of December.

Even more destruction to the performing arts was evident the following year in Shanghai, where the so-called January Storm on 11 January 1967 saw the cultural apparatus in the city fall firmly into the hands of the cultural insurgents associated with Jiang Qing. For the following five months, thirteen stage shows, identified as 'model performances and others' ('*yangbanxi*' *deng*), were presented in the city until such performances came to a halt in mid-June. Performances of these approved works were confined to a few shows on a few days around holidays, such as New Years, Spring Festival, May First, and National Day.

In the midst of 'struggle, criticism and reform,' a 'large group' (*dapi*) of Shanghai performing artists and others were sent to the countryside or factories for 'reform through labor'. In 1972 fifty-six performing companies in the city and surrounding counties were disbanded. More than a thousand actors and other professionals had changed their occupations. Some (*yixie*) theatres and smaller performance venues had been occupied or put to other uses. Shanghai's best-known theatre complex, the Great World (*Da shijie*), had been turned into a warehouse. From May 1973 things began to change. Thirteen city-managed performing companies returned to regular performances. Of the original sixteen such city-run companies, only those that performed the 'model performances' and a minority of others had not stopped performing or been dissolved. In the spring of 1973, the thirteen companies prepared to perform the model performances, transplanted versions of the model operas, or other approved dramas. The thirteen municipal companies comprised twenty-four performing troupes, including four Peking-opera companies, four spoken-drama companies, four *pingtan* (Suzhou-dialect story-telling and ballad singing) groups, three dance companies, two Shanghai opera (*Huju*) troupes, two acrobatic groups, and one company each of Shaoxing opera (*Yueju*), Huai opera, modern musical (*geju*), puppet, and unspecified music groups.

Statistics on performances during these four years suggest a flurry of activity, in contrast to the usual general claims about disbandment and inactivity. In 1973, there were 1,186 theatrical or large-scale performances and 299 smaller-scale shows at one venue. In 1974, there were 1,807 large-scale shows and 347 others. The next year, 1,467 large-scale shows were presented and 460 others. In 1976, 1,312 theatrical performances and 408 other shows were presented by these twenty-four troupes. This averages 1,822 shows each year, or seventy-five annually by each of the twenty-four troupes.[101]

A better picture of actual practice in the performing arts companies during the Cultural Revolution can be gained from contemporary Cultural Revolution documents, reproduced in the 1990s in the multi-volume *China Opera Gazetteer* (*Zhongguo xiqu zhi*). Each volume includes an appendix with official documents produced after 1949 by the national and local governments related to opera, especially the administration of troupes, theatres, and other organizational matters.[102]

The amount of documentation from the early 1970s reinforces the general picture suggested by the national statistics presented above. Provincial cultural administrations were unlikely to have been so busy producing guidelines on performances, troupe organization, and management if there had been the kind of dramatic cut in active troupes claimed by sweeping post-1976 generalizations about troupes being disbanded. These documents were clearly directed at a substantial body of practitioners serving not inconsiderable audiences.

In May 1966, the Zhejiang provincial Culture Bureau, for example, was tackling the pressing matters of wages for drama performers.[103] In approaching the cultural enterprise in China after 1949, an underlying assumption pervades studies that all cultural 'workers' were paid a minimal salary and practised their art for the glory of the revolution or because they had no choice. In reality throughout the decades since 1949, Chinese artists have been as concerned about their material conditions as any other professional artists in socialist or capitalist societies. At the start of the Cultural Revolution, when calls for revolutionary sacrifice were reaching new levels, such matters could still not be ignored. The Zhejiang report was prompted by the request by four performers in Shaoxing county, all Communist Party members, that their wages be reduced.

This unexpected request clearly caused some embarrassment to the Zhejiang cultural authorities. They knew that an arbitrary order to cut wages for all performing artists and other troupe members would be greeted with resentment. They acknowledged in their May 1966 draft report that different levels of remuneration operated among members of the same opera troupe and that some artists were known to have 'jumped troupes' (*tiao tuan*) in search of higher pay. The Zhejiang authorities were careful to suggest that reductions be done in a manner appropriate for the circumstances of individual troupes. State-owned troupes should follow national guidelines on wage levels and grades, while collectively owned companies should fix suitable salary levels. The younger members of opera and other companies in particular needed education about appropriate wage expectations. That the provincial Cultural Bureau in late May 1966 could not simply issue instructions to lower remuneration across the board according to a standardized formula raises major questions about assumptions of arbitrary state control over artists and their organizations.[104]

The dilemmas of dealing with central government or Party instructions on what to do with opera companies and other artists were illustrated at an August 1967 meeting called in Hangzhou by the Zhejiang provincial authorities. The meeting's purpose was to discuss central Party documents on the devolution in cultural groups, in which troupes would be rectified and assume responsibility for their own losses and profits. Such decentralization was in counterpoint to centralizing tendencies in terms of artistic matters. Much of the published minutes of the August 1967 meeting, like other Cultural Revolution documents, go through ritual acknowledgement of the truth and beauty of Mao Zedong Thought and the evil of Mao's alleged opponents.[105] But simple-minded calls to cut down or disband troupes were condemned for the unease these policies created. Responding to the decrease in performances and the narrowing of repertoire, the Hangzhou meeting participants called on troupes to both conduct criticism and continue to create new, particularly shorter, works, for paying audiences.

Budgets for the coming financial year should reflect more than a doubling of the monies set aside for such subsidies in recent years. Each troupe should conduct mass discussions to determine the level of assistance according to the different family circumstances of the recipients. Such mass determination of colleagues' income looks like a recipe for further jealousies and resentments in artistic organizations that were never free of such tensions.

As for variety performers (*quyi renyuan*) in difficulty, the first line of defence should be self-reliance. Such troupes tended to be smaller and more economically vulnerable than larger opera companies. Local governments should provide assistance at a level reflecting local living costs and incomes. Those artists resident in the countryside should rely on collective support from their communes and production brigades. The importance of these issues is indicated by these paragraphs on money and subsidies being the most specific in the entire three-page document.

In Hebei the process of sorting out and disbanding performing troupes took on new urgency as autumn 1967 approached.[106] Decisions on which troupes should be kept in existence and which should be disbanded were expected to take just two or three months and be resolved by November. Troupes that were to continue should meet two criteria: They should have the talent and resources to perform well the model performances, and they also had to be certain of continued resources to cover living costs. Clearly, the disbanding of troupes was a delicate matter, traumatic for the troupe members and potentially disruptive for the locations where these people ended up. The Hebei authorities gave specific instructions on what was to be done to ease the pain. Former troupe members from dissolved companies or deemed surplus to the requirements of continuing troupes were assigned to the countryside or to factories and other enterprises. Those sent to the countryside to live (or who remained in the countryside where their troupes had been domiciled) were to receive payments to cover their living costs based on their length of service in the performing company.

Former troupe members who were assigned to factories, businesses, or other enterprises were to receive wages from the new work unit, according to the prevailing rates. For those newcomers who found they faced a drop in wages from troupe to factory, their old wage levels could continue for a six-month transition period. For those former troupe members who had been receiving exceptionally high wages (presumably star actors), reductions of no more than sixty *yuan* per month (about the average monthly wage for a factory worker at the time) could be put into effect immediately. After six months, these persons too would revert to their appropriate new wage levels. Troupe members who were under investigation for political problems were to be given a living allowance while their cases were resolved. This could wait until the disbanding campaign had ended. The property and chattels of former troupes were to be sold, with the proceeds to go to local cultural and educational organs.

The overall thrust of the Hebei directives on what to do with the ex-members of disbanded performing troupes was to keep the solutions local. Reports to the provincial government were not expected. In a system that tended to be highly centralized and closely supervised, this was remarkably trusting of localities. Obviously, the Hebei and other provincial authorities felt they had enough on their hands without fussing about the fate of former actors, musicians, and front-of-house managers.

Two years later (in October 1969) Yunnan cultural officials seemed to have a lot to fret about.[107] Some audiences in mines, villages, government organs, schools, and towns still provided a market for 'poisonous weeds'. Allegedly, obscene or vulgar dances and unhealthy ballads were still available for the titillation of such audiences. Particular locales even manifested 'black performing troupes' (*hei jutuan*) presenting 'bad dramas' (*huai xi*). Some amateur propaganda troupes, a feature of the Cultural Revolution cult of the non-professional, were tending to become professional, leaving manual labour and self-sufficiency behind. This professionalization threatened wastage of state resources. For their part some professional companies took up the transplanting of the model performances, but without permission and with somewhat cavalier attitudes that distorted (and presumably over-localized) the originals.

In mid-1970, a report on professional performing companies in Yunnan painted a picture quite different from the usual post–Cultural Revolution claims of the dissolution or inactivity in theatre troupes.[108] Six hundred forty-nine persons staffed the six provincial-level troupes. These included the Peking opera troupe (135 persons), listed first, the Song and Dance Company (156 persons), the Yunnan-style opera (*Dian [Dianju]*) troupe (134 persons), the flower-drum company (101 persons), the spoken-drama company (81 persons), and the acrobatic troupe (42 staff). The latter had been halved in size in the late 1960s. Of the forty-two persons who were left, four were targeted for investigation of dubious political background, twenty-two had been found other work, and sixteen members had been assigned to other performing groups.

Professional troupes in Yunnan at the level below the provincial had originally numbered 68, with 3,094 members (an average of 45.5 members each). Among these groups were nine Peking opera companies (again mentioned first), twenty-one flower-drum troupes, twenty-five Yunnan opera troupes, eight song and dance troupes (*wengongtuan*), three folk groups (*minzu jutuan*), one *pingju* (Northern opera) company, and a ballad opera (*quju*) troupe. In the Cultural Revolution, noted the mid-1970 Yunnan report, forty-one of the sixty-eight troupes had been disbanded, involving 1,650 staff (an average of forty members each). These disbanded troupes included all nine Peking opera companies, many of whose members joined a newly organized provincial 'model opera' class. After further retrenchment and consolidation, in June 1970 there were fourteen song and dance companies, eight Yunnan opera companies, four flower drum troupes, and, as before, one *pingju* company.

While there was clearly a drop in numbers of groups and personnel, these figures indicate that blanket suggestions that all or most performing troupes suffered disbandment during the Cultural Revolution are misleading. The political campaign obviously presented an opportunity for the rationalization of performing groups. After 1949, many troupes had been formed at provincial and local levels without the planned permission of the provincial or national cultural authorities. Some troupes were the creation of particular individuals, a prominent local leader with a penchant for a particular kind of opera and an ability to move budget sums about to pay for a group of performers. The centralization of the national cultural project was one of the lasting legacies of the Cultural Revolution.

One way to break through the influence of hide-bound companies dominated by conservative old-school actors and leaders was to cultivate amateur groups. During the Cultural Revolution, the enthusiasm and politically trustworthy nature of amateur performers, writers, and others were emphasized. The focus on the amateur started well before the Cultural Revolution and received a boost from cultural radicals seeking to question the political loyalty of more established, professional performers.[109]

New recruits, untainted by old habits or personal loyalties and attracted by the continued glamour associated with the lives of actors, were brought in. Of the 102 members of the sixteen amateur performing troupes in Yunnan in mid-1971 (which meant tiny troupes of an average just over

six persons each), 21 persons had been professionals before the Cultural
Revolution and another 28 had engaged in amateur performance before
1966. Just over half the members (53 persons) were newly recruited. In
the first half of 1971, writing classes (*wenyi chuangzuo xuexiban*) produced a raft of large, medium, and small-scale works in Peking opera
(mentioned first, of course), Yunnan opera (*Dian [Dianju]*), flower-drum
opera, spoken dramas, and song and dance dramas. They all featured
worker, peasant, and soldier heroes. But these new works paled when
put beside the highly polished perfection of the model operas, a report
stated. The newly emerging younger writers and artists tended to lose
heart. Moreover, most were temporarily assigned to the study classes and
were uncertain of their long-term futures.[110]

Some leaders, the Yunnan report indicate, showed signs of local pride
and old-style tastes, instructing writers to create works set in their own
localities and publicizing local heroes. This may have arisen from frustration on the part of audiences and leaders at the abstract or distant settings of Cultural Revolution model works. In a nation the size of China,
local audiences wanting to see local people was not an unexpected phenomenon. Some leaders sat on their hands, mindful of the perils of cultural
work (*wenhua gongzuo weixian lun*), and dared not intervene in solving
problems in the new works. In sum, the Yunnan leaders reported in 1971,
literary and artistic efforts in the province were too slow, too late, and
too unfocused.

At about this time in Hebei, the cultural authorities began preparations for the thirtieth anniversary of Mao Zedong's Yan'an *Talks* ten
months later in May 1972.[111] They specifically asked for new works in
opera, songs, dance, music, and variety performance. Each district in the
province was to register by mid-November what items, written and performed entirely by local people, they would bring to the provincial meeting in December. This three-month gathering of Hebei artists, writers,
and managers was a sign of a major thrust at enlarging the kinds of work
available to audiences grown restless on a steady diet of mainly model
performances. Eleven hundred representatives participated in the festival,
watching more than 130 short and medium-length items. Reading between
the lines of the newspaper report, a highly developed and essential skill in
these years for all Chinese readers, we can find acknowledgement of shortcomings at the event. The troubled relationship between art and politics
in the presented items needed more attention. 'Politics are in command,
but politics and art must not be at odds and politics cannot substitute
for art.' Amateur performers needed to stay close to the grass roots, the
report observed, perhaps confirming the natural tendency for such groups

to take on professional ambitions. More new works were to be written and created, mostly by amateur artists.[112]

The *Hebei Daily*'s pictorial coverage of the 1972 Spring Festival showed the variety of the items performed, including song and dance (*gewu*), sung performances (*yanchang*), short musicals (*xiao geju*), and even a short Shanxi opera (*xiao Jinju*). The titles of the items and the statuary arrangement or performances in frozen stances of revolutionary determination are strongly reminiscent of the kinds of Red Guard agitprop performances from the 1966 to 1967 period at the start of the Cultural Revolution.[113] A troupe from Chengde, for example, stands in line with arms stretched out towards an imaginary future in their song and dance item, 'The [Yan'an] *Talks* Show the Direction'. Some of the eleven performers are dressed as a worker, a peasant, or a soldier, while most are in the standardized costumes of the heroes of the model operas: Fang Haizhen from *On the Docks*, Li Yuhe from *The Red Lantern*, and Yang Zirong from *Taking Tiger Mountain by Strategy*, though without the usual fetching tiger-skin waistcoat. This was one of the few references to the 'model performances' at the 1972 festival. Only one of the nine pictured performances is identified as in a local or regional style: the short Shanxi opera from Zhangjiakou, near the border with that province. In 1972, slow progress was being made in expanding the cultural repertoire, judging from this Hebei amateur festival.

The unevenness of the efforts across the nation to widen the repertoire and bring new works to audiences highly familiar with the model Peking operas is striking. While Hebei and Yunnan, inspired by Beijing examples, were making orderly moves to encourage novelty, Sichuan's Culture Bureau in the fall of 1974 was setting out arrangements for study classes to be held in Chengdu and Chongqing for performers of the strictly orthodox model operas. The classes would rehearse two of the second tranche of model operas, *Fighting on the Plain* and *Azalea Mountain*. They would be conducted by personnel who had participated in a national study class on the two operas, organized by the Culture Group of the State Council in Beijing. The possibility of opera troupes, long under-employed in the performing of a by-then hackneyed repertoire, leaping at this opportunity to travel to the big cities and indulge in highly professional preparation of two more modern operas seems to have troubled the provincial culture bureaucrats. They placed strict limits on the numbers that could participate. Each of the named local troupes could send no more than fifteen members: a leader, one stage director, three musicians (a conductor, a percussionist, and a string specialist), two people who covered stage design and lighting, and seven leading actors (the fifteenth member's function is not explained). The seven roles in each of the operas were actually listed to avoid actors turning up and finding little to do. The participants were instructed to bring three study documents to the classes. In addition to Mao's Yan'an *Talks*, the students were to study Jiang Qing's 1964 speech on 'The Revolution in Peking Opera' and the 'Minutes of the Conference on Army Literature and Art Work' from early 1966. The emphasis given to documents associated with Jiang Qing and the eve of the Cultural Revolution suggests a last-minute push in 1974 to guard a crumbling edifice of artistic rectitude.[114]

Experimentation, however, was not ruled out. In May 1975, Hebei performing troupes gathered at a Shijiazhuang festival items carefully labelled 'trial performances' (*shiyan yanchu*), including a Northern opera, several Henan operas (*Yuju*), and a Hebei clapper opera (*Hebei bangzi*) on new subjects and with new titles.[115] Perhaps the real purpose of the spring 1975 event was contained in the last sentence of the front-page *Hebei Daily* report on the festival. The Party should energetically popularize the experience of Xiaojinzhuang, a village-sized production brigade in the province. Xiaojinzhuang was closely associated with Jiang Qing and the other Cultural Revolution radicals who later were identified as the Gang of Four.[116] While ostensibly signalling a broadening of cultural activity, the Hebei gathering represented further defensive efforts to resist a rising tide of popular and political resentment at Cultural Revolution strictures.

Hebei was perhaps too close to Beijing to allow much space for real experimentation in the cultural field. Xinjiang was about as far from the capital, geographically and culturally, as was possible in China. The cultural festivities around the twentieth anniversary of the founding of the Xinjiang Uighur Autonomous Region offer an opportunity to assess the degree of loosening of control over artistic practice in 1975. Of course, we should not ignore the special qualities of this province, particularly the rapidly changing ethnic mix of Turkic peoples of Central Asia and a rising influx of Han Chinese from farther east. Catering to such diverse audiences put special demands on artists and their managers.

This ethnic and linguistic diversity was indicated by a half-page advertisement of performances in an early August 1975 issue of the *Xinjiang Daily*.[117] All of the 'model operas' listed were in local languages: Uighur, Kazak, Kirghiz, and Mongolian. Most were highlights from the transplanted versions of these Cultural Revolution classics, rather than the complete works. These other items included a spoken play, although most were advertised by the vague words 'songs and dances' (*gewu*). Songs and dances from Xinjiang had been a welcome and colourful relief from a steady diet of model performances for Chinese audiences back east. The extracts of transplanted model operas seem to have provided a legitimate occasion for the performance of more appealing works with stronger roots in the local communities. Cultural troupes from autonomous prefectures (*zhou*) within Xinjiang, populated by high concentrations of particular minorities, dispensed with the model-opera cover and simply performed their songs and dances in Urumqi. Many of these performances were scheduled for presentation in large factories in the city, at the Railway Bureau, and at other big enterprises with many employees and facilities, such as theatres.

Some of the performances were taken to a wider audience through broadcasting on Xinjiang Television. Kirghiz song and dance were featured on its Tuesday evening broadcast. On Thursdays the station broadcast in Uighur language and on Saturdays in standard Chinese again. If Urumqi audiences did not fancy a live show or the limited television programmes broadcast three nights a week after 7 p.m., they could try watching an open-air film show. Three feature films from Pyongyang were among the five films for 12 and 13 August listed in *Xinjiang Daily*.[118]

One of the amateur groups praised in the media coverage of the Urumqi festival in the summer of 1975 was the Baozihong No. Fifteen Production Brigade Peasant Amateur Propaganda Team.[119] Their act included such gems as the song and dance item 'Implement Total Dictatorship over the Bourgeoisie' (*Dui zichanjieji shixing quanmian zhuanzheng*), a short musical play 'Weddings Should be Held Like This' (*Hunli yinggai zheme ban*), and the chorus 'Raise Vigilance, Protect the Motherland' (*Tigao jingti, baowei zuguo*). A review by a labour-union review team noted approvingly that the team 'has never received any specialist artistic training'. Their dances, for example, were direct products of labour and struggle, 'without any of that kind of affected stuff' (*meiyou neizhong jiaorouzaozuo de dongxi*). Instead, their performances had the honest flavour of the fields about them. It was a characteristic the reviewers felt some professional troupes would do well to emulate.

A stage photograph of the Hetian District Song and Dance Ensemble is captioned to indicate the troupe adapted the traditional Uighur song and dance form 'Maixilaifu' in presenting 'Celebrating a Bumper Harvest' (*Qing fengshou*). But the tableau shows strong similarities with conventional Chinese song and dance numbers. Three male actors hold aloft a large cardboard or papier mâché corncob, wheat sheaf, and what looks like a loaf of bread. But their costumes, the beard on the central man, and the swirling skirts of women crouched in a line in front of them mark this performance as having a definite Xinjiang flavour. On the same newspaper page, stage photos of transplanted versions of the model operas *Song of the Dragon River*, *The Red Lantern*, and *Taking Tiger Mountain by Strategy* show that the transplanting was confined to the musical aspects of the operas. The costuming and poses are all strictly modelled on the Han mainstream originals. Likewise, an amateur propaganda team performance 'Battle Song of the Drilling Platform' (*Zuantai zhan'ge*), on oil production, has its actors in standardized stage-worker overalls, frozen in revolutionary determination.[120]

The Amateur Literature and Art Progaganda Team of Progress Commune (*Qianjin gongshe*) in Shanshan County during the 1975 festival published an account of its short history.[121] Established in 1973, the team consisted of about two dozen members, most of whom are described as the sons and daughters of poor and lower-middle peasants. A smaller proportion were sent-down or educated youths from eastern China living on the commune. The commune was fifty kilometres from the county seat, so going into town to watch a performance was not an easy proposition for poor peasants. The propaganda team would fill the gap, but they lacked experience, with their creative and performing levels at a low level. The team members decided to learn from the fighting spirit of Yang Zirong in *Taking Tiger Mountain by Strategy*. Ulan Muchir, the Inner Mongolian mounted cultural troupes, served as an inspiration in taking their art to the public.

But sometimes it was hard to persuade budding artists that amateur work was the way ahead. A report on the Amateur Literature and Art Propaganda Team of Tieti (steel dipper) Commune in Xinjiang's Yecheng County noted the criticism it attracted from outside and within its own ranks.[122] When it was formed in 1969, the team of amateurs had been mocked by some (labelled 'class enemies' in the 1975 report), who stated that 'a rabbit's tail can't grow long'. Conservative commune members thought that 'being amateurs offered no future, unlike being professionals'. Even some of the propaganda team thought they should be paid wages (rather than earn work points like other commune members) and not be expected to do heavy physical labor. Having overcome these initial challenges, the twenty-six members of the Tieti Commune team spent about two-thirds of their time working in the commune's fields and one-third as amateur performers. In six years they had written 460 items and performed more than 1,400 times. In 1974 their audience numbers had reached 250,000.

The final stages of the Urumqi festival in the summer of 1975 included a conference on literature and art work.[123] There, and at the closing ceremony, Xinjiang provincial leaders emphasized the need for the Communist Party at all levels to pay more attention to cultural activities. Wrongheaded notions about literature and art being non-essential (*keyoukewu*) and being separate from revolution or production were roundly condemned. In an intriguing commentary on the centrality and concomitant sensitivity of cultural practice during the Cultural Revolution, speakers also criticized the 'theory of literature and art work being a dangerous area' (*wenyi gongzuo weixian lun*). The complementary aims of encouraging artists to move closer to the broad masses and the latter to become more involved in artistic creation would remain blocked if Party leaders continued to tiptoe around such issues for fear of making egregious errors. A source of particular pride from the more than 200 items presented at the Urumqi festival was the evidence it was said to offer against Soviet assertions that China's literary and artistic revolution had 'obliterated minority arts' (*huimie minzu wenyi*). On the border with the USSR and inhabited by several ethnic groups whose territories extended across this international boundary, this was a particularly sensitive point in Xinjiang.[124]

All this local effort in part had a national focus. The National Day commemoration in Beijing on 1 October 1975 presented thirty-three cultural performances from across China.[125] These were the products of performance festivals (*wenyi diaoyan*) conducted in the capital over the preceding year. The previous two sessions of the series of national-level festivals had included companies from Qinghai, Shandong, Anhui, Jiangsu, Fujian, Ningxia, Zhejiang, Jiangxi, Guizhou, and Tibet. The range of performance forms presented in these festivals was apparently wide. Tibetan opera, Yangzhou opera (*Yangju*), Wuxi opera (*Xiju*), Huai opera, Kun opera (presumably a variation on *Kunqu*), Huaihai opera, Qinghai *pingxian*, *gaijiaxi*, *Xiangju* (Hunan opera), Shandong clapper songs, *liuzixi* ('willow plays'), and *Ganju* (from Jiangxi) were all listed as being presented. But delight at the variety (and occasional obscurity) of the folk and local forms on show should be tempered by awareness of the purposes to which these forms were put. The model operas in whole or as highlights were the objects of these various local performances.

But in addition, the October 1975 celebrations in Beijing included newly created Peking operas, spoken plays, and *Huangmeixi* from Anhui, among other large- and small-scale works. Sung and instrumental solos, part songs sung by two or more singers (*chongchang*), and instrumental equivalents (*chongzou*) presented new works on four stages. The Shanghai Symphony Orchestra and the Liaoning Song and Dance Troupe presented an evening of music and dance. The Beijing City Hebei *Bangzi* Troupe and the Beijing Northern Opera (*pingju*) Troupe added their colour to the mix. The forms were numerous and the content somewhat prescribed. But what turned out to be the last National Day performances in the Cultural Revolution had a breadth not seen just a half decade earlier.

In far Urumqi, the National Day celebrations had a more local flavour among the standard model performance ballets and Peking operas.[126] Uighur musical (*geju*) versions of *Song of the Dragon River* and *The Red Lantern* were presented, along with a couple of short Shaanxi operas (*Qinju*). Even a feature film, *Fighting the Flood* (*Zhan hong tu*), was shown in a Uighur-language version. Kazak speakers could enjoy screenings of *Red Flowers of Tianshan*, a feature film in Kazak dialogue made in Xinjiang in 1964. In Beijing the Cultural Revolution insurgents were adopting defensive positions and Li Guang continued to sing his role in *Fighting on the Plain*; however, out west something of local interest from before the Cultural Revolution could still be enjoyed.

In the promulgation, refinement, and expansion of the model works and in the provincial and local management of performance troupes and events, three broad tensions were apparent: The local versus the central, experimentation versus control, and the amateur versus the professional. Transplanting model works into regional opera forms could obliterate the merits of the original model or the attractions of local language and music. Innovation was demanded by the transplanting task, but artists could also feel they were 'dancing in chains'.[127] Too much novelty could bring problems. The official encouragement of mass participation in not just viewing the model works but in creating new works also had its limitations. The status of models required a degree of professional polish that few non-specialists could achieve. These three tensions can be seen in all areas of cultural production, as we shall see in the following chapters.

CHAPTER THREE

Fixing Culture on Film

Cinematographer Li Wenhua was in his mid-thirties when the Cultural Revolution began. It was a bumpy start, as he had been responsible for shooting *Early Spring in February*, one of the films that came under sustained criticism in 1964–1965. But by the end of the decade, Li was back at work in the sound stages of his Beijing Film Studio, charged with putting the model ballet *The Red Detachment of Women* on celluloid. As he noted in an interview more than two decades later, 'filming was easy, but making it good was hard'. The burden of responsibility for bringing one of the 'model performances' to the screen was difficult enough, but doing a dynamic stage art justice made the challenge even greater.[1] His work was so successful he went on to film *On the Docks* and another major dance work. But he also found himself crewing for films that were harshly attacked after the Cultural Revolution ended. Professional enthusiasm could be an awkward trait.

Film achieved new importance in the Cultural Revolution. During these years film's function in the People's Republic as the main conveyor of a new, mass culture to all corners of China reached its apogee. More Chinese probably saw the eight 'model performances' not live on stage, but as feature films. These and other films served to 'fix' Cultural Revolution culture, taking it in standardized form to the farthest reaches of the nation. Film had never been as prominent before 1965, and in the 1980s was rapidly overtaken by television as the main shaper of popular cultural discourse. An understanding of film in these years thus reveals a great deal about artists and audiences during the Cultural Revolution.

The five sections in this chapter start with the attacks on popular films that emerged two years before the start of the Cultural Revolution. Then the experience of artists and other staff in the studios is outlined. The important task of putting the 'model performances' on screen fell to these specialists. As the cultural repertoire expanded in the early 1970s, new feature films reached Chinese audiences. They joined a range of films, both Chinese and imported, that were brought to widening audiences for this modern art. We shall see that the pleasures viewers found in these films may not have been those intended by the cultural authorities.

For these authorities, film's potential as the medium to establish and promulgate the new mass culture had always been threatened by other qualities of the medium: its expense and its specialist nature. The flurry of expansion in film, as in other industries, during the Great Leap Forward in 1958 had seen many new, provincial studios established across the nation. Most of them were disbanded, downsized, or retrenched in the early 1960s. The Cultural Revolution decade, however, saw major new investment of resources in the film industry. Much of these resources went not into production but into distribution. New cinemas were constructed, more 16 mm and other smaller-format projection equipment was produced, and mobile projection teams greatly expanded. The specialists charged with making China's films had always been a dubious group, in the eyes of the leaders of the nation, including those in charge of the cultural apparatus. But the sorts of skills that a professional like Li Wenhua possessed, in cinematography, writing, directing, sound-recording, lighting, and editing, were essential for an acceptable level of film quality to serve the mass audiences and were not easily learned. It was difficult to cultivate rapidly a new corps of film professionals, unlike the efforts to support the new, worker-peasant-soldier poets, painters, and performers in other cultural fields.

As a more conspicuous art, potentially available to a much wider and diverse audience, filmmakers did not have the luxury of time and resources to adapt to the new political expectations, as opera modernizers had enjoyed. The insurgent cultural authorities had to rely to a greater extent than was the case for other arts on the existing artistic corps of filmmakers. This had been true in the transition to the People's Republic immediately after 1949 and was again the case in the Cultural Revolution. Film artists could not be fully replaced by more reliable supporters of the new cultural regime. As a highly complex and specialist art and medium, film needed special treatment and special consideration.

Film was prominent from the early rumblings of what became the Cultural Revolution storm in 1964. Several feature films were among the first products of the so-called black line in literature and art to be attacked in the mass media across the nation.[2] The nation learned during the Cultural Revolution that the 1951 *People's Daily* editorial attacking the film *The Life of Wu Xun* (*Wu Xun zhuan*), the first major national criticism of a work of art or literature after the founding of the People's Republic, had indeed been written by Mao Zedong.[3] In similar vein, the opening salvoes of the Cultural Revolution were directed at films deemed unsuitable for China's mass audiences. Although many histories of the Cultural Revolution identify the criticism of the hybrid Peking opera, Wu Han's *Hai Rui Dismissed from Office*, as marking the start of the 'ten years of catastrophe', film beat opera to this dubious distinction of being first target of the cultural radicals' scorn.

This suspicion of film professionals and acknowledgement of the power of the medium help explain why feature film production effectively stopped for the first four years of the Cultural Revolution. More than other arts, film required a proper 'cleansing of the ranks' before being given the task of taking the new culture to China's audiences. But when the first film versions of the model performances began to appear on China's screens, audiences saw a great many familiar names in the credits for the new features. Directors who had been prominent during the now discredited seventeen years before 1966, and even some who had been fiercely criticized in the pages of the nation's newspapers a few years earlier, were responsible for most of these new films.

The range of film production expanded greatly after 1972, which was the case for most other art forms. Some of the first works were direct re-makes of popular films from the 1950s and early 1960s, in colour and wide-screen format, with more elaborate musical scores and plots and characters adjusted to the new political circumstances. But the new films were severely circumscribed by Cultural Revolution requirements, particularly related to the presentation of heroes. The concentric emphasis on the chief protagonist may have worked well on the formulaic opera stage. It could also be fairly easily transplanted to the dance stage and to fiction, painting, and other arts. But in film, an art that lent itself to a more naturalistic approach to representing life, the opera-inspired aesthetic was an ill-fit. With its mass distribution, film indeed exposed the limits of Cultural Revolution aesthetics to popular grumblings and private derision.

Having been prominent at the launch of the Cultural Revolution, film possibly hastened its demise. The weaknesses of the new-style feature films, mocked as 'model films', were so obvious that they helped encapsulate popular disquiet with the cultural products that had been their fare since the mid-1960s. Resentment reached the highest levels: Mao Zedong had some filmmakers busy filming dozens of traditional-style Chinese operas for his own, solitary viewing pleasure. When the cultural insurgents tried to assert their firm control by attacking two new features, *The Pioneers* (*Chuangye*) and *Haixia*, they got no traction in cultural or political circles. Even more empty film rhetoric in 1976 did not help. The popular mood was so unforgiving that, upon the arrest of Jiang Qing and her allies, the outpouring of hatred against the Gang of Four was overwhelming. Films associated with the ex-leaders were more vigorously attacked than the eight 'model performances' that had been so vital in their attempted cultural dictatorship.

I. FILMS BESIEGED

One of the first films to come under attack in 1964 was a somewhat obvious target. *Early Spring in February* (*Zao chun eryue*) had been made at the Beijing Film Studio in 1963 by a team led by Xie Tieli and including Li Wenhua. It was an adaptation, penned by Xie, of a 1929 novella by Ruo Shi. The political credentials of the original story were based largely on the fate of Ruo, who had been imprisoned as a Communist and executed by the Nationalist government in 1931. The story centres on a would-be revolutionary, Xiao Jianqiu, who decides to give up political activism in the city and become a village schoolteacher in Zhejiang Province, west of Shanghai. His attempt at leading a quiet life is complicated by two women. One is the uneducated widow Wen, whose late husband Xiao once knew. The other is Tao Lan, the young sister of a colleague. When the widow's younger child dies, Xiao makes the reluctant decision to marry widow Wen, spurning the more obvious attractions of the lovely Miss Tao. But Xiao's reluctance is obvious and widow Wen hangs herself. The film ends with Xiao deciding to leave the school and Tao Lan and return to the revolutionary mainstream.

What might have seemed, in 1929 at least and perhaps even in the relatively liberal context of the early 1960s, a moving examination of the plight of a May Fourth–era intellectual torn between tradition (the widow Wen) and modernity (Miss Tao) came across on screen as something more than this. The filmmakers strengthened Xiao's dedication to his young students and softened Miss Tao's romanticism. The characters even on occasion pick up an issue of *New Youth* (*Xin qingnian*), the journal of the May Fourth movement. But countering this is a lack of restraint on the filmmakers' part. Xiao and Miss Tao have a penchant for tempestuous piano music, which provides opportunities for self-conscious flirting. Xie Tieli's assured directing could not disguise the film's inconsistency of tone and politics. In essence, the filmmakers had been trapped by their respect for the original novella and their urge to change it.[4] The criticism of the 'bourgeois' shortcomings of *Early Spring in February* in 1964 was one of the first shots in a broader skirmish against the so-called black line in literature and art.

Attacking established cultural authorities through films associated with them had several advantages. The films were generally well known to audiences: The film audience thus became a political audience for the radicals' messages. Esoteric discussions of a history play or Party documents lacked the immediate public impact that denunciation of a familiar film could provide. The films criticized tended to have a distant association with the targeted 'black liner'. This allowed audiences to make the connection but also provided a line of escape should the radicals find that their attack had backfired or been defeated by superior firepower from the establishment. The team nature of filmmaking also had advantages for the insurgents, as an ambitious team member might be found to voice 'accusations' against others on a project. As a complex art, even the most highly censored feature could be found to include unacceptable elements, if not in the script, then in the images, songs, or some other aspect. In an age before the VCR and DVD, attacks published in the media could not usually be checked against a further viewing of the film, unlike criticisms of a published work of fiction, a speech, or a newspaper article. Popular awareness and an inability to assess the accusations made a film an ideal target for those seeking to usurp control of cultural policy.

Xia Yan was the main target of the criticism of *Early Spring in February*. Xia and Zhou Yang had both been leaders of the underground League of Left-Wing Writers, founded in 1930. Xia's 1959 adaptation of Mao Dun's 1932 story *The Lin Family Shop* (*Lin jia puzi*) was targeted in 1965.[5] The pains Xia and his collaborators had made to try to diminish viewers' sympathy for shopkeeper Lin were not enough to protect the film from attack. Xia was also criticized at the February 1966 Conference on Army Literature and Art Work.[6] The last major attack on Xia Yan before his arrest at the start of the Cultural Revolution came in a long 'analysis' of the political shortcomings of his 1963 *Essays on Film* (*Dianying wenji lun*).[7] The 1930s Shanghai film legacy that Xia had helped shape was the focus of the first history of Chinese film published in the People's Republic. Cheng Jihua's two-volume *History of the Development of Chinese Film* (*Zhongguo dianying fazhan shi*) was published in 1963. Attacks on the book for its positive assessment of 1930s Shanghai films were a useful means to undermine further the influence and public standing of cultural authorities like Xia Yan and Zhou Yang.[8]

The other films that came under criticism in 1964–1965 all had links with what could be called the Shanghai, or May Fourth, legacy in Chinese filmmaking. *City without Night* (*Buyecheng*, 1957) told the story of a

Shanghai capitalist from the 1930s until the 1950s. Its fascination with the lifestyle of the protagonists suggested to the critics in 1965 an unhealthy longing for a bourgeois restoration. The script of the film was by Ke Ling, who had held high office in the Shanghai cultural bureaucracy. This had protected him from public criticism during the anti-Rightist campaign in 1957 when the film had been released. By 1965, the Maoist cultural insurgents had enough sway to launch an attack on *City without Night*. In a pattern seen in the literary campaigns in the 1950s, some of Ke Ling's associates in the film industry seized the opportunity to voice resentments of Ke or to display suitable revolutionary fervour to disarm possible attack on themselves. One such performer was Xie Jin, a Shanghai film director. His words were typical of ritual denunciations at the start of the Cultural Revolution:

> For many years now, some people in literary circles have used the excuse of writing about things with which they are personally familiar in order to oppose Chairman Mao's directives regarding the need for literary and art professionals to go deep among the worker-peasant-soldier masses, to join in their fierce battles, and familiarize themselves with the life of struggle of workers, peasants and soldiers.[9]

Ironically, Xie Jin's own 1965 film *Stage Sisters* (*Wutai jiemei*) came under attack soon after its release. Xie's words of criticism of Ke Ling quoted above may well have been designed to demonstrate his own political correctness in anticipation of difficulty with his new film. *Stage Sisters* had a distinctly Shanghai feel to it: Most of it is set in the city in the 1940s, as two Shaoxing opera actresses play out their rivalry against a background of the battle between the gangsters and Nationalists, on the one hand, and progressive political elements, on the other. The happy, post-1949 ending, in which the two actresses reconcile, seems forced, at odds with the film noir darkness of the rest of the work. One of the finest films made in the seventeen years before the Cultural Revolution, *Stage Sisters* was perhaps doomed when it was released in the midst of efforts to promote modernized Peking opera.[10]

A peasant drama set in North China, *Jiangnan in the North* (*Beiguo Jiangnan*, 1963) appeared to cleave closely to the Maoist line on presenting the lives of peasants as they push through land reform and collectivization. But the script by Yang Hansheng had a humanist edge. The importance of personal motivations, the tensions between the hero and his wife who is slowly going blind under the pressure of her husband's obsession with digging wells during the winter slack season, and his reliance more on persuasion than Maoist 'struggle' to solve village conflicts set the film apart from orthodox Maoist works. Compounding the distinction of the script was the superior directing by Shanghai director Shen Fu.[11] In a curious, though not unexpected, conflation of fiction and reality, an investigation team went to the district in Hebei province where the film was set to report on what life there was really like.[12]

Writers such as Yang Hansheng had been active among leftist intellectuals in Shanghai in the 1930s. Jiang Qing had been a relatively well-known actress in Shanghai in those years. Once the Cultural Revolution got under way, some of the actions of Red Guards in searching the homes of former associates of Jiang Qing indicated her concern at having her actions in those days used against her. Among the former colleagues whose homes were ransacked was the eminent actor Zhao Dan, who had shared at least a stage with Jiang Qing in 1935.[13]

At the February 1966 Conference on Army Literature and Art Work, more than a dozen films from the previous ten years or so were cited as examples of filmmakers' shortcomings and lack of commitment to the revolution. The 1959 film biography of Nie Er, composer in the 1930s of what became China's national anthem, was dismissed for over-stating Nie's historical role, as if the Chinese revolution sprang from his 'March of the Volunteers'. The real target of the criticism was probably Zheng Junli, a veteran Shanghai director who had known Jiang Qing in her actress days in the 1930s. The ethnic minorities film *Five Golden Flowers* (*Wu duo jinhua*) from the same year was allegedly fixated on the love affair between two people at the expense of any social value. *Adolescence in the Flames of War* (*Zhanhuo zhong de qingchun*, 1959) promoted individual heroics and had a whiff of 'butterfly lovers' about it. *Flowers Are Fine and the Moon Is Round* (*Hua hao yue yuan*, 1958), based on a short story by the Yan'an-era peasant writer Zhao Shuli, was a title that did not express class struggle.[14] The Changchun studio's 1964 film *City Besieged* (*Binglinchengxia*) told a tale of betrayal and courage in the northeast during the civil war of the late 1940s. At a time when cultural radicals were calling for art and literature to present simple dichotomies between enemies and Communists and between good and bad, the complexity of the film helped seal its fate.[15] By May 1966, when the Cultural Revolution officially began, Jiang Qing had identified fifty-four films worthy of criticism from the seventeen years since 1949.[16] A formal notice from the Central Cultural Revolution Group on 3 December 1967, eighteen months into the Cultural Revolution, ordered a stop to screening all Chinese and imported 'poisonous weed' (*ducao*) films. In June 1968 came a recall order for prints of such films from cinemas and other screening units.[17]

Under this onslaught of criticism production of feature films had begun to change in 1964. The Changchun studio, as well as releasing *City Besieged* that year, also included three Peking-opera films among its eight features for the year. Two of those operas had modern settings on communes. The Beijing studio's seven 1964 features included a 'folk song and dance collection' (*minjian gewu jijin*) of twelve performances by ethnic minority groups.[18] Filmmakers' shift to safer subject matter became more pronounced in 1965. Changchun made even more modern-subject opera films and a full-length colour documentary of the November 1964 National Minorities Mass Amateur Art Festival held in Beijing. Its title said it all: *Every Red Flower Turns towards the Sun* (*Duoduo hong hua xiang taiyang*), the sun being Chairman Mao. In similar vein, the Beijing Film Studio's 1965 productions included a modern musical, spoken dramas created by amateur groups, and modern-subject versions of local musical plays.[19] After years of the studios producing a relatively wide range of features, film was clearly being used as the best medium to record and disseminate the new-style, modern-subject performances that had begun to take over China's stages.

Even the two Shanghai studios, noted for their urban comedies and glossy productions, joined the shift to plainer fare, including operas and musical plays on modern subjects and stage-show compilations. *Spring in Shanghai* (*Shanghai zhi chun*), from the Tianma studio, for example, recorded items performed at the sixth 'Spring in Shanghai' music festival in 1965. They included an early, short version of the ballet *The White-Haired Girl*.[20] The army's August First Film Studio in Beijing, the Pearl River studio in Guangzhou, and the Xi'an Film Studio in 1965 all produced a majority of plain, stage-based compilations and short films, many in black-and-white. It was as if the film studios were serving the function in other societies provided by television stations.[21]

2. CLEANSING THE RANKS

With the start of the Cultural Revolution, films in production were suspended as the crews, actors, and management engaged in ritualistic displays of their loyalty to the Communist Party. Life in the film studios in these years centred not on production of films but on the production of big-character posters, speeches, and other public performances of correct political attitudes. Studio histories, published after the Cultural Revolution, make brief reference to the Cultural Revolution years, using standard phrases about 'ultra-leftists' and 'chaos' which reveal little of what actually went on at the studios.[22] Only the ancient Chinese tradition of documentary precision, or at least apparent precision, tells us something about developments. At the Changchun studio in the northeast, for example, close to 300 persons were 'illegally sent to "cow sheds" (*niu peng*)' and (with a few exceptions) the 190 films made in Changchun since 1949, along with 447 foreign films that had been dubbed there into Chinese, were all labelled 'poisonous weeds' (*ducao*). Five hundred fifty-two cadres of the studio (55.2 percent) were sent down to the countryside or out of the studio. This was similar to the disbanding of opera and other performing troupes in the late 1960s and early 1970s. The mathematical exactness of events at Changchun contrasts with vagueness about production being 'a blank period' (*kongbai qi*).[23] At the Pearl River studio in Guangzhou more than ninety percent of the artistic, technical, and management cadres were subjected to criticism or struggle sessions.[24]

At the Beijing film studio, a 1985 history claims in March 1970 the entire staff, 'without exception', were sent to do physical labor at a May Seventh Cadre School that had been built to receive them in Huang Village in Daxing County in the southern suburbs of Beijing city. Huang Jianzhong, who had joined the studio as a nineteen-year-old in 1960, at the height of Red Guard activism walked around eighty kilometres each day for ten days from Taiyuan, the Shanxi provincial capital, to Yan'an. His group had been looked after by local Red Guards on this pilgrimage. In 1970 he went to the May Seventh Cadre School, where his cooking duties allowed him to slip out of political study sessions.[25] Only in 1973 did these people start to return to the studio.[26] Quite how the studio managed to make television versions of *Taking Tiger Mountain by Strategy* and *Shajiabang*, and film versions of the ballet *The Red Detachment of Women* and *On the Docks* (with the Shanghai studio), in the alleged absence of all staff goes unexplained. In Shanghai actress Zhang Ruifang was imprisoned for six months starting in December 1967. As one of the best-loved faces on China's screens, she was vulnerable to attack for being an established filmmaker. After a further eighteen months of confinement, she was sent to the Shanghai film system's May Seventh Cadre School in the Shanghai suburbs for a year's work.[27] Down in Guangzhou, the Pearl River Studio put all production on hold in the second half of 1966.[28]

Similar closure of production and disruption of regular work occurred in all ten or so feature-film studios as the Cultural Revolution began in 1966.[29] At the Xi'an Film Studio, criticism had a definite viciousness, with accused staff sent to 'cow sheds' or brought to judgement in a 'fight selfishness and criticize revisionism class' (*dousi pixiu ban*). According to a 1985 report, other, more private means of intimidation included beatings. In all about one-third (130 out of 400 people) of the studio personnel were locked up or 'struggled against' (*beidou*).[30] Even the army's August First studio could not continue its regular work. A 1985 account claims that because of the interference of Jiang Qing's supporters, the filming of the modern opera *Raid on the White-Tiger Regiment* was abandoned in 1965.[31] Being part of the military could not protect the studio from radical harassment, which had started immediately after the February 1966 conference on army cultural work.

At the Changchun studio, as was the case in the other studios, the provincial level authorities had taken an immediate interest at the start of the Cultural Revolution. In June 1966 the Jilin Provincial Party Committee had sent a work team (*gongzuozu*) to take up residence in the studio, replacing the top-level cadres. Criticism and struggle sessions followed at irregular intervals. At the end of 1968 the Changchun studio established a 'revolutionary committee', like virtually all institutions across the nation at that time. The new leadership grouping was based on the official 'three combinations' (*san jiehe*), in this case several army veterans with professional knowledge, and members of the army and worker propaganda teams. A further sign of the restoration of order came in early 1970 when a Party committee for the studio was set up, anticipating the filming about to start on the 'model performances'. In August 1971, Su Yun, who had been a studio deputy head for six years before the Cultural Revolution, returned to top-level work in the studio.[32]

Feature-film production had stopped in 1966, but at some studios, other work occupied some of the employees. From 1968 until 1976, Pearl River made more than 140 newsreels and 39 popular-science films (*kejiaopian*).[33] Mao Zedong became the most frequently seen Chinese film star in the late 1960s, through wide distribution of documentary films on his public appearances. Seven documentaries on his eight inspections of Red Guards and others in Tian'anmen Square in 1966–1967 were made by the Central Newsreel and Documentary Film Studio and distributed widely, with low ticket prices to encourage attendance. The first of these films, *Chairman Mao Inspects the Red Guards* (*Mao zhuxi jianyue Hongweibing*), was watched for free by over 100 million people.[34]

Reports published after the Cultural Revolution typically cite cases of respected directors and other artists being 'hounded to death' (*pohai zhi si*).[35] The vagueness of the expression covers a range of actual grim experiences. When some filmmakers stood up at meetings and denounced colleagues with the vituperation embedded in set phrases used in the newspapers – snakes and demons, poisonous specialists, traitors, spies, and tools of the black-liners – obviously many targets of such attack were shocked and distressed. More distressing was that colleagues could not openly express support for them at the meetings or in the work units. In such circumstances, many targets of attack became physically or psychologically ill. Some committed suicide.

An official history of contemporary Chinese film provides statistics on Cultural Revolution victims in the studios.[36] Of the 1,000 personnel at the Shanghai studios, 309 artistic and technical staff members 'suffered persecution' (*shoudao pohai*), of whom sixteen died. Among the 108 writers, directors, and actors at Shanghai, 104 were subjected to illegal investigation, being 'struggled' against, and imprisonment. Of the forty-four Shanghai-based directors, thirty-one were 'overthrown' (*dadao*), twelve were 'washed away' (*qingxi*), and one was left as 'an example to others' (*fanmian jiaoyuan*). Seven of twenty-one famous actors were 'overthrown'. Twelve were investigated and then all were removed from the studio. Only two of twelve cinematographers were allowed to stay on at the Shanghai studios. In Beijing, 300 of the studio's over 800 staff were labelled 'counter-revolutionary'. Seven were 'hounded to death'. In Changchun 116 of the 290 middle- and higher-level artistic and technical cadres were accused. More than two-thirds of the creative and production personnel, 521 people, had their Changchun city residence permits cancelled and were obliged to go to the countryside for long-term labor. In a system in which urban residency was a valuable privilege, this was a drastic move. In 1969, during the first 'cleansing' of the Changchun studio, the main creative ranks were reduced by twenty percent and acting ranks by a full half.

But the generality of such verbs as 'overthrown' and 'cleansed' needs to be interrogated, even while we acknowledge the degree of appalling behaviour and suffering in the late 1960s and afterwards. A direct causal link between Red Guard or other colleagues' attack and the fate of the victim is sometimes far from clear. Some of the victims were already elderly men and women and not in the best of health: The upheaval and viciousness of the attacks undoubtedly hastened their passing. But the implications of 'hounded to death' suggest more direct causes. Using vague phrases like 'hounded to death' served a useful purpose after the Cultural Revolution, for it helped acknowledge political stupidity and drew a veil over the complicated reality. Participants had enough trouble after 1976 simply adjusting to working alongside persons who may have joined in attacks against them at some stage in the past. Post-1976 accounts of these years generally leap forward to the phrase at the start of a new paragraph or section: 'After the smashing of the "Gang of Four" ...' (*Fensui 'Sirenbang' hou ...*). It as if the writers are heaving a sigh of relief having tiptoed through the minefield of Cultural Revolution discord and suffering in their film studios, opera troupes, and work units. A 1985 outline of thirty-five years of the Shanghai Film Studio, for example, covers the Cultural Revolution in two short paragraphs occupying a third of a page in a twenty-five-page chapter. The emphasis in these nine lines is on the damage to people's lives and the film enterprise caused by 'ten years of upheaval' (*shinian dongluan*).[37]

Book-length studio histories published in the 1980s and 1990s provide a more concrete picture of happenings during the late 1960s. The Beijing studio history, for example, includes a substantial chapter on events during the Cultural Revolution.[38] But elsewhere the book shows that since the early 1960s regular work at the studio had been disrupted by frequent loss of personnel going to the countryside to participate in various political campaigns. In September 1964 a 'rectification work team' (*zhengfeng gongzuozu*) had been sent to the studio for ten months after several of its films had been criticized in the national newspapers.[39] In some ways, the coming of the Cultural Revolution in May 1966 was just another interruption.

But Beijing studio personnel soon saw that this movement was different. When the 16 May directive came from Party Central announcing the start of a cultural revolution, the first big-character posters were put up at the studio. Film studios were strategic assets in the new campaign, so in June a People's Liberation Army Work Team (*gongzuodui*) arrived and reorganized all staff into five broad groups: Party and government, artistic, administration, production, and theatre company. More than twenty leading filmmakers were sent to a two-month study class organized at the Socialist Academy (*shehuizhuyi xueyuan*) by the Ministry of Culture. In July 1966 the studio staff 'selected', with guidance from the work team, a Cultural Revolution Leadership Group. Large-scale criticism meetings were held involving all studio personnel in witnessing the humiliation of former studio leaders, including Wang Yang and Wu Xiaopei, who had led the 'rectification' of the studio in the summer of 1965.[40]

Red Guards from outside of the studio started singling out actors and directors for criticism in August 1966. Their targets included Xie Tieli, director of *Early Spring in February*, and Xie Tian, a director and lead actor in *The Lin Family Shop*. These outsiders encouraged the formation among younger personnel of the studio's own Red Guards later that month. This new group agitated for the 'eradication of the four olds' (*po si jiu*: old thinking, culture, customs, and habits), a campaign encouraged in August by members of the Central Committee of the Communist Party. Disorder soon followed, as the theatre company was the first to declare itself 'rebels' (*zaofan*). Also in September various groups set themselves up in the studio, calling themselves, among other names, the

Mao Zedong-ism Commune and the Mao Zedong Thought University. Different groups claimed unique access to Maoist truth, and each set about finding incriminating evidence on their opponents or rivals. In January 1967, the Mao Zedong-ism Commune seized power at Beiying, as the studio is called in shorthand form. They and the Mao Zedong Thought University group each used allies among Red Guard factions in Beijing city to promote their interests in the studio. The 'university' group established a 'New Beiying'. The 'commune' group countered with a 'Red Beiying'.

Order, in the form of a cowed silence, was partly restored to the Beijing studio in the summer of 1967. In June the Cultural Revolution radicals associated with Jiang Qing had established a Literature and Art Group (*wenyi zu*) to take over the responsibilities of the old Ministry of Culture. Acknowledging the importance of the film studios, the group dispatched military representatives to Beiying. But in October the central Literature and Art Group was disbanded. The start of 1968 saw little change in the confusion of factional rivalry at Beiying. The military representatives at the studio occasionally organized mass criticisms of various prominent filmmakers, some of whom were sent off to the Public Security Bureau for incarceration. But not all the attacks were centrally condoned. In May the 'rebels' at the Beijing Film Academy savagely beat Hai Mo, who died soon afterwards.[41] But the prospect of more order arrived at the Beijing studio in August 1968, when a worker and military Mao Zedong Thought Propaganda Team moved in. Similar teams began entering all major institutions and work units in Chinese cities at this time. The team at Beiying ordered that all employees were to live at the studio. Those whose apartments were outside the precincts could return home once a week. An indication of the importance attached to the film medium was the dispatch of a group from the PLA's 8341 troupe, the part of the army charged with the security of the Politburo, to the Beijing studio in September 1968.[42] In November the propaganda team began to 'sort out' (*qingli*) the cadre ranks at the studio, ordering some to be released, while freshly identifying others as 'counter-revolutionaries'.

Even the army's August First studio was not above Red Guard or 'rebel' factionalism. A rebel group calling itself the 'Red Army', made up mostly of film professional cadres, and other groups presumed to pass judgement on the pre–Cultural Revolution films made at the studio, examining the standing of directors, scriptwriters, actors, and others. Labels such as 'serving the revisionist black line in literature and art' were applied to those judged wanting in proper revolutionary credentials. Such people were sent to do physical labor at a May Seventh Cadre School in Gao County, Sichuan province. Some returned to the studio in 1970, only to be sent down to the countryside to work in October that year. Artists assumed they were rehabilitated if they managed to avoid being sent to a May Seventh cadre school.[43] Even in late 1973, when the studio started shooting a new-style feature film, the crew reportedly included several 'rebels' who identified still with different factions, making the director's job difficult.[44]

There may be a tendency to overstate the disruption in the studios by concentrating on key figures at the top in these institutions, as we have seen among the opera ranks. The total numbers of staff at the studios did not seem to change much during the period. The Changchun studio had 1,610 personnel in late 1966. In late 1970, there were 1,310 staff, although a large number of cadres had been sent to the countryside in 1968 and been replaced in the statistics by several hundred demobilized soldiers who came to 'stir up the sand' (chan shazi) in the studio. With the return of the former cadres, numbers rose again. By late 1976 there were 1,906 employees, including 353 working at the Super 8 film developing and printing works attached to the studio.[45] Disruption began to give way to dullness.

Jiang Qing was as aware as any Chinese leader after 1949 of the potential of film to carry reliable messages directly to her political audience. In June 1968 she met with the newly established revolutionary committee in charge of the August First studio and some of the creative personnel there and raised the idea of making feature films again. In mid-September that year, she mentioned the notion of filming revolutionary dramas to a group of artists and writers at a meeting in the Great Hall of the People.[46] Jiang Qing even expressed concern about the state of production of film stock and equipment. On 28 February 1969, she asked that in the future all issues related to film machinery manufacture be reported directly to the State Council, China's cabinet. Jiang Qing also insisted that once Super 8 projectors had been successfully produced, she be sent an example.[47]

Other state leaders were also showing increased interest in the nation's film enterprise. A meeting of representatives of several relevant ministries in July 1969, called by the highest levels of the government, set up a thirteen-person group to take charge of ensuring China's film machinery production reached world levels of quality.[48] Around midnight on the night of 28–29 October 1969, the state leadership watched China's first documentary made with Chinese-produced colour film stock. They saw themselves on the screen in The Ninth National Congress of the Chinese Communist Party (Zhongguo gongchandang di-jiu ci quanguo daibiao dahui). At the end of the screening, Jiang Qing reportedly turned to Zhou Enlai and remarked: 'Premier, I suggest that a . . . study film (jiaoxue pian) of *The Red Detachment of Women* be made with our own film stock, developed with our own methods. We'll use our own, not the foreign. We should urge them on a bit.' The premier readily agreed.[49] Major momentum was building for the resumption of feature-film production.

The moves were capped by a 'national film industry coordination meeting' of 554 representatives of 303 units in the film apparatus held in Beijing from mid-November to mid-December 1969. The resolutions for work in 1970 passed by the delegates included commitments to produce the colour film stock, lenses, and other materials and equipment required for the filming of the 'model performances'. The emphasis was on Mao's call for independence, keeping the initiative, and being self-reliant (*dulizizhu, ziligengsheng*), which was being applied to the revival of China's industrial and agricultural production. Obligatory slogans about mobilizing and relying on the masses did not disguise the plan to apply a great deal of specialist scientific and technical knowledge to growing the equipment side of China's film industry.[50]

A major signal of a more relaxed political climate came with an editorial in the 24 April 1972 issue of *People's Daily*. The editorial reported the conclusion, after investigation by Premier Zhou Enlai himself, that over ninety percent of cadres were 'good or relatively good'. Education, rather than attack, should be used to help lapsed cadres see the error of their ways.[51]

3. FIXING THE MODEL PERFORMANCES ON FILM

Putting the model performances on celluloid offered the Cultural Revolution cultural leaders the means to standardize a version of each of the models that could be seen in this fixed form in all corners of China. The rewriting and fussing with staging that had occupied so many talented artists and writers for years could end and the perfection of the completed models be seen by the world. Amateur or local attempts at and even abuse of the models would be superseded by a visual record of the official versions, against which any live performance of an aria or a whole opera could be measured.

The first of the films of the model operas was *Taking Tiger Mountain by Strategy*, made at the Beijing studio and released on National Day 1970. Being in the capital allowed for the reportedly constant visits to the soundstages during the filming by representatives of Jiang Qing and others in charge of cultural policy. The formal decision to make film adaptations of the 'model performances' had been made by the Politburo and the 'Central Cultural Revolution' (*Zhongyang Wen-ge*) in the early autumn of

1968. *Tiger Mountain* took two years to complete.[52] The crew was headed by director Xie Tieli. Born in 1925, Xie had a long connection with the Communist Party, which he had joined as a teenager, and had directed his first film in 1959.[53] Xie's third work as director had been *Early Spring in February*, which Jiang Qing rather liked, he later claimed, despite the public denunciations of the film in 1964.[54] Like director Xie, cinematographer Qian Jiang was associated with several films, including *The Lin Family Shop*, which had been heavily criticized at the start of the Cultural Revolution. But his film roots in Yan'an, as well as his work on 1965's song and dance epic, *The East Is Red* (*Dongfang hong*), counted for more in 1969.[55]

Initial work on the *Tiger Mountain* project had come in the second half of 1967, when Xie Tieli was released from over a year's confinement in a 'cow shed'.[56] In the summer of 1968, two 'model performance' film crews were formally established at the Beijing studio: one for *Tiger Mountain* and the other for the ballet *The Red Detachment of Women*, and crew members began preliminary planning.[57] Apparently orders came from the central authorities that the production team was not be distracted by factional upheavals and other disturbances at the studio. In May 1969, an official announcement was approved by the Party central leadership about the establishment of a 'model performances' production crew at the Beijing Film Studio. Meanwhile plans firmed to move the Beijing Film Studio to a new site, perhaps a suitable distraction for those not involved in making the opera film.[58]

Adapting a model opera, and matching the opera's innovations in film, was a major challenge. The aim, as with all film versions of Chinese opera that aspired to being more than just a dull-eyed, static recording of a stage performance, was to find ways to convey the special qualities and spirit of the original work in the new medium. The first problem was to decide on the sense of space and place in the film: Opera characters moved in one or more defined spaces; film could ignore boundaries. The production team converted the stage opera's ten scenes to forty-one, adding certain necessary details but reducing the length from three hours to a more standard cinema timing of two. Compounding their difficulties were the reportedly inconsistent responses of Jiang Qing, who one moment endorsed boldness and the next cautioned about undermining the original opera. The degree of her interest was such that she allegedly even made adjustments to the hero Yang Zirong's make-up design.[59] Also a challenge was preserving the stage business and artificiality of the original in a medium that lent itself to naturalism. Thus, Yang Zirong enters the film riding an imaginary horse before bursting into song.

Trial and error characterized the production. When the first rough cut of several scenes was shown, major criticism was expressed. The new work looked too much like previous, traditional opera films. The filmmakers' response was to follow strictly Jiang Qing's instructions to 'return to the original stage' (*huanyuan wutai*). But when the team experimented with filming one scene in the manner of a stage documentary, Jiang Qing declared that such mechanical transferring to film did not properly enhance the original. A third way was attempted, in which the camera concentrated on the main actor in any sequence. But this too was deemed a failure. 'When we tried using film methods, they said we didn't respect the opera. When we tried the old stuff, they said this wasn't "even better than on stage"' (*gao yu wutai*), Xie Tieli noted more than thirty years later.[60] The model operas' 'three prominences' were to guide the filmmakers' next endeavours. Heroes were shot as if in centre stage, full-on and fully lit, seemingly towering above their crouching enemies, seen sideways and badly illuminated. This took the principles applied to the stage presentation of the opera and used the mobility of space and the camera to reinforce those emphases. From these principles, further guidelines were produced: 'three contrasts' (*san peichen*), 'multiple sides' (*duo cemian*), 'multiple starting points' (*duo qidian*), and 'multiple layers' (*duo cengce*). These simple slogans may have had little real meaning in actual practice on the film soundstage or on the opera stage, but they provided the filmmakers with an ideological cover for what they produced on celluloid.[61] Xie later recalled their daily regimen: 8 a.m. political study, determined by the army propaganda team at the studio, followed by filming. At lunch time the opera performers had 'model food' (*yangbanfan*), which was of higher quality than the film crew's meals. The actual filming took an extraordinary twenty months. 'We got everything we needed', even a huge living bamboo plant shipped by the PLA from Jiangxi.[62]

Most post–Cultural Revolution assessments are highly dismissive of the results. The standard objections to stereotype and generality are trotted out when discussing the model-opera films made in the early 1970s. The films left real life behind, distorted reality, misrepresented history, and so forth. Moreover, they were weapons in a plot by evil usurpers to seize power.[63] But when looked at without the lenses of obligatory political denunciation of the Gang of Four, the film version of *Taking Tiger Mountain by Strategy* and of the other model operas marked a major achievement in Chinese film artists' ongoing project to film China's musical theatre. The original stage works may have produced shows that teeter on the brink of self-parody and high camp. But they also took a historic theatre form in new, potentially productive directions. The filmed versions of these operas did them justice. They captured the forceful and theatrical nature of the originals with remarkable felicity. Yang Zirong, with his tiger-skin waistcoat, beams his proletarian determination into the lens and the world can be set right, at least on the silver screen.

After two years of work, during which it was reportedly filmed three times with apparent disregard of the financial costs, *Taking Tiger Mountain by Strategy* was released nationwide in 1970, needless to say, to rapturous critical acclaim.[64] But the Beijing film studio had little time to enjoy their success, for other adaptations of the 'model performances' were already under way. Director Xie Tieli had proved himself and went on to take a supervisory role in the making of the ballet *The Red Detachment of Women* at the studio in 1970–1971. Then he co-directed a joint Beijing–Shanghai film studios production of *On the Docks*, released in 1972, and directed *Song of the Dragon River*, also released that year. For these last two titles, Qian Jiang served again as cinematographer. Xie and Qian also took on the filming of *Azalea Mountain* in 1973.[65]

Also released in 1970 was *The Red Lantern* from the August First studio, directed by Cheng Yin, the director in 1951 of the original *Fighting North and South* that was still being shown on China's screens in the late 1960s. In 1938, at the age of twenty-one, he had gone to Yan'an and was involved with Communist Party theatre work.[66] Cheng was lent to the army studio by his Beijing Film Studio to work on *The Red Lantern*. Being an army establishment had not protected the August First studio from the depredations of the cultural insurgents. The work on *The Red Lantern* marked the start of the restoration of production at August First. The film was released at Spring Festival in 1971.

The importance attached to the filming of the Cultural Revolution 'model performances' confirmed their role in the cultural enterprise and the significance ascribed to making available nationwide a standardized film version of the works. *On the Docks*, the only contemporary story among the initial eight model performances, proved particularly irksome to get on film in an acceptable version (Figure 3.1). Two studios, Beijing and the newly re-established Shanghai, combined forces to complete the work. Two directors were responsible for the final version: Beijing's Xie Tieli and Shanghai's Xie Jin. The latter had started working in film in his twenties in Shanghai just before 1949. The most well-known member of his generation of relatively young film artists, Xie Jin was the director of *Stage Sisters* and the comedy *Big Li, Little Li and Old Li* (*Da Li, xiao Li he lao Li*, 1962), which had both been heavily criticized at the start of the Cultural Revolution, and of the original non-dance 1961 version of *The Red Detachment of Women*.[67] Having made his name in film

3.1. The dockworkers and Fang Haizhen in *On the Docks* (photograph by Shi Shaohua). Source: *Xiandai Jingju: juzhao mingxinpian* (Modern Peking opera: stage-still postcards), Shanghai: Shanghai renmin meishu chubanshe (Shanghai People's Fine Arts Publishing House), 2003.

with his engaging portrayals of strong-willed women, Xie had the task of putting on screen the determinedly strong-willed Fang Haizhen, female Party secretary to the waterside workers.

Xie in fact had helped create the stage opera. Film directors had been brought in to contribute to the stage blocking of the new operas: Xie Jin had been assigned in the spring of 1969 to the directing team (*daoyan zu*) to assist with *On the Docks*. The revised opera was approved for performance in the summer of 1971 and for filming later that year. But this proved a difficult assignment. A first attempt was made at the Beijing studio by Fu Chaowu and Xie Jin. Yu Huiyong, the former Shanghai composer now responsible for cultural matters in Beijing, praised the newly completed film. But Jiang Qing was not satisfied: One major concern was that Fang Haizhen looked too old on film. Furthermore, the scenes were not opened up enough and the lighting was not bright enough. Xie Tieli and Xie Jin took on a second filming of *On the Docks*.[68]

The task of the two directors Xie was not easy, especially when Jiang Qing herself, another strong-willed woman, took such an interest in the filming. *On the Docks* was reportedly filmed three times. One of these re-makes was ordered because Jiang Qing did not like the particular shade of red of the scarf worn by the heroine.[69] In fact the two Xies do not appear to have actually collaborated on the filming of On the Docks. The Beijing studio history claims that the opera was first filmed in Shanghai and then re-shot at the Beijing studio by Xie Tieli. But only one cinematographer, Qian Jiang, appears in the official catalogue listing of the film. A second film of On the Docks was made in 1973 with the same Beijing–Shanghai studio co-operation and with the same crew and cast as the 1972. A third version was shot to answer Jiang Qing's objections.[70] The 1972 version was released nationwide in May that year, along with the Peking-opera films Song of the Dragon River and The Red Detachment of Women, to commemorate the thirtieth anniversary of Mao's 1942 Talks on art and literature in Yan'an.[71] Xie Jin went on to make a regular feature film and then returned to the model operas in 1973 to work on a film adaptation of the new opera, Boulder Bay. In an innovation, Xie decided to film in real locations on an island off the coast of Fujian. The film was completed in the spring of 1976.[72]

Communist China's senior film studio, in Changchun, joined the effort to make film versions of the model performances with Shajiabang, which was completed in August 1971 after a year's filming, and Raid on the White-Tiger Regiment, a 1972 production. An account of the studio, published in 1985, notes that 'these two films were produced with fear and trepidation (zhanzhanjingjing) under the menace of the "Gang of Four's" rods, hats, braids and little shoes'.[73] The Jilin Provincial committee sent inspectors to the studio several times during the filming of Changchun's first two model operas to ensure nothing was amiss.[74] Wu Zhaodi, who directed Shajiabang, had studied in Yan'an after the age of nineteen in 1939, so he had a long association with the Party. His most well-known work was Guerillas on the Plain (Pingyuan youjidui), which he co-directed in 1955 and again co-directed in its Cultural Revolution colour re-make in 1974. A Peking-opera version of the film was among the second tranche of model operas.[75]

White-Tiger was the work of two directors, Su Li and Wang Yan. Su Li had also started his artistic career in Yan'an and had co-directed the original version of Guerillas on the Plain. He had experience with musical films, having made the immensely popular Third Sister Liu (Liu Sanjie), based on a Guangxi folk tale, in 1960.[76] Wang Yan could also claim a Yan'an pedigree. Raid on the White-Tiger Regiment, both as opera and film, never enjoyed the enduring public interest apparent for The Red Lantern, Taking Tiger Mountain by Strategy, and Shajiabang. The original opera must take the blame for this failure, though a somewhat pedestrian film adaptation did not help make *White-Tiger*'s case for entering the popular imagination in the ways its sister operas managed.

As a newer, more modern stage art, ballet could perhaps allow its film adaptors more scope to experiment with ways to present the stage performances on screen. Cinematographer Li Wenhua later claimed that the film of *The Red Detachment of Women* which he shot was even better than the stage performance, from the point of view of audience enjoyment.[77] But making the film took several years: It was released in New Year 1971. The process at the Beijing studio started with key members of the crew living in the same quarters as the ballet dancers, familiarizing themselves with each movement of the dance, and differentiating the key moments from the rest. As a relatively new import, ballet was not a genre with which Chinese filmmakers had had a lot of experience. As Li later recalled, balancing the rather large stage space that the ballet required with the intimacy that film allowed was a process of trial and error, not helped by a steady stream of feedback and comments on rough cuts of scenes from Jiang Qing herself.

Taking the ballet *The White-Haired Girl* to China's screens was a two-stage process in unlikely hands. In 1970 Shanghai Television and a filming team made up of employees of the former Haiyan and Tianma film studios in Shanghai made a television version of the ballet in black-and-white. Two years later a colour film version was completed and released. Both versions were the work of Sang Hu as director and Shen Xilin as cinematographer. Sang Hu was an unexpected choice as director, given the pattern with the other model performance films of assigning the directing duties to filmmakers with a long association with the Communist Party from wartime Yan'an days. A scenarist and director of comedies in pre-1949 Shanghai, Sang's post-1949 claim to fame was co-directing in 1954 China's first full-length colour film, *The Butterfly Lovers* (*Liang Shanbo yu Zhu Yingtai*), an adaptation of a well-known Shaoxing opera. His success with this musical film, along with his writing of film scripts for *Huangmeixi* (opera from Anhui) and Peking opera, probably helped strengthen his qualifications to direct one of the model works.[78] Shen Xilin had been cinematographer on the original *Red Detachment of Women*.[79] Taking on the *White-Haired Girl* project for filmmakers was a way to display their loyalty to the Cultural Revolution cultural radicals. But such responsibilities also could mean high risks, in an apparently fickle atmosphere of arbitrary demands from Jiang Qing and her local supporters.[80]

Other films began to emerge from the studios in 1972 based on model performances. A Peking-opera version of *The Red Detachment of Women* was directed by Cheng Yin at the August First studio, following his filming there of *The Red Lantern*. The opera was hailed as a successful example of 'transplanting' the model performances, so a filmed version could take this achievement to all parts of the nation.

Also put on celluloid to achieve popular access was a three-part film of concert versions of scenes from *The Red Lantern*, along with a piano-concerto version of *Yellow River* and the symphonic version of *Shajiabang*, which was the eighth of the original 'model performances'. Made in 1972 at the Central Newsreel and Documentary Film Studio, the film was helpfully titled *Piano Accompanied 'Red Lantern', Piano Concerto 'Yellow River', Revolutionary Symphonic Music 'Shajiabang'* (*Gangqin banchang 'Hongdeng ji', gangqin xiezou qu 'Huanghe', geming jiaoxiang xinyue 'Shajiabang'*). This music required specialist artists: The film could take these performances to a wider audience than would ever see them in a concert hall or attempt them as amateur musicians. The piano concerto was a transplanted version of music from the *Yellow River Cantata* (*Huanghe dahechang*), a large-scale, Western choral work written by Nie Er and Xian Xinghai and first performed in 1939 in Yan'an. The *Shajiabang* symphony featured several arias from the opera, accompanied by many more Western instruments than the ersatz model-opera orchestra. In contrast, the *Red Lantern* arias accompanied by piano were sung by the Peking-opera actors who had appeared in the feature film of the opera. The pianist in the film was Yin Chengzong, and the conductor of the newly reconstituted Central Symphony Orchestra was Li Delun. The director, Sha Dan, was one of China's most experienced documentary filmmakers.[81]

After the first wave of model performance film adaptations had appeared on China's screens, the State Council's Culture Group organized a 'conference on filming the revolutionary model performances'. Almost fifty people participated from October 1972 to February 1973 in what one attendee called more a study class than a conference. Recalling the occasion a dozen years later, Su Yun from the Changchun studio notes the performance aspects of the conference. Filmmakers made suitable noises in long speeches, while their listeners quietly guffawed. This national gathering revealed the sort of false display of revolutionary earnestness that characterized daily political discussions in work units across China in the early and mid-1970s.[82]

On New Year's night 1973, participants at the filming model works conference attended a reception with other film, opera, and music workers. National leaders were also there, among them Zhou Enlai, who remarked:[83]

> Film's educational function is considerable. Men and women, the young and the old, all need them. This is really worthwhile. The masses express the view that there are too few films. The Culture Group will take a hold of film work. With three years of hard work, we should fill that void.

These words from the saintly premier were the immediate spur for the emergence of new feature films from the studios.

But meanwhile the effort to create film versions of the model Cultural Revolution performances continued in 1973 and beyond, as regular feature-film production resumed after seven years or so. *Azalea Mountain* was the fifth model performance that Xie Tieli had been involved in filming, so he was more confident in 1974 in using all the cinematic resources available to go well beyond the limitations of a stage documentary. He encouraged each specialist section of his crew (set design, costumes, lighting, and so forth) to develop their own coherent style, just like for a regular film. But Xie also wanted to make the film and its characters stand out, with slightly more obvious than usual lighting, rhythmical editing, camera movement, and other effects. Xie even modified the standard treatment of bad characters in the model-opera films, giving them more presence than had been the norm. His risk taking with *Azalea Mountain* did not go unnoticed: It helps explain the difficulties Xie Tieli was to encounter with a new feature film in 1975.[84]

Fighting on the Plain (*Pingyuan zuozhan*) reached China's screens in 1974 from the August First studios. Both its directors, Cui Wei and Chen Huai'ai, had considerable experience filming old-style operas and had been objects of mass criticism in the late 1960s at their home Beijing Film Studio.[85] Cui had been one of the twenty or more artistic leaders at Beijing to feel first the onslaught of criticism in 1966. In June that year he was sent off with the others for 'study', having been, like Xie Tieli, criticized by Red Guards from outside of the studio. For Cui his early acquaintance with Jiang Qing, a fellow Shandong provincial, was cause for concern.[86] Filming *Fighting on the Plain* was Cui Wei's opportunity at rehabilitation. But it also showed how dependent the Cultural Revolution insurgents were on the specialist talents of film artists.

Despite the complete denunciation of old-style operas, Cui Wei, Chen Huai'ai, and their colleagues quietly borrowed some of the techniques they had used in making opera adaptations before the Cultural Revolution. It would have been astonishing self-denial if they had not done so. The shooting plan they had used to film fighting in the old opera *Wild Boar*

Forest (*Yezhu lin*), a 1962 co-production with a Hong Kong studio, helped them present a modern armed clash between a Chinese detachment and the Japanese army in *Fighting on the Plain*. There was some irony, for the main aim in making the films of the model performances was to establish the new (*li xin*).[87] Shooting was relatively trouble-free: According to the lead actor it only took four months and could have been a lot faster, were it not for instructions from on high.[88] This was in marked contrast with the lengthy process of the first model-opera adaptations.

Filming the model performances in the early 1970s also provided the opportunity for the revival of production at studios beyond the big four (Changchun, Beijing, Shanghai, and August First). In 1974 the Pearl River Studio in Guangzhou started filming full-length features again with a Cantonese opera (*Yueju*) version of *Shajiabang*. This was part of the transplanting of the model operas being promoted at the time. A reworking of the opera with lyrics sung in Cantonese, orchestration with a Cantonese dimension, and with some gestures towards Cantonese opera performance conventions, this transplanting also acknowledged the popularity of Cantonese opera in southern China and among overseas Chinese in Southeast Asia and elsewhere. A film version could help the model operas find new audiences at home and abroad. The work was directed by Yu Deshui and starred the outstanding actress Hong Xiannü as Sister Aqing. The latter accordingly somewhat outshone the nominal central hero of the opera, military commander Guo Jianguang.[89]

Premier Zhou Enlai, on a visit to Guangzhou, reportedly was so impressed at Hong Xiannü's singing in a concert performance of arias from the opera that he had suggested it be filmed. This required the Pearl River studio to get back into production mode after a seven-year hiatus. The director who started the project became ill and could not continue. An invitation to a director from the Beijing film school was unsuccessful, so Yu Deshui took this important task on as his directing debut at the age of forty-four. A statistical compilation of films made at Pearl River between 1958 and 1980 shows the care with which these model-opera films were made. The actual shooting of *Shajiabang* lasted 137 days, from early August to mid-December 1973, a considerable length of time given the studio-based filming. The amount of film stock used was more than double the length of any feature film made at the studio in the five years following. Perfection was clearly the aim.[90] The provincial propaganda department was delighted with the result, calling a meeting of the entire studio to announce its congratulations. Part of the delight was the usefulness of the film in showing to Chinese audiences abroad that a star like Hong Xiannü was not being held prisoner for previously performing traditional roles.[91] She was there on screen singing her heart out in one of the most artistically coherent of the transplanted model operas.

The Pearl River studio in the later years of the Cultural Revolution received a boost from an influx of new artistic and technical talent. As a relatively small studio, established in the late 1950s, it had always been dependent on staff transferred from the more established studios in Changchun, Shanghai, and Beijing. In this period, newcomers were sent from the army's August First studio, the Changchun and Shanghai studios, and actors and art directors from the Central Drama Academy. Actors were recruited from spoken-drama companies in Fujian, Jilin, Guizhou, and Guangxi provinces.[92]

Another provincial gesture was the filming of the Uighur versions of *The Red Lantern* and *Shajiabang*. These had three main purposes: to encourage multicultural enthusiasm, to show at home and abroad the official benevolence towards China's ethnic minorities, and, perhaps most important, to offer a taste of the exotic for the majority, Han audiences. The Xinjiang provincial authorities had endorsed filming of *The Red Lantern* in 1972, but the work was too important to entrust to the somewhat resource-poor Tianshan Film Studio in Urumqi. Instead it was made in the army's August First and Beijing studios in the capital in 1975, under the direction of former Yan'an veteran Cheng Yin.[93]

Along with *Boulder Bay*, the last of the Cultural Revolution new-style Peking operas were *Investigation of a Chair* (a short piece created by the Shanghai Peking Opera Company) and *Red Cloud Ridge*. The latter was the work of the same Shandong company that had created the original model opera, *Raid on the White-Tiger Regiment*. *Red Cloud Ridge* was filmed at the August First studio in 1976. One of its two directors, Li Wenhu, had also shared the directing credit on the film of the dance-drama *Ode to Yimeng*, made a year earlier.[94]

These works could cross art genres, just like the transplanting of the original 'model performances', though their smaller scale allowed for more imaginative treatments. *The Ferry* (*Dukou*) was a creation of the Tianjin Hebei *Bangzi* Opera Company and featured three characters: a young girl, an old man, both of whom work on the ferry, and a passenger, who turns out to be a Nationalist spy. Several versions of this story were used in dance, opera, story-telling, and other forms in the mid-1970s. In the same year, a short animated version of the story was created at the Shanghai animation studio.[95] The film of the Hebei clapper opera probably encouraged the further transplanting of that work. A similar transplanting was applied to a spoken drama by Li Shaoran, *Main Subject* (*Zhuke*), about an old brigade leader giving class education to a sent-down young woman who had been misled by a former landlord element on the commune. It was first made into a puppet animation in 1975 and then filmed in colour with live actors as an exercise by the Guangxi Zhuang Autonomous Region Film Study Class the following year.[96]

In essence, these films' simplicity and emphasis on enemies within were highly reminiscent of the films and plays of 1965–1966 on similar themes. Another film, the first new work from the Pearl River Film Studio in more than six years, was also reminiscent of the compilation films of performances made on the eve of the Cultural Revolution. Simply called *Dance* (*Gewu*), the film featured the song and dance companies of Guangdong and Hainan Island performing five dances, including 'Red Guards on the Grasslands See Chairman Mao'. The inclusion of the Hainan dancers ensured a crowd-pleasing ethnic-minority component in the film.[97] This short work, shot between November 1972 and June 1973, was something of a trial run before full-length features went into production with 1974's Cantonese version of *Shajiabang*.[98] Likewise, the Emei Film Studio in Chengdu in Sichuan made a dance film as a trial run, after stopping production at the new studio for financial reasons in 1962. *We Are All Sunflowers* (*Women dou shi xiangyanghua*, 1975) recorded in documentary-style songs and dances by Chengdu and Chongqing amateur singers, choreographers, and performers. They included arias from model operas, Sichuan opera transplants of model-opera arias, and modern songs and dances.[99]

4. NEW-STYLE FEATURE FILMS

The first new feature films, not adaptations of operas or ballets, for seven years began to reach Chinese audiences at Spring Festival in early 1974. Planning for these new films had started almost three years earlier. In May 1971 two leading filmmakers at the Beijing studio had written to the Politburo urging the resumption of feature-film production, which, they argued, 'the masses' longed to watch. In July Premier Zhou Enlai, at a reception for the Dutch documentarist Joris Ivens, indicated to the two filmmakers that he had received their letter and supported their idea to make features. By early 1972 key creative personnel began to return to the Beijing studio, from May Seventh cadre schools, imprisonment, home, and elsewhere. Mao Zedong remarked in July 1972 on the paucity of literature and artworks, though he apparently did not mention films specifically.[100]

When they finally reached audiences, these new films had a welcome novelty after several years of somewhat familiar adaptations. But in other ways, the new works were all too familiar. Filmed with a directness and tendency to spell everything out for audiences, the new features often seemed too much like the model-performance adaptations. All the limitations of the model-opera and dance adaptations could be found in the new films: A heavy concentration persisted on the central heroes distinguished by extraordinary wisdom, confidence, and success. What was expected in a musical film, based on a ritualized stage art, could seem wooden or unnatural when presented in the vehicle of an ordinary film.[101]

The Beijing film studio produced twelve such films between 1973 and 1976. The Changchun studio made eighteen in the period and Shanghai sixteen. The total from all seven feature film studios then in operation was fifty-eight films in these four years, somewhat short of the usual production levels in the 1950s and early 1960s.[102] There were two kinds of such features: a few re-makes of films from the pre–Cultural Revolution period and completely new works. In both types two kinds of subject matter predominated: war stories from the Chinese revolution and contemporary stories of the countryside. Urban subjects were virtually absent.

The re-makes were a secure bet for the studios and the personnel given the opportunity to use their professional skills on these films, as long as the cultural authorities had given clear approval for the venture. The first of these re-makes was *Green Pine Ridge* (*Qingsong ling*), produced at the Changchun studio in 1973, where the 1965 original had also been made. There were similarities and indeed overlap between the two versions, as well as some telling differences.

Both the 1973 and 1965 versions of *Green Pine Ridge* were directed by Liu Guoquan, though he had a co-director in the second project, made when he was fifty-nine years old. Liu's co-director had been an assistant director on the 1965 original. The music for both versions was from the same composer. Even the cast of actors was similar. Nine out of the fourteen main parts were played by the same actor in both versions, including the lead Li Rentang as the cart driver who helps expose a class enemy. In 1965, scriptwriting credit was given to Zhang Zhongpeng, author of the spoken drama on which the film was based. The 1973 version was listed as a collective creation of the Chengde Regional Spoken Drama Company.[103] This emphasis on collective creation, with its egalitarian, anti-specialist thrust, was a typical Cultural Revolution touch. The film had little difficulty in securing central censorship approval.[104]

Changchun's next re-make was a colour version of the 1955 Changchun feature *Guerrillas on the Plain* that had inspired the new-style Peking opera *Fighting on the Plain*. With this re-make, too, there were direct connections with the original, even after almost twenty years. Wu Zhaodi had co-directed the film in 1955 with Su Li. He co-directed again in 1974, sharing responsibility with Chang Zhenhua, a veteran director of stage and screen. Whereas the 1955 script had been attributed to Xing Ye and Yu Shan, the 1974 version was the work of the 'Guerrillas on the Plain writing team' (chuangzuozu). Even the actor who had played a small part as an old peasant in the original film appeared in the same role in the new.[105] But the re-make required 'major surgery' (da shoushu), according to Jiang Qing, to emphasize the close relations between the guerrillas, the regular Communist army, and the people's militia.[106]

Among the first films to mark the re-establishment of the Shanghai Film Studio was another of the 1970s re-makes. The colour version of Scouting across the Yangzi (Dujiang zhencha ji) emerged twenty years after the 1954 original, with its original director, Tang Xiaodan, listed as second director. The sixty-four-year-old had directed City without Night, one of the films singled out for attack on the eve of the Cultural Revolution. In a nice touch, perhaps to suggest that enemies never changed, the head of intelligence in the Nationalist army in both films was played by the same actor, Chen Shu.[107]

One of the main films from the pre-1966 films that were available to Chinese audiences throughout the Cultural Revolution years was re-shot in widescreen colour at the Beijing studio in 1974. Cheng Yin co-directed both versions of Fighting North and South (Nanzheng beizhan), joined in the second by Wang Yan, who had been one of two assistant directors on the 1952 project. Shen Ximeng received writing credit in both versions, though his two 1952 co-authors were replaced by 'and others' (deng) in the new film. Zhang Ruifang went north from Shanghai to play a much smaller role than she had in the 1952 version but indicating for audiences her rehabilitation after years of political difficulty. Vast quantities of military equipment and personnel were made available to the production to make sure the new version impressed with its spectacle, for which Eastman film was especially imported. The result, according to a 1997 account, was ahistorical nonsense in which the officers and men seemed to 'play' at being soldiers. This was far from the black-and-white plainness of the original.[108]

Re-makes became less significant but did not vanish entirely once new feature production gathered pace. As late as 1976, the Shanghai studio re-made in colour A Youthful Generation (Nianqing de yidai), which had first been produced in black-and-white by the Tianma studio in 1965. One of the two writers of the original film (and co-writer of the novel from which it was drawn) shared writing credit with Shi Fangyu on the new version. Zhao Ming, director in 1965, was listed as 'artistic adviser' for the 1976 re-make. Despite the passage of eleven years, Da Shichang played the young geologist hero in both films. Zhang Ruifang acted her age as a late middle-aged, poor-peasant 'aunty' figure.[109]

But most audience attention in early 1974 was directed at a group of all-new feature films. Preparation in some studios had taken a long time. According to an internal Pearl River studio report from September 1974, in late 1968 the studio had formed several scriptwriting groups. These had gone to 'experience life' in factories and on communes and begun to write scripts drawn from such experience. Reportedly, in late 1969 the mistaken directive was made that 'for three to five years we won't make feature films'. This caused the disbanding of the writing groups by the spring of 1972, despite the Culture Group in Beijing in late 1971 and early 1972 telegraphing its plans for feature-film production. Moreover, now that the Pearl River studio, like the other film studios across the nation, was under the local control of the provincial revolutionary committee, the script department's plans to seek scripts from beyond Guangdong province were stopped. Only after a meeting at New Year's 1973 with Jiang Qing (referred to in the document as 'the Central senior officer', *Zhongyang shouzhang*) did the studio leadership push ahead with finding new scripts and securing permission to send teams to five provinces to seek new works. The small size and lack of skilled personnel in the script department meant finding new amateur writers offered some solution. The studio leadership apparently found difficult the transition in their thinking from producing newsreels and documentaries to making new-style features.[110]

At the Beijing Film Studio the first of the new films was *The Scout* (*Zhenchabing*), directed by Li Wenhua. Li had been the cinematographer on the much-criticized *Early Spring in February* and had also served in the same capacity on the ballet film of *The Red Detachment of Women*. Li was also given sole writing credit on the script, an unusual move at a time of 'collective writing group' credits. Filming started in 1973 and the film was released in 1974. After eight years filmmakers were delighted to be back at feature work, though not without trepidation after years of 'struggle, criticism and reform' at the studio.[111]

Their Changchun colleagues had completed *Bright Sunny Skies* (*Yanyangtian*) at the same time as their re-make of *Green Pine Ridge* and another new feature, *Fighting the Flood* (*Zhan hong tu*). The studio had sought permission to start new feature-film production from the Jilin provincial committee in January 1971. They received approval in April. Work on the *Bright Sunny Skies* script began in September 1971, shooting started in May 1972, and the film was completed in November that year.[112] *Bright Sunny Skies* was based on the 1965 novel by the Cultural Revolution era's most prominent writer, Hao Ran, and was set in a North China village in the fall of 1956. Both novel and film presented typical, stereotypical characters in familiar conflicts over collectivization, but they also managed to convey enough of the flavour of peasant life, including a sort of spoken dialogue that combined local colour with intelligibility, to engage audiences.[113]

As a work drawn from the most acclaimed Cultural Revolution novelist, *Bright Sunny Skies* was a safe bet for the Changchun studio. But making a film of such hallowed provenance proved difficult. There was criticism, when director Lin Nong showed some early rushes at the studio, that the hero, the 'number one' character (*yihao renwu*), was not shown to be sufficiently 'tall, large and perfect' (*gao, da, quan*, or 'high, wide and handsome'), as the current slogan described such figures. Director Lin snorted back: 'Tall and large, tall and large. The studio chimneys are tall and large. We'll tie the number one character to a smokestack and point all the cameras at him and film, okay?'[114] The studio recommended a re-shoot, with the finished version sent to Beijing for inspection in November 1973. Reportedly at the insistence of Jiang Qing, the film went through five re-cuts between January and July 1974, despite its nominal release at Spring Festival in February.[115] Lin Nong went on to co-direct in 1975 the adaptation of part one of Hao Ran's *The Golden Road* (*Jinguang dadao*), which had been published in 1972, one of the first new novels published during the Cultural Revolution.[116]

Several of the new productions effectively retold events on the eve of the Cultural Revolution to project a version that accounted for the victory of the current leadership in that movement. Settings in the early 1960s provided an opportunity to re-write history. *Fighting the Flood* presented peasants and Party united in determination to conquer natural disaster and in their adoration for Chairman Mao, with no mention of the agricultural disaster and famine that had followed the Great Leap Forward.[117] A children's film, *Sunny Courtyard Story* (*Xiangyangyuan de gushi*, 1974), focused on the destructive plottings of class enemies in the summer of 1964 to undermine the gleaning activities of a retired worker and his grandchildren to help industrial production.[118] By 1976 some films were being used to project a view of the Communist Party in the early 1960s as deeply divided between true believers supporting Cultural Revolution-type policies and backward cadres standing in the way of progress. One such film was *Chained Dragon Lake* (*Suolong hu*, 1976), which told how a new Party secretary in 1963 discovers all is not well in his new county.[119] As a mass medium of great immediacy for audiences and one difficult to abuse locally, films were the most effective way to reinvent recent history in the popular imagination.

Other new features even tackled the potentially difficult period of the Cultural Revolution in the late 1960s, although often as an adaptation of a published novel or short story which had tested the waters for the subject matter. *Song of the Mango* (*Mangguo zhi ge*, 1976) follows the exploits of a 'workers propaganda team' at a technical institute in Shandong in 1968 in rooting out enemies of the revolution through 'struggle, criticism and reform' sessions led by young students. The film in effect told a sanitized version of the struggles in workplaces and universities during the transition from Red Guard upheaval to the restoration of nominal order.[120]

Some of the new features were later subject to bitter denunciations as tools of the Gang of Four. *Chunmiao* was made at the Shanghai studio with the well-known director Xie Jin as the first listed of the three directors. Chunmiao is a young brigade leader who in 1965 gains training as a 'barefoot doctor', a kind of rural health worker much lauded in the Cultural Revolution for increasing peasants' access to basic medical care. Once the Cultural Revolution starts, Chunmiao leads the Red Guard rebels (*zaofanpai*) in denouncing the 'revisionism' of the conservative leaders of the local hospital. Misogynous post-1976 sneering at Jiang Qing seeing herself in these heroic women should not obscure the genuine commitment to raising the status of women on the part of many people involved in the enterprise. Director Xie Jin had made his name with his portraits of strong women. A second Cultural Revolution theme central in *Chunmiao* is the privileging of the amateur as against the professional. This dichotomy had exercised Chinese Communist leaders for three decades: Their ideal was a new Chinese citizen who was both 'red' (*hong*, meaning politically committed) and 'expert' (*zhuan*) in his or her field. The attention paid to 'barefoot doctors' was not just a public health issue but also a move to put specialist knowledge into the hands of ideologically reliable persons. Often in these Cultural Revolution feature films, the politically reliable were the young. They were in need of regular reminders about the horrors of the 'old society', usually conveyed by the standard elderly 'uncles' or 'aunts', in their kindly way always available for a tearful reminiscence about life before 1949. But youth definitely had the future on their side in these films.

Many of the other features of these new films were borrowed from or inspired by the representational and performance aesthetics of 'model performances'. Indeed, they were derogatively labelled as 'model films' (*yangban dianying*), particularly after 1976. The heightened rhetoric of the presentation came directly from the opera stage: Conflicts are matters of life and death; emotions are singular and directly conveyed; individuation of characters serves to underscore the perfection of the heroes. The films' lead characters tend even to strike a pose at key points similar to the *liangxiang* of Peking opera performance, a parallel made obvious by frequent use of a rapid zoom into the hero's face. The central heroes, such as Chunmiao, lead a small group of activists granted moral authority through their ability to apply Maoist truth to the situations around them. The wise, older characters have counterparts in the model operas. Like their opera counterparts, the heroes of the 'model films' from the mid-1970s live strangely unrounded lives. The absence of biological families, the indifference to romance, and the resistance to material comfort are all typical of the model performances.

The camera, editing, and sound served this rhetorical stance. At key moments of revelation, rapid zooms into a tight close-up of the hero, dark eyebrows akimbo, lips pursed in firm resolve, were similar to such shots in the model-opera and ballet films. Musical effects, usually with a full Western symphony orchestra, underscore the effect of the zoom. In other places, filming tends to be fairly static, with group tableaux reminiscent of the theatrical stage. Standard shot-reverse shot in medium close-up covers most of the dialogue scenes, though the distance from the actors and the somewhat front-on angles emphasize similarities with a theatrical audience experience. In large-scale scenes, tight close-ups of the central heroes are inter-cut with shots of massed supporters, nodding wisely or leaping to their feet in enthusiasm. Many of these films included a standard two songs: the first about twenty minutes into the film, the second nearer to the climax in a ninety-minute or two-hour feature. Exegetical and often with roots in folk tunes, the songs had two main purposes. They served as backing for images of the heroes going about their revolutionary business, usually accompanied by the supportive peasant, worker, or soldier 'masses'. The songs also had a life beyond the film. Audiences could, as it were, take them home, sing them in their schools or workplaces during massed singing practice, and hear them on the radio or on the county or commune broadcasting loudspeakers. This publicized the film and the political messages it conveyed.

The 'three prominences' from the 'model performances' can be seen in many of these new films. The steelmaker hero Zhao Sihai (the name is a homonym for 'shines on the whole world') in *The Fiery Years* (*Huohong de niandai*, 1974) seems to tower above his enemies in the steelworks which in 1972 are under attack from foreign and domestic spies. He seems taller than his comrades and is always the centre of somewhat static tableaux when he speaks to his adoring allies.[121] When these workers succeed in producing a new alloy, or when the new dam is dedicated in *The New Doctor* (*Hongyu*, 1975), the hero is surrounded by what has been called a 'Chinese chorus'.[122] The film cuts to a number of close-up shots of the hero's colleagues expressing their collective joy. This signals to the audience how they too should react. In a rare analysis of the shooting and montage of the model-opera films and these new features, Wang Tugen notes how the films inscribed their audiences into a 'front of stage' position in order to be lectured at by them. He also shows, simply by counting the kinds of shots in a sequence, the unrelenting nature of the concentration on the central heroes.[123]

But we should not overlook the differences between the model operas and the 'model films'. The film medium, with its expected relative naturalism, could not sustain the kinds of unchanging characterization of the more formal opera stage. Heroes on film were seen to have moments of confusion and even split seconds of self-doubt on their road to inevitable triumph. The bad characters, class enemies to a man (and they were almost invariably male), could not be presented in the formulaic manner of the opera and ballet stage. Gone were the green and gruesome faces and crouched body posture. Instead, an excessive interest in fountain pens, polished leather shoes, and classical Western art prints or sculptures were some of the signs that indicated evil.

In a major innovation, some characters were even permitted to change their political stripes in these film narratives. *Breaking with Old Ideas* (*Juelie*, 1975), for example, presents the setting up of a new-style 'communist labor university' (*gongchanzhuyi laodong daxue*) in a remote, mountainous district to end the usual loss of local young talent to urban universities and city careers. The Party secretary at the new university, helpfully named Long Guozheng (literally 'Dragon nation correct'), leads the fight against conservative professors who decry the study of practical, agricultural subjects in such an institution.[124] One of the teachers, who wears spectacles – in some of these films a sign of class incorrectness – starts out in the conservative (in the film identified as the 'bourgeois representatives within the Party') camp. Sun Ziqing even teaches a class titled The Function of a Horse's Tail, a rare instance of satire in these films. But learning from his determined peasant students, he realizes the error of his attitudes and joins the progressive side by the end of the narrative.

This kind of character, though usually among peasants, before the Cultural Revolution had been called 'middling characters' (*zhongjian renwu*). They had emerged in fiction and films as part of the breakaway from Soviet-style 'socialist realism' to Mao's notion of combining realism and romanticism. Middling characters, however, were soon denounced as a typical 'black-line' denial of the importance of class struggle.[125] The striking emergence of such characters in late Cultural Revolution films is best explained with reference to the naturalistic expectations audiences brought to viewing films, in contrast to opera.[126]

But in general the proletarian nobility of the heroes of the model films was firmly preserved in the face of real-life experience. One of the most popular of these films was directed at both children and adults when it was released on National Day 1974. *Sparkling Red Star* (*Shanshan de hongxing*), like most of the model operas and ballets, was set in wartime before 1949. Winter Boy (Pan Dongzi) is a peasant growing up in the 1930s whose father goes off to fight with the Red Army. His mother later dies in a fire lit by the landlord's militia while Winter Boy gazes on helplessly. His revolutionary ardour tempered by this loss, the boy, now a teenager, joins his father, donning the cap with the red star on its front. One of the film's two directors noted:

> Practice has proved to us the necessity of learning from the revolutionary operas and ballets and applying them to film: only by depicting the boy at climaxes of the struggles between the two lines and class struggle were we able to portray his heroism in full length, to make his image more inspiring.... the evocative power [of a work] is only effective if it enhances the image of the hero: otherwise extraneous incidents are only scattered pearls torn from the string.[127]

The popularity of *Sparkling Red Star* in the mid-1970s lay in the boyish hero and the melodrama. Winter Boy is a preternaturally handsome child (his voice was dubbed by another actor in the film), an ideal designed to appeal to the motherly instincts in a good part of the film's audience (Figure 3.2). The martyrdom of his mother, accompanied by a stirring song, can move the most heartless of viewers. The deliberate crosscutting between real scenes and imagined, modern sequences in which youngsters greet the soldiers, and Winter Boy marching through a field of wildflowers, further endeared the film to its younger audience. The cheery theme song that accompanies this scene, sung by seemingly all Chinese children in those years, further served to suture the audience into the film.[128]

The older pleasures of Chinese film viewing were not obliterated in these Cultural Revolution features. The music of feature films, particularly their songs, continued to appeal to audiences, as the case of *Sparkling Red Star* indicates. The new feature films offered a new source of musical entertainment and reminded viewers of the characters, conflicts, and images of the film. They also began to expand the range of subject matter available to

3.2. The 1930s boy hero Pan Dongzi from the 1974 film *Sparkling Red Star* as an inspiration to contemporary children. The slogan reads: 'Study Pan Dongzi, be good children of the Party.' Source: Poster published in 1975 by Renmin meishu chubanshe (People's Fine Arts Publishing House, Beijing). Poster in the author's collection.

songwriters, beyond earnest praise of Chairman Mao and all his works. Another pleasure from these new films was seeing familiar faces. Just as the directors and crews behind the camera had not changed much, so the people in front of the camera were frequently not new. Yu Yang, who had started his career in 1942 as a child actor in the Manchukuo Film Studio, under Japanese control, played Zhao Sihai, the confident hero in *The Fiery Years*. Yu recalled almost twenty years later that he had originally been cast in a secondary role but was later asked to play the central hero, despite concerns that he had been identified as one of the twenty-two stars who had been part of the 'black line in literature and art'. The film was so popular on its release in early 1974, particularly as one of the first new feature films in seven or eight years, that in Shanghai wearing a small towel around one's neck in the manner of Zhao Sihai in the film became quite a fashion.[129] The face of Miss Tao from the much-maligned *Early Spring in February* re-appeared on China's screens in 1976. Xie Fang played the eponymous lead, Gao Shanhua, in *Mountain Flower (Shanhua)*, who leads the peasants in 'learning from Dazhai' to transform mountain fastness into productive farmland. Xie's role was typical for the Cultural Revolution films: the young and female leading the masses in smiting class enemies. This was a far cry from Miss Tao's piano and dreams of foreign travel.[130]

Even at the other end of the political spectrum, familiar faces could be enjoyed in these new films. The veteran actor Xiang Kun, who had played the hapless Nationalist commander in the original *Fighting North and South* in 1952 and a Nationalist jail commander in 1964's *Red Crag* (*Liehuo zhong yongsheng*), was capable of making his evil characters more subtle than usual, even presenting an almost pitiable caste. He re-emerged on Chinese screens in 1975's *Youth Like Fire* (*Qingchun si huo*), playing a cadre who resists efforts in 1971 to automate a steelworks by some young Maoist enthusiasts.[131] A big push was made in the mid-1970s to cultivate a new cohort of film actors, similar to the efforts to recruit new opera and other performers. But the old faces were still needed and were still recognizable to audiences bored by most other aspects of these new films.

A third continuing pleasure from the new model films was provided to Han Chinese audiences by a handful of films set among the minority cultures of China. Since 1949 such films had provided the kinds of pleasures of colour, exotic locations, and customs that had once been available through watching Hollywood and other foreign films.[132] As before the Cultural Revolution, the title usually signalled the exotic delights awaiting. *Spring in the Desert* (*Shamo de chuntian*), made at the Changchun studio in 1975, was set on the Inner Mongolian steppes in contemporary times. Scripted by a Mongolian writer, the film told how a young, female cadre in a herding commune leads efforts to transform the desert into pasture land. With its dedication to the movement for 'in agriculture learn from Dazhai', the story may have been orthodox Cultural Revolution fare, down to the gender of the central hero. But the setting and the look were different: Mongolian actors played almost all the parts. The score was also the work of a Mongolian composer.[133] In *Secret of the Axia River* (*Axiahe de mimi*), from the Shanghai studio in 1976, a trio of young people work at a forestry station in western China. They are a multi-ethnic crew: Han, Tibetan, and Chinese Muslim (*Huizu*). One summer night they hide in wait to see why logs have been floating away from the mill and succeed in exposing a gang of thieves. This was a less pleasurable work, in terms of the attractions of minority films. The combination of three ethnicities, played by Han actors apparently cast for their looks, whose voices were dubbed by others, did not give a satisfyingly ethnic flavour for Chinese audiences.[134]

The Cultural Revolution authorities claimed that these new feature films represented a repudiation of the bourgeois, Hollywood-inspired styles of those made in the seventeen years before the Cultural Revolution. But the continuities are striking. The same influential directors were active from the 1940s through to the 1980s. The same actors appeared on China's screens before and after 1966. And the same audiences continued to grumble. Mao Zedong in his 1942 Yan'an *Talks*, which was the basis for policy in literature and art from 1949 on, had eschewed naturalism: 'Literature and art can and ought to be on a higher plane, more intense, more concentrated, more typical, nearer the ideal, and therefore more universal than everyday life.'[135] The slogan promulgated after 1958 about 'combining revolutionary realism and revolutionary romanticism' was similarly anti-naturalistic, though it allowed for a greater acknowledgement of national Chinese aesthetic modes, from opera and elsewhere.

The model films of the Cultural Revolution continued this aesthetic thrust but to a particular level of excess. One illustration is *Youth* (*Qingchun*), a widescreen colour feature made at the Shanghai studio by Xie Jin. *Youth* was a 1977 production, mostly filmed and completed after the arrest of the Gang of Four. Xie applied his experience in creating strong-willed female central characters to an unusual story.[136] Yamei is a deaf-mute orphan who, at age thirteen, comes to the attention of the army during the Cultural Revolution. With treatment and training from the army doctors and nurses, Yamei manages to cultivate an ability to hear and speak. She becomes a telephone operator in the army, an occupation that to many viewers may seem a triumph of revolutionary hope over medical reality. The deaf-mute telephonist would seem to sum up nicely the silliness of a great many of these feature films, and Xie Jin and his actors invest the work with typical Cultural Revolution po-faced earnestness. The usual Xie Jin focus on strong women has a feel of being done by numbers in *Youth*. The orthodox collection of kindly old uncles and energetic young women mill about in the background. They beaver away accompanied by a seemingly endless heavenly chorus: Three choirs are listed in the credits. The result is a typical nonsense, lacking artistic, visual, or thematic interest.

5. GROWING THE INDUSTRY, PLEASING AUDIENCES

A focus on upheaval and on the limitations of the films being made can obscure some parts of the film enterprise that showed expansion even in the 1966–1969 period of greatest Cultural Revolution upheaval. Artists and technicians in the studios had stopped real work, devoting their days to rituals of study, meetings, and visits to learn from other workplaces. But elsewhere work continued in fits and starts. The management committee of the Nanjing Film Machinery Factory, China's oldest maker of projectors and other equipment, may have been disbanded in December 1966, but production continued. Innovations there and at the equivalent factory in Shandong included more work to design and produce lighter-weight, more reliable projectors for use by rural projection teams, some of which travelled from village to village to show films.[137] Construction of a new factory in Gansu to produce optical instruments (including lenses for projectors and cameras) continued.[138]

A view from this technical part of the film industry gives a somewhat different picture of the start of the Cultural Revolution from the usual general accounts of events in the film studios. Premier Zhou Enlai, in the midst of factional disputes at the top of the nation, took time again to call for the design and production of lighter-weight portable lights for documentary filming. Documentaries to record the doings of Chairman Mao and others on National Day 1966 received top-level attention. Among the instructions given in September 1966 was that the central newsreel studio and the August First studio should share their footage, to avoid duplicate filming, of National Day activities. Sixteen-millimetre film production should increase, presumably to allow more flexible screenings in a range of venues, including the countryside. And all screenings should be free, covered by the state.[139]

The push to get films to a broader audience continued strongly. In September 1966, the Ministry of Culture, in charge of the nation's film enterprise, ordered the transfer of old American and Soviet equipment to the Xi'an Film Studio, markedly increasing its production of prints. In November 1966, the Ministry of Chemical Industry set up a group to direct an all-out effort to produce more colour film. The group was disbanded in late July the following year. The Shanghai Film Projection Equipment Factory saw a huge slump in their regular, 35 mm production. It responded by starting work on a Super 8 (8.75 mm) projector, which began regular production in 1968. At the end of 1966, 600 staff members of the Nanjing Film Machinery Factory were on their way to the new optical factory in Gansu Province.[140]

The importance of film meant that a new corps of politically reliable specialists needed to be trained. Actors were easiest to produce. The Shanghai studio, for example, had always had an attached theatre troupe, members of which performed in films and in spoken plays. The re-established studio set up such a troupe in the early 1970s and by 1975 was scouting for 'worker, peasant, soldier' performers to replenish its acting ranks. Zhang Jianya and Jiang Haiyang, two future directors who helped create Chinese cinema's 'new wave' in the 1980s, were recruited into the Shanghai studio acting troupe. Neither were of worker background: Their fathers were a doctor and actor, respectively.[141]

At the Beijing Film Studio, efforts in the first instance went into cultivating new film writers. Ma Depo, appointed from outside the studio to head the editorial department, organized the first intensive film writing class (*dianying bianju xuexiban*). More than thirty participants came from all over the country and managed to produce a pile of potential film scripts.[142] Towards the end of the Cultural Revolution, the Pearl River Film Studio received permission to conduct its first Film Specialists Class (*dianying zhuanye xueyuanban*). Forty Guangdong high school graduates were selected for training, which took the form of work study: Students worked around the studio between attending classes taught by studio veterans.[143] From February through April 1974, the studio in Guangzhou also conducted a scriptwriting conference, attended by twenty-nine participants, mostly from southern provinces. At the end of the conference, an internal studio report noted the importance of continued criticism of Lin Biao and Confucius, the major public political campaign from the summer of 1973 through 1974 and beyond. The report next listed the need to 'study the spirit of the Central senior officer (*Zhongyang shouzhang*, meaning Jiang Qing) and the experience of the creation of the revolutionary model performances'.[144] Clearly, as this studio was restoring production, the restrictions were tight, although criticism was allowed about new scriptwriters creating unbelievable enemy characters.

At this Pearl River studio conference and in a studio report on scriptwriting practice in Shanghai, the extent of the effort to seek the opinions of 'the masses' is striking. Each studio was to select several factories and commune production brigades and, with the help of each unit's propaganda corps, organize what in another world would be called 'focus groups' to discuss scripts. In Shanghai the script department had groups charged with finding scripts and writers in and outside Shanghai, among those submitted to the studio and those written internally.[145] Even later in July 1975, the Pearl River script department was lamenting the lack of trained and experienced personnel. The solution remained commissioning works from amateur writers, discovered on recruitment visits to the neighbouring provinces to meet with leaders of the now restored writers' associations.[146]

The last group of degree students at China's only film school had graduated from the Beijing Film Academy in 1968. The start of the Cultural Revolution had somewhat disrupted their education, but they were assigned, as usual, to the studios and other suitable work units. Among them was the woman directing graduate Wang Junzheng, who upon graduation, was assigned to the Beijing studio. She served as director's assistant in 1974 on *Youth in the Flames of Battle (Fenghuo shaonian)*, in 1975 on *Breaking with Old Ideas*, and in 1976 with the ill-fated *Counterattack*. These Cultural Revolution graduates of the film academy formed part of the corps of so-called fourth-generation filmmakers, though it took the emergence of the fifth generation in the 1980s for them to be identified as such.[147]

Film and culture in general were too important for the Cultural Revolution cultural leadership in the 1970s to allow the reopening of the Beijing Film Academy and the central academies for music, drama, and painting. In their stead, a new institution was set up to train a purer corps of specialists, the Central May Seventh Art University (*Zhongyang Wu-qi yishu daxue*), closely associated with Jiang Qing, to take over the functions of existing academies. The music and opera sections of the new university were located by the mid-1970s on the site of the Beijing Agricultural College at Zhuxinzhuang, thirty kilometres northwest of the city. The art and drama departments of the new school had found premises close to the city. At first, the film specialities taught were strictly technical: sound recording and lighting. The teachers were recruited from the former film academy's staff.[148] Other specialities were added later.

This new training institution would take time to have a significant effect on the artistic ranks in the film studios. New graduates of the film academy had always been faced with long delays before being able to take on real responsibilities in their studios' productions because of the massive overstaffing of the studios. The situation hardly changed after the May Seventh Art University started producing new filmmakers. Established directors tended to secure the major projects: The cost and political sensitivities made handing a project over to inexperienced newcomers a big risk for the studios. But the numbers of studio employees increased considerably in these years, despite the lower levels of production compared with pre-1966. The seven feature-film studios from 1966 to 1976 gained 2,082 persons to reach a staff total thirty-four percent higher than 1965 levels.[149]

A view from the film distribution enterprise in Beijing city provides further unexpected insights into a mixed picture of disastrous disruption and considerable development. Cinemas, along with clubs and halls in Beijing, stopped their regular business in August 1966, as the first waves of youthful Red Guards began travelling about the nation, mostly heading towards the capital. The cinemas became reception centres and temporary hostels for out-of-town Red Guards. Staff of the cinemas worked in three shifts over twenty-four hours, providing mostly free food and shelter to Red Guards who spent daytime hours touring about the city 'establishing ties' (*chuanlian*). In the young people's absence during the day, cinemas soon began to show documentary films. Initially, these were shown free to Red Guards and others. When charges did apply, a ticket to see films of Mao Zedong's reviews of Red Guards in Tian'anmen Square was set very low: ten cents for adults and five cents for students. These seven documentaries were shown 7,218 times in Beijing city to an audience of 5,315,707.[150] The city may have been in chaos, but the Chinese bureaucratic tradition continued: Such apparently precise statistics were still being collected.

Most accounts of film in these years declare that the more than 600 feature films made in the seventeen years before 1966 were banned and vanished from China's screens. Despite this apparent blanket proscription, films still featured in the media but as objects of criticism. Even films made before 1949 were deemed suitable objects of criticism. On 1 April 1967, for example, the front page of *People's Daily* carried a major article by Qi Benyu titled 'Patriotism or National Betrayal – A Critique of the Reactionary Film *Sorrows of the Forbidden City* (*Qinggong mishi*)', a film made in Hong Kong in 1948.[151] A costume melodrama, the film told a story of thwarted love in the Qing court at the end of the nineteenth century. Mao Zedong had singled out the film for criticism along similar lines in 1954, but this did not lead to a large-scale campaign. In the last scene of the film, a group of peasants approach the disguised emperor in his carriage, fleeing the foreign forces sent against the Boxer rebels in 1900, and express their sympathy for his plight. Peasants like these did not fit the Cultural Revolution view of class struggle and revolutionary masses.

Officially the 600 or so films that had been made in the seventeen years of the so-called black line in cultural policy were banned. But this did not prevent certain films from being brought out for special showings. Thus, *Sorrows of the Forbidden City* and *The Life of Wu Xun* were occasionally shown as 'negative examples'. *City without Night* and *City Besieged* in April 1967 were declared as such and distributed nationwide for audiences to watch and go through the motions of criticizing.[152] The sources are silent whether audiences went to watch to engage in political study or to appreciate the now forbidden works. The ready phrase 'negative examples' (*fanmian jiaocai*) provided a useful camouflage for a range of motivations and the showing of politically dubious works throughout these years. Indeed, some audiences were positively attracted to watch any work labelled 'negative'.

Other occasions were more positive: In October 1970, for example, five old features set in the Korean War were distributed to commemorate the twentieth anniversary of China's participation in that conflict. They included *Heroic Sons and Daughters* (*Yingxiong er nü*, 1964), based on a novel by the veteran writer Ba Jin, who was then under arrest.[153] Three feature films from the seventeen years (1949–1966) were given broad distribution throughout the Cultural Revolution. The trio was known colloquially as the 'old three fights' (*lao san zhan*), as they all had 'fight' (*zhan*) in their Chinese titles: *Tunnel Warfare* (*Didao zhan*, 1965), *Mine Warfare* (*Dilei zhan*, 1962), and *Fighting North and South* (*Nanzheng beizhan*, 1952).[154] Quite how these three titles came to be singled out for special treatment is unclear, although they had all been popular works on their first release. *Mine Warfare* and *Tunnel Warfare* were set during the Anti-Japanese War, and the third film told a story of the civil war of the late 1940s, similar eras to most of the model operas. By 1969, when the People's Liberation Army had been called in to help restore civil order in China's cities, the films' positive images of army–peasant unity could help matters. As we have seen, *Fighting North and South* was remade in a colour version in 1974.[155] Other pre-1966 films that enjoyed wide circulation included *Little Soldier Zhang Ga* (*Xiaobing Zhang Ga*, 1963) and *Urgent Letter* (a.k.a. *Letter with Feather*, *Jimaoxin*, 1954), two much-loved children's films.

The distribution of the model opera and similar film adaptations during the Cultural Revolution, like much of the aesthetic of the works, was a triumph of overkill. Starting in 1971 cities across China held periodic 'model-performance' film festivals, bringing together the available titles for viewing by groups organized by work units and schools. A festival of nine such films in Beijing took place for eight days in May 1975, coinciding with the usual annual commemoration of Mao's Yan'an *Talks*. To encourage attendance at such films, Beijing factories and communes were known to stop production, and theatres increased their screenings day and night. From 1970 to 1976 in Beijing, these *yangbanxi* films were given more than 137,000 screenings, to an audience of more than 100 million.[156]

Those film fans who wanted relief from this 'model' diet had some choice, apart from the new regular feature films that began to emerge from Chinese studios after 1973. Foreign films were also screened in China throughout the Cultural Revolution. In fact, as in all other periods of Chinese film history, foreign titles tended to dominate audience interest. After May 1966 Chinese audiences continued to watch Indian and other films from abroad, but soon the most common source of film imports had changed. In March 1968, at a time when the only new Chinese film, other than newsreels, was a black-and-white fifteen-minute cartoon made at the Shanghai Animation Studio to commemorate Mao Zedong's expressed support for African-Americans, a North Korean film was released in Beijing. Dubbed by the Changchun studio, which had a specialist film-dubbing section, the film was *Women of Nanjiang Village (Nanjiangcun funü)*. When the widespread showing of foreign films resumed in August 1970, three nations' films predominated: North Korea, Vietnam, and Albania. None was renowned for their film industries. One source names fifteen Korean titles as being distributed. North Korean films had always had an effect on Chinese audiences: The emotional stories of maternal sacrifice and tearful devotion to Kim Il-sung seem to have had a twin appeal. The emotion in these features was more obvious (indeed, abject) than in their Chinese equivalents. The worship of the nation's leader shown for Korea made China's efforts in that direction by the 1970s seem positively discreet by comparison.

One of the biggest Korean hits was shown during a Korean film festival in Beijing in September 1972. The popular interest in seeing *The Flower Seller (Mai hua guniang)*, a widescreen, colour adaptation of a musical drama, was immense, with lines every day snaking around the blocks at Beijing's cinemas. At a time when good movies were hard to find, audiences flocked to this film. One of the attractions was apparently the widescreen projection. When it was re-released in June 1973 in eleven copies in Beijing (three widescreen and the rest regular format), the film achieved a Chinese record for admissions for a foreign film since 1949: 6,060,518 admissions were recorded. Imported films were a welcome change of fare. Beijing audiences had an expression to characterize the films of each country: 'A Korean film: weep, weep, smile, smile; a Vietnamese film: just guns and artillery; an Albanian film: all hugs.'[157]

Between 1966 and 1976, half (thirty-six titles) of the seventy full-length features distributed publicly in China were foreign films.[158] This meant that the ten years of the Cultural Revolution were no different, in terms of the importance of foreign films, from the rest of Chinese film history, before or since. Feature films from the North Vietnamese film industry, producing despite the war, were shown: Eight titles are given by one source. Eleven titles came from Albania, the ruling Communist Party of which was one of the few that recognized the ideological legitimacy of the Chinese Communist Party.[159] Another source says thirty-six films were imported from four countries, including North Korea.[160] The 1986 history of the Changchun Film Studio notes in passing that among the foreign films dubbed at the facility in 1975 was the first American film they had done.[161] Also often seen were two Soviet films from the 1930s: *Lenin in October (Liening zai shiyue*, directed by Mikhail Romm, 1937) and *Lenin in 1918 (Liening zai yijiuyibanian*, also directed by Romm, 1939). Showing these films could express loyalty to Lenin's ideas and to Stalin, who was in power when they were made, in contrast to their current 'revision-ist' successors, who were attacking Chairman Mao. Indeed Red Guard spoken dramas in 1966–1968 seem to have been directly inspired by the portrait of the Russian leader in that film.[162] For audiences, the foreign films had novelty value, for they were one of the relatively few places in which Westerners and the world beyond China could be seen.

A selected group of Chinese enjoyed even wider access to international cinema. Throughout the Cultural Revolution, films from the United States and Western nations continued to be imported for 'study purposes'. Some-what in the vein of 'negative teaching materials', these films were made available to film professionals and members of the cultural apparatus. The official rationale was keeping abreast of current developments in film art. Jiang Qing, as the self-styled leading figure in cultural practice, reportedly enjoyed her study of such works. Others in the lower ranks also found such films of high interest. As was true in the years after 1976, 'inter-nal screenings' (*neibu fangying*) were attended by a remarkable range of persons, sometimes most of whom had no pressing professional reason for being there. Personal connections (*guanxi*) operated as effectively dur-ing the Cultural Revolution as at other times in the history of the People's Republic. In fact, the breakdown or uncertainty of other structures meant that *guanxi* was perhaps more important than before or since. A spe-cial screening for film professionals could attract friends, colleagues, and neighbours, as long as they could present the necessary ticket or other credential at the door.

As a 1999 history of the film enterprise in Beijing somewhat ruefully notes, because there was little else by way of public cultural activity in the city and benefiting from the attention given to film as a propaganda medium, audience numbers in these years broke all records. Work units, schools, and other institutions organized film attendance for their mem-bers. Despite the limited number of titles available and the narrowness of subjects and styles shown on their screens, Beijing's and China's cinemas did huge business in these years.[163]

The range of audiences for the new films continued to expand. Widen-ing the distribution of films was a major focus of Gang of Four attention. A 1978 report states that about a third of the 210 employees of the China Film Corporation in charge of distribution were sent to 'cow sheds' during the Cultural Revolution. At the end of 1969, a further 150 employees were dispersed to cadre schools. By this time there were few films other than documentaries being distributed in China. Many leading cadres and core functionaries were not allowed to return to the corporation. Similar dis-ruption occurred at lower levels in the distribution system. The employees

3.3. A mobile projectionist shows *The Red Lantern: The model performances come to the fishing village* (*Yangbanxi dao yucun*), woodcut by Lin Ju. Source: *Renmin ribao* (People's Daily), 11 June 1973, p. 4.

at the Liaoning film corporation, for example, were completely replaced. This did not help audiences find films: Some places saw an expansion in projection facilities but could not get hold of films to show in them. But other places saw contraction: In the Wenzhou region of Zhejiang, 428 projection units shrank to less than 100. According to 1976 statistics, each projection facility only presented 9.7 shows each month. Watching a movie could also be dangerous. In February 1975, one commune projection unit had an accident in which seventy-one audience members were killed, apparently in a fire and consequent stampede. A county film management office had a fire that destroyed seventy-nine film prints.[164]

The development of highly portable Super 8 projectors and facilities in Changchun, Beijing, and elsewhere to produce film prints in the smaller format meant that travelling projection teams could become more mobile. One source claims that the number of rural projection units, which included the teams as well as fixed places where films were shown increased four times over the 1965 level (see Figure 3.3). Guangdong rural people had averaged four film viewings in 1966: Eight years later they enjoyed ten annual film viewings. The film version of *Taking Tiger Mountain by Strategy* between its 1970 release and the end of 1974 had been watched by 730 million people.[165]

Greater Beijing also presented a picture of growth rather than destruction. By the end of 1975, the number of projection units (*danwei*) had increased to twice that of pre-1966. In 1975 more than 200,000 screenings were held. In the Beijing countryside, there were more than 900 film teams. All communes had a central film team, and even some production brigades in communes had their own teams. Of the 1,606 projection units in 1975, 300 were in production brigades, 309 were on communes, 136 belonged to schools, 63 belonged to districts or county-level units, and 798 were part of offices or industries.[166] In the Ningxia Muslim Autonomous Region (equivalent to a province) projection units went from 163 in 1965 to 861 in 1976. In Fujian province rural projection team numbers had doubled the 1966 level by early 1974. Nationwide, projecting units increased 4.2 times in these ten years, audiences by 2.9 times, and distribution income went up 59 percent.[167]

But expanded facilities did not mean that audiences would flock to the theatres, clubs, and threshing grounds to watch films. In the eleven years between 1966 and 1976, of the seventy full-length films in distribution six were re-makes of feature films and more than a dozen were model works of some sort. Film distribution had been a prosperous industry before 1966, even with low individual ticket prices of a few pennies. But from 1974 to 1976, the China Film Corporation's losses reached twenty million *yuan*.[168]

Audiences found the new Chinese-made films irresistible because work units, schools, and other institutions organized members to attend screenings. But the new films also offered certain pleasures to their viewers in the early 1970s. The model performances had been ubiquitous in the print media, in radio broadcasts, and in cities with professional opera companies that had not been disbanded or dispatched to the countryside. Amateur performance had been the major other mode of spreading familiarity with these model works, with sometimes brilliant, but often somewhat flawed results. Peking opera, even in the modernized version that placed stories and performance styles closer to real life than the old-style opera, was a demanding art. The best-intentioned amateur or local-style opera performers could not necessarily capture the aural perfection heard on the radio from professional singers and musicians. The film versions of these operas at last served the works properly, even if opera was a performing art best encountered live in a theatre, not a cinema screen. As we have seen, the operas and ballets were the creative pinnacle of the efforts of an array of stage and performance specialists using vast resources, including time to experiment, despite the narrowness of their political content. The film versions, starting on October 1970, brought these efforts to a far wider audience and with a greater intimacy than had ever been possible.

The best actors and singers, the best acrobats, and the best musicians were made accessible to film audiences. By the time this occurred, of course, the operas, and to a lesser extent the two ballets, had become over-familiar for many. But the pleasure for some of viewing perfected versions of the model performances should not be overlooked in the rush to mock the excessive emphasis on these relatively few artistic works. Moreover, there were particular pleasures in some of the new model films. Wu Qinghua, the heroine of the ballet *The Red Detachment of Women* film version 1971), spends the first part of the film in flaming-red silk 'pyjamas'. With its carefully crafted close-ups and travelling shots, the film captures every quiver of her red tunic as she mimes her resistance to being bound in chains by the landlord's men. Her split-legged leaps about the stage, in the bright red silk trousers, created a film still that graced many Chinese dormitory and home walls in the mid-1970s. An appreciation of ballet was probably not the motivation for sticking up such stills for many eager (mostly male) viewers.

When audiences began to watch the new feature films that were released at the start of 1974, disappointment may have reigned. We can assume that the novelty of full-colour and widescreen versions of war films first made in the early 1960s soon wore off. But a film like *Sparkling Red Star* had immense appeal in a cultural climate in which only limited acknowledgement had been made of the interests of children. The boy, Pan Dongzi, class consciousness and determination fixed on his cherubic face, became a huge hit with Chinese of all ages. He was the first child hero in a Chinese film for many years. The two songs that featured in the film and were played on radio and learned by schoolchildren enhanced the impact of the film, which was genuinely popular. The film's combination of so-called realism and romanticism provided escapist pleasures for many viewers. We have noted already the pleasure to be had from seeing familiar faces, often in familiar roles, in the new-style feature films.

Despite the flurry of film screenings across the land, the strictures on cultural production in these years caused chafing even at the highest level of audience. As late as July 1975, after eighteen months of new-feature films and several years of new operas, Mao Zedong was dis-satisfied:[169]

> There are two few 'model performances' (yangbanxi). Moreover things with just a tiny flaw get criticized. There's no sign of one hundred flow-ers blooming.... The Party policy on literature and art should be readjusted a bit, so that in one, two or three years the items in literature and art will be progressively expanded.

By the early 1970s Mao had been replaced in prominence on docu-mentary-film screens by Cambodia's Prince Sihanouk and his travels, with his French-born wife, around China. As we shall see, one response to Mao's complaint of lack of choice was the filming of dozens of features made especially for his viewing pleasure. For the rest of the nation, Li Wenhua and his colleagues in the studios plodded on against the politi-cal odds, ensuring something Chinese continued to be shown on China's screens.

CHAPTER FOUR

Elaborating Culture: Dance, Music, Stage, and Fine Arts

Three years after the end of the Cultural Revolution, Liang Lun, a forty-year veteran of Chinese dance, lamented the quality of recent dance students. Many young dancers by the late 1970s had a narrow, formalistic approach to their art: Dances that did not feature big leaps and spins seemed bland to his students. They were not particularly interested in works that drew on Chinese national or ethnic roots. The inflated rhetoric of the Cultural Revolution included large, empty gestures on the dance stage. Real meaning and authentic emotion were hard to find. For Liang, the bombastic and ultimately barren notions of art in those years still lingered and had distorted the views of another generation.[1]

Others might argue that Liang's newly recruited students to some extent were reflecting the internationalization of dance in China. Far from simply being a period of vacuous gesture, the Cultural Revolution in dance, music, plays, and the fine arts helped open up Chinese culture to the possibilities of the modern. Unconfined by the historical and national baggage that Chinese opera carried, and more flexible and easier to produce than film, these other stage and exhibition arts were more able to invest talent and experimentation in modern, global borrowings and hybrid adaptations.

We first examine the two Chinese-style ballets that joined the modernized operas as Cultural Revolution models, along with the innovations in dance that gathered momentum in the mid-1970s. Making Chinese music modern, including further integrating Western music with the local heritage, is discussed in the second section here. Traditional performance forms also underwent modernization, while spoken drama, a modern import, served Cultural Revolution needs for topical representations of politics. The chapter ends by showing how the search for the modern extended to the visual arts and architecture.

1. DANCING FOR THE REVOLUTION

The two full-length ballets among the eight 'model performances' gave dance unprecedented importance in Cultural Revolution culture. Its inclusion ranked dance as close to equal with the relatively ancient performing art of Chinese opera. But this model dance form was distinctly Western. Ballet had been introduced into China only in the third decade of the twentieth century; it could not be said to have any strong roots or large following in China. As model works, the ballets indicated the modernizing and internationalizing ambitions of cultural practice in the Cultural Revolution. At the same time, efforts intensified to make full use of the indigenous resources in China's historical, folk, and ethnic dance traditions. Perhaps in dance more than any other cultural activity the mixed, even contradictory impulses of China's artists and their managers are clearest.[2]

On the eve of the Cultural Revolution, a major dance and musical performance encapsulated some of these ambitions and tensions. *The East Is Red* (*Dongfang hong*) was first mounted on stage in 1964 and released as a feature film in 1965. Described as a 'music and dance historical poem' (*yinyue wudao shi shi*), *The East Is Red* at first glance typified the large-scale, rhetorically certain works of the ten years after the release of the film version. Drawing on folk songs from Yan'an days, it told in song and dance the history of the Chinese Revolution, from the Opium Wars to the Communist victory in 1949, ending with two long sequences of celebration of achievements since that year.[3] The scale of the work meant it was not easily presented as a live performance. Its September 1964 premiere in Beijing, marking the fifteenth anniversary of the People's Republic, involved more than 3,000 professional and amateur musicians and dancers. Film adaptation of *The East Is Red* made the work more accessible, but the scale obliged three Beijing studios to co-operate on the production: the army's August First Film Studio, the Beijing Film Studio, and the Central Newsreel and Documentary Film Studio. Like the Cultural Revolution film versions of the model performances made a half-decade later, the perfection of the dancing, songs, costuming, and lighting is an obvious obsession.

Likewise, the actual dances in *The East Is Red* drew on a range of dance heritages in similar ways to the major dance works of the Cultural Revolution. Non-Han ethnic-minority dances and Han folk dance, adapted from the dances performed by peasants on festive occasions, were the sources for most of the dances. One of the choreographers used as inspiration for the opening dance of sunflowers turning to the sun (of

Chairman Mao) the 'rice sprouts' dances of Jiaozhou in Shandong, but with modifications to suit the need to present the birth of the Communist Party as a coming together of various social forces from the four corners and centre of the stage.[4] Ninety-six young women hold fans together to look like huge sunflowers. Blocking the dancers to form small triangles that became a large triangle borrowed movements from the 'flower-drum operas' (*huadengxi*) of Yunnan. Other influences on the dances in *The East Is Red* were Chinese operatic movement traditions, mime, and other moves from Western dance, particularly ballet. Much was also made, as in the Cultural Revolution, of learning from real life, so that some movements replicated real-life actions, though with artistic license to heighten and elaborate in the spirit of Mao's *Talks* on art and literature. The mix of Chinese and Western dance and real-life influences became typical of dance in the Cultural Revolution.

This hybridity was further elaborated in the two 'model ballets', *The White-Haired Girl* (*Baimaonü*) and *The Red Detachment of Women*. Ballet had only been introduced on any scale in China after 1949, encouraged by China's close ties in the early 1950s with the Soviet Union.[5] With the Great Leap Forward and China's efforts to find its own path to modernization came a parallel push to draw upon indigenous Chinese traditions in cultural production. Ballets based on Chinese legends and historical episodes were created, with attempts to introduce Chinese-style movements. Chinese audiences remained small and, outside a relatively small coterie of aficionados, generally bewildered. On the eve of the Cultural Revolution, there were about ten major ballets in the repertoire of the two ballet companies based in Beijing and Shanghai. The two cities also each had a ballet school: Beijing because it was the capital and Shanghai as China's most Westernized and prosperous city. Ballet had no hold anywhere else. The *White-Haired Girl* started life in Yan'an, the wartime Communist headquarters, as a musical reworking of the Shaanxi peasants' 'rice-sprout songs' (*yangger*) popular in the locality. Chinese audiences first encountered *The Red Detachment of Women* as a feature film released in 1961. Part of its charm was the setting among minority peoples on Hainan Island in the far south of China. For Chinese audiences unfamiliar with the dance form, adapting these two works into ballets was thus eased by the appealing familiarity of the musical and film.

Like the modernized Peking operas that became Cultural Revolution 'model operas', the two 'model ballets' were the product of lengthy and assiduous work by a range of specialists. Like their opera counterparts, these artists were given the resources, including time, to create works of singular polish. *The Red Detachment of Women* was developed by the

Central Ballet Company in Beijing, itself established in 1959. *The White-Haired Girl* was a product of the Shanghai Ballet Company. Concern in 1963–1964 among cultural authorities that China lacked its own ballets encouraged the search for suitable subject matter. In the case of *Red Detachment*, the story was well known from the 1961 film's popular success, the film theme music was appealing, and the story concentrated on women and the Communist revolution: This was ideal for making a new Chinese ballet. In early 1964, the Ministry of Culture organized a *Red Detachment* creative group, based on the Central Ballet Company but drawing on a range of other dance, music, and stage specialists.[6] After a visit to the tropical warmth of Hainan, the group drafted a six-scene ballet and rehearsals began in May 1964.

Wu Qinghua, a servant in 1930s Hainan, is treated as a slave by a powerful local magnate. Qinghua flees her oppressor and is aided by a Communist army officer, Hong Changqing. They had met when Hong reconnoitred the landlord's home by visiting him in the guise of a wealthy overseas Chinese merchant. Hong is the Communist Party representative in a detachment of the Red Army comprising women soldiers. Under Hong's patient guidance, the former slave Qinghua becomes a disciplined fighter who learns to subsume her personal grievance against the landlord in the broader class war. Hong Changqing is captured and tortured to death by the landlord's militia. Qinghua resolves to continue his fight for revolution.[7]

To present the process of the central character's political maturing, life in a women's army detachment, and the peculiar qualities of the Hainan Island setting, the expressive repertoire of classical Western ballet fell short. The task called for bold experimentation and a breaking of ballet's artistic rules. Jiang Zuhui, the main choreographer, worked on the early scenes of Qinghua's servitude and rebellion in the home of landlord Nan Batian. Making full use of the appropriate steps and movements of classical ballet, Jiang tried to find ways to strengthen the forcefulness and vigour of the presentation of the young woman. Classical ballet, in contrast, tended to emphasize the beauty, softness, and compliance of female roles. Jiang and colleagues borrowed moves from Chinese musical drama, from folk dance, and from other traditional dances. Qinghua expresses her determination against the landlord by striking a frozen pose which was a borrowed from Peking opera's *liangxiang*. A third source of inspiration was real life, as observed during the Hainan fieldwork. To enhance the sense of place, the choreographers incorporated steps from local folk dances and even borrowed ideas from foreign dances. As Jiang later recalled: 'With a foundation in our own culture, assimilating all the best of foreign art, broadly gathering and abundantly concentrating (*guangcai boji*), putting all to our purposes: this was our creative aim.'[8]

By July 1964, a selected audience was shown the work to test its acceptability and seek feedback. The army officers present felt that the women soldiers did not march and move like real soldiers. At their invitation, 130 members of the Beijing ballet company went to live at an army camp for a fortnight. On their return from the camp, the ballet corps were full of inspiration and gave further ideas to the writers of the new ballet, who had stayed at home working on re-writes. The work was premiered in the smaller of the auditoria in the Great Hall of the People to mark National Day 1964. China's top leaders were publicized attending performances.[9] The kind of attention afforded the ballet on its first release reflected a sense of pride, and indeed relief, that Chinese artists had created a full-length work of their own. Reliance on *Swan Lake* and other classics of 'bourgeois' ballet could end.[10]

The White-Haired Girl had a longer artistic pedigree than its sister work. The title was familiar to Chinese audiences, having been one of the iconic first works promulgated on the founding of New China. The musical drama began life in Yan'an in the 1940s. Musical and theatrical specialists in the wartime Communist headquarters adapted local, peasant performance forms to the ideological needs of the regime. They had two main reasons for encouraging this effort: as models for work by alienated artists new to Yan'an from highly Westernized parts of China and for unengaged audiences, bewildered by unfamiliar, modern artistic forms like spoken drama. The musical drama *The White-Haired Girl* was one of the first large-scale works produced in Yan'an and was based on the local 'rice-sprout songs', small-scale musical plays performed by amateurs at key festivals in the yearly agricultural cycle, such as at Spring Festival (the lunar New Year). In 1950 one of the first new works from the nationalized studios was a film version of the musical. It was made at the Changchun studio with a crew that included Japanese staff left over from before 1945.[11] The musical told how a young peasant woman, Xi'er, flees her home village because of the landlord's unwelcome attentions and goes into the mountains. By the time her fiancé Wang Dachun finds her there, her hair has turned white. They return to the celebrations of the liberation of the village by the Communist army.

The ballet adaptation was the work of the Shanghai Ballet Company, encouraged in 1963 by the city leadership to produce works on contemporary Chinese life. The push to create new-style Peking operas with modern settings and stories had emerged from this same impulse.[12] In the spring of 1964, some members of the dance school, which included the ballet company, came up with the idea of adapting one scene from the original musical *The White-Haired Girl* into a short ballet as an exercise for their students. In addition to the film of the musical, a recent visit by the Matsuyama Ballet Company of Japan, led by a left-leaning artist and 'friend of China', had included its own adaptation of extracts from *The White-Haired Girl*.[13] With advice and input from a range of prominent Shanghai stage practitioners, including the spoken-drama actor-director Huang Zuolin, the well-known opera clown Liu Binkun, and eminent musicians, the adaptation of the Yan'an opera went from a small-scale dance to a mid-length piece and finished up as a full-length, eight-scene dance-drama (*wuju*). The interest shown by officials in the Shanghai cultural apparatus, reportedly including detailed critiques of early versions of the ballet, indicates the important symbolism attached to making a homegrown Chinese ballet.[14]

The new work drew upon five dance, or movement, traditions: Western ballet, traditional Chinese dance, Chinese folk dance, martial arts, and movement from Chinese musical drama. The traditional language of ballet could be seen when Xi'er and Wang Dachun dance a *pas de deux* or when Xi'er dances alone, on points in the mountains. But when, for example, Wang Dachun is sent off to join the Eighth Route Army, the choreographers draw on Chinese martial arts movements. In the massed dances, for example, at the end of the drama to signify the unity of peasants and soldiers, folk traditions of group dancing are prominent.

To make the characters and narrative clearer and to ensure that Chinese audiences, who were generally unused to watching ballet, understood and liked what they saw, singing in solos and a chorus was introduced into the dance-drama. Chinese folk traditions, at village festivals, for example, had always included simultaneous singing and dancing. The original opera made this relatively easy: Several songs and tunes from the Yan'an opera were preserved in the ballet, while several new songs and music were written for the dance version. Music from the Anti-Japanese War era, including the song of the People's Liberation Army, added a note of historical context to the story. A sense of authentic place was enhanced by incorporation of the plaintive style of Northern Shaanxi folk songs and the tunes of Hebei and Shanxi clapper opera (*bangzi*). The orchestration reflected the combination of Western and Chinese musical traditions. The three-stringed guitar (*sanxian*), the bamboo flute (*dizi*), two-stringed violin (*erhu*), and soundboard violin (*banhu*) were used to help differentiate the characters. This had the additional effect of further sinicizing the ballet.[15] On 23 May 1965, marking the twenty-second anniversary of Mao's *Talks* at Yan'an, *The White-Haired Girl* reached the Shanghai stage as a full-length work presented as part of the 'Shanghai Spring' (*Shanghai zhi chun*) festival of new works.[16] From May to November 1965, it played in major theatres in the city.

Several accounts of the emergence of *The White-Haired Girl* include records of Premier Zhou Enlai taking a personal interest in the new ballet. Zhou stressed three principles that should shape the ballet adaptation: being revolutionary, being in national style, and having popular appeal (*geminghua, minzuhua, qunzhonghua*).[17] Such interest from the nation's top leaders confirmed the dance specialists' confidence in taking the foreign dance form and making it Chinese.[18] Between April and June 1966, just as the Cultural Revolution got officially under way, *The White-Haired Girl* played in Beijing. The ballet's Yan'an origins as a musical made it a safe bet politically, despite ballet's inherent bourgeois associations. But not all audiences were pleased with the ballet version of *The White-Haired Girl*. In the spring of 1967, even at the Shanghai dance school where it had been created, debate arose on the merits of the new ballet, driven by early Cultural Revolution factional strife at the school. As a work created by the dance school's leaders, with warm endorsement from the school's Party committee, *The White-Haired Girl* was an obvious target for disaffected or ambitious school 'rebels'.[19] It was time to bring in the big guns. On 18 April 1967, Zhou Enlai watched yet another performance. Six days later Chairman Mao had the pleasure and was photographed with the cast and creators afterwards. His reported remarks were rather briefer than those of his colleagues: '*The White-Haired Girl* is good!'[20] This action and statement effectively put an end to the negative argument against the ballet.

Jiang Qing, the person most associated in public discourse with the model performances, had no hand in the creation of *The White-Haired Girl*, according to post–Cultural Revolution accounts. She never watched a performance, even though she spent much of 1964–1966 in Shanghai.[21] Jiang Qing reportedly saw *The White-Haired Girl* for the first time on 18 April 1967, six days before her husband took the opportunity and just a month before the official promulgation of the model performances. Post-1976 accounts then suggest that once Chairman Mao had endorsed the ballet, his wife leapt into action, meeting with teachers and students of the Shanghai Dance School, when she told them: 'In Shanghai I only want two companies: one Peking opera company; the other is yours'.[22] At the same meeting, she allegedly called for major revisions of the work, objecting, for example, to the combination of dance with songs and to the concentration on Xi'er at the expense of Wang Dachun, the army officer.[23] Jiang Qing's supposed discomfort with the work did not exclude the new ballet from the eight model works proclaimed in late May 1967.

In a similar re-invention of the history of the creation of *The Red Detachment of Women*, Jiang Qing's involvement was presented as central. A speech by Zhong Runliang at the launch of the model eight typified the new version of events. Having mentioned the evil influence of the cultural 'black liners' in urging the ballet company to learn from Soviet revisionism and to present Western dances, Zhong noted a change in the company's fortunes. 'Spring thunder sounds to quake the heavens. The day we had looked forward to for so long finally arrived. In the spring of 1964 Comrade Jiang Qing took personal leadership of the ballet revolution, by bringing Chairman Mao's red line on literature and art into our company.'[24] An article in the July 1970 issue of the Party's theoretical journal *Red Flag* wrote of the dance-drama being 'the rich fruit of Jiang Qing's personal fostering (*qinqin peiyu*)'.[25]

The ballet version of *The White-Haired Girl*, now reportedly 'inspired by Comrade Jiang Qing's directing of the adaptation of *The Red Detachment of Women*', required changes to the Yan'an musical and its 1950 film. The love story between Xi'er and Wang Dachun is replaced by their mutual 'class feeling' (*jieji ganqing*) in the ballet. The politically backward suggestion that Wang Dachun express his love for Xi'er in the final scene was quickly expunged from the work, as being too much like the bourgeois stories of *Swan Lake* and its ilk. In the Chinese ballet, Dachun and Xi'er meet in her cave in the mountains and maintain a suitably asexual distance, as they mime their joy at being reunited as neighbours and comrades, not lovers. The emphasis instead in the final scene is on the red sun rising over joyful poor peasants as they celebrate the return of Xi'er to the village. The sun represented Mao Zedong and the Chinese Communist Party. Attacks on the alleged ideological shortcomings of the Yan'an musical of *The White-haired Girl* were part of the attacks on Zhou Yang, the chief promulgator of Mao's Yan'an policies on art and literature.[26] By 1967, Jiang Qing had taken over from Zhou as the commander of literature and art. Rendering an icon of the Yan'an era into a new, improved version was an undoubtedly gratifying symbol of her triumph. Nonetheless, Jiang Qing apparently remained dissatisfied with the work. For eight months from February 1975, the *White-Haired Girl* team worked on revisions in Beijing. Nothing that was publicly performed resulted.[27]

In order to expand the audience for the ballet, and as a means of establishing a definitive version for the present and future reference of dance specialists, the ballet was recorded. In May 1968 Tianjin television had broadcast the ballet to viewers in the city and in Beijing for the anniversary of Mao's Yan'an *Talks*.[28] The Shanghai television station made a black-and-white 'stage documentary' of the ballet in July–August 1970. A few months later, at the end of 1970, another black-and-white version of the ballet was produced,[29] which was done by a production team identified as a combination of the Shanghai television station and the Shanghai City Film Production Unit (*Shanghaishi dianying shezhizu*). Capturing a standard version of the ballet on black-and-white film was deemed too important in the fall of 1970 to await the formal re-establishment of the Shanghai Film Studio.

Eventually in 1972 the same director and cinematographer produced a colour version of *The White-Haired Girl* at the Shanghai Film Studio. The 1970 and 1972 films also shared an identical cast.[30] Also in 1972 the ballet was taken abroad to North Korea and Japan. By the early 1990s, *The White Haired Girl* had been presented onstage more than one-thousand times to audiences of over one million, at home and abroad.[31] Its place among the eight Cultural Revolution model performances was not held against it in the aftermath of the arrest of the Gang of Four, unlike the ambivalent attitudes held by the new cultural authorities towards the modernized Peking operas with which the Gang had once been closely associated.[32] Still performed in the early twenty-first century, the dance-drama continued to serve as an example of the sinicization of ballet.

These two efforts at making ballet Chinese, commonly called by dance professionals in shorthand '*Red*' and '*White*', shared certain characteristics. Both incorporated dance steps and other movements from Chinese folk performances, from musical theatre, and from martial arts. The platoon of women soldiers in *The Red Detachment of Women* is a good illustration of the innovation these works represented. Instead of tutus, this martial equivalent of the *corps de ballet* wore a distinct uniform of tight shorts, shirts with army epaulettes, knee-length leggings, and army-style caps. Their carrying rifles required a reinvention of the movement and steps expected of a *corps*. It was natural that martial arts gestures, with weapons, and stylized steps echoing the deliberateness of opera actors were incorporated into their movements. Local colour was added with hand and upper-body gestures derived from Hainan folk dance or at least associated in the minds of Chinese audiences with the dances of the minority peoples of southwest China as presented in somewhat homogenized versions on stages across the nation since 1949.

In similar vein, *The White-Haired Girl* borrowed from northern folk traditions. The innocent Xi'er teases Wang Dachun and her uncle with steps and gestures like those used in peasant celebrations of Spring Festival and other calendar highlights. Even the evil landlord and his minions use movements reminiscent of buffoon characters in peasant dances and on the opera stage. The final scenes of celebration feature successive centre stage performances by corps of young peasant women, sturdy young peasant men, and Eighth Route Army soldiers. Each group draws upon the appropriate folk-dance vernacular, while preserving the grammatical or structural conventions of ballet. Both model ballets drew directly on Peking opera by having lead dancers strike the frozen pose of heightened attentiveness or determination called *liangxiang*.

Both ballets shared some features that clearly rooted them in their historical context. The emphasis was on the Cultural Revolution aesthetic of a super-realism, in which things were 'even higher, stronger, more concentrated, more typical and more ideal than ordinary real life'.[33] Accordingly, the uniforms of the women soldiers on Hainan Island are spotlessly clean and well repaired. The young peasant men and women in Xi'er's home village wear conventionalized versions of peasant clothing, as do the few, typified older peasant men and women.

In both ballets, the narratives and characters are also idealized, compared with their original sources. We have noted the major changes in *The White-Haired Girl*, designed to desexualize and revolutionize the main hero. The 'three prominences' rubric, used to focus attention in the model operas on the single hero, was also applied to the model ballets. Ballet's conventional *corps de ballet* could be easily presented as the outer of the concentric rings of heroic characters. Some modification of the three prominences was required, however, as both young women were less ideologically advanced than their supporting male characters: Wang Dachun, the Communist army political instructor, and Hong Changqing, his equivalent for the Hainan women's detachment. The latter becomes a focus of attention when he is burned at a stake after being captured by the landlord's men. Joan of Arc–style martyrdom of the male lead shifts attention somewhat awkwardly from the heroine Wu Qinghua. A final scene of group determination to continue Hong Changqing's fight against oppression was intended to undermine the association of the young woman with the central role.

Despite the best efforts of the Cultural Revolution adapters of the two ballets, sex was not entirely removed from the picture. Audiences' own assumptions or unsanctioned thoughts about what might happen, in another dance world perhaps, between Xi'er and Wang Dachun or between Qinghua and her instructor, could never be stamped out. Across China in the mid-1970s a still from the film version of *The Red Detachment of Women* decorated peasant homes and student dormitory rooms. It featured not the short-wearing *corps* but a solitary Wu Qinghua. She

4.1. Qinghua, the heroine of *The Red Detachment of Women*, leaps in defiance of her landlord captors. Source: *Chinese Literature*, 1971, 1 (January), p. 7. Published by the Foreign Languages Press, Beijing.

was clad in the floating silk blouse and pants she wore as a prisoner of the evil landlord Nan Batian (see Figure 4.1). In a widely admired solo dance in the dungeon of the landlord Qinghua leaps high in the air, her back arched backwards, her arms held high, her legs flaying. That her clothes are red and light silk adds to the sexual allure of the film still. Having it pasted on a wall could be taken to indicate appreciation of a core Cultural Revolution artwork. But more private motivations cannot be ruled out, especially given the frequency with which this particular still found fans. Likewise, two stills of Xi'er *en pointe* were also popular: One featured her with one leg stretched back horizontal to the ground (*Arabesque*); the other had her in the same pose but supported by the upraised hand of Wang Dachun standing beside her.[34] Given the requirements of the art, it is not surprising that the two 'model ballets' of the Cultural Revolution had a male–female relationship at their centre. And notwithstanding their best efforts to de-sexualize the connections, the creators of these ballets could not entirely direct their audiences into completely chaste thoughts. When new ballets appeared in the mid-1970s, they too featured central pairings, though every effort was made to obliterate any sexual references.

The Red Detachment of Women and The White-Haired Girl were not the only dances performed on China's stages in the late 1960s. Two kinds of dance performance continued to educate and, perhaps, entertain Chinese audiences. One kind built on the mainstream efforts from the 1950s and early 1960s at melding an indigenous and modern form of dance. The 1964 performance of The East Is Red represented this orthodox achievement. The late 1960s and 1970s saw considerable expansion in this repertoire, as we shall see. The other kind of dance was even more highly politicized and more in the nature of moving tableaux than of actual dance. Performers in contemporary dress assumed the poses of revolutionary group statuary. The former kind of dance remained largely in the hands of professionals: The latter was the realm of the local and the amateur.

The type of dances seen in The East Is Red involved incorporating and adapting three historical strands of dance in China. One strand was the folk dances enjoyed by country people in times of annual festivities: Spring Festival, Autumn Harvest, and the like. A second strand was associated with the other end of society: imperial and aristocratic dance performed with elaborated orchestration at court and elsewhere. This historical legacy had been enriched by the recovery by scholars of evidence of traditional Chinese dance in such places as centuries-old murals in the Buddhist caves of Dunhuang, in northwest China. The third strand were the dances of China's fifty-something ethnic minorities, that proved so irresistible to Han dance professionals and to Chinese audiences in general.

Dances based on the folk dances of the non-Han minority cultures of China seem to have always been available to Chinese audiences, even at the time of the strongest Cultural Revolution strictures on what cultural activities were permitted. The head and shoulder movements of Mongolian and other minority dances from the Northwest were instantly recognized across the nation. Folk-derived dance gave instant 'national characteristics' (*minzu tese* or *minzuhua*) to performance forms that drew heavily on imported, Western artistic traditions. As with film, another Western form imported into China in the twentieth century, China's minority cultures as subject matter offered instant 'Chineseness' for the dance medium, even in somewhat modernized or homogenized versions. The other reason for the acceptance of such folk dances was that most Chinese audiences found them fun. The somewhat racist view that regarded many minority peoples as having a propensity to burst into song or break into dance helps explain this response to folk-based dance. But at a time when most performances were deadly serious, serving as lessons in the importance of class vigilance, many dances were a welcome relief from the somewhat dour fare usually on offer. The same can be said of musical performances throughout the Cultural Revolution that drew on folk music heritages. Chinese audiences regarded them as a lively change from a strict diet of newly minted 'revolutionary songs' in mainstream style.

Weaving the various dance strands together was the work of professional, Soviet and other Western-educated dance scholars and choreographers. Like other performance-based arts in China, including opera, scholarly attention from non-performing specialists was a distinctly twentieth-century phenomenon. For dance, the specialists appeared relatively late, based in the apparatus of training and sorting out represented by dance schools and dance professional (*wudaojia*) associations. This kind of dance creation and performance continued after the start of the Cultural Revolution, despite the emphasis given the two *Red* and *White* full-length ballets. Some of the dances, on a large-scale similar to 1964's *The East Is Red*, were broadcast on television in the later 1960s and into the 1970s, frequently as part of celebrations on important holidays.[35]

The second kind of dance performance that continued vigorously in the late 1960s was the more mechanical 'praise dances', the equivalent of the 'praise songs' to Chairman Mao that they often accompanied. They were resolutely contemporary and orthodox, with performers dressed in overalls, headscarves, or army uniforms to serve as standardized markers of workers, peasants, or soldiers. These archetypical actors would move about in militant, resolute ways on stage or often in makeshift venues in streets, factories, or on worksites. They would strike a collective pose, grouped in a manner much used by Soviet and Soviet-trained Chinese monumental artists. Like statues, they would be grouped pointing their chests, faces, and arms towards an imagined glorious, revolutionary future. Often props, such a banners with current slogans, were used, unfurled to mark the dramatic climax of the performance. Music, songs, chants, or simple drumbeats could be the accompaniment. This was a dance form that lent itself well to amateur performance, by Red Guards in 1966–1967 and by propaganda teams organized by the army, Party organs, and worker unions as part of the restoration of political order in 1969 and afterwards. These performances were as much street theatre as dance and persisted throughout the ten years of the Cultural Revolution. They enjoyed something of a revival in 1976.

A focus on the *Red* and *White* model ballets ignores the elaboration and innovation elsewhere on China's dance stages. Only some sources acknowledge the works that emerged in the early 1970s. Seventeen dance-dramas (*wuju*) were presented in the period from 1970–1976.[36] In 1970 *Little Guards of the Railroad* (*Tiedao xiao weishi*) was premiered by the China Railroad Song and Dance Ensemble (*wengongtuan*), a typical group attached to government ministries and major enterprises since 1949. The dance is a story of the battle between young student guards and 'bad elements' seeking to damage the railroad. The choreographers had been active in the early 1960s, evidencing some continuity in personnel as well as dance aesthetics between the eve of the Cultural Revolution and the 1970s. Another 1970 dance-drama was the work of the Changchun City Song and Dance Company (*gewutuan*) in northeast China. It celebrated the actions of Yang Lin, a soldier who had died the previous year in a border skirmish with Soviet troops on a disputed island in the Ussuri River between the two countries.[37] Other dance-dramas from the early 1970s incorporated songs, just as *The White-Haired Girl* ballet had done, and drew on the dance interest in ethnic minorities.[38]

By 1974 the two 'model ballets' were joined by several major new works. *Sons and Daughters of the Grasslands* (*Caoyuan ernü*) had an Inner Mongolian setting and so was able to combine ballet steps with elements of Mongolian dance (or at least movements that Chinese audiences identified as Mongolian). *Ode to the Yimeng Mountains* (*Yimeng song*) was set in Shandong on the banks of the Yi River. By this time considerable expansion was occurring in the range of stories and styles available to audiences of musical drama, spoken drama, literature, and other arts. Dance was no exception, with an explosion of officially sanctioned short-length dances appearing on China's stages.

Sons and Daughters of the Grassland was the story of a Mongolian boy and girl braving the elements to protect their collective's sheep flock. The themes of the ballet first emerged in a 1964 animated cartoon recounting the real-life drama of two Mongolian sisters, *Heroic Little Sisters of the Grassland* (*Caoyuan yingxiong xiao jiemei*). The Cultural Revolution ballet version of the story soon changed to a male and female hero, in line with ballet convention, and inserted a class enemy who tries to sabotage the young people's work. The ballet was created by the China

Dance-Drama Company (*Zhongguo wujutuan*), which had been established in 1972, but was little more than a renaming, with reconstituted personnel, of the former Central Musical Theatre Ballet Company
(*Zhongyang gejuyuan balei wujutuan*).[39] This reorganization of the dance
companies was part of a response to complaints about the relative narrowness of cultural activities voiced reportedly by Mao Zedong, Zhou
Enlai, and others in the Chinese leadership.

The Mongolian ballet allegedly was well liked by 1970s audiences.
Unlike the *Red* and *White* ballets, it presented contemporary life, though
in an exotic context akin to the Korean War setting of the *Raid on the
White-Tiger Regiment* model opera. It also allowed scope for the kind of
folk dance borrowing that had helped give the *Red* and *White* ballets their
distinctive flavours. *Sons and Daughters of the Grassland* was filmed in
colour at the Beijing Film Studio and released in May 1975. Like the stage
version, the film featured in close-up a strangely doe-eyed and incongruous
toy sheep which the heroes save for the collective.[40]

The other major new ballet that appeared in May 1974 was a less exotic
work and apparently less popular among Cultural Revolution audiences.
Ode to Yimeng was set in the north Chinese heartland and had started
life as a novel titled *Red Sister-in-Law* (*Hongsao*). The early attempts
at creating Chinese opera with modern settings had included efforts to
adapt the story to musical drama and into a dance version in 1965.
The ballet version, like *Grasslands*, was the work of the China Dance-
Drama Company, many of whose members had also been responsible
for *The Red Detachment of Women*. Sister Ying, a poor peasant, discovers a seriously wounded Communist army platoon leader in 1947 and
feeds him her own breast milk. Succoured also by Sister Ying's soup,
surviving enemy fire and mounting counterattacks, he eventually is able
to return to his unit. An epilogue celebrates the liberation of the mountain village, somewhat in the manner of the ending of *The White-Haired
Girl*.[41]

Once again a male–female heroic centre lends itself to using ballet's
conventions. The attractions of *Ode to Yimeng* lay in its action and its
characters. The dedication and sacrifice of its three central heroes (including Sister Ying's guerrilla husband) had moved readers of the novel and
attracted opera modernizers. Added to this was the potential on the ballet stage of presenting scenes of fighting between the Communist guerrillas, the Guomindang army, and their local landlord allies. For the
Cultural Revolution cultural authorities, the portrayal of the close links
between civilians and Communist soldiers was the big attraction. This

link, allegorized as 'fish in water' (*yushui guanxi*), was much promoted during these years, in popular songs and other mythologies. *Yimeng* was filmed in 1975 at the army's August First feature film studio.[42]

Dance was prominent in the expansion after 1972 of the repertoire of performances for Chinese audiences, through regional and national performance conventions and festivals that also included operas and other stage forms. One of the earliest examples of new dances was identified as a dance of the Li people of Hainan Island. *Happily Giving Grain* (*Xi song liang*) was first performed in 1972 by the Hainan Nationalities Song and Dance Company.[43] Unlike the full-length ballets, *Happily Giving Grain* was a dance without a strong narrative. It featured young women of the Li minority transporting grain, bananas, and other crops from a bumper harvest (no other harvests were permissible in these years) to a state warehouse. This was their means of paying tax to the state and was a source, apparently, of unbounded delight. Dance expectations of interaction between male and female performers were achieved by having the young women engage in banter and mild teasing with the driver of the vehicle carrying them and the grain. Here too the setting among non-Han peoples allowed for more easy allusions to a heavily disguised sexuality. Likewise, the absence of an enemy, in this case a class enemy, could be excused by the minority context, as well as by the relative shortness of the work.[44] Props were also used in novel ways: Lengths of cloth served as headscarves and as bindings, as well as producing floating visual effects. The nine young women's straw hats served as winnows of the millet, were held together to become a machine for blowing away chaff, and, twirling in a line, became the turning wheels of the cart taking the grain to the warehouse.[45]

Another notable dance, first performed in 1974, marked considerable innovation in featuring only male dancers and not including songs as part of the musical score. *War-horse Cries* (*Zhanma siming*) was created by the army's General Political Department Song and Dance Company, a group that had been active in dance innovations since the 1950s. As in the case of the Hainan dance, there are no class enemies to enhance the trajectory of the story. Spectacle and experimentation characterized *War-horse Cries*. The choreographers drew principally on the drum-accompanied 'rice sprouts songs' of Shandong and on classical Chinese dance. These two sources were combined with movements inspired by real-life horse training to create, according to one source, a new dance vocabulary. A post–Cultural Revolution comment notes the degree of technical difficulty that the dance involved for the sixteen male performers. Spins, tumbles, and high leaps presented a challenge to the dancers and made a definite impression on audiences. Clearly, the choreographers injected a strong muscular element into a performing art that was usually associated with women dancers, unlike the male preserve of opera acrobatics.[46]

Between 1972 and 1974, a number of other dances appeared on China's stages and gained a place in the widening performance repertoire. Some were the work of propaganda teams identified as amateur, though many such prominent amateur groups in fact harboured experienced professionals, given discreet employment in such teams after the disbanding of their full-time companies or their expulsion from professional groups for political offences.[47] Full-time specialist groups in various parts of the armed forces were also active in creating and touring new dances. Most major sections of the People's Liberation Army had professional song and dance troupes attached to them, mainly charged with entertaining the forces but also encouraged to practice outreach into the civilian community. The army had been required to restore order in many Chinese cities in 1969, as rivalry between Red Guard and other factions either turned more violent or stalemated necessary decisions and economic production. Marshall Lin Biao, the top military leader and Mao's chosen successor, in September 1971 had died while allegedly plotting to kill Mao. The People's Liberation Army had some work to do in shoring up public affection and respect. Entertainment with new dances that emphasized close army–civilian relations was one way to do this. Sometimes ethnic-minority and military subjects could be combined, as in the 1974 Hainan dance *The Army Comes Camping in the Mountains* (*Yeying dajun jin shan lai*).[48]

Early 1976 saw a new stage in the development of Cultural Revolution dance. For the first six weeks of the year fifty-one dance organizations, involving 1,300 people and 262 dances, participated in a national dance (solo, duet and trio) festival in Beijing. Such festivals allowed professionals to observe in one place the work of colleagues from across the nation. This event also involved public performances with almost 300,000 admissions.[49] The festival's emphasis on small-scale works, involving one to three dancers, was in marked contrast to the usual stress on dances using relatively large groups of dancers. This change, and the encouragement of broad public attendance, suggested a desire to innovate further in dance performances. About one-third of the items presented in Beijing made direct reference to current policies: Twenty-eight were on class struggle, seven were based on the model operas, and fifty-eight covered such subjects as the educational revolution, sent-down youth, barefoot doctors, and the movement to criticize Lin Biao, Confucius, and 'capitulationists'.[50]

In reporting on the festival, the first issue of the re-established *Dance* (*Wudao*) magazine in March proudly noted the change of subject matter and approach wrought by the Cultural Revolution. At the first of such national gatherings to present solo and duo dances in 1961, the stage had been filled with flowers, birds, fish, and insects as well as handsome scholars and beautiful maidens, just as in traditional opera. Fifteen years on, heroic members of the worker, peasant, and soldier masses occupied centre stage. The 1976 report went on to praise the ways in which the dances made use of the 'model performances', attacking those who complained of the model works being 'a single flower blooming' (*yihuadufang*). Also of note were the number of youthful or amateur choreographers and performers.[51] Such young people and part-timers were a source of fresh, and politically malleable, talent. In addition to the performances, seminars were held to discuss aspects of dance work, including choreography, music, art direction, and how folk and minority dance could be incorporated in the new dance efforts.

Many of the works performed by solitary dancers, pairs, or trios were not as fresh as the 1976 reports suggested. Some, such as *Ferry Crossing* (*Dukou*), had long pedigrees in other performance forms. Transplanting a story or concept into the rather youthful genre of such non-group dances increased the odds of the work being politically acceptable, thus lowering the risks of innovation.[52] Indeed, despite the praise for the new dances, there seems to have been a certain caution in coverage of the 1976 festival. The solos and limited number of dancers in the other works presented did not fit well with the Cultural Revolution emphasis on collectivism and group action, even if led by outstanding individuals. Such solitary or relatively small-scale dances did not seem to reflect properly Cultural Revolution heroism. The newness of these dance developments in the early 1970s encouraged an unprecedented rupture in the usual periodization of Chinese cultural and political history, which always separates the ten years of the Cultural Revolution (1966–1976) from the periods before and after. Mao Hui's *A Chronology of New China's Dance*, published in 2005, used 1975 (not 1976) as the break point in dance developments.[53]

Some dances premiered in 1975–1976 were transplanted from other Cultural Revolution cultural arenas. *Sparkling Red Star* was adapted from the popular 1974 feature film and was the work of the Shanghai City Dance School which had been responsible for *The White-Haired Girl* ballet.[54] Modernized Peking operas were also rather safe bets, politically if not artistically, for dance adaptation, which was done to *Boulder Bay* and *Azalea Mountain*, among others. The transplanting compliment had been returned with the adaptation in the mid-1970s into modern Peking operas of the *Red* and *White* ballets.[55]

By spring 1976 political tensions were higher than since the late 1960s. Like other periodicals, *Dance* magazine reflected these disputes. The first new issue of the journal included an attack on 'revisionist' education of dancers before the Cultural Revolution in contrast to the correct instruction offered to students of the Central May Seventh Art University, nominally headed by Jiang Qing.[56] In time for the May First International Labour Day celebrations, the Tsinghua University Amateur Literature and Art Team presented a new dance work. Titled *Reversing Verdicts Does Not Enjoy Popular Support (Fan'an buderenxin)*, the dance was billed as the first 'struggle with capitalist roaders' dance.[57] It chimed with media attacks on Qingming demonstrators in early April in Beijing, who were accused of wanting to reverse the verdicts on alleged enemies of the Cultural Revolution, among them the newly demoted Deng Xiaoping. The dance's contemporary setting marked a new departure for literature and art at the time. Until then, dances and other stage works generally avoided specific reference to the Cultural Revolution. A dance could be set in contemporary times, like *Happily Giving Grain* and its ilk, but there was no overt reference to actual political events, just a generalized celebration of the everyday under the glorious leadership of Chairman Mao. *Reversing Verdicts Does Not Enjoy Popular Support*, created at a bastion of Gang of Four support, reflected the mounting weakness of the cultural leadership of Jiang Qing and her allies.

The stage photographs show that *Reversing Verdicts Does Not Enjoy Popular Support* was a distinct throwback to the 1966–1967 period at the start of the Cultural Revolution. The performers, playing a Mao Zedong Thought Propaganda Team with an outstanding leader, chant slogans or appropriate rallying cries, holding up banners, flags, tools, and other props. The intensity of the expressions of determination on the faces of the performers matched the predictability of the narrative and the stunning familiarity of the message. This was simple agitprop. The contrast with the innovations in modern dance at the early 1976 Beijing festival was striking. Such a reversion was another sign of weakness on the part of the dance's promoters.

2. SCORING THE REVOLUTION: MUSIC

Two areas of Chinese musical life were transformed during the Cultural Revolution. One was symphonic and classical music associated with elite tastes and the Westernization of Chinese culture. The other kind of music had roots in indigenous traditions and popular participation. The former underwent renewed popularization and sinicization in these years. Songs and folk music were further made modern. Indeed, much of the musical innovation associated with the Cultural Revolution came as part of the modernization or adaptation to Chinese aesthetics of other performing arts, namely, opera and other musical theatre forms and in dance. One of the eight model performances was a symphony, *Shajiabang*, based on the model opera of the same title. A second group of model performances promoted in the early 1970s included two musical performances: a piano-accompanied concert version of arias from the model opera *The Red Lantern* (*Gangqin banchang 'Hongdeng ji'*) and a piano concerto *The Yellow River* (*Gangqin xiezouqu 'Huanghe'*). The latter was a reworking of the *Yellow River Cantata* (*Huanghe dahechang*), first performed in Yan'an in 1939.[58]

Striking in this list of major musical items in the Cultural Revolution is the dependency of the music on another performing art. Even the purely musical items are adaptations from modernized Peking opera or from older works. This feature is not unconnected with the dogma of the times that was critical of so-called non-programmatic music (meaning music without titles). The Cultural Revolution insurgents regarded the latter as an attempt to deny the inherent class nature of all art and literature. Nonetheless, as the grip of the insurgents over cultural activities was loosened in the early 1970s and as their influence weakened, more variety of musical expression emerged. Meanwhile another aspect of musical culture in these years, the effort at creating suitably rousing songs that would appeal to mass audiences, was sustained at the professional and amateur levels. In all these musical phenomena, the position of folk or indigenous music in relation to modern music remained a central challenge to composers, performers, and indeed to audiences or users of the music.[59]

Like other performing arts and cultural activities, music making had been re-organized upon the establishment of the People's Republic in 1949. To existing conservatories in Beijing and Shanghai were added new schools in places like Xi'an, closer geographically to the Chinese heartland. A central conservatory, the China Music Academy, was set up only in 1964, on the eve of the Cultural Revolution.[60] Two somewhat contradictory focuses characterized musical endeavours in the new apparatus. One was the teaching and performance of modern, Western music and the on-going creative work to sinicize this music, to express Chinese experience in the international language of modern, classical music. The second focus of musical culture after 1949 was more inwardly directed, on the musical traditions that had emerged in China over centuries and across regional and ethnic diversity. This in effect was an effort to modernize Chinese music, both folk and traditional (if this distinction can be properly made). As with old-style opera, part of this focus was the censoring of tunes, lyrics, and styles considered salacious, vulgar, or 'bourgeois'.[61] Notwithstanding the careful, ethno-musical research of many dedicated scholars, one result of this work was a tendency to homogenize and obliterate differences in treatment of folk music. A similar tendency was seen in dance, another folk activity that was elevated to receive attention from modern-trained specialists.

Western music continued to hold powerful sway. This was in spite of the official effort to put Chinese traditional and folk music on an equal footing with Western music, at least structurally though not necessarily in the minds of musicians and other music professionals. A Central Symphony (*Zhongyang yinyuetuan*) was established in 1956 and a Central National Music Orchestra (*Zhongyang minzu yinyuetuan*) in 1960.[62] Chinese composers continued to produce Western-style music, not infrequently based on folk tunes in the manner of nineteenth-century nationalist European composers. But the stalwarts of the Western canon: Beethoven, Mozart, Brahms, Tchaikovsky, and company continued to hold pride of place in the repertoire.

Ironically, despite the efforts to promote folk-based music, the Cultural Revolution in music saw a considerable emphasis placed on Chinese reworking of Western classical music. Even the music of the modern Peking operas was strongly influenced by Western music. The more 'tuneful' and regularized sounds of the model-opera scores owed much to the creative borrowing of instruments, harmonics and effects, drawing upon at least half a century of musical experimentation in Chinese musical theatre. Given the resolutely modern subject matter of the new-style operas, the incorporation of sounds and musical effects that were identifiably modern was hardly surprising. On occasion the processes were in parallel. The '*Shajiabang* symphony', for example, emerged at the same time as the Peking-opera version. The symphony was completed in 1965, when it was labelled a 'symphonic chorus' (*jiaoxiang hechang*). The model opera itself was only finalized in 1969.[63] The 1965 symphonic work was composed by Luo Zhongrong and colleagues at the Central Symphony, who had been using Peking-opera music as a source of inspiration since 1959.[64]

In May 1976 the newly re-published *People's Music* (*Renmin yinyue*) included an article by members of the Shanghai Symphony Orchestra on their 'battle' to create proletarian symphonic music. They cited their version of *Tiger Mountain* as an example of their achievement in bringing together specialists and masses in creating the symphony.[65] Two years after the Cultural Revolution the same orchestra expressed a somewhat different view of such Cultural Revolution symphonies. They revealed that soon after the *Shajiabang* symphony was first widely performed in 1967, Yu Huiyong, himself a noted composer, claimed that the work was the personal project of Jiang Qing. The resources wasted on trying to produce a new version of the *Shajiabang* symphony in 1973 indicated the seriousness of the cultural leadership's efforts to adapt Chinese musical traditions to Western classical music.[66] It was clear which music heritage, folk or modern, was more prestigious for Jiang Qing and her supporters.

One classical music genre that received unprecedented attention in the Cultural Revolution was choral versions of the classical-style poems written by Mao Zedong. Composers had begun to produce song versions of the poetry in 1958, though initially in something of the manner of German lieder, for the solo voice. By the late 1960s, the preferred vehicle was the massed chorus.[67] At a time when some forms of Western music were subject to criticism, having such a lyricist offered ideal protection from critics. Massed singing of musical versions of individual poems by Mao Zedong was also encouraged. After 1 January 1976, when two new Mao poems, written some years earlier, were released with a massive media flourish, students and others across the nation learned to sing the simultaneously publicized musical versions of them.[68]

One part of the musical enterprise during the Cultural Revolution involved the creation of new modern musicals (*geju*), a form that had had considerable popular success in the 1950s and 1960s. *Third Sister Liu* (*Liu Sanjie*), based on Zhuang folk tales from Guangxi, *Ashma* (*Ashima*), a legendary tale set among the Bai minority in Yunnan, and *Red Guards of Lake Hong* (*Honghu chiweidui*), about a Red Army-led uprising in central China in the 1930s, had attracted appreciative audiences, especially to the colour-film versions of the musicals. Despite the early Cultural Revolution focus on modernizing Peking opera, the entirely modern musical was never ignored. Three musicals created in 1975–1976 reached public theatres. *Red Hawk of the Grasslands* (*Caoyuan hong yin*) was the work of the Hulunbei'ermeng Nationalities Song and Dance Troupe of Heilongjiang. The Mongolian setting had echoes of the successful pre–Cultural Revolution modern musicals. *Bright and Brave* (*Sashuang yingzi*) was from the Ankang District Song and Dance Ensemble in Shaanxi. The Musical Play Troupe (*gejutuan*) of the PLA General Political Department in 1976 presented *Tempest Song* (*Kuangbiao qu*). But even such impeccable provenance did not guarantee audience delight. This army musical, like the others, seems to have had no life after October 1976.[69]

The changing fortunes of classical music during the Cultural Revolution reflected factional disputes. Yao Wenyuan, the house ideologue in the Gang of Four, had made a name for himself in May 1963 with an article on assessing the musical achievement of Claude Debussy. Yao had been prompted to write at his usual great length on the nineteenth-century French composer by the publication by the Shanghai Music Press of writings by Debussy. Yao in fact was using this criticism of the Frenchman to attack contemporary Chinese musical figures, including He Lüting (born 1903). Yao and Zhang Chunqiao allegedly never forgot He Lüting's fiercely expressed disagreement among the thirty or so articles published in national newspapers and journals in response to Yao Wenyuan's initial blast in the Shanghai newspaper *Wenhui bao*.[70] He Lüting was removed as head of the Shanghai Conservatory in 1966 and in late April 1968 a 'struggle' session against him was broadcast on Shanghai television. Viewers watched in awe as he collapsed in pain to the floor, his arms pinned behind his back. He was released from prison in January 1973.[71]

In that same year, these arguments about classical music re-emerged with an October article in the *Guangming Daily* titled 'On a discussion about program music and non-program music' (*Guanyu dui biaoti yinyue yu wubiaoti yinyue de taolun*). This topic had had been raised in an attachment to a report by a unit responsible for the visit to China of two Turkish musicians. The article gave rise to a nationwide criticism of non-program, or untitled music, that is music (for example, Symphony No. 5 or Concerto in G Minor) without a title that indicates its content.[72] The Cultural Revolution insurgents considered this a bourgeois indulgence in fantasy and obscurity: Real proletarians wanted music that had a title that explained what it was about. This was the custom with traditional Chinese instrumental music, each part of which usually bore a poetic suggestion as to supposed content. Only certain Western composers who had emerged at the time of the rise of the bourgeoisie were considered to have a positive historical role. These latter on occasion included Beethoven: Not even Jiang Qing, it seems, could abolish Beethoven. Unlike the Debussy criticism on the eve of the Cultural Revolution, music professionals could not avoid the much larger scale 1973 criticism and were obliged to go through the motions of mouthing the contents of the media fulminations on the subject.[73] The 1973 movement also had a direct factional function. Premier Zhou Enlai, in charge of China's foreign relations, had encouraged visits by Western orchestras. Among the first had been by the London Philharmonic and the Philadelphia Orchestra under Eugene Ormandy in September 1973. Attacking Western classical music's ideological shortcomings was a means of indirectly undermining Zhou's position. Around this time Beethoven and other composers again came under attack for failing to reflect a proletarian outlook in their work.[74]

Nonetheless, visits by Western orchestras continued in the mid-1970s. In the autumn of 1975 the New Zealand National Youth Orchestra toured to Beijing and Guangzhou. This was the first Western orchestra to visit China since 1973. Sensitivity was heightened by the recent factional tensions over programmatic music. Chinese organizers of the tour were extremely cautious about the repertoire that the young orchestra would perform, in addition to selections from a concert version of the score of *The White-Haired Girl* and of the new ballet *Sons and Daughters of the Grassland*. The biographical backgrounds of the New Zealand composers of the nominated works and descriptions of the contents and intentions of the works themselves were carefully scrutinized in Beijing. The two New Zealand works had clear programmatic content. The two other pieces performed on the tour were symphonies by Sibelius, who could be presented as a Finnish nationalist, and Haydn. There was a distinct frisson of excitement in the invited Chinese audience at their concerts in Beijing when they started to play the familiar works by Sibelius and Haydn. These professionals engaged in animated discussions on the choice of the repertoire in the intermission. Vice-Premier Zhang Chunqiao himself attended one of the Beijing concerts, an indication of factional support for the tour and the kind of music presented.[75]

Meanwhile, China's own symphony orchestras, in Shanghai and Beijing, had regrouped, working on film scores in addition to public performing. Slowly they too were testing the limitations of repertoire by going beyond the standard Chinese-composed, Western-style classical music that had consisted of the score to the model ballets, along with some other pieces usually distinguished by their romantic bombast. These orchestral pieces became familiar to Chinese audiences who in the past had only been exposed to such music in cinemas or wherever else they watched films. But the musical spectrum of the Cultural Revolution could accommodate much more than ersatz Chinese-style romanticism and modernized opera orchestrations.

Popular songs had had a role in modern Chinese history, expressing national aspirations in the 1930s during the confrontation with Japan and subsequently encouraging mass support for the Communist revolution, being popularized through modern, mass media. After 1949, the production, distribution, and mass enjoyment of these songs became even more regularized, with radio being used effectively. Composers and lyricists strove to find the turn of phrase and catchy tune that would capture the popular imagination as well as please political masters. In March 1965

4.2. A piano accordionist entertains waiting passengers: *Before Boarding the Train* (*Chengche zhi qian*) by the Art Study Class of the Beijing Railway Bureau (New Year picture), from *Bejing xin wenyi* (New Beijing literature and art), 1972, trial issue 2 (March), p. 74.

Red Flag took the unusual step of publishing words and music of thirteen songs which had been most well received in recent years.[76]

Similar well-crafted songs, presenting current policy, continued to be produced during the Cultural Revolution (Figure 4.2). The range of subject matter narrowed somewhat and the central focus on the wisdom of Mao Zedong grew even stronger, but the songs still found a place in the lives and hearts of Chinese. As before, a clever turn of phrase in lyrics or music, an ease of mastering words and tune, and a rousing beat ensured songs a life beyond their publication in newspapers and journals, their broadcast on radio, or (later) their use in a feature-film score. Songs that borrowed from the Turkic tunes of Xinjiang province or from some other ethnic minority's musical tradition were particularly welcomed by ordinary citizens. As in other fields, minority music allowed for a greater range of subject matter and tunes and even permitted more fun in the performance of such songs.[77] Singing in organized groups of workmates or schoolmates was the least unpopular kind of political study activity in the 1970s, with many natural singers finding roles in guiding their colleagues in the learning and performance of these works.

With the start of the Cultural Revolution, musical attention turned most immediately to what we might call 'praise songs' for Chairman Mao and 'rebel songs' for Red Guard groups. To the existing repertoire of songs glorifying Mao's wisdom were added such gems as 'Wishing Chairman Mao a Long Life' (*Zhufu Mao zhuxi wanshouwujiang*) and 'Chairman Mao is the Red Sun in the Hearts of the People of the Whole World' (*Mao zhuxi shi quan shijie renmin xinzhong de hong taiyang*).[78] These songs, known as 'loyalty songs' (*zhongzige*), served as the musical part of 'loyalty dances' (*zhongziwu*), performed by amateurs in factories, offices, and in the street during the late 1960s. While musically having much in common with earlier popular songs, being created by the same composers and lyricists, the single-minded focus on one man in the Cultural Revolution versions and their constant use in the public performance of political commitment were new.

Another novel kind of song was 'quotation songs' (*yulu ge*), setting the quotations and passages from the so-called Little Red Book to music. These were first publicized in *People's Daily* on the eve of National Day in 1966.[79] But Mao's sayings were hardly poetic and, with several notable exceptions, the task of setting them in a musical context made singing and listening to them a strain for even zealots. The Red Guard 'rebel songs' took liberties with musical convention, combining singing with chanting. There was even a kind of song called 'enemy songs' (*niugui gequ*, literally 'cow-spirit songs') associated with the intellectuals imprisoned in the first years of the Cultural Revolution. These latter songs were, of course, written by Red Guards and their supporters to encourage public resentment of the victims labelled 'cow ghosts and snake spirits' (*niugui-sheshen*).[80] Both these kinds of songs vanished by the late 1960s.

Ethnic minority-influenced songs and traditional Chinese music, including more obvious folk-style music, appealed to audiences not particularly engaged by bombastic classical-style music or other mainstream tune-smithing. In the early stages of the Cultural Revolution, when the emphasis was on the model operas and on Red Guard performances of modern songs, national music (*minzu yinyue*) did not receive much attention. The model operas' musical innovation, combining traditional instruments with some Western additions and borrowing effects from Western music, seemed to indicate the way forward for Chinese music. But traditional music, both in its refined, so-called classical, or imperial, form and in less cultivated folk forms, never disappeared. This music enjoyed a revival in the early 1970s, when local forms of opera and other arts also re-emerged officially.

In the 1970s, other Chinese musics derived from the folk offered further ways to enhance the local and engage the locals. Regional musical performance forms, such as the *pingtan* (story-telling and ballad singing in Suzhou dialect) in Zhejiang and the drum singing (*gushu*) popular in Tianjin city in the north, began to be performed again. The settings were usually somewhat sanitized versions of the teahouses and other entertainment places of old. The contents of the performances also reflected current political needs. But audiences welcomed the opportunity to enjoy the skills of the performers, both old and younger, newly trained professionals and amateurs. As with traditional, familiar operas and the new-style operas, for audiences the contents was less important than delighting in the skills of actual presentation.[81] From his recent fieldwork among village musicians not far from Beijing, Stephen Jones notes briefly how many traditional practices in musical presentation survived locally, while content tended to be updated.[82]

There was a long-standing tension here which pre-dated the Cultural Revolution years. Modern intellectuals, trained in Western traditions and intent on making China modern, had tended since the May Fourth era in the 1910s and 1920s to undervalue Chinese and folk forms. This was true in literature, where most twentieth-century Chinese writers had resolutely rejected old forms, adopted a new written language close to everyday speech, and assumed a modernist stance. Part of the Maoist literary and artistic enterprise after the Yan'an *Talks* in 1942 had been to rehabilitate and revalue folk and other forms.[83] Like the new-style Peking operas, music was an important part of this reassessment of the Western and of the search for a Chinese way to the modern.

There was apparently a fine line between innovation and surrender to Western music. As was the case with opera and other arts, key established authorities were targeted for criticism on the eve of the Cultural Revolution. One such target was Li Ling, a pioneering musicologist who had written extensively on the issue of national style in music. Li had become a leader of the Central Orchestra after 1949. Rather than being acknowledged in the vanguard of bridging the gap between Western classical music and Chinese musical traditions, Li Ling found himself in December 1964 denounced as an apologist for a musical imperialism.[84] Coming at a time when composers were putting a lot of effort into modernizing the Chinese musical heritage, at least in the stage art of opera, such criticisms reinforced caution in adapting too much or too obviously from Western experience.

We have already noted the innovations associated with the new-style opera music. But, the music historian Ju Qihong has argued, the privileging of model operas and ballets amounted to a negation of both international musical history since the composition in the nineteenth century of 'The Internationale' and of Chinese musical advancements since the May Fourth era in the early twentieth century. Making the model-opera music a model for other musical composition narrowed the scope for further innovation and undermined future effectiveness by valorising bombast and falsity.[85] In 1968, piano-accompanied aria singing from *The Red Lantern* marked a new stage in musical developments. The work featured arias sung by the three central characters in the opera: Li Yuhe, his daughter Li Tiemei, and Grandma Li. The use of the piano, an obviously Western instrument, to accompany modernized Peking opera singing was unexpected. But in these years, the piano was declared a 'revolutionary instrument'. This was in line with the Maoist thrust, seen in the Great Leap Forward in 1958 but having roots in Yan'an, that foreign and Western technologies should be put to Chinese purposes. The piano joined modern artillery, the blast furnace, and modern military organization in a century of useful borrowing made to serve China's quest for wealth and power.

Prominent in this effort to use the piano to popularize the music of the modernized operas was the Central Symphony's Yin Chengzong, himself an award-winning pianist and twenty-five years old at the start of the Cultural Revolution. He had studied at the Leningrad Conservatory between 1960 and 1963.[86] In the late 1960s, after Chairman Mao had met more than one million Red Guards assembled in central Beijing on several occasions, Yin came up with the idea of performing revolutionary songs on his piano in Tian'anmen Square.[87] His dream of a massed concert in the sacred heart of the capital proving impossible, Yin threw himself instead into transplanting the new-style music of the model operas into works for the piano. In this way, his instrument could be sinicized and put down real roots in China. The piano-accompanied version of *The Red Lantern*, with Yin at the keyboard, was filmed by the Central Newsreel and Documentary Film Studio in 1972.[88] The same feature had two other sections: the piano *Yellow River Concerto*, with Yin as soloist, and several arias with symphonic orchestral accompaniment from *Shajiabang*.

Piano adaptations became a major new musical genre in the later period of the Cultural Revolution. These included reworking of classical Chinese music with the foreign instrument. The piano version of the well-known *Moonlight on Second Spring* (*Er quan ying yue*) by Chu Wanghua was one of the better known of such adaptations. This work had first been composed in the 1930s by a blind itinerant *erhu* player named A Bing (1893–1950).[89] A similar classical number reworked for the piano was *Flute and Drum at Sunset* (*Xiyang xiaogu*). This piece, but for lute (*pipa*), had first been transcribed in 1875, although it had been performed since the eighteenth century. Almost 100 years after its first transcription, the piano version emerged from the pen of Li Yinghai in 1972.[90] The other main type of piano adaptation in the early 1970s took folk songs and more recently composed popular songs as their basis. Chu Wanghua wrote *The Red Star Sparkles Splendidly (Hongxing shanshan fang guangcai)* and *Little Sentinels of the Southern Seas (Nanhai xiao shaobing)*. Yin Chengzong himself composed *North Wind (Beifeng chui)*.[91] With works like this, the Cultural Revolution emphasis on the indigenization of modern art forms achieved considerable success in the musical field.

The *Yellow River Concerto* had been completed in December 1969 after ten months' work by Yin Chengzong, Chu Wanghua, and two other musicians, drawing on Xian Xinghai's 1939 *Yellow River Cantata*. Yin Chengzong had premiered the concerto on New Year's Day in 1970 and performed it again in May that year, coinciding with the annual commemoration of Mao's Yan'an *Talks*. Jiang Qing reportedly was so impressed at such a Chinese musical achievement in an international form that she arranged for it to be performed at the Guangzhou Trade Fair in April for the foreign visitors there.[92] The Central Symphony Orchestra (*Zhongyang yuetuan jiaoxiang yuedui*) at that premiere and in the filmed version was conducted by Li Delun, one of the most prominent Western-style musicians of the Cultural Revolution. Li Delun was trusted by his friend Jiang Qing to defend her interests at the orchestra. As one of the few new films made in 1972, the documentary received widespread distribution, taking the piano even to audiences who may never have seen the instrument before.[93]

In addition, other musical versions of the model operas and ballets were experimented with in these middle years of the Cultural Revolution, transforming Chinese music into distinctly Western classical musical formats. *Taking Tiger Mountain by Strategy* was transplanted into a 'revolutionary symphony' by the Shanghai Symphony starting in 1967, though it only had its official premiere in January 1974.[94] *On the Docks* took on a new life as a quintet for piano and strings and *The White-Haired Girl Suite (Baimaonü zuqu)* was written for string quartet. The quintet version of *On the Docks* reportedly strained acceptance, for it seemed to be either a piano accompaniment writ large or a symphonic version that had been shrunk down. But as a chamber work, in the hands of Yu Li'na and her string quartet, the work made a lasting contribution to the ongoing effort to sinicize modern classical music.[95]

The *Yellow River Concerto* was based on Xian Xinghai's 1939 cantata, which lent itself to the expressive means of the piano, unlike the model operas' scores. The cantata, after all, was written in the Western classical tradition in which the piano belonged. But the concerto version also reflected its times, with the somewhat awkward incorporation of *The East Is Red* into the third movement. This was to reinforce the notion, in the concerto as in the original cantata, of tracing the modern history of China through the music. The song that symbolized Chairman Mao had to be worked into the early 1970s concerto.[96] This incorporation of revolutionary songs was not new; it had become fashionable in the 1950s in Chinese classical music compositions.

In an unexpected gesture towards China's modern musical heritage, several public performances of Xian Xinghai's original *Yellow River Cantata* were presented in October 1975. The occasion was ostensibly to mark the thirtieth anniversary of the death of Xian Xinghai and a little over forty years since the death of Nie Er, the composer of what became the national anthem of the People's Republic. But the re-emergence in a Beijing concert hall of a work from 1939 was also an indication that more of the revolutionary past could be acknowledged.[97] Guang Weiran, who had written the lyrics for the cantata, was released from detention at age sixty-four to attend the Beijing concerts and bask in some of the glory. The performers came from several musical organizations in the capital: the central and film studio symphony orchestras, the central modern musical (*geju*) company, a song and dance company, a spoken drama company, a radio children's choir, and the musical academy of the Central May Seventh Art University.[98] The People's Music Press even published a commemorative version of the lyrics and score, with title-page calligraphy by the poet-politician Guo Moruo. A note from the press indicated that the lyrics were as performed in 1975 and had been 'corrected' (*zhengli*) from the 1939 version and a revision made by the writer. A second booklet from the same press also in October 1975 contained songs and music by Nie Er and Xian Xinghai. Eight of the ten Nie Er songs and two of Xian Xinghai's twelve had new lyrics from 1970, credited to 'collective revisions' (*jiti chongxin tianci*).[99] More pragmatic leaders and an older generation of intellectuals could be placated with gestures such as these concerts, while at the same time heritage works could be re-worked for contemporary purposes.

Meanwhile, new choral works were being created, following the late 1960s *Shajiabang* chorus, which had combined a variety of choral combinations (solos, repetitions, male, female, and mixed parts) in reworking the model opera. One of the more notable of the new works in the early 1970s was *Mountain Lilies Are Blooming Bright Red* (*Shandandan kaihua hongyanyan*). As the repetition in the Chinese title suggests, this was based on folk songs and music from northern Shaanxi. A child's chorus sang another Cultural Revolution success, 'The Red Star Song' (*Hongxing ge*) from the 1974 film *Sparkling Red Star*. The musical adaptations of the poems of Mao Zedong, including those for two new poems published in January 1976, also relied frequently on massed choral performance.[100]

By this time, China's stages and airwaves were full of new popular songs that replaced the turgid late-1960s concentration on Mao Zedong and his sayings. Writers of the new songs still had to be careful, however. A 1978 account cites examples of Gang of Four sensitivities that seem laughable: *The People of the Mountains Welcome the Liberation Army* (*Shanqu renmin huanying Jiefangjun*) reportedly provoked the question: 'Does this mean the people of the plain don't welcome them?'[101] Other songs managed to find their audiences. Such gems as the children's song, 'I love Tian'anmen in Beijing' (*Wo ai Beijing Tian'anmen*), was allegedly composed in 1970 by Jin Yueling (then aged eleven), with words by Jin Guolin.[102] When new feature films emerged in 1973, another vehicle for the popularization of such songs became available. Part of the success of films such as *Sparkling Red Star* was owed to the well-crafted children's songs given pride of place in the film. While lyrically, the new songs were hardly fresh, they represented innovation in their broader subject matter and from a musical standpoint.[103] 'The Proletarian Cultural Revolution Is Really Good' (*Wuchanjieji wenhua dageming jiu shi hao*) was composed around this time and remembered long after for its rollicking tune and repetition of the last phrase (*jiu shi hao*: really good). Dissemination of these new songs was enhanced by publication in annual issues of *New Songs from the Battlefields* (*Zhandi xinge*) after 1972 and by the revival of provincial and local literary magazines in 1972–1973. The latter always included poems identified as 'songs' (*ge*), some of which were also accompanied by a musical score. Enterprising composers could set those poems not supplied with a score to music. The first new issue in 1973 of *Yunnan Literature and Art*, for example, included seven 'songs', each identified as belonging to a particular ethnic minority from that culturally diverse province.[104]

The genuine popularity of a well-written song, and time and collective occasions to sing such works, gave rise to an important cultural activity for the millions of 'sent-down youth'. By the early 1970s, songs composed and popularized by such young people in Inner Mongolia, the northeast and elsewhere were in circulation, either in the newly revived local literary magazines or in unofficial forms, copied by hand. Sent-down youth were a reservoir of amateur compositional talent, but also (as we shall see in the next chapter) a pool of disaffection. Like poems, hand-copied fiction, and even fine art, underground songs were conveyed along unofficial channels and were a welcome outlet for scepticism about their own and their nation's condition. Old favourites from before 1966 never lost their popularity: Young people in the anonymity of darkness were wont to enjoy group singing of songs such as 'Moscow Nights'.[105]

The Cultural Revolution focus on the model performances and subsequent denunciations should not obscure a great many developments in music as in other arts. Productivity was much reduced from the norm before 1966 and what was written, unless underground, was severely restricted in range of subject matter and style. But serious or elite music of all sorts in the Western tradition continued to be written, performed and listened to, and even enjoyed. A listing of compositions produced in Shanghai in the period notes that most were either adaptations and revisions of earlier works and were written in the 1970s, as the emphasis on the eight model performances weakened.[106] The new songs included Chen Mingzhi's 1975 four-part male voice *Fishing Song* (*Yuge*), with lyrics by Yu Huiyong, then head of the Cultural Revolution culture group in Beijing. Instrumental compositions included a piano suite *Four Shaanxi Folk Songs* (*Shaanxi minge sishou*) by Wang Jianzhong in 1972 and Chen Mingzhi's 1975 *Eleven Polyphonous Pieces* (*Fudiao xiaopin shiyi shou*). Violin works included Chen Gang's Concertos in G major (1973) and in D major (1975). Note the absence of programmatic titles in these works. A Kejian composed in 1972 a version for violin of the song *Flowers Bloom on the Thousand-year-old Iron Tree* (*Qiannian tieshu kai le hua*). This listing of Shanghai compositions also includes various instrumental and symphonic versions of music from the dances *Little Sisters of the Grassland*, *The Red Detachment of Women*, and from the operas *Taking Tiger Mountain by Strategy* and *On the Docks*. The latter, a piano quintet, was a 1975–1976 work by a group headed by Yu Huiyong. Qu Wei's 1974 symphonic suite *The White-Haired Girl* was performed by the Shanghai Symphony on its tours of Japan, Australia, and New Zealand in 1975.[107] As Richard Kraus notes, this revival of Western music in the 1970s was a way out of rural exile for many young Chinese musicians and marked an unprecedented high point in Western instrumental music in China.[108]

Musical education was essential for the Cultural Revolution insurgents to shape a new corps of specialists in their service. In the 1970s the Central May Seventh Arts University in Beijing included a music academy (*yinyue xueyuan*), along with departments teaching filmmaking, opera, and other specialties. In Shanghai the 'May Seventh Music Training Course' (*Wu-qi yinyue xunlian ban*) was the equivalent training centre, though it appears to have been formed on the basis of the old Shanghai Conservatory.

The approach of these schools, at least in rhetoric, was 'enter, manage, and reform' (*shang, guan, gai*), meaning that the worker-peasant-soldier student recruits would attend the schools, take responsibility for their running, and use Mao Zedong Thought to reform the institutions. Reportedly, the students assigned to study the piano were recommended by villagers and factories and lacked any background in the instrument. There were those enthusiasts who rejected traditional (meaning Western) training methods. The emphasis on piano versions of revolutionary songs and model-opera arias, later critics argued, produced as narrow a repertoire as any pre–Cultural Revolution syllabus that centred on the European classics.[109]

One strong theme in the post-1976 denunciations of the Gang of Four was their alleged scorn for China's indigenous musical heritage. A 1978 article in *People's Music* cites a variety of quotations, without source, from the cultural insurgents labelling traditional music as 'low class', 'unhealthy', 'unable to express the spirit of the age', and 'decadent sounds' (*mimi zhi yin*). An elderly performer of a traditional Chinese rap (*shuochang*, talking and singing), Han Qixiang had performed for Mao Zedong in Yan'an. But the Cultural Revolution insurgents reportedly wanted him labelled a 'three-anti element' (*sanfan fenzi*: against Party, socialism, and Mao Zedong Thought). When told he was a 'capitalist roader', Han snorted: 'I am blind. I can't walk down a road. How can I be a capitalist roader?' Yu Huiyong, composer of Western-style music and cultural commissar, supposedly wanted Han Qixiang to learn new tricks to 'reform' his art: singing with Western vocal technique and accompanied by a pianist.[110]

Chinese-style music, like Chinese opera before the reforms after 1949, was the domain of master–student transmission of skills and repertoire. Its customary subject matter was the private and emotional: Bombast and rallying listeners were usually foreign modes. In practical terms, traditional music was generally not suited for performance in concert halls and at other large-scale gatherings. Nonetheless, efforts to continue the work of adapting and modernizing traditional and folk music to the new social and political circumstances continued during the Cultural Revolution. As in other areas of performing arts, the 1970s saw a restoration of activities. In the field of traditional instrumental ensemble music, for example, there were some significant developments. In 1975 the Shandong cultural authorities established an 'instrumental composition group', combining, as was the then practice, amateur and specialist musicians. The group published a book of newly written instrumental scores. A 1973 collection published in Tianjin, *Dazhai's Red Flowers Bloom Everywhere* (*Dazhai honghua biandi kai*), was a re-working of Shanxi folk tunes to support the campaign to popularize the Shanxi production brigade as a model for agriculture. Fisher-folk songs, in northern and southern styles, provided material for named individual composers to rework for ensemble playing. And the model operas, of course, were transplanted into this musical form. Peng Xiuwen wrote his popular *Tumultuous Clouds Fly* (*Luan yun fei*) drawing on the music of *Azalea Mountain*. Some Chinese-style instrumental works were rather more politicized, including pieces titled after slogans (*Grasp revolution, promote production*; *Zhua geming, cu shengchan*) or those that were burdened with direct political content, such as *Rainy Night House Call* (*Yuye chuzhen*), on barefoot doctors.[111]

The individual experiences of eminent musicians, such as conductors, are one way to map the destruction and growth in these years. Li Guoquan, for example, had conducted the ballet version of *The Red Detachment of Women* and been the conductor of *The East Is Red* in 1964. He died in August 1966 at the age of fifty-two, under pressure of political criticism.[112] Shanghai conductor Huang Yijun re-emerged in public in 1972 to conduct a concert on National Day. He had spent some of the time before then working on a symphonic adaptation of a famous folk instrumental piece, *The River* (*Jianghe shui*).[113] Experienced artists were relied on in key Cultural Revolution projects. Chen Chuanxi, conductor of the Shanghai Film Studio orchestra, re-emerged in 1972 to direct work on the score of a documentary film being made for submission to the United Nations, although he had been subjected to Red Guard harassment a half decade earlier.[114]

Li Delun, one of China's most prominent musical figures, went from 'black gang troupe' label wearer to leading Cultural Revolution musician in the space of about a year in 1966–1967, allegedly after Jiang Qing endorsed his work on the symphonic version of *Shajiabang*.[115] In 1974 a planned Chinese martial arts tour of the United States required help from Qin Pengzhang, former conductor of the Central National Music Orchestra, in preparing a musical accompaniment for the displays. The Shanghai orchestra's late 1975 tour to Australia, New Zealand, and Hong Kong included a Chinese music section: Qin worked on training preparations for that also.[116] Folk-inspired music was a field less vulnerable to accusations of 'bourgeois' or Western contamination.

Past connections with the Communist Party leadership could also help in these years. Yan Liangkun was targeted as a 'bad element' at the start of the Cultural Revolution. But in 1972 he returned to conduct at a soirée for Prince Sihanouk at the Great Hall of the People. There, the wife of Premier Zhou Enlai recognized him as a former member of the children's theatre group in wartime Chongqing. Three years later came the call to conduct the commemorative performances of the *Yellow River Cantata*.[117] A former child soldier in the Red Army during Yan'an days, Tang Jiang found fame in the Cultural Revolution as composer-conductor of a choral work, *The Long March Suite* (*Changzheng zuge*). He had written this in 1964, but was only able to perform it in 1975. Similar to the historical ambition of choral works like *The East Is Red*, the Long March work was distinguished by its experimental incorporation of local musical styles, including minority musics. The song marking the Zunyi Conference in Guangxi, for example, featured a distinct, nasal style of part-singing by two female soloists. Tang Jiang worked on a film version of the choral suite in the winter of 1975–1976.[118] Hu Defeng, army conductor chiefly at the August First Film Studio, was released in 1971 and returned to work the following year. He conducted the music for the 1974 film *Sparkling Red Star*.[119]

Younger specialists tended to do better than their older peers in securing work in the Cultural Revolution, as the cultural leadership had more confidence in their loyalty. Chen Xieyang graduated from the Shanghai Conservatory in 1965 at age twenty-six and was assigned to the Shanghai City Dance School (soon to be renamed the Shanghai Ballet Company). During the Cultural Revolution, he was kept busy conducting performances of the model ballets and other new dances.[120] Yuan Fang, thirty-three years old in 1966, found himself in demand to help direct musical performances by different, often rival Red Guard groups. In winter 1969, Yuan was assigned to the China Peking Opera Theatre to conduct *The Red Lantern*, a task for which his earlier training at an East Berlin conservatory had not prepared him. The attention given these model performances included assigning specialists to work solely on a single performance item. Two years later Yuan returned to his original orchestra at the Central Radio Station.[121] A relatively young, unestablished professional like Nie Zongming (born in 1930) was sent to work with Mongolian and Shaanxi musicians in efforts to indigenize and professionalize musical endeavours in those places.[122] The modern appropriation of ethnic-minority artistic motifs as a means of instant 'Chinese style' continued unabated during the Cultural Revolution, in music and dance in particular.

Music was a field in which several Cultural Revolution themes were played out. In contrast with modernizing Peking opera, music was an art in which the relative attention given Chinese traditions and modernity was more contestable and the outcomes less predictable. Western classical music had always been associated with middle-class aspirations in China. The folk and other traditions appealed to patriotic inclinations but needed modernizing. The association of the Cultural Revolution cultural leadership with classical music and modernity should not surprise. The whole thrust of the Cultural Revolution cultural project was to make China modern. The classical music tradition also appealed on another level. The self-image of Chinese modernizers, from the May Fourth era onwards, had been a Romantic, Promethean concept which struck a chord with traditional notions of Chinese intellectuals and their social leadership role. The music of the nineteenth-century classical period in Europe and their twentieth-century successors had distinct attraction for Chinese Prometheans and other convinced of their duties to save the nation. Jiang Qing saw herself on the mountaintops she liked to photograph, alone with her muse and ready to descend to raise China up to a modern culture equal to the Western cultural heritage. Western classical music, in its bombastic and saccharine Chinese reworking in the Cultural Revolution, provided the background music to this fantasy. As Liang Lun noted in dance, however, the effect of the inflated rhetoric of Cultural Revolution music took time to fade. But this should not obscure the considerable musical innovation, in both Western and Chinese music, of the period.

3. STAGING CULTURE: SPOKEN DRAMA, *QUYI*, AND OTHER PERFORMANCE FORMS

Chinese audiences had a somewhat tentative relationship with spoken drama, which was a relatively recent arrival in China: Plays without singing were a distinct novelty in twentieth-century China. But the potential of spoken plays to convey modern ideas about social and political reform was obvious. The prominent figures in the modern drama movement in the 1920s and 1930s included many underground supporters of the Chinese Communist Party. After 1949, these efforts, largely with the same dominant personalities, continued with official endorsement and subsidy. Every province, provincial-level autonomous region, and major city had a spoken-drama troupe (*huajutuan*). Chinese audiences were generally weak in their enthusiasm for the genre, for the writing could be wooden, the characters flat or stereotyped, and the drama forced and predictable. Of course, the same could be said for feature films from this period, although these latter could provide a gloss of authenticity in real locations and include a lot of action, unlike a play on a stage in a hall. Indeed, most of the better received plays of the 1949–1965 period reached audiences not in theatres, but in cinemas when they were adapted to the screen. Despite this lack of roots in Chinese soil, the flexibility and immediacy possible on a spoken-play stage meant that the genre acquired new attention during the Cultural Revolution.

In short the strongly propagandistic nature of spoken drama in China, that had been characteristic of the art from its earliest introduction, reached something of an apogee during the Cultural Revolution.[123] Official subsidy and local supervision also reached their zenith in these years. As happened with opera companies, most theatre companies were officially disbanded or re-organized in the late 1960s. Likewise, the degree of reactivation seen in film, opera, music, and other arts in the early 1970s also applied to spoken plays.

In the countdown to the start of the Cultural Revolution, two trends emerged in spoken drama. One was the writing and production of more plays on modern subjects, as was being pushed also on opera stages. The other was the criticism of established playwrights and their works, many of which had been adapted to film. Among the targets of official criticism by early 1966 were the plays of Tian Han, a veteran of the Shanghai theatre world of the 1930s who had helped invent Chinese spoken drama in those years. Yao Wenyuan's critical essay on Wu Han's historical opera *Hai Rui Dismissed from Office* was matched by an equally prominent essay by Yun Song, titled 'Tian Han's *Xie Yaohuan* is a great poisonous weed'.[124] Tian's spoken plays and operas were banned and whole pages of newspapers filled with denunciations of his work and his person.

But at the very start of the Cultural Revolution a rather different, and arguably more indigenous, form of drama monopolized China's stages. This was a hybrid form of spoken play created and performed by Red Guards. Like the Red Guards themselves (at least in their early activism), the drama created and presented by Red Guard theatre groups was a spontaneous development, from beginning to end outside the official cultural realm. The movement peaked in the summer of 1967, at a time when the 'model performances' had been proclaimed as the Cultural Revolution cannon but had not yet taken over all cultural activity.[125] The plays combined elements of spoken drama, dance, chorus singing, tableaux, and speech-making to present a message relevant to the current struggles. The content of the Red Guard dramas, however, mixed history and the foreign in unexpected ways.

Early performances drew heavily on 1964's *The East Is Red* song-and-dance drama and on similar paeans to the revolution created in the army in 1965–1966 and were not necessarily amateur shows. The Shanghai Modern Musical Theatre Rebels (*Shanghai gejuyuan zaofanpai*) created *The February Storm* (*Eryue fengbao*), a full-length song-and-dance drama about recent events in the city. The Shanghai Drama Academy and the

Shanghai People's Art Theatre joined forces to present a full-length historical song-and-dance drama, *The Red Lantern Shines* (*Hongdeng zhao*). In
Beijing, Red Guards from ten institutions created and performed *Chairman Mao's Red Guards* (*Mao zhuxi de Hongweibing*) in early August
1967.[126]

Despite the sloganeering titles, the stories told in these song and dance
epics could be drawn from real events, giving accounts of real Red Guards'
experiences. A drama presented by a Beijing middle school, for example, told of the abuse a young woman student had suffered at the hands
of a rival Red Guard faction. Some Red Guard groups received official
blessing: This middle-school drama was broadcast on Central Radio on 1
July 1967, the anniversary of the foundation of the Chinese Communist
Party, having been noticed by cultural officials. The song from the show,
'Our hearts and the Central Cultural Revolution [Group] are joined as
one' (*Women he Zhongyang Wen-ge xinlianxin*), received several playings
on the nation-wide radio station, a signal achievement. Most of these dramas recycled *The East Is Red*, rewriting the lyrics of the songs, although
some included newly composed songs.

Other Red Guard dramas borrowed more widely. In late May 1967,
rebel factions at the China Musical and Dance Theatre and the China
Youth Art Theatre joined forces to present *Rent Collection Courtyard*
(*Shouzu yuan*). This showed remarkable intertextuality, as the 'Rent Collection Courtyard' was a group of sculptures created in 1965 in Sichuan
to illustrate peasant suffering in the 'old society'. Red Guard newspapers
at the time acclaimed the stage version of the sculptural tableau's rejection
of old theatrical strictures and praised its 'national style' (*minzu fengge*),
a concept of consuming interest to Chinese artists since before 1949.[127]

Spoken drama from Red Guards was different from the regular plays
that had entertained relatively small numbers of Chinese before the Cultural Revolution. The Red Guard plays incorporated musical and dance
features and were more direct in presenting political ideas, preferring the
harangue to more subtle means. Naturalistic reflections of real life were
not the central concern of these dramas. A typical play was the one-act
Taking the Road of 1917 (*Zou yijiuyiqinian de lu*), created in the winter of 1967 by the Beijing Film Academy Jinggangshan Red Guards. The
date in the title alludes to the play's Russian protagonists, but the story
covers several generations, so that the grandson of the hero, after a visit
to China, can declare excitedly about his leader: 'He is in my heart. He is
Mao Zedong!'[128]

The Central Drama Academy, centre of professional training for
spoken-drama actors, directors, and others, was home to three rival Red

Guard drama troupes in 1967. They each produced professional-level plays that year, one presenting the so-called January storm in Shanghai in 1967 and another a drama showing the peoples of the Third World adoring Mao Zedong. The latter included scenes in Japan (against a backdrop of Mount Fuji), Gambia (with an American naval vessel in the background), the Soviet Union (in front of Lenin's tomb), and the United States. The notable works in the Red Guard repertoire in 1967 had identified authors, unlike the collective creation emphasis of the 'model performances'. Reportedly, performances at factories and to army units were well received, which encouraged further competition among the different Red Guard troupes.[129]

In Lenin's Hometown (*Zai Liening de guxiang*) premiered in January 1968. The story was set in 1966 in revisionist Moscow, where a Russian worker receives a copy of the 'Little Red Book' of quotations from Mao and, along with comrades from an underground party, is inspired by their truth. When Soviet leaders order the workers to print articles attacking China, some resist this task. Instead, they succeed in reprinting Mao's quotations. The professionalism and polish of the play's production were typical of the more important Red Guard plays.[130]

This kind of Red Guard drama had its origins in the 'worker-peasant-soldier' art of the eve of the Cultural Revolution and even earlier. In 1958 during the Great Leap Forward, 'news report plays' (*tongxun baodao ju*) had been widespread and delivered up to the minute messages. In similar vein were the 'mobile, costumed living newspaper skits' (*youxing huazhuang huobaoju*) of 1964–1965, during the Socialist Education Movement. At the same time 'loyalty plays' (*biao zhong ju*) featured quotations from Mao Zedong and his poems. The performances by amateur actors from the People's Liberation Army in 1965 had inspired student imitation. These included clapper recitation (*kuaishu*) and *sanjuban* (rapid-fire delivery of three and a half sentences by four performers). Professionals had also gotten in on the act. In 1965 and the first half of 1966 the Beijing People's Art Theatre, one of the nation's leading spoken-drama companies, had presented several such newly written plays. But the Red Guard dramas in 1966–1968 also had roots in the streets, through a process in which 'street propaganda' (*jietou xuanchuan*) slogan and chant recitation and skits became short sketches and then multi-scene stage plays.[131]

'Madman' of the New Age (*Xin shidai de 'kuangren'*) was a May 1967 creation of the Beijing People's Art Theatre Mao Zedong Thought Red Guards and Red Flag Red Guards. This short play incorporated dance and two-actor dialogue (*duikou ciyan*) in a declamatory drama. The title

referred significantly to Lu Xun's seminal May Fourth short story of 1918, 'The Diary of a Madman' (*Kuangren riji*), which denounced Confucianism's grip on Chinese minds by revealing the madman's wisdom. The Cultural Revolution play's madman, Hong Weimin, has written more than thirty letters since 1962 denouncing head of state Liu Shaoqi. He is confined in the 'Red Flag Insane Asylum', but with Red Guard help, Hong manages to get a letter to Chairman Mao. The Cultural Revolution Group agrees to meet him and supports his revolutionary actions. Five classical poems by Mao, seven of his quotations, and Red Guard propaganda team performances were worked into the play. Even the fledgling state television stations showed an interest in filming some of these plays, which produced what a 1990s researcher characterized as a kind of artificial folk culture.[132]

Professional troupes in relatively distant parts of the country were also active in 1967 in creating spoken plays. The May Ninth Revolutionary Rebel Troupe of the Guizhou Provincial Spoken Drama Troupe (*Guizhousheng huajutuan 'Wu-jiu' geming zaofantuan*) presented their new work in May 1967, during the annual commemoration of Mao's Yan'an *Talks*. The new play (or song-and-dance drama, *gewu ju*) was *Spring Thunder in the Southwest* (*Xi'nan de chunlei*), directed at exposing the established Party leadership in Guizhou. The mostly professional theatre creators of *Spring Thunder* had reportedly used an 'open-door creation' (*kaimen chuangzuo*) method, rather than leave things entirely in the hands of specialists. All together, more than 200 people, amateur and professional, from fourteen units, including schools, the military, Red Guard organizations, and performing arts groups, participated in the creation of the drama. The finished play incorporated performances by actual participants in the Cultural Revolution events covered in the work.[133]

By late summer 1968, the Red Guard tide was beginning to recede, including in the cultural realm. From late September, provinces and cities began establishing 'revolutionary committees', a model which was adopted at university, factory, and other work-unit levels. Regularization and discipline were watchwords; factional divisions were to end. The creative flourishing that had produced the Red Guard plays and performances began to dry up.[134] Dramas continued to be produced, but they were more polished, professional, and orthodox in supporting the general Cultural Revolution goals rather than particular local factional interests. In Taiyuan, the capital of Shanxi province, for example, Red Guards at the Taiyuan print works joined forces with the provincial and city spoken-drama theatres to present the seven-scene *The Serf's Halberd* (*Nongnu ji*) in 1968–1969.[135] We can note the irony in these plays of cultural insurgents relying on the professionals whom the newcomers had vigorously condemned as politically backwards. The historic Chinese aesthetic's emphasis on perfection and polish in performance seems to have predominated over strictly political concerns.

These Red Guard plays make two points about culture during the Cultural Revolution. First, the dramas served political purposes, in their content, style, and the process of their creation and presentation by different groups. Their politics was total, with consequences for any traces of art they may have contained. Second, despite this, the Red Guard performances, including the scale and relative professionalism of their creation and presentation, were a notable cultural phenomenon. They are one indication that 'eight hundred million people' were watching much more than 'eight performances', even when Cultural Revolution upheaval was at its most destructive. At the same time amateur stage productions were encouraged. Unlike most regular spoken drama, these could use local performance forms and even delight audiences with local dialect.[136] Items performed included simple *duikouci* (stylized dialogue exchanges between two or more performers) that had been popular among Red Guard performing troupes, and ballad songs. Sent-down youth after 1968 took their new versions of these forms to the countryside.[137]

A standard general history of Chinese drama, published in 1990, reflects a typical view of the Cultural Revolution. Having noted the effect of the army literature and art conference on cultural activities in early 1966 and the attacks on dramas (both operas and spoken plays), commentary thins markedly. Less than four lines describe events between 1966 and 1976, with destruction the only experience of performers, writers, and even audiences during those ten years.[138] But the Cultural Revolution experience in this field of cultural activity was as varied as in most others. The shallow roots that spoken plays had put down into Chinese soil over the previous half-century meant that the cultural insurgents paid less attention to the art than to musical theatre. But activities continued after 1966, as in the Red Guards' use of spoken performance in innovative ways.

The institutional representatives of spoken drama had mixed fortunes, though the personnel associated with theatre troupes were not all sent off to imprisonment or labour camp, as most brief overviews suggest. Some members continued to practise their craft in drama troupes run by the army or in reconstituted companies organized by local cultural authorities who drew on existing and new talent. By the mid-1970s, most provinces and major cities had a spoken-drama troupe.[139] The renowned Beijing People's Art Theatre by 1968 had stopped performing in its own name. But

some members of the company were redeployed under the banner of the
'Beijing Spoken-Drama Troupe' (*Beijing huajutuan*). In this capacity, they
performed mostly shorter works appropriate for the times and endorsed
by the army propaganda team that was in control of the troupe. These
dramas included a play about curing the deaf in an army hospital, titled
Flowers Bloom on a Thousand-year-old Iron Tree (*Qiannian de tieshu kai
le hua*), written by Liang Bingkun, who had joined the theatre company
at age eighteen in 1954. When Liang was called on at short notice to
stand in for a sick actor, he found learning the lines he had written not
difficult, apart from his fear of misquoting one of the passages from the
writings of Chairman Mao that studded the script. When the doctor whom
Liang played dares to experiment with acupuncture on himself, he was
to quote the opening paragraph of Mao's 1944 essay 'Serve the People'.
There were risks on stage even in short phrases associated with Mao. One
actress managed to reverse the subjects in each side of 'Vietnam must win,
American imperialism must fail', causing great political embarrassment
to the troupe. Likewise the expression 'ten thousand lives without limit'
applied to the chairman became, in the mouth of one nervous actor, 'ten
thousand limits without life'.[140]

But the Beijing People's Art Theatre's experience in the Cultural Revolution was not all laughs. Of the more than 200 members, between 70 and
80 were removed from the troupe and labelled as 'spies', 'historical anti-
revolutionaries', and 'three fames and three high personages' (*san ming
san gao*' referring to famous writers, directors, and actors and to high
salaries, royalties, and bonuses).[141] The worker propaganda team and
army propaganda team that were put in charge of the theatre organized
those personnel deemed of dubious background or attitude in mid-August
1968 to go to a May Seventh Cadre School. The average age of those sent
was fifty, and they were organized, military style, into three companies
(*lian*). According to the army propaganda team, the transfer to the state
farms had three purposes: remoulding (*gaizao*), remoulding, remoulding.
In addition to labouring in the fields, the troupe members also undertook
militia training while at the farms.[142]

Members of the Shanghai People's Art Theatre had a similar experience
in the late 1960s. The theatre, which had incorporated after 1960 (in a
post–Great Leap cost-cutting consolidation of troupes) a Shanghai Dialect
Drama Company (*fangyan huajutuan*), went through the standard process of replacement of the leadership by outside personnel who supervised
criticism and the reform through labour of the staff.[143] As at the film studios and other institutions, in September 1968 a Workers' Mao Zedong
Thought Propaganda Team and a Liberation Army Mao Zedong Thought

Propaganda Team moved into residence at the theatre. Those members of staff who had not been identified for inspection were considered 'revolutionary masses' (*geming qunzhong*). These latter were organized into four platoons (*pai*) and engaged in 'struggle and criticism' sessions. During three summers and three autumns, the entire theatre company visited communes in the Shanghai suburbs, as city dwellers since the 1950s had done to help with the harvest and gain the supposed ideological benefits of toiling alongside peasants. In 1968 the Shanghai spoken-theatre people lived at the Fengxian Tangwai commune, helping build the May Seventh Cadre School there for the use of the literary and art personnel of Shanghai city. The next year the entire theatre company went to live and work at the new cadre school.

The company must have returned to the city by mid-1970, for in August that year a first group of more than eighty staffers were assigned to factories around Shanghai to help in a 'battle the heat' (*zhan gaowen*) campaign. Summers in Shanghai can be debilitatingly hot, and, at a time when air-conditioning was virtually unknown, extra hands were required to assist in sustaining summertime production. In the cold of March 1973, a proportion of those who had gone to 'battle the heat' returned to the theatre. They included some dialect-play personnel. The return marked a renewed effort to 'seize revolution and promote literature and art' (*zhua geming, cu wenyi*).[144]

By the early 1970s, professional spoken-drama troupes were back in action on China's stages. In 1972, for example, the Beijing People's Art Theatre was performing what were called 'obedience plays' or 'loyalty dramas' (*zunling xi*). On one such occasion, Jiao Juyin, a long-serving leader of the company before the Cultural Revolution, was summoned to accompany Zhou Enlai to watch a performance. When asked what he thought of the show, Jiao could not restrain himself: 'Sixty percent for politics, no marks for art', he snorted, bringing the wrath of the cultural leadership on his head yet again.[145]

Local drama companies were also active. In spring 1970 the Qingdao Spoken Drama Troupe were rehearsing a stage version of the 1952 film, *Fighting North and South* (*Nanzheng beizhan*), one of the few pre-1966 films regularly screened during the Cultural Revolution. The eighteen-year-old actor Tang Guoqiang joined the company to play a minor character. That year the Jinan Military District advance guard song-and-dance ensemble (*qianwei wengongtuan*) considered recruiting young Tang, but rejected him. Tang hoped for more luck with the Nanjing Military District Front-line Spoken Drama Troupe, which came to Qingdao looking for soldiers for the artistic ranks. The young actor finally got his military break when he participated in the Qingdao company's performance of *Drama on the Wharves* (*Matou fengyun*) at the national spoken-drama festival held in Beijing in spring 1975. Spoken drama thus joined opera and other performing arts in having national and regional festivals in the mid-1970s to encourage emulation. Talent spotters from the army's August First Film Studio saw Tang Guoqiang's performance and approached him. In October Tang transferred from Shandong, the Qingdao troupe's leaders having finally agreed to let him go.[146]

New plays were mounted, on stage and elsewhere, including television, where regular colour broadcasts began in 1974. The following year Shanghai Television produced and broadcast two dramas, *Daughter of the Commune Party Secretary* (*Gongshe dangwei shuji de nü'er*) and *The Sacred Duty* (*Shensheng de zhize*). Both were stories of sent-down youth in the countryside, made at a time when the national media were full of positive stories of youthful achievement and dedication.[147] It was faster and cheaper to use television to parallel the newspaper and magazine emphasis on sent-down youth's positive experiences than to make feature films on the subject.

A series of drama conventions (*wenyi diaoyan*) were held in Shanghai and in Guangxi, Hunan, and Liaoning provinces in 1974–1975. In Tianjin audiences had been able to watch a number of spoken dramas by mid-1976. These included *Red Pine Fort* (*Hongsong bao*), *Spring in Dragon Bay* (*Longwan zhi chun*), and *In One's Prime* (*Fenghuazhengmao*), along with the modern musical (*geju*) *Sea-river Village* (*Hai he cun*). These four all had settings in the 1970s in the movement to learn from Dazhai. But many plays also managed to make reference to national political issues, such as the 1976 attack on 'capitalist roaders'.[148]

As was the case with a number of films, certain plays written and presented before the Cultural Revolution were performed during these years. One such drama was Chen Qitong's *Ten Thousand Rivers and a Thousand Mountains* (*Wanshui qianshan*), the lengthy and somewhat turgid paean to the Communist Party's Long March. It had been filmed in 1959 in wide-screen, full-colour as the August First film studio's contribution to the tenth anniversary of the People's Republic. The army studio was working on another, two-part version of the play, from a script by Chen Qitong, when the Cultural Revolution ended in October 1976. But already a year earlier, the stage play had been revived to commemorate the fortieth anniversary of the end of the Long March. Just as several films had been distributed and then remade in more lavish, colour versions during the Cultural Revolution, so this 1950s play was brought out of cold storage for theatre audiences perhaps not intoxicated at the thought of sitting through such an interminable drama. The play was even transplanted into Peking-opera form by the Tianjin City Third Peking Opera Troupe.[149]

Spoken drama, a form of performing art without much history and few roots in China, took a minor role in culture in the Cultural Revolution. But an examination of what actually was presented to Chinese audiences during those ten years shows that spoken drama played its part in presenting the politics of the era to an extent seldom acknowledged in accounts of the Cultural Revolution. The concentration on modernizing sung drama in these years and access to feature films, however, meant spoken drama was a somewhat unloved, orphan form.

The same was not true of *quyi* (narrative performances with music), *pingtan* (story-telling and ballad singing in Suzhou dialect), and other forms associated with particular regions and languages. These had deep roots in society, in the manner of local opera. As with opera, the cultural authorities after 1949 had attempted to further reform, modernize, and control such arts. In the first part of the Cultural Revolution, Red Guards had drawn upon these small-scale performing traditions in their own productions, though their determination to smash the 'four olds' would not allow acknowledgement of this inspiration. By the mid-1970s, these kinds of arts became regular features of holiday performances.[150] Clearly, they were more popular than some of the less-familiar stage arts. Scenes from the model operas were among the first to be transplanted into *quyi* forms, for this model content was already highly sanctioned.[151] As with opera, conventions of specialists and newcomers exchanging experiences provided a vehicle for promoting stage variety. In Tianjin, for example, where Jiang Qing's command of performing arts organizations was strong, training classes were conducted and conventions held for professional and amateur variety performers in the early 1970s.[152] In 1975 the Tianjin *Quyi* Troupe reportedly adapted an episode from the eighteenth-century novel *The Dream of the Red Chamber* (*Honglou meng*), a surprising Cultural Revolution choice, into *dagushu* (drum-ballad story-telling) on the instructions of Jiang Qing.[153] Another much-loved northern form, *kuaibanshu* (clapper story-telling) was also revived by professionals. Radio broadcasts took this *quyi* story-telling, with new content, across the nation.[154]

Shanghai's *quyi* traditions were also turned to Cultural Revolution purposes. Several lengthy *pingtan* performances were created, including retelling some of the model-opera stories in this beloved form.[155] Straight story-telling (*gushihui*), without a musical element, by skilled narrators of new and historical novels had been popular on radio and in live presentation before 1966. It continued throughout the Cultural Revolution, as production was relatively easy. In the summer and fall of 1969, several workshops on story-telling were held in Shanghai. Again, the model operas featured prominently in the new repertoire from 1970 onwards.[156] Comic dialogues (*xiangsheng*) had always been popular since 1949, but, as vehicles for gentle satire, they were vulnerable in 1966. Some famous performers were targeted for criticism, but the same Red Guards who led the attacks made use of the art for their own propaganda. By the 1970s comic dialogues were again on stage, poking fun at stereotypical bureaucrats or backsliders, using the same format of funny man and straight man, with the same confusions, double-takes, plays on words, and comic timing to highly amusing effect.[157]

Other, highly specialist artists also continued to entertain during these years. The Shanghai Puppet Theatre, for example, produced 'Little Eighth Route Army Soldier' (*Xiao Balu*) in 1968 and renovated its building three times, in 1971, 1973 and 1975, to accommodate new performances and eager young audiences. They adapted the children's film *Sparkling Red Star* into a puppet show soon after its 1974 release.[158] Acrobats also remained active, participating in a six-troupe gathering in Beijing in 1972, for example.[159] But the emphasis on the mass and the amateur in massed singing (*qunzhong geyong*) was of more central Cultural Revolution appeal. Even Yao Wenyuan praised its usefulness in 1973, as new songs were created. On 23 May 1976 to mark the anniversary of Mao's Yan'an *Talks*, 18,000 Shanghai choristers sang about the 'Rightist deviationist wind to reverse the correct verdicts'.[160] It sounded better set to music.

4. VISUALIZING THE MODERN: FINE ARTS AND ARCHITECTURE

The fine arts in twentieth-century China shared with music and dance the twin concerns of remodelling tradition and creating a modern culture that absorbed Western traditions and made them more Chinese. In the visual arts, these intertwined themes were perhaps most obvious, so the attempted solutions were most subject to criticism, from political authorities, art specialists, and the public at whom the art was directed. A glance at the typical statuary or poster-style figure paintings from the Cultural Revolution suggests there was little substance and much rhetorical cliché in the works. But a careful analysis of the more significant artworks from the period reveals the ways in which these ten years continued the debates and efforts at answers that had obsessed Chinese artists throughout the twentieth century, including after 1949.[161] These obsessions included what to do about ancient Chinese and classical Western art. In November 1966, at a meeting with Red Guards from the Central Academy of Art (*Zhongyang meishu xueyuan*), Jiang Qing is quoted as saying:[162]

> Some people always take some ancient and some foreign works (including famous classic works from the nineteenth century) as their models (*jingdian*), but that's no good. Those feudal and bourgeois things cannot serve the Chinese revolution. But we cannot use a nihilist attitude: we should use critical eyes to assimilate (*xishou*) those things.

Several secondary themes also show up in the visual culture, including fine arts, of the Cultural Revolution. The influence of the model performances, both the heroes of the works and the approach to art exemplified by their creation, can be seen in this field. The paradoxical success of the model operas and ballets that ensured their ultimate failure as efforts at modernity also plagued some key art works from these years. The emphasis on the amateur was another theme that the visual arts shared with other cultural activities, as the specialist professional came under criticism. The broadening of the repertoire apparent in the performing arts, including film in the early 1970s, can also be traced in fine arts and architecture. As in literature and in the performing arts, on a smaller scale, as well as in painting and other visual arts, underground or unofficial experimentation helped lay the groundwork for apparently considerable changes in the following decade.

In these ten years, the most common artistic images available in China featured one man, Mao Zedong. His face, usually in bas-relief profile, appeared in hundreds of permutations on the Mao badges that were the mark of Red Guards. Such badges had not been usual in the seventeen years before the Cultural Revolution. Indeed, Mao's appearance in paintings and sculpture had been confined to one narrow genre in fine arts, the political or historical event commemoration. Episodes in the rise of the Communist Party and the revolution led by Mao were immortalized in the kinds of oil paintings that eulogized the achievements of Lenin and Stalin in the Soviet Union. But such art was only a small proportion of the range of fine art activity in the years after 1949.

By 1967, Mao was on most young chests, often in multiple versions on the same jacket or shirt. The Mao badges, produced locally by or for army units, workplaces, universities, and other organizations, identified membership of a particular unit, group, or faction. As Red Guards and others took advantage of the breakdown in regular order and travelled widely to sites associated with the revolution or simply to interesting places, a Mao badge was the ideal souvenir. They even became a kind of currency for many young people, traded among friends, swapped with visitors from afar, and prized for occasional rarity.[163]

Artists uncertain of the parameters that applied at the start of the Cultural Revolution saw the use of Mao images as a relatively safe bet. Some of the most accomplished painters and sculptors turned to refining the visual representation of the chairman, carefully recycling and making more noble images of him that derived from Yan'an days. Others took the risk of producing narrative paintings of Mao at key episodes in the civil wars, the war against Japan, and, less often, in the 1950s.[164] The latter included renditions of Mao's visits to communes, factories, and army units. These paintings, always in oils, were often based on contemporary news photographs. The artists added rhetorical context, often with an appropriate 'chorus' of adoring citizens. In this respect, the model-opera theory of the 'three prominences' can be mapped in many paintings, with a concentric attention from the general public and chosen representatives of the 'revolutionary masses' to the leader himself. The second ring of prominence not infrequently featured worker, peasant, and soldier young people, presented as revolutionary successors particularly attentive to Mao's message.[165]

One of the most famous of the Mao images from these years appeared in the late 1960s, as fine arts activities resumed momentum along with other cultural realms. The painting of the youthful Mao Zedong on his way in 1921 to visit the miners of Anyuan in northwest Jiangxi was exhibited with considerable fanfare in October 1967. It was by Liu Chunhua, a twenty-three-year-old student of the Central Academy of Arts and Crafts, though collective input into its creation makes this attribution a little misleading. Unusually, Mao is alone, striding forward in a landscape positioned in relation to him somewhat like that of the landscape in relation to the Mona Lisa, distant, generalized, and at the base and background of the central figure. In oil, the landscape is rendered in a Western fashion rather than in the manner of traditional Chinese (watercolour) painting. Mao is clad in a long scholar's gown, which allows the artist scope to show his skills with the light and shade of drapery. He carries a furled wax-paper umbrella and has a clenched fist, a sign of his determination to bring Marxist truth to the oppressed miners. This historical episode was a contentious one, for the now-deposed head of state Liu Shaoqi had also visited the striking miners. Visually placing Mao in the mine workers' history was a way of 'correcting' the alleged falsity of Liu's support to the strikers. The painting was given widespread distribution in 1968, including being incorporated into Mao badges and a portrait bust.[166]

Liu Chunhua's painting was among those widely reproduced in a range of media. These included woven silk versions of the standard Mao portrait, itself standardized further with great care at the highest levels of state in these years. The silk portraits eventually included reproductions of news photographs: Mao after his 1966 swim in the Yangzi River, Mao and Zhu De welcoming Zhou Enlai back to China at Beijing airport, Mao playing table tennis. As this latter suggests, some of the silk tapestries were highly domesticated, even intimate portraits of the highest leader.[167] These representations of the chairman contrasted with the standard, usually oil paint, versions, which increasingly showed him towering over the landscape, in a more god-like position than Liu Chunhua's Anyuan icon.[168]

Large statues of Mao Zedong began to be erected at the start of the Cultural Revolution. The first of these were set up at Tsinghua University, an insurgent centre in Beijing, on 4 May 1967, as a sign of loyalty to the chairman. Concern was expressed soon after at the highest levels of government that such statues be of appropriate quality, but by the early 1970s, most large state offices, universities, and some other major public buildings were graced with giant statues of Mao in front of them.[169] He was often portrayed with his right arm outstretched in greeting or benediction. The overcoat that in general clad the figure allowed the sculptors scope with drapery of more interest than a simply giant pair of trousers. As with religious iconography, including China's long history of Buddhist sculpture, these statues were presented to tell stories. The one outside the Shaoshan railway station in Mao's home village in Hunan, for example, was raised on a plinth so that its height could make reference to Mao's birthday.[170] These ubiquitous statues graced Chinese cities at the same time as red billboards at key intersections carried quotations from the chairman or key political slogans in large white characters, and major buildings in many provincial centres and Beijing raised large rooftop 'Long live Chairman Mao' (Mao zhuxi wansui) signs in neon lights.

One suite of statues, given considerable attention in the late 1960s and 1970s, had first been created in mid-1965. This was 'The Rent Collection Courtyard' (Shouzu yuan), a 118-meter-long set of 114 human figures set up in a former landlord's house in Dayi County, Sichuan. Made for class-education purposes to narrate a story of oppression and resistance, the statues were a location piece designed for the specific circumstances of the mansion. Peasants of all ages are shown being exploited, humiliated, and physically abused by the landlord, his family, concubines, and officers. The peasants hand in their meagre harvest as rent and taxes. Resistance is not a strong element: There are only clenched fists and noble chests gazing into a (presumably liberated) future. There is no representation of peasant or underground Communist organization. The group of statues was the work of teachers and students at the Sichuan Academy of Fine Arts in Chengdu. While the individual statues were in the socialist realist, public-hero mould, the idea of a whole suite of statues in one place narrating a story was a new concept. Sichuan citizens were organized to visit the statues, meet with the local peasants, and hear their tearful, somewhat mechanical recollections of the 'old society'.[171] Photographs and a documentary film took *The Rent Collection Courtyard* to audiences across China. In October 1966, for example, Tianjin cinemas were showing the documentary as part of National Day commemorations. Copies of the original exhibition in Dayi county were created and set up for class-education purposes in Beijing and other cities across China.[172] A similar clay sculptural ensemble, modelled on the Sichuan original but telling the story of serf resistance in Tibet, had been created by late 1975.[173]

As was the case with the model operas, a good idea by specialists before the Cultural Revolution tended to lose its impact through dogged repetition. The style of the statues, however, was copied widely by other sculptors, though with a greater emphasis on political action and revolution. The centre of Shenyang city, capital of Liaoning in the northeast, for example, was graced after 1970 by a massive statue of Mao Zedong with arm upraised, supported by a gigantic prow-shaped set of statues of workers, peasants, and soldiers thrusting forward.[174] At the same time, a more romantic, softer kind of statuary, often situated in public parks or at important natural sites in a long Chinese tradition of marking the landscape with stone calligraphy or carving, was no longer possible, except produced privately.

Chinese painters since at least the mid-nineteenth century had been responding to Western art in a range of ways. Traditional landscape painting, done with ink and watercolours, had developed in different directions from Western art. To Chinese eyes, Western painting was in oils, seemed alien, and was associated with the modern. Many Chinese painters felt challenged by this other tradition and sought to counter it by elaborating new ways with landscapes, ink, and watercolour. In effect these were moves to modernize China's painting heritage. In addition, with the rise of revolution and the triumph of the Communist Party, landscape painting was obliged to confront another challenge, the politicization of landscape representation. One standard response, particularly after 1949 and continuing into the twenty-first century, was to simply add a few red flags flying in a more or less conventional landscape. More subtle moves included painting power pylons, laden river barges, smoke stacks, newly created irrigation canals, and other evidence of socialist construction in the midst of the usual imagined mountains, mist, trees, and water.

But these kinds of superficial adjustments to political circumstances could bring criticism that they were but token gestures by the politically unreformed. Indeed, the mere act of painting in the old, landscape genre could occasion challenge from the more activist cultural revolutionaries. By 1968 the Central Academy of Art in Beijing, the Zhejiang Academy of Arts (*Zhejiang meishu xueyuan*), and other tertiary educational institutes had been purged of many older teachers and were continuing a somewhat tentative existence as production centres for art best described as propaganda. Students and some staff, particularly younger, less-established teachers, formed Red Guard groups in 1966–1968, producing agitprop art for use in newspapers and broadsheets, as well as more considered works.[175] Much of this painting was in oil, as a modern, international medium. The old, Chinese landscape-painting heritage was undervalued and even denounced in these years. Historical portraits, done in a somewhat romantic modernized Chinese style in watercolour, were the specialty of Cheng Shifa. His obvious error, in the eyes of Red Guard critics in mid-1967, was to have painted several portraits of the Ming dynasty official Hai Rui. Cheng suffered the same sort of attack as had Wu Han for his historical drama about Hai Rui.[176]

The poster or propaganda painting of the Cultural Revolution took considerable inspiration from the operas and ballets of the 'model performances'. Fine art thus joined film, music, and dance in modelling the characters and styles of the *yangbanxi*. Actual portraits of Yang Zirong, Li Tiemei and others, in action or as stationary tableau, were rendered into oil paintings and widely disseminated. Some paintings featured the modern-opera characters in the imaginations of young students and others, just as the heroic soldier martyr Lei Feng had appeared in similar paintings in the early 1960s and continued to do so after 1966. In a widely used poster with the slogan 'I want to be that sort of person' (*Zuoren yao zuo zheyang de ren*), a young female militia member, Mao badge on left breast and holding a rifle and copy of Mao's collected works, gazes into the distance. In a parallel pose above her, Li Tiemei, heroine of the model opera *The Red Lantern*, holds high the lamp her father had left her.[177] The opera characters were joined by standardized representations of workers, peasants, and soldiers. Workers almost always appeared with the accoutrements of work: overalls, a wicker safety helmet, a tool of some sort in hand or nearby if the hand clutched a political tract. A small white towel knotted at the neck, to absorb the sweat generated by hard work, was a standard trope. Likewise, peasants, at least in the north, were pictured with towels knotted at the back of the head, a hoe or wheat-cutting blade close at hand. Soldiers, like their counterparts from farm and factory, were invariably of uniformly rugged good looks. They were ever vigilant at the frontier or warmly cooperating with delighted peasants.[178] Young women also achieved unprecedented prominence in the pictorial art of the Cultural Revolution, often doing unconventional work more usually associated with men, such as power-line maintenance or mining. All these fine figures were not individuals but symbols of political appropriateness. It was as if they were the ordinary equivalents of Mao Zedong portraits, ubiquitous and in reality, drained of much meaning through excessive repetition.

One exception to this standardization of imagery, that itself became standardized, came to public attention in 1973. The peasant paintings from Hu county in southern Shaanxi province were most welcome in a sea of oil-painted, eager heroes. One reason for the attention given the Hu county peasant painters, along with some similar groups in other parts of the nation, was their status as amateurs. In the early 1970s, as fine arts and other cultural institutions and activities were being revived and reconstituted, the cultural leadership saw a danger of the pre–Cultural Revolution authorities in their various fields reasserting themselves and the professionalism they represented. Amateur artists, inspired by real life among ordinary people, were an alternative vision to the academy. They represented a supposed empowering of the 'broad masses' and a releasing of natural creative talents, in deliberate contrast to the elitism and alienation seen as inherent in trained professionals. The peasant artists were not alone in being made use of in this on-going tension between the 'red' (*hong*: politically correct) and 'expert' (*zhuan*: professionally competent).[179]

But this celebration of peasant painting was not an unblemished or naive throwback to valorizing folk ways. Rather than a rejection of the modern, the Hu county painters and their works can best be understood as offering a Chinese route to modernity in art. Drawing on the customary repetition of patterns, seen in more everyday folk art such as paper-cuts and painted papier-mâché or sewn and stuffed animal toys, the painters created large-scale works that went well beyond folk art in their ambition and aesthetics. Two of the most widely reproduced works illustrate the newness of the paintings. One shows a huge net filled with a bounty of fish. The repetitive shape of each fish, individually painted with a peasant's eye for detail and realism, and the curved line of men and women hauling on the corners of the net set up a dynamic pattern of action across the canvas that a professional artist would be proud to achieve. Another painting of women crouched in a field weeding includes a striking effect of mist or drizzle, so that parts of the painting are largely blank. Folk art in most cultures does not use empty space like this, but fills it from edge to edge. The use of blank areas is fully attuned to mainstream Chinese painting traditions, whether explained with standard reference to Daoist and Buddhist aesthetics or not. All the Hu county paintings are attributed to individual, named artists, sometimes working in pairs or as a trio. Some would argue that true folk art is anonymous, though the rise of the 'living national treasure' folk artist in Japan, South Korea, and elsewhere has undermined that notion.

These modern features of the supposedly folk paintings encouraged suspicion at the time abroad and later in China that the Hu county artists had received help and training from professionals.[180] By 1972, recognizing the potential of these paintings to make a point about the amateur and non-specialist artist, Beijing had sent professional art teachers to Hu County, though they were charged with preserving the peasant or folk qualities of the art above all.[181] In 1974 students from the Art Department of the Central May Seventh Arts University went to the county as part of 'open-door schooling' (*kaimen banxue*).[182] Indeed one heavily publicized Hu county painting has little to link it with the agricultural scenes of the fisher folk and weeders (Figure 4.3). *The Old Party Secretary*, painted by Liu Zhide and first exhibited in 1973, is distinguished from the rest of the Hu county school by being an individual portrait. Liu described how he had experimented with placement of a group of fellow peasants in the background. But their presence suggested that the cadre was distancing himself inappropriately from his comrades, so they vanished from the painting. The emphasis on the collective, seen in the fishing and weeding paintings, is absent visually, though the implication is that the old man is resting after engaging in such activity and his reading of a political document is part of his work for the commune. Overall, 'The Old Party Secretary' is difficult to distinguish from similar works from academically trained artists in the early 1970s, including those returning to their paints after May Seventh Cadre School or other reform and those freshly trained amateur painters, newly produced from the re-opened art schools.[183]

By the time the Hu County painters came to national attention, regular art exhibitions and training of new artists were being restored. After 1970 the Zhejiang Academy of Arts had reopened, and the art department of the Central May Seventh Art University was in operation at the downtown Beijing site of the former Central Academy of Arts.[184] Many of the established artists who had been denounced, imprisoned, and sent away

4.3. Model peasant art gallery visitors admire *The Old Party Secretary: Models* (*Bangyang*) by Chen Guoying in Wang Mingxian and Yan Shanchun, *Xin Zhongguo meishu tushi, 1966–1976* (Illustrated history of New China's fine art), Beijing: Zhongguo qingnian chubanshe, 2000, p. 110.

to labour had returned to professional work, often being used to assist less experienced, even amateur artists to produce the works to match the latters' political ambitions.[185] This coincided with the revival of activity in a range of fields, including the performing arts, film, and magazine and book publication. The latter provided ready outlets for illustrations created according to the new aesthetic, with its focus on heroic worker, peasant, and soldier figures. The woodblock print, associated with left-wing art activities in the 1930s encouraged by the eminent writer Lu Xun and inspired by German models of political radicalism, had something of a revival with the restoration of literary periodicals. This paralleled the earlier prominence of woodblock illustration, in self-conscious imitation of the 1930s and Yan'an art traditions and for practical reasons of ease of reproduction, in Red Guard publications in 1966–1968.[186] The related illustrative art of picture stories (*lianhuanhua*) remained in consistent production during the ten years of the Cultural Revolution. As Julia F. Andrews notes, this genre was perhaps the most successful fine art after 1949 in combining artistic innovation, popular appeal, and political requirements.[187] Throughout the Cultural Revolution perhaps the most artistically satisfying art available in China came in book illustrations and comic-book retellings of fiction and films.

In Beijing in 1972, the first official, public fine art exhibition since 1966 was mounted in the China Art Gallery to commemorate the thirtieth anniversary of Mao's Yan'an *Talks*. Works from across the nation were exhibited for a full two months. At the same time, the 'Beijing City Worker-Peasant-Soldier Art and Photography Exhibition' opened. It included 330 artworks and 180 photographs.[188] Such large-scale exhibitions of new work in the most prestigious exhibition space in China sent a powerful message about the revival of art activity, of course, along new lines. In the autumn of the following year, a customary time in the past for new art exhibitions after the heat of summer, two major shows opened in the capital: one of picture-story paintings (*lianhuanhua*) and Chinese painting (*Zhongguohua*), the other of works by Hu county peasants.[189] These exhibitions were organized by Gao Jingde, a young teacher of oil painting at the Zhejiang academy, who was given considerable resources to assemble, and improve upon, works from across the nation.[190]

Photography in the Cultural Revolution experienced a similar narrowing of scope in the first half of the period and revival in the early 1970s. The first photographic exhibition in many years was held in May 1972, at the same time as painting exhibitions were revived.[191] Two characteristics worked for and against the art. First, like filmmaking, photography was not a domain for the amateur or non-specialist. Chinese-made cameras were not cheap and developing and printing services were not readily available, unlike in Western countries at the time. Photography tended to be an area for specialists and so came under scrutiny of the new cultural leadership critical of past work. Second, conversely, photography was the ideal means to record, to create, and to disseminate appropriate images of the Cultural Revolution. But in general the kinds of photographs exhibited and reprinted in these ten years are not particularly distinguishable from the work of the previous seventeen years. The subject matter may have shown more emphasis on the collective, on representative types (workers, peasants, soldiers, and the young), and on economic production.[192] Nude or draped figure studies, for example, vanished from before Chinese cameras but had hardly been featured since 1949 anyway. Landscape photography continued as a major genre after 1966, with again little to distinguish works from this period from their predecessors in the 1950s. Perhaps the one area in photography that lagged behind expected developments was colour photographs, for work on Chinese-produced colour film stock was continuing in these years.[193] The function of news photographs to send messages about the relative standing of Party and state leaders of course continued.[194] The apogee was reached in late 1976, when Jiang Qing and other members of the newly arrested Gang of Four were brushed out of photographs of the memorial service for Mao Zedong held in September, less than a month before their arrest.[195]

Restoring fine art activity in the early 1970s was not without its dangers. Apparently the cultural insurgents were concerned at the return to professional life of a number of artists whom they felt were not sufficiently reformed. The China Art Gallery in the early spring of 1974 was graced by a 'black-painting exhibition' (heihua zhanlan). This featured works gathered from storage at the Zheng-Xie Auditorium, International Club, Beijing Hotel, and other places around the capital. Jiang Qing and her allies reportedly used the exhibition as a means to educate visitors, mostly specialists in organized groups, on the shortcomings of pre-1966 art and artworks currently being produced for hotels and other areas accessed by international visitors.[196] In the same year, the Beijing art exhibition office organized more regular displays of artworks themed to such political campaigns as 'Criticize Lin Biao and Confucius', 'Industry learns from Daqing', 'Agriculture learns from Dazhai', and 'Socialist new things' (shehuizhuyi xinsheng shiwu).[197] To mark National Day and twenty-five years of the People's Republic, a nationwide exhibition at the China Art Gallery included 430 items of traditional painting (guohua), oils, woodcuts, sculpture, poster art (xuanchuanhua), picture-stories, and New Year pictures (nianhua). The latter two kinds indicate further attention to more folk-style art. In 1975 a Beijing city children's art and photography exhibition included 800 items, and in May–June 1976 another municipal exhibition had 600 pieces.[198] The scale of these exhibitions was standard before 1966 and after 1976 so exhibitions should not be seen as desperate attempts to overwhelm viewers with a flood of approved works.

The pace of change quickened by 1976 with the re-publication in late March of the main mass-circulation periodical, Fine Art (Meishu), which had last been published in the spring of 1966. In an inaugural issue editorial, the editors used the standard Maoist slogans that suggested inclusiveness and innovation: 'Let a hundred flowers bloom and a hundred schools of thought contend' (baihuaqifang, baijiazhengming), 'make the past serve the present, make foreign things serve China' (guweijinyong, yangweiZhongyong), 'weed out the old to get something new' (*tuichenchuxin*), and 'revolutionary political content and as much as possible perfect artistic form are as one' (*geming de zhengzhi neirong he jinkeneng wanmei de yishu xingshi de tongyi*).[199] These had been trotted out for the previous nine and more years, though we should not overlook the combination of old, new, Chinese, and Western allowing for innovation and experimentation, depending on the caution or otherwise of the current leadership. This first issue of *Fine Art* reprinted a March *Red Flag* article reflecting the current obsession with 'the rightist deviationist wind to reverse the correct verdicts', a movement being used by Jiang Qing and her allies against, among others, Vice-Premier Deng Xiaoping. The July issue included sculptures, woodcuts, posters, and 'artistic big-character posters' on the same movement.[200]

Among the artworks reproduced in these 1976 bi-monthly issues of *Fine Art* were typical examples of the continuing innovation in genres. 'The Furnace Fire Is Pure Red' (*Luhuo zhenghong*) was identified as a 'Chinese-style painting' (*Zhongguohua*), as it uses watercolour, not oil. The non-traditional subject matter, a mass of workers seated or standing around a leader lecturing in a heavy-industry workshop, is striking.[201] In their summary of Cultural Revolution painting, Lü Peng and Yi Dan write of the theatricality (*xijuxing*) of such massed or even solitary figures. As they note, 'straightforward (*mingkuai*), popular (*tongsu*), uniform (*tongyi*), direct (*zhibai*), and bright (*xianming*) can perhaps best summarize the artistic style of the Cultural Revolution'.[202]

By the 1970s, the push to encourage amateur efforts in art produced a series of handbooks and instruction manuals on how to draw typical workers, peasants, and soldiers. These self-help publications were widely available and included guides to writing different styles of calligraphy. Much of the latter was intended for the blackboards used in all work units to convey timely messages about the latest political campaign.[203] Also available by the mid-1970s were reproductions of historical calligraphy, commonly in slim, large-format volumes for each famous calligrapher.

Just as in the case of the model performances, our haste in condemning political overkill and agitprop art should not blind us to the considerable skill and fresh techniques evident in some of this art. 'Sisters of the Grassland' (*Caochang jiemei*), a coloured woodblock print from around 1976 by Zhang Zhenqi presents a standard trope of the period (see Figure 4.4). A young woman, presumably a sent-down youth, on a harvester, is speaking to a woman dressed in more old-fashioned, Mongolian style, who is seated on a horse-drawn harvester. Thus, the notions of old and new, urban and rural, Han and minority, and mutual respect and friendship are all served. But the cropping of the image, with the rolling long grass almost filling the bottom two-thirds of the picture and the figures at the

4.4. A local farmer and a sent-down youth meet in the fields: *Sisters of the Grassland* (*Caochang jiemei*) by Zhang Zhenqi (coloured woodblock), in *Meishu* (Fine Art), 1977, 1 (May), p. 29.

top against the sky, is reminiscent of the film innovation of 1984's *The Yellow Earth*.[204]

Likewise, a post–Cultural Revolution eye can find ambiguity, even possible subversion in some works from the mid-1970s. Another woodblock print, Li Ronglong and others' 'In Battleground Order' (*Dabai zhanchang*), presents a mass of factory workers dwarfed by a high wall covered in big-character posters, mostly related to the Criticize Lin Biao and Confucius campaign of 1973–1974.[205] The posters would be impossible to read from ground level. Moreover, all the workers who are writing seem to be copying from documents or other pieces of paper, as if to imply they have no original thoughts of their own or lack spontaneity. The theatricality of a wall of criticism does not obliterate these thoughts, which artist or some viewers may have shared.

In this respect, a history of art activities among the millions of youth sent down to the countryside, to factories, or to the army after 1968 remains to be written. The kinds of literature and films that emerged in the 1980s from these young people are well known. The officially endorsed activities of 'sent-down youth' artists are documented. Many were given considerable encouragement in the 1970s, being brought back to their urban homes and provided with resources to practise and improve their art skills.[206] But beyond these official activities, unofficial individual and group experimentation with drawing, sculpture, and other forms certainly occurred among these young people. Many others by the mid-1970s had found ways to return to the cities, where some groups were formed to circulate new-style poems, for example.[207] Similar unorthodox activities happened with art in these years among these groups, even if a painting or woodblock was harder to hide than a handwritten copy of a novel or poem.

Architecture is a field in which politics need not be as obvious as in other arts. Certainly the variations on Beijing's Great Hall of the People planted incongruously in other parts of the country highlighted the political uses of buildings. Historical monuments in the form of buildings, such as the ersatz twin pagodas monstrosity created in 1971 in the middle of Zhengzhou in Henan to commemorate the railway workers' strike of 1923, also showed politics ruled over practicality or grace.[208] Chinese architects, like their painter colleagues, had wrestled for decades with the issue of finding a Chinese style that combined modernity and nationality. Zhengzhou's twin pagodas showed how not to do it. But in other parts of China, even during the Cultural Revolution, architects could find less obvious ways to engage with modern developments. In April 1973 the China Art Gallery displayed seventy items in a Finnish architecture exhibition.[209] Far from Beijing the Hot Springs Guesthouse (*Kuangquan bingshe*) in Guangzhou was designed and built in 1972–1974 by architects Chen Weilian, Li Huiren, and others in the Guangzhou City Planning Bureau. It and the smaller-scale guesthouses designed for Guilin by Shang Kuo (born 1927) showed what could be done in concrete with a modern sensibility and attention to Chinese landscaping and space aesthetics (see Figure 4.5).[210] Even the users of the Capital Gymnasium in Beijing

4.5. Reed Cliff Reception Room (*Ludiyan jiedaishi*), Guilin (designed by Shang Kuo, early 1970s). Source: Zou Deyi, *Zhongguo jianzhushi tushuo: xiandaijuan* (Illustrated history of Chinese architecture: modern volume), Beijing: Zhongguo jianzhu gongye chubanshe (China Architecture Industry Press), 2001, p. 180.

(built in 1966–1968) and the Hangzhou airport terminal building (built in 1971–1972) could be grateful for their designers' success in combining the modern with subtle Chinese features.[211]

Perhaps unexpectedly, large-scale works in concrete created in these ten years represented well the kinds of outlooks their designers shared with composers, choreographers, painters, and even traditional performers. The newly built spaces, like the classics of Chinese traditional public architecture carefully proportioned to a human scale, expressed a common determination to make Chinese art and life proudly modern. In this endeavour, the architects seemed to have done better than their more obvious and familiar colleagues. Without the usual bombast and over-promising that Liang Lun recognized as remaining in dance even after the end of the Cultural Revolution, some Chinese architects, painters, and performers in these years made real progress on China's twentieth-century journey to modernity.

CHAPTER FIVE

Writing Wrongs: Public and Private
Fictions and Resistance

Zhang Yang was a published author before he was sent down in his mid-twenties to the Hunan countryside from his native Changsha in the late 1960s. His unpublished novel *The Return* (*Guilai*), which had started as a short story in 1963, took on a life of its own after 1970 when it was circulated in hand-copied and mimeographed form among his fellow 'educated youth'. By 1974 Zhang had produced his sixth draft of the story. Later in the 1980s it was claimed that this was the first novel in the world to receive its title not from its author but from its readers. *The Return* became *The Second Handshake* (*Di-er ci woshou*), the story of a patriotic Chinese scientist and her decision to return to the motherland.[1] The emotional story of sacrifice, unrequited love, and triumph over adversity in modern settings in foreign countries held great appeal to young readers in the midst of the Cultural Revolution. Its adaptation to film in 1980 revealed flaws that had not troubled its readers in the years before 1976. In a nation in which publication and literature were strictly controlled, the frisson of the forbidden had added to the novel's attractions.

With its unsanctioned popularity, *The Second Handshake* alluded to the modern or international thrust of much official cultural production in these ten years. It also serves as an underground example among numerous works from the stage and the bookstore that came under attack in these years. From 1975 onwards Zhang Yang was subject to numerous investigations of his writing. Instead of being a sign of the continued effectiveness of central control, these criticisms reflected a wider difficulty: the waning grip on power of the Cultural Revolution insurgents. The success of Zhang's uncoordinated literary effort also indicated the failure of the Cultural Revolution's officially endorsed literary works to engage their potential readerships. Interest, innovation, and introspection could be better satisfied by underground writing. By the mid-1970s the initial, model works of the Cultural Revolution for many seemed old-fashioned and meaningless. In the last year of his revolution, Mao Zedong turned his back on the new and watched old-style films made for his irregular enjoyment.

We begin with the orthodox literature available to Chinese readers in these years, mapping the changing landscape of literary publication. Many readers found more interest in other publications, including foreign literary translations, and in the kind of underground writing that Zhang Yang's work exemplified. Sections 3 and 4 turn directly to political matters, showing how official criticism of key works in the last three years of the Cultural Revolution indicated the growing weakness of the politicians most responsible for the changes in Chinese cultural production since the 1960s.

1. MODELS ON THE PAGE: OFFICIAL LITERATURE

Literary publication in the ten years after 1966 reflected the narrowing of subject matter, elevating of simple, folk-influenced style, and a push to enhance the status of the amateur writer with real connections to socialist purity. The modernism evident in the revised Peking opera and other stage arts was less evident in Cultural Revolution bookstores, at least for the general public. An approach through the literary publication enterprise is a useful way to reveal the productivity of these years, although it does not directly address the lack of quality in many of the public literary works.

In literature, as in the rest of the cultural arena, the Cultural Revolution began with attacks on the seventeen years after 1949 and on the men and women who represented that, and an earlier, era. Writers who had become famous in the May Fourth period that produced modern Chinese literature were subject to increasingly scathing criticism as this modern tradition was condemned as elitist and bourgeois. The novelist Ba Jin (1904–2005), for example, was taken to the campus of Fudan University in Shanghai to be denounced by the kinds of students and teachers who had been his biggest fans just a few years earlier.[2] Lao She (1899–1966), the equally popular Beijing novelist and playwright, could not bear the pressures of Red Guard and other attacks. In August 1966, he committed suicide by drowning in a lake in the city that he had celebrated in his writing. Zhao Shuli (1906–1970), who had emerged in the Yan'an era as a peasant writer of tales infused with folk elements, was among those others subject to denunciation, despite his Maoist pedigree. Zhao's creation of 'middling characters' (*zhongjian renwu*), who were a mix of good and bad, had revived an early 1960s debate on such characters. In the Manichean world of Cultural Revolution politics, such mixed characterization was unwelcome.[3] Other eminent writers continued their habit of adapting to changes in policy. Guo Moruo (1892–1978), long associated with the Communist Party, produced an abject self-denunciation that was widely published in April 1966.

These famous literary figures were at the peak of a literary apparatus that was closed down, though not dismantled, with the coming of the Cultural Revolution. The Writers Association, at the national and provincial levels, ceased functioning, as did other literary organizations that had served to facilitate and control professional writing. In the spring of 1966, literary journals at the national and local levels ceased publication. Sources claim that only *Liberation Army Literature and Art* (*Jiefangjun wenyi*) continued to appear, building on the February 1966 conference on army art and literature which had signalled the heightened importance of the military in cultural life. But this journal ceased publication in May 1968 for a five-year period. *Liberation Army Songs* (*Jiefangjun gequ*) continued publication until December 1968 and resumed again in May 1972.[4] Writers, editors, and managers found themselves occupied with political study meetings, learning 'loyalty performances', or, in the case of younger persons, travelling about the nation. Almost the only literary outlets were the Red Guard newspapers, broadsheets, and other publications, in which the literary qualities of the poetry, essays, short plays, and other works usually took second place to agitprop purposes.

A popular characterization of literature in the Cultural Revolution was encapsulated in the joke phrase 'Lu Xun walks the Golden Road' (*Lu Xun zou 'Jinguang dadao'*). Lu Xun (1881–1936) continued to be celebrated throughout the Cultural Revolution as China's greatest twentieth-century writer. He had been the central inventor of May Fourth fiction, starting with his *The Diary of a Madman* in 1918. His elevation into the pantheon of Cultural Revolution ignored Lu Xun's somewhat ambiguous attitudes to communism and to the social function of his writing. The Beijing meeting on 31 October 1966 to mark the thirtieth anniversary of Lu Xun's death resolved to 'carry on Lu Xun's fearless revolutionary and rebellious spirit'.[5] Throughout the Cultural Revolution, the reinvented Lu Xun retained this apotheosis as fearless writer, even as fear was visited upon his former students and colleagues from the 1930s and upon his literary successors. One famous poster from the period puts Lu Xun in the position usually occupied by Li Tiemei, or some other model-opera hero. He gazes nobly in the imagination of a contemporary student who has a brush in hand, ready to write.[6]

The 'Golden Road' of the popular encapsulation of literary narrow-ness during the Cultural Revolution refers to the novel *The Golden Road* (*Jinguang dadao*) by Hao Ran. Born in 1932 in a small Hebei village, orphaned at thirteen and with only three years schooling, Hao Ran had joined the Communist Party in 1948. He developed his writing skills dur-ing a career in newspaper journalism. His first short story appeared in *Beijing Literature and Art* (*Beijing wenyi*) in late 1956. Five years later he joined the editorial staff of the Party's main journal, *Red Flag*. Hao Ran gained fame in 1964 with the publication of the two volumes of a novel about collectivization in the countryside in the 1950s, *Bright Sunny Skies* (*Yanyangtian*). Part 1 of his *The Golden Road* appeared in May 1972 and was one of the first new novels published in China since the start of the Cultural Revolution. Hailed as a peasant writer because of his humble origins, Hao Ran had little competition in the literary scene, at least when *The Golden Road* was first published. The book sold more than four million copies in its first year.[7]

But Hao Ran's novels had several attractive qualities for his millions of readers. The stories were long and complicated tales of effort, frustra-tion, and determination. While reviewers at the time hailed their use of the 'three prominences' in giving centre stage to the handsome peasant heroes, the novels offered the pleasures of a lengthy tale full of well-drawn characters, conflict, and the plotting of class enemies with the narrative space to accommodate surprising twists. In a cultural arena in which the main stories were set at a distance from the present, usually in the pre-1949 period, Hao Ran's settings were in more recent times, covering collectivization in the 1950s and conflict in the early 1960s. He traversed experiences familiar to urban readers who were acquainted with the countryside, having helped with harvests or in political cam-paigns. Episodic, multiple-character novels of heroism and comradeship had been popular reading matter in China for three or four centuries. Hao Ran's modern novels were a good, self-indulgent read for many people.[8]

The other engaging feature of Hao Ran's novels was their language. The push to establish a national language (*putonghua*, literally common speech) after 1949 had encouraged the tendency in many media to oblit-erate the regional. Feature films, for example, had the main characters, no matter where they lived, speaking in *putonghua*, with the occasional gesture towards local or regional usage in the choice of words or speech patterns. Sometimes a minor, often less educated or older, person in films spoke in a way closer to the habits of people who actually lived in that place. Part of the attraction of many local opera forms for locals was their use of local 'dialects', but these kinds of play only began to re-emerge in transplanted form in the early 1970s. Hao Ran's novels featured well-written narration and dialogue that cleverly captured something of the flavour of speech by country dwellers on the North China plain. It was not a transposition of actual speech, but it had the feel of the location, even though some of the lengthier dialogue exchanges were full of Marxist expressions. The speech, combined with capturing the quotidian detail of life in a village, drew readers to Hao Ran.[9] In addition to the big novels, he also published short stories and stories for children in these years and mentored new writing talent.

Beating Hao Ran's *The Golden Road* by three months, the first novel published in many years was *Cowfield Sea (Niutian yang)*, which appeared from the Shanghai People's Publishing House in February 1972. This was a collective effort by a group formed by the Guangzhou Military District specifically to write the book; however, the author was given as Nan Shao (literally 'southern scout'). Set in the early 1960s, it told of an army group reclaiming fields on the shores of the South China Sea. Many of these collectively written novels included skilled writers, who were enjoying a degree of rehabilitation after periods in May Seventh Cadre Schools or elsewhere. Their participation was covered by the idea of 'three combinations' *(san jiehe)*.[10] This rubric usually included worker-peasant-soldier or other amateur writers and less-schooled informants about the lives being depicted. Several well received novels from the 1970s shared a similar tropical setting to *Cowfield Sea*, including Li Ruqing's *Island Militia Women (Haidao nüminbing)*, the novel on which the disputed film *Haixia* was based (see below), and Hao Ran's own *Sons and Daughters of Xisha (Xisha ernü)*. All such novels and shorter fiction were expected to embrace the 'three prominences', 'the theory of the basic task' *(genben renwu lun,* meaning promoting the revolution), 'the theme determining everything' *(zhuti xianxing lun)*, and other theoretical notions that supposedly set this literature apart from the 'black' writing from before 1966. This meant a flattening of characterization in which evil characters lost redeeming features and heroes became more perfect.[11] One estimate claims that about 100 full-length novels were published during the Cultural Revolution.[12] Li Xintian's *Sparkling Red Star* was typical of the most popular works, including comic books, which were adapted into a range of forms before its success as a film.[13]

Other literary forms also had Red Guard producers and then re-appeared in the early 1970s, including reportage *(baogao wenxue)*. This is a kind of literary journalism, also seen in the Soviet Union, which had a function in a society in which the media were tightly controlled.

Reportage was a literary genre after 1949 which could, depending on the political climate, expose problems in society. Newspaper journalists were muzzled, but a writer with a journalist's instincts and a novelist's pen could on occasion reveal abuses of power and other shortcomings in socialist society. Unsurprisingly, the reportage published in the first half of the 1970s took a less-critical approach, instead using reportage's descriptive power to praise 'socialist new things', such as barefoot doctors (*chijiao yisheng*) and other innovations ascribed, usually misleadingly, to the Cultural Revolution.

Writing poetry had a long historical association with the intellectual class in Chinese society. China's most prominent poet in the ten years after 1966 was, of course, Mao Zedong. Several of his poems, written before the Cultural Revolution, were publicized with great acclaim during these years. An accomplished poet in the classical mode, Mao was generally dismissive of the modern-style poetry introduced during the May Fourth era. Poetry written in a kind of invented folk style was another genre that had received attention in the Yan'an period and after 1949.[14] During the Great Leap Forward in 1958, for example, popular mobilization included mass poetry composition. More poems may have been written during that campaign than perhaps had ever been composed in Chinese in the previous two or three millennia.[15]

Classical, modern, and folk poetry continued to be published during the Cultural Revolution. Red Guard broadsheets and newspapers included poems written for the current struggles, often in a style intended for public recitation by individuals or groups.[16] In this activity, the youthful Red Guards were continuing a long tradition of poetic commentary on public events, though their rhetoric was much more direct than tradition allowed. Sent-down youths published poetry in their local newspapers and in the newly re-published literary journals in the 1970s. Poetry was considered such an important part of literature that it needed careful supervision. The main journal, *Poetry* (*Shikan*), was one of the last literary periodicals to resume publication when it reappeared in January 1976. Editors tried to express their independence from the past by not numbering the eighty-first issue, the first issue to be published since the 1950s.[17] But the range of poetry styles in the new journal still reflected the poetic heritage, even if the contents had narrowed considerably as a result of Cultural Revolution considerations. Poetry writers were expected to use the 'model performances' as inspiration, with heroes given pride of place, and 'tall, large, and perfect' were the watchwords for highly politicized works.[18] The quantity of published poetry in the last period of the Cultural Revolution was impressive: Between 1972 and 1975, 390 poetry collections were published, including works by some poets who had established their reputations before 1966.[19]

As the Great Leap Forward had shown, poetry was an area of cultural production in which the amateur could participate and even provide a directness of voice that might measure up to more polished work. Groups of people could compose poetry together which satisfied another Cultural Revolution emphasis on the collective. *Selected Poems and Lyrics from Xiaojinzhuang*, published in 1976, was one of the most widely publicized collections of poetry. Members of the production brigade in the suburbs of Tianjin city composed *Selected Poems*, and Jiang Qing and her allies promoted the brigade as a model organization for amateur cultural activities. The country poets showed what non-professionals could do untainted by the alleged bourgeois thinking that had drenched pre–Cultural Revolution specialist writers. As with all such publishing in China since 1949 and before, editors polished and improved the work.[20]

The compiler of a 2005 chronology of non-classical poetry in the Cultural Revolution found enough to fill 500 pages, which suggested much was going on.[21] By far the most widely published and read individual poet in these years was another amateur, Mao Zedong. Two poems he had written in 1965 were released with great publicity, on New Year's Day 1976, when the front page of *People's Daily* was given over to these two poems written in his own distinguished hand. During the Cultural Revolution, Mao's poems were popularized to an unprecedented extent, first by Red Guards in the early years of the decade and then in his last years by the insurgent cultural authorities.[22] In both periods, his poems were set to music and the songs were taught to all comers. Indeed, many Chinese were only acquainted with the poems as songs learned with the rest of their class, workshop team, platoon, or village chorus. Collected editions of Mao's poems were published in a variety of formats, from lavish calligraphy reproductions and cheap scrolls to small booklets, often with explanations of the classical and historical allusions Mao skilfully wove into his work. Bonnie McDougall associates the revival of classical poetry in the late 1960s with the influence of Mao as model. She also links this development with the Criticize Lin Biao and Confucius campaign after 1973.[23]

Literary publication from the early 1970s flourished, at least in terms of quantity and accessibility. By then the main literary publishing houses at the central and provincial levels had begun to produce new books and journals. Periodical titles grew from 21 in 1970 to 194 by 1972, though the number was still far from 1965's 790 titles.[24] One kind of new book was editions of classical Chinese texts, annotated with explanations for the less literate that convey a Cultural Revolution interpretation of the pre-modern works. Popularization was stressed, with some important modern or classical works appearing in various formats for different readerships: a comic-book story for younger or less-literate readers, an illustrated child's edition, and more ordinary versions sold at subsidized prices. Of course, the biggest print runs in these years were for the writings of Mao Zedong. A table in a fifty-year chronology of publishing after 1949 shows that the number of books and other materials published per one thousand persons was higher in the ten years of the Cultural Revolution than in the preceding seventeen years. But this figure may be somewhat distorted by the avalanche of Maoist tracts. Periodicals per thousand by 1973 had reached average pre-1966 levels.[25] The model performance operas and ballets also were given special attention. The chronology of publishing after 1949 even cites instances of Zhou Enlai expressing concern at too many colour plates in some of these books and at the planned print run of one of the ballets. 'How many people are actually going to dance it?' he reportedly asked. The Shanghai People's Publishing House printed five million comic-book versions of *Taking Tiger Mountain by Strategy* in 1970. China's pre-modern vernacular literary heritage was not ignored. In the spring of 1972, *The Dream of the Red Chamber*, *Water Margin*, and *The Three Kingdoms* appeared in bookstores.[26]

Among the official published literature, a new genre appeared in the early 1970s. This was writing by sent-down youth who had gone to the countryside in the millions after 1968. The most interesting and innovative work by such writers was not published in official journals or collections but passed around, as we shall see, in hand-copied or unofficial editions. By the early 1970s, the newly revived provincial literary journals also provided an officially sanctioned outlet for young writers. Many such authors were members of propaganda or performance teams on state farms or in communes, so they were perhaps not purely amateur (or part-time) writers. But the official media were happy to acclaim these new authors, especially when their published works hailed the alleged achievements of the youth rustification movement. Guo Xianhong's *The Journey* (*Zhengtu*) was one such account, set in 1968, and was published in two volumes in 1973 by Shanghai People's Publishing House.[27] In September 1974 the same press launched its 'Up to the Mountains, Down to the Villages Educated-Youth Writing Series' (*Shangshanxiaxiang zhishiqingnian chuangzuo congshu*) as an outlet for these new authors. One of the first volumes was *Spring on the State Farm* (*Nongchang de chuntian*).[28] New, youthful talent needed cultivating. Zhu Lin, for example, having returned to her hometown from the Anhui countryside, attended a writing class in 1975 organized by the Shanghai Youth and Children's Publishing House.[29]

These newly published writers included several who were to achieve fame in the 1980s as inventors of new Chinese fiction. The young worker Jiang Zilong, for example, appeared in his hometown *Tianjin Literature and Art* (*Tianjin wenyi*). His 'Pressure' (*Yali*) was published in its first issue of 1974. In the northeast, Wang Xiaosheng was included in a collection of stories by sent-down youth edited and published at the construction corps (*jianshe bingtuan*) where he was stationed, which had its own printing shop and newspaper.[30] In Hunan Han Shaogong began his public writing career in *Xiangjiang Literature and Art* (*Xiangjiang wenyi*) when a spring issue in 1974 included his 'The Red Furnace Goes to the Mountains' (*Honglu shangshan*). Ten years later Han became a major shaper of the 'search for roots' (*xun'gen*) movement that self-consciously played up the non-Han, extra–Yellow River basin origins of Chinese culture. Zhang Kangkang had her short story 'The Lamp' (*Deng*) published in *Liberation Daily* (*Jiefang ribao*) in 1972, as newspapers revived their pre-1966 literary pages. Her sent-down youth novel *The Dividing Line* (*Fenjiexian*) appeared from the Shanghai People's Publishing House in 1975.[31] Other writers who appeared in print in the last years of the Cultural Revolution and then made their names in the New Era (*Xin shiqi*) after 1976 include Zou Zhi'an, Zhu Sujin, Jia Pingwa, Li Cunbao, Zhou Keqin, and Gu Hua.[32]

The latter's 'Legend of Yangtian Lake' (*Yangtianhu chuanqi*) was included in a volume released in October 1974 in the Chaoxia series (*Chaoxia congshu*) of books. This series and its associated periodical *Chaoxia* (literally, facing the morning, or evening, glow) were identified after the Cultural Revolution as key outlets for literature supporting the faction around Jiang Qing. The journal had started publication in Shanghai in 1974, joined soon after by the book series, both edited by an editorial unit at the Shanghai People's Publishing House (*Shanghai renmin chubanshe*).[33] Post-1976 accusations denounced the use made of such publications to promote so-called plot literature and art (*yinmou wenyi*), the written equivalent of films like *Counterattack* (*Fanji*). Unlike feature films, writing was easier to print and to disseminate to a supposedly gullible public. In 1975 *Chaoxia* published a collection of fiction, plays, and other works set during the Cultural Revolution. *Prelude* (*Xuqu*) encapsulated the features of official Cultural Revolution writing in its twenty items: Amateur writers were included; authors elaborated on their use of *yangbanxi* models; heroes were beyond flaw or doubt; redness prevailed over expertise.[34]

This overview of literary publication shows how unexpectedly prolific activities had become by the mid-1970s. Novels, short stories, and poetry were being produced by a generally new corps of officially recognized writers, both amateur and professional. Subject matter and style tended to be somewhat constrained, but even in these orthodox outlets, the seeds were sown of a new literature that would bloom in the 1980s.

2. HIDDEN PLEASURES: UNOFFICIAL, UNDERGROUND LITERATURE

The most interesting, and in the long term the most significant, literary activities during the Cultural Revolution were not on display in bookstores or on the magazine racks in post offices. An underground movement of writing, distribution, story-telling, and even translation operated outside of official channels, even if some writers, readers, and editors may have worked in both arenas. As speakers at a roundtable discussion organized by the modern literature section of the Chinese Academy of Social Sciences in August 1998 agreed, literature in the Cultural Revolution consisted of two parts, the above-ground (*dishang*) and the underground (*dixia*). Although both parts deserved attention and research, the achievements of the latter were greater.[35] The label 'underground' essentially meant 'unofficial', rather than necessarily dissident, though the mere act of unofficial circulation was a gesture of resistance.

Zhang Yang's *The Second Handshake* represented one of the main features of this activity, the circulation and re-copying of fiction, both novels and shorter works, poetry, and other writings. The massive transfer of educated young people to communes, state farms, mining areas, factories, and into the armed forces provided an eager audience for such unofficial literature. Many of these youth had a keen interest in writing or reading, had time on their hands (especially in the slow agricultural seasons), and had access to paper, even mimeograph equipment to aid the reproduction of these works. Youth from one city, suburb, and even school tended to be dispatched to the countryside as a group and lived as groups in their own dwellings, which eased circulation of these writings.[36]

The attractions of underground literature were manifold. No matter what their content, the fact that these were unofficial, even forbidden works was excitement enough for some readers. Many were written in the episodic style that had attracted listeners to story-telling centuries earlier and readers to vernacular novels when story-tellers' tales were written down and published in the Ming dynasty (1368–1644). The content of this literature also set it apart from officially available reading.

Love stories, sacrifice, adolescent confusion, and all the other emotions could also be found in above-ground writing, at least in some guise, by the mid-1970s. But the underground versions, in part simply by being unofficial, seemed to carry more genuine and deeper emotional heft. *The Second Handshake* allowed its readers (and hand-copiers in an era before photocopying) to indulge in a love triangle that included a dedicated female scientist who goes abroad. In the United States, she even has an African-American maid to assist her in running her lovely home, though she longs to return to China. Romance, exotic locations, and unfamiliar social arrangements proved irresistible to readers fed a dreadfully familiar diet of local heroes.[37]

A work like Zhang Yang's could undergo considerable transformation in the hands of those who copied a circulating manuscript. In a far more meaningful way than the claims to mass or collective authorship made for many official literary products during the Cultural Revolution, these underground manuscripts were truly popular creations. Having started out in 1963 in his own hands as *Spindrift* (*Langhua*), Zhang's novel took on a series of titles: *Red Leaves on the Fragrant Hills* (*Xiangshan honghua*), *A Dynasty of Lords* (*Yidai tianjiao*), *Mother of the Hydrogen Bomb* (*Qingdan zhi mu*), *Return to the Homeland* (*Guiguo*), and *The Return* (*Guilai*). A young copier in a Beijing factory, rather than Zhang Yang himself, is said to have produced the lasting title in 1974.[38] But not just titles could change in the process of unofficial copying and circulation. New episodes and characters could appear in a new, unauthorized version. If a copier or group of readers did not like a particular ending or the treatment of a character, these could be changed in the next version. Local references, satirizing an acknowledged corrupt official or eulogizing a self-sacrificing young person, could be worked into some of these circulating stories and poems. The liveliness and spontaneous nature of these changes were in marked and welcome contrast to the 'buttoned-down' character of fiction and verse in the official media. Other titles to circulate in this way include 'Down and Out' (*Jiuji lang*), 'Fleeing from Home' (*Taowang*), and 'Waves' (*Bodong*).[39] The titles themselves promised melodrama and escapism. Detective stories were another genre that flourished underground.[40] Some of these stories circulated in oral versions, creating an 'oral literature' (*koutou wenxue*) which might eventually be written down for a wider audience. One of the earliest hand-copied works was 'Open Love Letters' (*Gongkai de qingshu*), first collected together from actual letters written among sent-down university students in 1970. It became a major hand-copied and mimeographed title in circulation by 1972.[41]

Another way to escape was to read about faraway places described by distant hands. Foreign novels and classical Chinese literature both circulated among sent-down youth throughout the Cultural Revolution. Many urban young people in 1966, when regular schooling stopped and time for their own activities stretched on, turned to books their parents had at home. Nineteenth-century novels by writers such as Stendhal, Balzac, Hugo, the Dumas, and Dickens and more recent Russian works had been popular with educated Chinese readers throughout the twentieth century. The start of the Cultural Revolution provided an opportunity for a new generation to become acquainted with these works. Many people recall finding parallels between their own lives, required to perform roles, and the characters in, for example, *The Scarlet and the Black*. Ethel Lillian Voynich's 1913 novel *The Gadfly* (*Niumeng*) continued to hold its young readers in thrall, as many remembered the somewhat romantic Soviet film adaptation. Li Hangyu, a former sent-down youth, in his 1979 short story 'A Pitiful Fortune' (*Kelian de yunqi*) describes how a youth in a small town discovers a page of Pushkin's poetry used as a wrapper for his melon seeds. He goes back over and over to buy more seeds and eventually assembles the entire poetry volume.[42] More recent work, such as the stories of social and state oppression by Franz Kafka, surprisingly seems to have had less appeal.[43] The length and episodic nature of nineteenth-century Western novels and their social commentary seem to have offered inspiration to underground writers of the hand-copied Chinese novels.

The other kind of literature that helped fill the hours in the late 1960s was from China's pre-modern tradition. Lu Xun, while inventing modern Chinese literature, had been deeply immersed in ancient fables and histories. The *Book of Songs* (*Shijing*) and Sima Qian's *Historical Records* (*Shiji*) offered readers who could tackle the classical language glimpses into another world. Both kinds of literature were also circulated widely among sent-down youths. As the poet Duo Duo later recalled, in the early winter of 1970: 'Two of the most fashionable books, *Catcher in the Rye* (*Maitian li de shouwangzhe*) and Kerouac's *On the Road*, along with Vasilii Aksenov's *A Ticket to the Stars* (*Dai xingxing de huochepiao*) caused a new stir among Beijing sent-down youths'.[44] These translated works were known by the colour of their covers: Contemporary topics had 'yellow covers' (*huangpi shu*), class topics had 'grey covers' (*huipi shu*), and socially relevant topics were labelled 'internal restricted readings' (*neibu duwu*). They included contemporary works by Sartre, Ilya Ehrenberg, and others. Duo Duo recalled about forty such books in circulation.[45] Many of these were published by the Shanghai People's Publishing House (also in charge of the *Chaoxia* series) or the Shanghai

News Publishing House as part of a series of 'May Seventh Cadre School' translations intended for restricted access by those who were deemed professionally required to be aware of intellectual or social developments abroad.[46] But the porous nature of such restrictions was well known in China in these years, as before and since.

The ability of sent-down youth in the countryside or young people in cities to indulge their unorthodox literary and cultural tastes depended on their circumstances. Yang Jian, a pioneering researcher on underground and sent-down youth literature in the Cultural Revolution, contrasts three different situations.[47] Those youths assigned to militarized construction corps (*jianshe bingtuan*) in the border regions of the northwest or southwest faced the most restrictions. Creativity was less possible in the presence of officially organized 'educated-youth literature' and activism from the corps' propaganda teams. But even in these corps, private and anti-establishment writing and creating were possible, including poetry, oral story-telling, or recitation. Li Ping, then in the navy, started a love story about Red Guards by telling it to his friends, elaborating in the tradition of the inventors of Chinese fiction four centuries earlier.[48] Often the same writer would have an officially endorsed output, published locally or nationally, and would produce unofficial works for trusted friends, or the writer had to wait until after 1976 for public consumption. On occasion writings that had started as underground items emerged in public, officially sponsored venues. A second group, those young people who were sent to more regular communes, often in poorer regions that could use the extra labour, was less controlled in their cultural activities. There was space (time and place) in which to read, copy, or discuss unofficial writing. Yang Jian shows how novels and prose (*sanwen*) were composed and distributed in Inner Mongolia among herding groups. One of the early works was a medium-length story, 'One Year' (*Yinian*), written in 1972 by a Beijing youth surnamed Wang. It recounted the story of sent-down youth, describing them as 'wanderers over the earth' (*dadi de liulangzhe*). Its story of disappointment struck a chord among its readers. Other Inner Mongolian educated youth mimeographed poems for relatively wide and open distribution.

From about 1972 more sent-down youth found excuses or reasons to return to the cities, where the third phenomenon, 'salons' (*shalong*), emerged where young writers and their readers exchanged manuscripts and shared opinions about literature and life.[49] The 'up to the mountains, down to the villages' experience had such a profound effect on many young people that, even after they had returned to their hometowns, getting together with like-minded persons who understood the movement

was only natural. These groups, Yang Jian suggests, maintained ties with
sent-down youth still in the countryside, hosted those allowed leave to
visit the cities, and passed around unofficial writings. These links had a
mutual effect on creativity in the salons and back in the villages. New ideas
or experimental forms tended to be introduced by city colleagues, while
the countryside continued to provide the raw material for writing. These
salons helped produce new-style works, notably modernist poetry later
identified by the somewhat dismissive label 'misty poems' (*menglongshi*,
literally obscured or hazy poetry).

One of the first salons was established as early as 1967 by a young
woman writer, Li Li, who fled from being sent-down in the winter of
1969 and returned to a precarious existence back in Beijing. Her salon
had disbanded by 1970. In the winter of that year, a slightly older poet,
Zhao Yifan (1935–1988), established a salon that attracted some of the
more innovative new writers.[50] In the summer of 1972, there even small
'cultural salons' (*wenhua shalong*) were meeting in the housing quarters of the State Council and the Ministry of Railways. The participants
exchanged hand-copied and 'internal' publications and shared poems and
film scripts, among other works. Some also had an interest in the fine
arts.[51] Yang Jian identifies 'underground literature' activities even in the
army.[52] He also notes the revival of classical-style poetry writing among
sent-down youth, intellectuals at May Seventh Cadre Schools, and in the
literary salons.[53] Writing according to rules imposed by history rather
than by contemporary power-holders was attractive. The private writing
of older writers during these years should not be overlooked, including
the veteran artist-essayist Feng Zikai (1898–1975) and the poet Niu Han
(1923–), among others. These 'underground' works could be published
only after 1976.[54]

But one of the last Cultural Revolution moments for underground literary activity produced a more politically engaged corpus. The demonstrations in memory of Zhou Enlai (who had died in January) at the
Qingming festival on 5 April 1976 included the more open circulation
of underground poetry. Poems full of affection for the late premier and
barbed with various degrees of obvious reference to Mao's wife and other
Cultural Revolution power-holders were pasted up around Tian'anmen
Square or handed out on broadsheets. Readers were electrified by what
they saw or collected. Much of the writing, which included prose and
other genres as well as poetry, was as politicized and full of cliché as the
official poetry of the time. But the purpose captured the rebelliousness
of the Red Guard era, even if all concerned knew that 1966–1967 was
now long past. Doggerel, modern-style poems, and classical poetry forms

were all used to voice protest at the treatment of Zhou and, by extension, at those in power restricting these popular voices.[55] Jiang Qing was described with all kinds of historical and literary allusions to white-boned demons, witches, and unsavoury animals. It was the underground literary movement's finest hour, even if the media three days later began a drumbeat of denunciation.[56]

3. MODEL ASSERTIONS: CRITICIZING WORKS

As we have seen in previous chapters, Chinese cultural space expanded after 1972, following the trauma of the fall of Lin Biao in late summer 1971, allegedly in an abortive plot to assassinate Mao Zedong. For the chairman's chosen successor and comrade-in-arms to have met such an ignominious end was a shock to all readers of the Chinese media. Instead of provoking a witch-hunt and a further tightening of control and surveillance, Lin's death prompted a realization of the limitations of perpetual mobilization and frantic demands for heightened vigilance. The mounting in 1973–1974 of the campaign to criticize the unlikely pairing of Lin Biao and Confucius could not disguise the increasing vulnerability of the Cultural Revolution insurgents. The old guard, embodied in Vice-Premier Deng Xiaoping, became more assertive in its push to regularize Chinese political, economic, and cultural life. The expansion of the cultural arena that earlier chapters have outlined, with the re-publication of provincial and local literary magazines, the completion of new feature films, and the expansion of the performing repertoire, was part of this winding down of Cultural Revolution fervor.[57]

But the cultural leadership did not go down without a fight. The passage from bombast to blandness was not without its share of bumbling resistance. Performing-arts classes and conventions in various provinces revealed a subtext of tensions and concerns to defend the artistic changes wrought in the 1960s. Several operas, plays, and other artefacts were identified as models of deviation for educative criticism in the media. These criticisms culminated in the pillorying of two new feature films in 1975. The response to these attacks underscored the increased desperation of the defenders of Cultural Revolution faith.

As had been the case with *Hai Rui Dismissed from Office* at the start of the Cultural Revolution, in the early 1970s, several plays were singled out for criticism as a means to model the errors they supposedly contained. In 1973 a new play came under attack for presenting a distorted picture of life in socialist society. *The Unquiet Seashore (Bu pingjing de haibin)* told the story of Chinese policemen capturing foreign spies in a coastal city in 1963. The play was the work of the Shandong Provincial Spoken Drama Company and had first been performed in March 1973.[58] But in creating the Public Security Bureau (PSB) officers as heroes along the lines of the model performances and a drama full of surprise twists and tension, the play's authors had apparently overstepped the mark. On 27 March the Shandong newspaper *Masses Daily* (*Dazhong ribao*) published an article by its critic headlined 'A black example of reversing the verdict on "restoring the rites"' (*Yige 'fu li' fan'an de hei biaoben*).[59] In 1973–1974 newspapers and journals nationwide published criticisms of the play and its efforts to present the dedication and professionalism of the security apparatus. 'Our line in the work of eliminating counter-revolutionaries (*sufan*) is the line of the masses eliminating counter-revolutionaries,' wrote one upset PSB staffer of the play's failing to emphasize the importance of mass mobilization in rooting out enemies. To not rely on the masses was to practise 'closed-doorism and mysticism' (*guanmenzhuyi, shenmizhuyi*). Indeed, the ordinary citizens allegedly came across in the play as a 'common herd' (*qunmeng*) and 'scatterbrained' (*madaha*).[60]

Two other dramas received even more attention as models for criticism in the national media. *Song of the Teachers* (*Yuanding zhi ge*) was a modern-style Hunan opera. In essence a children's morality tale, the opera comprised just four main characters: two teachers and boy and girl students. The male teacher has lost heart because he feels his students are not conscientious enough. His female colleague approaches her work from the students' point of view and patiently changes her teaching methods to connect students' literacy studies with their learning of revolutionary ideals. The results are most heartening, a triumph sung about at great length by all concerned. In its simplicity and relative brevity, *Song of the Teachers* was hard to distinguish from similar short works filmed in 1965–1966 as part of the pre–Cultural Revolution promotion of new-style operas on contemporary subjects.

The Hunan opera had first appeared in 1972, when, in best Cultural Revolution practice, it was credited to a collective of amateur and professional writers in Changsha. Liu Zhongfu served to record the script, which was published in an early issue of *Xiangjiang Literature and Art*, the newly restored Hunan provincial cultural magazine.[61] It was hailed as a fresh new work and noticed nationally. From July 1973 *Song of the Teachers* was at the eye of a storm of debate in literary circles, for the cultural insurgents had seized upon the work as a symbol of problems in literature and art and as a weapon to use against their factional rivals.[62] By mid-1974 *Song of the Teachers* came under sustained denunciation, first locally and then nationally, a reaction probably prompted by the distribution of the recently completed film version.[63] This pattern of starting with small, local criticism and then broadening to a nationwide campaign was also a standard Cultural Revolution practice. The criticism's point was that *Song of the Teachers* made more of teachers than of the ultimate teacher for the nation, the Communist Party. It supposedly revealed the airs of a manager of slaves, not of good teachers.[64] But Mao was apparently unimpressed by the fuss. In December 1974 he watched the fifty-minute performance, thereby indicating his endorsement of this stage work from his home province.[65]

Cultural Revolution campaigns like this against specific creative works are usually not readily explained by the contents of the work itself. However, shortcomings, or at least differences with more mainstream or conventional works that were not attacked, can often be found, despite the obscuring clouds of post-1976 counter-criticism. In the case of *Song of the Teachers*, the absence of a class enemy, even in a four-person piece, was striking. The gardener of the title referred to the two teachers, cultivating young minds. The young girl student's grandfather used to own a factory which is a small gesture towards acknowledging class interests. But the 'class conflict' in the opera is that between naughty students and caring teachers in a classroom.

In the more relaxed cultural climate of the early 1970s, this relatively softer conflict must have seemed presentable. But the performers and promoters of this short opera had not counted on the growing insecurity of Jiang Qing and her allies. Arch political rivals, including Deng Xiaoping, had been reinstated. Any let-up in the careful regulation of the performing arts could spell trouble. *Song of the Teachers*' timing was bad.[66] By 1974 this opera was included on lists of spoken plays and *quyi* performances that allegedly represented a 'resurgence of the black line' (*wenyi heixian huichao*).[67] Calls for constant vigilance and lavish praise for 'model' works were falling on deaf ears among cultural professionals and their long-suffering audiences.

A similar case of bad timing and artistic resistance was the modern-style Shanxi opera *Climbing Peach Peak Three Times*, first performed at a North China performance convention in early 1974. The story was based on an actual episode in Hebei in 1965 at Peach Peak production brigade. This was the place where Wang Guangmei, wife of the then head of state Liu Shaoqi, had gone during the Socialist Education Movement on the eve of the Cultural Revolution. Like the heroine of the later opera, Wang had presented the brigade with a prize horse. The parallels infuriated those who had led the charge against Liu Shaoqi. On 28 February 1974 *People's Daily* carried a major article by Chu Lan, a pen name for the

writing group led by Yao Wenyuan and other allies of Jiang Qing. The
Shanxi opera, the article insisted, was trying to 'bring back the spirit of
the dead' Liu Shaoqi. This marked the start of the campaign against the
'resurgence of the black line', 'restorationists' (*fubipai*), and 'overturners
of verdicts' (*fan'anpai*). The appearance of *Peach Peak* showed that even
in 1974, as in the early 1960s with Hai Rui plays, historical allegory could
still be part of artists' armoury.[68]

Dance professionals could also find themselves singled out for criticism in the early 1970s. One such work was a Uighur dance eulogy to
bumper harvests and socialist progress. *Under the Grape Trellis* (*Putaojia
xia*) seems to have gotten into trouble for taking the romanticism associated with minority dance to an extreme. 'Revolutionary romanticism',
when combined with 'revolutionary realism', had remained acceptable
to the new cultural authorities from the start of the Cultural Revolution, even though it was an artistic rubric first coined in the late 1950s.
The dance's misfortune was to be chosen as an exemplar by Jiang Qing's
followers, who wanted to 'kill one to warn a hundred' (*shayijingbai*).
Under the Grape Trellis was taken to represent an attempted 'resurgence
of the black line' in art and literature. By featuring 'soft music and slow
dancing' (*qinggemanwu*), the Uighur dance allegedly lacked the necessary
revolutionary hard edge, including the requisite image of revolutionary
heroism.[69] It is difficult to ascertain how it differed from such soft celebra-
tory dances as *Happily Giving Grain*, produced in Hainan Island at about
the same time. Hardness, however, was more expected from the deserts
of Xinjiang, on the Soviet Union border, than in the tropical southwest.

A foreign-made documentary film came under sustained criticism in
March 1974 about the time troubles mounted for *Song of the Teachers*,
Peach Peak, and other local works. Michelangelo Antonioni, the Italian communist feature-film director, had been invited to China in 1972,
in the flurry of 'opening up' that included visits by Richard Nixon, the
Philadelphia Orchestra, and other cultural groups. Antonioni's documentary, *Chung Kuo Cina*, had not yet been released in Europe when it was
denounced in a series of major articles in March 1974 in *People's Daily*
and elsewhere.[70]

The criticism reflected a fundamental difference of attitude and approach between Antonioni and his Chinese viewers. The Italian had tried
to create an impressionistic contemplation on contemporary China. The
Chinese documentary tradition was one of instruction and clear interpretation, along lines similar to those applied to the model operas and other
Cultural Revolution works. Antonioni's presentation of the Yangzi River
Bridge in Nanjing in a shimmering haze and other sequences may have

reflected somewhat questionable European notions of a special 'Eastern' connection with nature, but to his Chinese critics they were an outrage. The bridge, they alleged, was filmed as if it was about to fall down, denying the Chinese engineering achievement of only the second major structure to cross the Yangzi. Likewise, an infant with split pants in Tian'anmen Square to European eyes may have been a wonderful example of Chinese earthiness and connectedness with the body. But in Chinese eyes it was an insult to the most sacred political space in China. The criticism of *Chung Kuo Cina* was, of course, an indirect attack by the cultural insurgents on Zhou Enlai and others associated with the expansion of foreign contacts and invitations to people like Antonioni.[71]

Despite these aggressive criticisms of particular works, evidence of the growing defensiveness on the part of Jiang Qing and her allies is not hard to find by the mid-1970s. The push to promulgate the two new model operas, *Azalea Mountain* and *Fighting on the Plain*, through especially formed opera troupes in Chengdu and Chongqing in November 1974, for example, seemed decidedly rearguard. The participants were instructed to bring three study documents to the classes that would mount the operas. In addition to Mao's Yan'an *Talks*, the students were to study Jiang Qing's 1964 speech on 'The Revolution in Peking Opera' and the 'Minutes of the Conference on Army Literature and Art Work' from early 1966. The focus on these writings from the eve of the Cultural Revolution suggests a last minute push in 1974 to prop up a crumbling edifice of artistic rectitude.[72]

Likewise, in the spring of 1974, the Hebei Culture Bureau sought reports on how local cadres in cultural work were providing leadership in three areas (*san daitou*): the study of the theory of proletarian dictatorship, the avoidance of bourgeois corruption, and continuing of the revolution by vanguard soldiers. To be reported were the methods and frequency of study of the theory of the proletarian dictatorship undertaken by local Party members, cadres, and artistic professionals. The clichés were standard, but their mention in this context indicated a real concern, on the part of the Hebei leadership, that such failings as suggested by 'bourgeois corruption' were prevalent in the province. The 'proletarian dictatorship' was coming under threat as grumblings about the narrowness of Cultural Revolution cultural prescriptions grew in Hebei and elsewhere. Delegates to a cultural convention in Shijiazhuang, the provincial capital, were asked to bring concrete examples of how the 'poisonous influence of the black line in literature and art' was manifested in their locations and to report, among other things, on the local struggle against 'feudal professional bad habits' (*fengjian hangbang xiqi*), particularly among writers and actors.

The somewhat repetitive rhetoric suggests that the Hebei authorities realized they were losing their grip on cultural developments in the province, at a time when audience expectations were expanding rapidly.[73]

Meanwhile the national cultural leadership, in the hands of allies of Jiang Qing and the Cultural Revolution insurgents, were actively encouraging national-level efforts at further expansion of the cultural repertoire. By so doing they were attempting to assert national control over the endeavour. Performers from four provinces were invited to present new works at a convention in Beijing in February–March 1975. On finding that the local hostel had provided each room with a small hand towel, soap, and tea leaves, the delegation from Shaanxi reportedly were deeply moved. But they gathered them up and returned them, unused, to the hostel office, reportedly saying: 'We have studied the theory of the dictatorship of the proletariat and on restricting bourgeois privileges (faquan). We must start with the smallest point and the tiniest drop (yidian-yidi)'. That such stilted, Boy Scout behaviour should be proudly reported indicates the extent to which the rhetoric of the Cultural Revolution had been ineffective. The slightest gesture was inflated into vast political significance, whereas real issues of cadre privilege and abuse of power were never addressed. Tellingly, the Shaanxi report of this convention noted proudly that whether Party and state leaders were watching made no difference to the actors, who did their best for all audiences.[74]

But ten years of political study by cultural workers clearly had not changed old ways. The Shaanxi Culture Bureau acknowledged in July 1975 continuing 'professional bad habits' (hangbang xiqi) among performers and other artists. Similarly, the tendency to regard writing and art as private matters ('chuangzuo siyou' and 'yishu siyou') deserving individual credit was reportedly still strong, after more than a decade of collectivist creation.[75] By 1975 the Cultural Revolution insurgents were clearly on the defensive. They had in effect become the conservatives, defending the artistic achievements of the Cultural Revolution and warning of the rise of retrograde elements in the cultural arena.

The fifth, and last listed, agenda item at a July 1975 conference in Urumqi on encouraging new writing and expanding the artistic ranks was the simplest and yet most complicated: 'the issue of strengthening the leadership of cultural work'.[76] In times past, such a phrase usually meant a reassertion of strict Party control of artists and writers. In the context of rising factional tensions at the national and provincial levels by 1975, the phrase in reality was an acknowledgement that two leaderships were vying for control of cultural activities in China. One wanted to defend the model performances and the Cultural Revolution destruction of the pre-1966 power-holders. The other group wanted to loosen control, take more risks in allowing a wider space for creativity and innovation, and perhaps even recognize that more pre-1966 culture and creators still had a place in China.

A performance festival in Hebei province in the spring of 1975 revealed the tensions permeating cultural production that year. While the scope of subject matter was widening in the mid-1970s, the rhetoric of class struggle and danger was becoming more hysterical. Some in the artistic ranks were still susceptible to seduction by the 'black line' or by notions of 'bourgeois rights' (*zichanjieji faquan*). What little was actually reported of the Shijiazhuang event noted the need for more bold efforts at writing new works. These should be led by local Communist Party branches assigning cadres to specialize in the management of cultural work, in identifying good representative works (*dianxing*) and summarizing good experience. But 'grasping well' the revolution in literature and art, by past experience, could mean strangling creativity. Perhaps the real purpose of the spring 1975 event was contained in the last sentence of the front-page *Hebei Daily* report on the festival. The Party should energetically popularize the experience of Xiaojinzhuang, a village-sized production brigade in the province.[77] As we have seen in relation to poetry writing, Xiaojinzhuang was closely associated with Jiang Qing and the other Cultural Revolution insurgents who were later identified as the Gang of Four. While ostensibly signalling a broadening of cultural activity, the Hebei gathering represented more defensive efforts to resist a rising tide of popular and political resentment at Cultural Revolution strictures.

Tensions among cultural workers were clearly encouraging caution. The summer 1975 Urumqi conference on literature and art work roundly condemned wrongheaded notions about literature and art as non-essential (*keyoukewu*) and separate from revolution or production. In an intriguing commentary on the centrality and concomitant sensitivity of cultural practice during the Cultural Revolution, speakers also criticized the 'theory of literature and art work being a dangerous area' (*wenyi gongzuo weixian lun*).[78] The complementary aims of encouraging artists to move closer to the broad masses and the latter to become more involved in artistic creation would remain blocked if Party leaders continued to tiptoe around such issues for fear of making egregious errors.[79]

By mid-1976 the factional tensions between defenders of Cultural Revolution orthodoxy and those, like Deng Xiaoping, seeking a broader path forward for China's economic and social development, had reached their height. The attack on the 'Rightist deviationist wind to overthrow the correct verdicts' (*fanji youqing fan'an feng*) had started two months after the death of Premier Zhou Enlai, in early January 1976. His passing emboldened both sides in the debate on China's future. The successful suppression of mass protests at Qingming (5 April 1976) provided an excuse to ratchet up the rhetoric, and Deng Xiaoping was once again removed from office.

The performing arts were enlisted by the insurgents to reinforce their campaign against Deng. 'Rightist deviationists' became the central negative characters in several plays and films in mid-1976. In Tianjin the spoken play *Red Pine Fort* (*Hongsong bao*) focused on a county Party secretary in a struggle with 'capitalist roaders', in a similar kind of story to that of the film *Counterattack* (*Fanji*). Indirect reference to Deng Xiaoping was shared by film and play.[80] After the arrest of the Gang of Four, *Red Pine Fort* was denounced as a plot by anti-Party schemers. This play and others like it had been prompted by the call in the early spring of 1976 to 'write works about the struggle with capitalist roaders'. A Ministry of Culture meeting on 18 March had encouraged a narrow focus on certain subjects related to the political interests of the future Gang of Four. An unnamed close supporter of Jiang Qing in the Tianjin municipal government helped promote the play. *Red Pine Fort* was set in Xiaojinzhuang. Jiang Qing reportedly visited the creators of the play there and gave 'instructions' (*zhishi*), a word often used to refer to high-level commands from such persons as Chairman Mao or the Party's Central Committee. Jiang Qing allegedly urged the writers to be ambitious in their portrayal of 'capitalist roaders' in high office: Even someone as high as a State Council minister was not off-limits. Later, when she inspected the finished work, she allegedly remarked that even a vice-premier could be identified as taking the capitalist road. The play's characters claimed the bounty of their grain crop was the result of their studying and singing of the model operas (*liangshi shi changxi chang chu lai de*). A young woman, Song Jinxiu, was at the center of the play. She led her fellow peasants of Red Pine Fort production brigade in promoting the study of the Dazhai model in agriculture and in exposing renegade Party leaders.

The play was rushed to rehearsal and trial performance before selected audiences in May 1976. A 1977 source claims that worker-peasant-soldier audience members and artists were as one in voicing strong objections to the new play.[81] Work continued, even in open-air rehearsals after the massive Tangshan earthquake had devastated a great deal of Tianjin city in late July. The final dress rehearsal was set for 8 September. The death the next day of Mao Zedong, and the arrest of Jiang Qing and her top allies a month later, put an end to *Red Pine Fort*, except as an object of derision and as evidence of the abuse of literature and art for factional political purposes. Spoken drama's relative ease of production, compared with opera or film, made it an attractive medium for pressured politicians.

The play *In One's Prime* (*Fenghuazhengmao*), titled after a four-character phrase about youthful development, in a similar mould presented a young woman in political battle against conservatives (and hidden 'capitalist roaders') in the education field.[82] This topic had been traversed in the film *Breaking with Old Ideas* (*Juelie*), released in early 1976. Films could reach a wider audience, but stage plays could be more easily adjusted to suit the changes in political ambitions of their promoters. By 1976 most of the plays on China's stages were newly written to endorse the increasingly obvious factional disputes at top Party levels. Twenty or so plays reportedly were created about 'capitalist roaders' in the Party leadership.[83] *A Grand Festival* (*Shengda de jieri*), a typical work, was set against the background of the 'January storm' of 1967 in Shanghai, during which Maoist 'rebel' Red Guards formed a 'Shanghai Commune'. After October 1976, this play was labelled a 'plot play' (*yinmou xiju*). Critics pointed out that the fictional heroes had obvious real-life references: The rebel hero Tie Gen (literally, 'iron root') was modelled on Wang Hongwen and the 'old cadre' Jin Feng was a stand-in for Zhang Chunqiao. Both men had risen to prominence as a result of events in Shanghai in January 1967 and were arrested in October 1976 as members of the Gang of Four. Ninety-nine percent (a remarkably precise figure) of the 'old cadres' in *A Grand Festival* were presented as 'capitalist roaders'.[84] In effect, spoken drama had come full circle from the summer of 1967, when rival Red Guard groups used the stage art to promote their own views of the Cultural Revolution and their own righteous place in the conflicts.

The changing political landscape in 1975–1976 saw a revival of highly charged, somewhat clumsy songs, also reminiscent of Red Guard rhetoric of 1967–1968, in support of the insurgent leadership's causes. These included the controversial *Battlesong of Tian'anmen* (*Tian'anmen zhan'ge*), performed in late May 1976 by massed choirs in the Xi'an Illuminated Sports Field to mark the Yan'an *Talks* anniversary. The song cycle was written at speed in response to the officially condemned popular demonstrations in the square in early April.[85] But it was not easy to put slogans like 'oppose the Rightist deviationist wind to reverse the correct verdicts' to music. In countervailing mode, dancers at the China Railroad Song and Dance Ensemble created *Cherished Memories of the Bridge Workers* (*Qiao gong de huainian*). The dance featured an actor playing Zhou Enlai who is saluted by adoring women dancers, perhaps the first time the late leader was impersonated on stage or film. The railroad dancers' other 1976 creation was a celebration of an episode in

Chongqing during the Anti-Japanese War during which Zhou had encouraged newspaper boys to distribute a newspaper banned by the Nationalist
government. Such work on dances commemorating the late premier ran
the risk of accusations of supporting the disgraced Deng Xiaoping, so the
dances' premieres seem to have been held after the October arrest of Jiang
Qing and her allies.[86]

4. SCREENING RESISTANCE: FILMS UNDER ATTACK

The filming of the eight model performances in the early 1970s had offered
a new, more effective way to promulgate the models. The success of the
film versions, artistically and in being watched by millions, ironically hastened their achievement of the status of kitsch icons. They were perhaps
the most watched films the world had ever seen. Other films from the mid-
1970s became well known in China, less through audience viewing than
through large-scale criticism campaigns. *Haixia*, a Beijing Film Studio
production, and *The Pioneers* (*Chuangye*), from the Changchun studio,
were denounced by the cultural leaders associated with the (future) Gang
of Four. After the arrest of Jiang Qing and her allies, these two films were
cited as models of the commitment to their art of their makers and of
the evil excesses of the fallen leaders. A third film, *Counterattack* (*Fanji*),
made also at the Beijing studio and never released, served as an example
of the use of film by the Gang of Four to further their plot to seize political power.[87] In the controversy surrounding these films, questions of their
artistic merit were either highly charged or ignored. Whether they were
in reality very different from most of the other features being produced
at the studios in the last four years of the Cultural Revolution was never
considered.

   The Pioneers was completed at Changchun on 29 January 1975, though
formally it was counted as part of the studio's 1974 productions, along
with four other features, including the colour re-make of *Guerillas on
the Plain*.[88] It told the story of the opening up of the Daqing oilfield in
Heilongjiang in the northeast. The early days of the Daqing field had
already become the stuff of legend, with one oilfield worker, Wang Jinxi,
being hailed in the Chinese media as an 'iron man' (*tieren*). The film's
central hero, oilman and Party member Zhou Tingshan, copies iron man
Wang's most celebrated deed, by leaping into a pit of liquid concrete in
order to stop it from setting. The film starts in 1949 with Zhou's youth in
the northwest where he sees China's dependency on foreign oil and oil-
drilling technology. Ten years later at Daqing he is a firm advocate of the
Maoist virtues of self-reliance. In contrast Zhou's highly trained geologist

managers insist that, according to foreign wisdom, the search for oil there is a lost cause. Needless to say, Zhou Tingshan is proved right by an almighty gusher. Self-sufficiency in sight, Zhou leads the workers in exposing the chief geologist's past counter-revolutionary crimes.[89]

The film was directed by Yu Yanfu, from a collectively created script written down by Zhang Tianyi, a novelist and long-time scriptwriter at Changchun. In the winter of 1972, he and director Yu, along with key figures from the film crew, had gone to experience life at the Daqing oilfield. This was in the best Maoist tradition, one also practised by the creators of the model operas and ballets. They lived and worked with the drill workers and interviewed upwards of 100 people in Daqing and elsewhere. The film went into production, shooting exterior scenes in snow in February–March 1974, and filming finished in mid-November 1974. In normal times, this pace might be considered leisurely. After going through three rounds of editing and four inspections (by the State Council Culture Group in Beijing), the film was reduced from an original three hours and ten minutes to two hours and twenty-eight minutes. Reportedly, it was shortened because Jiang Qing (referred to in the sources as 'the senior officer', *shouzhang*) had pointed out that the longest model performance film was two hours and thirty minutes. Audiences nationwide started watching the film on 7 February 1975, a release date timed to coincide with Spring Festival, a traditional time to introduce new performances.[90] Some post–Cultural Revolution accounts make much of the ways in which the film 'broke through the restrictions of the "three prominences"' and presented a more nuanced set of characters.[91]

Four days after its release Jiang Qing saw the finished film and was not impressed. 'I've watched this film over and over and still don't understand'. For this critic, the film was full of artistic and political mistakes. Of the dramatic point in the film in which iron man Zhou Tingshan receives copies of Mao's *Selected Works* from Party Central in Beijing, Jiang Qing reportedly snorted: 'Those days Party Central was in the hands of Liu Shaoqi [the Cultural Revolution's highest victim]: this film is beautifying Liu' (Figure 5.1). The next day orders came from the Culture Group that the printing of copies and distribution of *The Pioneers* were to stop. A representative was sent to Changchun to inform the crew that the film had 'serious problems', though he failed to specify anything. This was typical Cultural Revolution intimidation by vague accusation.

The post–Cultural Revolution accounts of what happened subsequently are full of quotations from such mysterious figures, alleged allies of Jiang Qing, as So-and-so Liu (*Liu X X*) and others. The picture is painted of innocent filmmakers responding bravely to accusation and innuendo.

5.1. Jiang Qing as revolutionary leader of cultural activities. The slogan reads: 'Let the new socialist literature and art occupy every stage.' 1967 or 1968 poster produced by the Revolutionary Rebel Liaison Headquarter of the Beijing Film Studio. Poster in the author's collection.

Jiang Qing had the Culture Group prepare 'ten objections' (*shi tiao yijian*) to *The Pioneers*.[92] In July 1975 the scriptwriter Zhang Tianyi responded with a letter to Mao Zedong reporting the affair. While doing fieldwork at the Dagang oilfield near Tianjin, Zhang and director Yu Yanfu made preparations, anticipating being jailed or worse. On 25 July, Mao Zedong wrote back, in the manner of an imperial rescript:[93]

> This film has no big errors. Propose it is passed for distribution. Do not nitpick (*qiuquanzebei*). And to list as many as ten accusations against it is going too far. It hampers the adjustment of the Party's current policy on literature and art.

The response at the Changchun studio when Mao's letter reached there on 28 July was jubilation. It was seen as applying to more than just *The Pioneers*. Clearly, both Jiang Qing and her allies, as well as the filmmakers, saw this case as a test or gauge of the cultural climate. The post–Gang of Four accounts invariably present the attack on the film as an example of Jiang Qing's arbitrary exercise of power over cultural matters. But the case can also be seen as illustrating her awareness of the shifting of cultural fortunes in the course of 1975. Vice-Premier Deng Xiaoping had returned to public life, signalling a turning away from the excesses of the late 1960s. Feeling their position increasingly under threat, the Cultural Revolution insurgents responded with threats of their own.

Another threatened film was the Beijing Film Studio's 1974 work *Haixia*, about the life of militia women in a fishing village on the southeast coast. The film was co-directed by erstwhile cinematographer Qian Jiang, Chen Huai'ai, and Wang Haowei from a script polished by Xie Tieli, director of the much-maligned *Early Spring in February*. This team had started work on the project in January 1973, soon after a meeting of film workers with Premier Zhou Enlai, at which he had urged that more feature films be produced.[94] It was an adaptation of the 1972 novel *Island Women's Militia* (*Haidao nü minbing*) by Li Ruqing.[95] The film seemed unremarkable in its presentation of a female hero, firmly supported by the proletarian masses, exposing enemies within the ranks on the front line of the Mainland–Taiwan divide.

But the increasingly insecure cultural leadership in 1975 needed a target around which to launch an 'anti-guild' (*fan hangbang*) movement in film circles. They chose *Haixia* with which to expose 'the cliquish system of the director as the central figure'.[96] Of the films in production in 1974–1975, *Haixia* was the project in the hands of the most senior, and hence vulnerable, filmmakers. Moreover, Xie Tieli and Qian Jiang had taken it upon themselves in May 1971 to write to Zhou Enlai to report that Chinese audiences were yearning for new feature films. They had based their report on conversations with workers at the 7 February Locomotive and Carriage Factory, to which the film crews from the Beijing studio that had worked on the model performance films were sent in March 1971 for a period of labour.[97] This boldness in writing to the premier seems to have rankled Jiang Qing. Three years later, in August 1974, when discussing their re-shooting of *On the Docks*, she reportedly remarked she had heard Xie and Qian wanted to make feature films: 'Is it that you have no interest in making "model-performance" films?'[98] As Xie Tieli noted to an interviewer twenty years later: 'From that time on, no matter what we did, Jiang Qing was always displeased. Whatever we did was wrong'.[99]

Once *Haixia* was completed after a lengthy twenty months in January 1975, the leading lights of the culture ministry began to grumble about how the film allegedly did not accord properly with the 'three prominences': Too much attention was given to secondary characters, with Haixia not standing out among her peers.[100] Part of the problem for the filmmakers was the inadequacy as a film performer of the opera actress who played the adult Haixia. She brought the exaggeration of stage work to her acting in front of the camera. One way of dealing with the problem was to avoid putting the actress in the centre of shots and shooting her from oblique angles or interacting with other characters.[101] Jiang Qing herself later watched the film and dismissed it: 'a city girl', and 'nice mountains, nice water, nice scenery'. Three plans for changes to the film were rejected by the culture ministry, which sent inspectors to the studio to report on the *Haixia* crew.[102]

Having made adjustments to more than 100 shots and still not passed censorship, the makers of *Haixia* wrote in frustration to Jiang Qing in June seeking clarification of the objections to the film.[103] It is clear from a lengthy history of the *Haixia* episode completed in the mid-1990s that debate on the film at the highest levels in the Chinese government became entangled in factional disputes.[104] Frustration levels were so high that the filmmakers eventually responded to the criticism of their work in the same way as the artists at Changchun. In July 1975 they wrote letters to Zhou Enlai and Mao Zedong reporting on the difficulties with *Haixia* and complaining how representatives of Jiang Qing and Zhang Chunqiao had made several visits to the studio to try to put pressure on the crew.[105] In his imperial way, on 29 July Mao noted on the letter: 'Distribute to all comrades in the Politburo'.[106] Clearly by mid-1975 the future Gang of Four had lost ground in disputes on both *Haixia* and *The Pioneers*.

The third of the mid-1970s feature films that served as iconic works in the aftermath of the fall of the 'Gang of Four' in October 1976 was also made at the Beijing studio. *Counterattack (Fanji)* was never distributed, though it was shown as a 'negative example' *(fanmian jiaocai)* rather widely to selected audiences. The film was cited as evidence of film being put to direct factional use by the Gang of Four in its struggle with Party rivals in the Politburo. Its making was allegedly ordered by Jiang Qing's ally Zhang Chunqiao within days of Hua Guofeng becoming acting premier in February 1976, a month after Zhou Enlai had died. The script and production were a collective effort, later attributed to a number of groups. The Liang Xiao (a homonym for 'two schools') writing group, under directions from Chi Qun, who had strong links with Peking and Tsinghua universities, where the writing group was based, wrote the script and took care of political questions.[107]

Shooting started on 4 June 1976, and a rough cut was completed by 20 September 1976, eleven days after the death of Chairman Mao.[108] Although the director's role was attributed to Li Wenhua, artistic questions were the responsibility of the Ministry of Culture, headed by Yu Huiyong and Hao Liang, the original star of *The Red Lantern* model opera.[109] Jiang Qing's supporters also had allies who worked at the Beijing studio. The 1997 studio history writes of one unnamed 'Gang' follower who had sent a dozen letters to Jiang Qing to report on developments in the studio between 1967 and September 1976.[110]

Counterattack told a more ambitious story than most films from the mid-1970s, suggesting its political purpose in the factional fighting in Beijing. Han Ling, a provincial Party secretary, newly returned from Beijing in the summer of 1975, sets about work on the 'four modernizations' (*si ge xiandaihua*) and closing down 'open-door schooling', insisting that the students take examinations. Leading the counterattack is Jiang Tao of Yellow River University, who exposes secretary Han as a capitalist roader seeking to restore capitalism. At the end of the film, the 'counterattack against the Rightist deviationist wind to overturn the correct verdicts' has started. Secretary Han is the first victim, Secretary Jiang the first victor.[111]

Until *Counterattack*, the allegorical politics of Cultural Revolution feature films had mostly been indirect, even circumspect. With this film, the gloves were off. The editorial contents of the *People's Daily* and other media were transferred directly onto the screen: Secretary Han represented Deng Xiaoping and other Gang of Four opponents. The counterattack at the end was exactly what the media were pushing in April–May 1976, after the Qingming demonstrations in Tian'anmen Square and the consequent dismissal of Deng from the vice-premiership. Even more obviously than *Breaking with Old Ideas*, which shared the educational setting and themes, or *Chunmiao*, about a 'barefoot doctor', this film was full of long speeches stuffed with mouth-breaking slogans and labels.[112] The masses serve as a chorus of support for Jiang Tao (who shares Jiang Qing's surname) and the central heroes. There is even a minor character called 'Xiaoping Tou' (little flat head, or 'Xiaoping head'). Like *Breaking with Old Ideas*, *Counterattack* ends with a mass meeting, slogans draped across the back of the film frame, as the victory of the correct path is celebrated. Never passed for release and excoriated after October 1976, the film served as a signpost of the weakness of the Cultural Revolution insurgents on their way to the arrest of the Gang of Four.[113]

The power of one person in this political system and concern at the negative consequences of too narrow a cultural realm were shown in a curious way in 1975–1976. Old-style Chinese opera, of the kind condemned at the start of the Cultural Revolution and replaced by the 'revolutionary modern Peking operas', re-appeared on China's screens. But they were for an audience of one: Mao Zedong himself. The official catalogue of feature films for the thirty years after 1949 includes pages of credits and synopses for these operas, all of which were straightforward 'stage documentaries' (*wutai jilupian*), rather than elaborate productions after the manner of the model operas. Almost all of these works were made on videotape, as it was cheaper and easier and the current intended audience, by now in his eighties, had difficulty watching big-screen films.[114]

Work started in the autumn of 1975, when Yu Huiyong announced to a startled gathering of opera actors and other specialists that they should prepare lists of operas and scenes to be recorded, along with the performers' names. Secrecy was to be maintained, though Yu reportedly argued that this new turning back to tradition was not just for Mao Zedong's benefit, but for the purpose of continuing the revolution in the performing arts. The response from actors and others was generally cautious: the young seeking reassurance that their leaders would take any blame and the old needing persuasion after being targeted for criticism ten years earlier. Old-style opera costumes and props had been sold or destroyed long ago, and even scripts were hard to find. Shanghai actors, who in their home troupes were performing the model operas, re-learnt the old scenes and filmed them in temporary quarters in the city. Pay and conditions for the casts and crews were according to the then generous terms enjoyed by the 'model troupes'.[115] Four studios joined the effort to make these traditional opera films, all fifty-two listed as 1976 productions. Six films were made at Changchun, twelve at Beijing, twenty in Shanghai, and fourteen at the Central Newsreel and Documentary Film Studio.[116] At the Beijing studio, directing these opera recordings was all in the hands of Chen Huai'ai and Chen Fangqian, experienced opera-film directors working with a specialist production team.[117] Jiang Qing, as she had done with the film adaptations of the model performances, looked at rushes and expressed opinions on the quality of the work.[118] In all, these opera films amounted to more than half the ninety productions listed for 1976 of the eight feature-film studios then at work.

There was another reason for making these opera films: Fifty-two were too much for an increasingly infirm Mao to enjoy. These opera documentaries recorded performances and scripts that had not been made public in ten years. Many of those made at the Shanghai studio were small-scale performances of a single scene or several scenes from an opera. They featured older actors and musicians to record their stage-craft while they were still capable of performing.[119] But the credit to the China Peking Opera Company and the Shanghai Peking Opera Company given with many of these 1976 films suggests an intriguing situation in which the same companies that were responsible for the model Peking opera *On the Docks* and the opera version of *The Red Detachment of Woman* were, at the same time, engaged in rehearsals and performance of traditional-style operas. Some of the minor actors listed in the old-style opera tapes' credits appear also in the cast lists for the Cultural Revolution operas. This was further evidence of the growing weakness of the Cultural Revolution insurgents by the mid-1970s.

One of the more remarkable films made at the Beijing Film Studio in 1976 embraced several worlds of cultural practice: that of the Cultural Revolution and of the seventeen years before then. *The Precious Lotus Lamp* (*Bao lian deng*) had started life as China's first full-length 'national dance-drama' (*minzu wuju*). Created at the Beijing Dance School in 1957, it was based on an ancient folk tale that had been featured in many old-style Chinese operas. The story had been transformed for the dance stage into a suitable socialist story of a beautiful young woman resisting 'feudal oppression' in her marriage choice. Much of the success of the dance-drama can be ascribed to the ancient setting and dazzling old-style costumes. Shanghai's Tianma Film Studio had filmed the dance-drama in 1959. It starred Zhao Qing, daughter of Zhao Dan, China's most famous film actor since the 1930s.[120]

In 1976 Chen Huai'ai and Chen Fangqian, along with shooting twelve old-style operas on tape, took time to make a three-part film of a new version of *The Precious Lotus Lamp*. This had transformed the dance-drama into a Hebei clapper opera (*Hebei bangzi*). The legendary setting, costumes, and story remained, and the means used to tell the story was a modernized version of the old-style opera. It was performed by the Hebei Clapper Opera Leap Forward Company (*Hebei bangzi yuejin jutuan*).[121] Thus, even as the Gang of Four were applying pressure on filmmakers and other cultural professionals to continue the triumphs of the Cultural Revolution, a regional-form opera was created that eschewed the modern settings and stories required of all other operas performed publicly in those years.

At the time that Jiang Qing and her three cohorts were arrested in October 1976, Zhang Yang was still under investigation for his unpublished but widely circulated novel *The Return*. He had been in custody for almost two years, while police investigated the case of the novel that became *The Second Handshake*. Another two years and two months would pass before he was released from jail, his health broken, and his case officially cleared. Six months later, in July 1979, Zhang's novel was finally published. A work that had started life as a short story, as it turned out appropriately titled 'Spindrift' (*Langhua*), become a novel and been passed from eager reader to reader in hand-copied editions, finally sat on a bookstore shelf in printed and bound form. To cap off the achievement, *The Second Handshake* was made into a film, starring Xie Fang as the nuclear physicist who returns home to China. While the eras were different, this Cultural Revolution underground heroine had something in common with Xie's earlier role as Miss Tao in *Early Spring in February*. Both heroines had appealed to the romantic, idealistic ambitions for society and themselves of many young Chinese. One film had helped mark the start of the Cultural Revolution. The other underscored its end.

CHAPTER SIX

Conclusion: Forcing Modernity

More than thirty years after the end of the period and forty years since its beginning, making judgements about the Cultural Revolution is still fraught with difficulty. As an event of such magnitude, the Cultural Revolution will naturally always arouse passion and confusion. It also continues to raise questions about how and why it occurred. The urge to condemn the political excesses and stupidities of the era remains strong, especially for those whose families suffered directly from the cruelties or who see the Cultural Revolution as an appropriate representative of such political excess in other places and other times. Making sense of Cultural Revolution culture requires acknowledging the extent of political control over artists, performers, writers, and managers, as well as audiences and readers. This study has attempted to cover the range of cultural practice and experience in the major centres and in the regions, in the public arena and well as in more private contexts, in order to suggest that a great deal more was being created, enjoyed, or resisted than hackneyed jokes about 800 million people limited to eight model performances.

This book has approached the era from a viewpoint that has combined an acceptance of its special qualities with a determination to locate these ten years in the broader sweep of Chinese developments. As the making of the eight so-called model performances shows, these works did not spring into complete and rounded existence in 1966 in the hands of artists and writers with no experience of the preceding half-century. These origins indicate that decisions on creative production and on the political usage of these cultural products were embedded in Chinese historical experience across the whole of the twentieth century and earlier. While a unique experience for many participants in its policies and madder directives, the Cultural Revolution is best understood in this wider historical context.

The first aim of this study has been to offer a comprehensive history of cultural production and consumption during the Cultural Revolution. The discussion has tried to map three periods during these ten years, evident in all the different kinds of artistic activities outlined in successive chapters. An initial breaking down of authority and the introduction of new cultural models (1966–1968) saw the emergence of the *yangbanxi* as central exemplars for artists and audiences. During the middle or transition period (1968–1971), these models were elaborated and fixed centrally, while their patterns were replicated in local artistic forms. Cultural organizations were reformed and a new corps of artists given more prominence. At the same time, the internal migration of millions of young people to the countryside set up conditions for the growth of less-controlled, unofficial cultural life. From 1971, the restoration of art and literature periodicals across the nation and the release of new feature films were part of a widening cultural production that allowed for a return to greater experimentation with old and new forms. In all three periods, national leaders and factional politics on occasion were key in determining the direction of cultural change and the range of choices available to artists and their audiences.

Cultural consumption and production, including the emphasis on the amateur, offer insight into Chinese life beyond the political and social elites, which has been the second aim of this study. An analysis of the kinds of art, literature, and performances available to ordinary audiences can indicate what elites thought were suitable for mass consumption. This study has suggested some of the ways in which audiences responded to these new works. The issue of what exactly audiences felt remains illusive, shaped by a mix of memory, nostalgia, and awareness of change in the decades since. This concluding chapter will extrapolate further on the question of mass cultural habits and tastes.

The following paragraphs will also offer further observations on the ways in which the ten years formally identified as the Cultural Revolution fit firmly in the pattern of twentieth-century Chinese cultural developments. This third, contextualising aim of our study has been addressed in the analysis, for example, of the rise of modernized Peking opera and the invention of Chinese-style ballet. In addition to cultural products, the ways in which these works were made available and enjoyed or otherwise by audiences matched habits that emerged much earlier in the century and evolved further into the present century.

The politics of the Cultural Revolution effort to produce a modern Chinese culture ultimately defeated the attempt. The composers, choreographers, and theatre directors undertook their work in a political system obsessed with concepts of correctness. This fever over ideological right and wrong, in an era when factional rivalries became even more vicious, made public innovation on occasion too risky. Experimentation was so politically charged in most instances that artists, writers, and audiences chose to avoid risk, at least in public.

But the innovation of the first period did not fade away, once Red Guard groups had been disbanded and members dispatched to communes, state farms, or the military. Instead, it went underground, avoiding the dangers of open performance and circulation. The private, unofficial pleasures of the hand-copied novel, some of which were highly salacious, co-existed with ritual enjoyment of more orthodox new art and literature. The latter never obliterated this underground, unsanctioned creativity to which the early year or two of relative openness to new cultural forms at the start of the Cultural Revolution gave an unexpected push. Red Guards took their mid-1960s urban experiments in new performance forms and strange combinations of Chinese and foreign contents and settings and, as sent-down youth in the countryside, reproduced these kinds of innovation for themselves, often far from official interference or knowledge. Even in official contexts, the innovation and degree of experimentation by the mid-1970s in fields such as music and dance were striking.

The kind of hybridity seen, for example, in the mix of Chinese and Western dance steps in the Cultural Revolution was a distinctly modern element in these cultural productions. Chinese folk dance, martial arts, and more high cultural dance movement were added to orthodox ballet or modern dance movement to create a new style of performance. These unique dances were clearly Chinese but based on international models. The modernized operas similarly incorporated movement, blocking, lighting, and other staging elements from the spoken drama stage to produce a new kind of Chinese musical theatre. Such borrowing and blending could be from somewhat distant sources, as the cinematic inspiration in the staging of some scenes in the new-style operas attests. Audiences unfamiliar with or unwilling to attend opera performances could be engaged by (probably unconsciously) recognizing the narrative strategies, character presentation, and climactic devices usually associated with feature films. These stage performance experiments were borrowed in other arts. Painters, usually working in a national painting (*guohua*) tradition, attempted to present individual figures or groups in ways recognizable from the opera stage or cinema screen. The results of these experiments in hybrid borrowings were both distinctly modern and definitely Chinese. The dream of the young musician Yin Chengzong to mount a performance of the piano version of *Shajiabang* for a massed audience in Tian'anmen Square can be understood in this context.

Another distinctly modern element in cultural production during the Cultural Revolution was the extent to which specialization was introduced into heritage performing arts and elsewhere. Chinese opera, in whatever regional variant, had in the past been the domain of actor-managers, training successors through a master–apprenticeship mode, and staging shows from a well-worn repertoire with standard performance and musical tropes. By mid-century, and especially during these ten years, lead actors lost this generalist eminence and became, in the major companies, one kind of specialist among a range of professionals. Stage directors, set designers, lighting designers, costume and make-up designers, musical composers, lyricists, and other experts were brought together to work on the iconic operas of the era. Many of these specialists brought no particular knowledge of operatic practice to their tasks. Instead, they borrowed and adapted ideas and effects from other stage arts, poetry, fiction, and music to the opera stage. The results represented a major transformation in Chinese musical theatre, a shift to the modern in a stage art most associated with Chinese regional cultures.

Artists responded to the new demands and opportunities presented by this experimentation with a mix of confusion and eagerness. Particularly for younger, less-established performers and other artists, the new-style operas, other performances, and arts offered an opportunity to achieve official and even popular acclaim. The political accommodations required of cultural practitioners between 1966 and 1976 were hardly unfamiliar to most players. Faced with a choice of silence, resistance, or participation, most chose the latter.

Among the characteristics of the modernized culture in these years was its apparent militarization. Seven of the eight model performances are set in wartime and feature soldiers in the lead or central roles. This emphasis on the army was seen on the eve of the Cultural Revolution proper, when the cultural insurgents used a conference on art and literature work in the armed forces to force the hand of the power-holders over cultural practice. Four of the five modernized Peking operas and the two ballets, used to promulgate a new-style culture, were set in the Anti-Japanese, civil, or Korean wars. The *Shajiabang* symphony was equally martial. Only the contemporary story of *On the Docks* escaped the presence of armed soldiers.

The militarization of culture matched the militancy of purpose of the cultural revolutionaries. Mao Zedong called on Red Guards and others to reject the effete, comfortable practices becoming entrenched among

Party members and the general public as memories of revolution and civil war faded. Mao's rallying cry to continue the revolution was matched by the militancy of cultural production. Heroes without concern for their personal interests, indeed seemingly without emotional ties to anyone or anything unconnected with that revolution, became models of militancy and determination in the Manichean struggle to defend Mao's work.

Here too the underground cultural production offers a mirror image of the official versions. Novels such as *The Second Handshake* made heroes not of soldiers, but of scientists and other intellectuals, like the readers among whom they circulated. Other fiction told melodramatic tales of love, betrayal, and reconciliation, again filling the emotional void of the model and other official works and appealing to youthful readers. More racy, even pornographic writing catered to further needs not addressed, at least directly, in official cultural production. Soldiers were virtually absent from such unofficial tales.

A cult of the physical and the body during these years was part of the militancy of official culture. The heroes of the model operas all show a toughness that expressed a rejection of reliance on the cultivated mind of traditional intellectuals and a need for physical endurance and risk taking. Chairman Mao's acclaimed swim in the Yangzi River in July 1966 was not just a display of his own health but a further message on the need for personal transformation on the part of educated young Chinese. Weekly sessions of token physical labour were required of urban intellectuals in these years, even if many persisted in keeping shirtsleeves down in the summer heat to avoid the sun-bronzed forearms associated with peasants.[1]

Running counter to the rise of the often modern specialist, these years saw a renewed emphasis on amateur creation and performance. Mao Zedong had set the Cultural Revolution in motion from his determination to undermine what he saw as elitist, increasingly entrenched superiority in political and professional life. Instead of well-paid, privileged holders of power and influence, 'the broad masses' (*guangda qunzhong*) would be encouraged to seize influence and topple those who felt born to rule, even as Communists. For many educated Chinese, used to lives of relative comfort and privilege, these years saw an appalling challenge to the normal way of the world in which, in many places, uneducated boors took charge and barked orders. Likewise, in the sphere of cultural production, the amateur challenged the entrenched elitism of the professional. Poetry writing, for example, was further popularized in these years. The quintessential cultural practice for educated Chinese over three millennia, poetry writing had been transformed in the twentieth century, at least in the rise of modern-style verse that could eschew the emphasis on rules, literary allusion, and precedent of traditional verse. After 1949 mass poetry composition was encouraged among less-educated Chinese, drawing often on folk versification. This amateur activity received a further push during the Cultural Revolution, facilitated by the greater availability in the revived literary journals and radio broadcasts of the early 1970s of models of poetry for emulation. The peasant painters of Hu County in Shaanxi province and other amateur painting schools in Zhejiang and Fujian provinces took another traditional scholar's skill to folk producers and, through posters, to mass consumers.

This mobilization of the amateur writer, artist, actor, or musician, and of mass participation more generally was an effective means to popularize the model cultural productions of the Cultural Revolution. In the second half of the 1960s, before the operas were given a lavish and perfect celluloid existence, non-professional groups staged the model operas in whole or as key scenes in factories, mines, military camps, and communes across the nation. Some of the performing groups were not amateur, though they could hardly be described as professional. Large enterprises, including factories and government bodies, had propaganda groups, generally staffed by local people who had displayed a talent for song and dance. Group members often did little or no work on production lines but devoted themselves to morale-boosting performances. Occasionally, such groups also enjoyed the services of more professional colleagues, transferred from a (perhaps recently disbanded) local opera or dance company or given an opportunity to practise their craft in a break from reform through labour at a May Seventh Cadre School. Radio broadcasts allowed prospective local performers access to the new-style music and recently invented singing styles of the model operas. These broadcasts also ensured prospective audiences for local productions were familiar with the characters, stories, and new-style sound of the model works. Even the most inept amateur production could be followed, though not necessarily enjoyed. These local performances helped the modernized operas become the heart of cultural practice in these years. They also encouraged emulation and local efforts, through so-called transplanting, to modernize regional musical theatre forms as well as other kinds of local performance traditions.

An unforeseen elaboration of the Cultural Revolution cult of the amateur was seen and read privately far from official gaze. The creation and circulation of underground writing, including poetry and stories, was often in the hands of young people who were being encouraged to develop their writing talents in more official arenas. Indeed, some sent-down youth used the facilities made available to them to produce official newspapers and periodicals to duplicate and circulate texts that were somewhat more resistant. A mimeograph machine at a propaganda station on the Inner Mongolian steppes might produce in daytime a broadsheet for the entertainment and edification of young people settled there from Beijing. But at night the machine could be turned over to the production of hand-bound stories that gave a more emotionally florid and satisfying expression to the sent-down youth experience on the grasslands. Amateur performing talent, cultivated to present model works or heroes in spoken drama or dance, could stage, when the circumstances allowed, unapproved, heartfelt works that referred to real experience rather than idealized lives. Many such amateurs had gotten a taste for producing works of topical immediacy as Red Guard performers before being dispatched to the countryside after 1968. Readers and audiences too had been attuned to different, less-polished expectations by exposure to officially endorsed amateur composition and presentation.

The processes of cultural modernization, as elsewhere in the world, had a mixed effect on local cultures. On the one hand, the official endorsement and centralized propagation of a standardized, national culture could mean the effective obliteration of the local. For a time in the mid-1960s, opera performers and audiences may have wondered whether the riches of hundreds of local types of musical theatre had any future, as Peking opera was singled out for a highly resourced and highly controlled effort at modernization. But the Cultural Revolution cultural leaders chose Peking opera for its symbolic function, not as the sole opera genre to be permitted in the new, national culture. By mid-century Peking opera had become, by default, the national opera form: the style of musical theatre most associated with the nation's capital and deemed most suitable to present martial stories of heroism and recent history.

The importance given to the modernized version of Peking opera, at least in terms of rhetorical attention if not in actual practice, seemed perhaps to threaten local opera styles and traditions. But on the other hand the centralizing tendencies even of the Cultural Revolution could not replace the attractions of local musical theatre heritages. Just as the modern Peking operas had been adapted in several cases from local or regional originals, so the newly ensconced model works were immediately subject to transplanting into local forms. The modernized versions of these local and regional styles may have often looked somewhat distantly connected to their alleged local roots, but the differences from the Peking-opera versions were gratifying to performers and audiences keen to preserve something of the local.

The modern pattern of centralization of cultural practice and a tendency to homogenize the local into easily recognized versions of their original, often rougher prototypes, were marked features of Cultural Revolution cultural production and consumption. This was of course not a new phenomenon during these years. The rise of modern newspapers and other media, including magazines, radio, and film, had encouraged similar changes from early in the twentieth century. The new regime after 1949 gave added impetus and considerable resources to these centripetal trends. A mass, national culture would help unite the new China and strengthen the bonds between government and citizens and between regions and the centre. The most obvious example of such centralizing and homogenization of the local can be seen in the treatment of the songs and dances of various ethnic minorities. Chinese audiences in the 1950s and early 1960s became familiar with certain dance moves or musical sounds or tropes as signifying particular ethnic groups. To both officials and audiences the authenticity of these dances and music was not an issue. By 1966, they had become standardized, easily recognized signs of ethnic diversity and assertions of multi-cultural tolerance. The Cultural Revolution radicals took these tendencies to new extremes, but they did not invent them. Indeed, during the Cultural Revolution these local signs were valued as providing a ready, even shorthand way to assert a Chinese version of modern culture. A ballet step combined with a shifting of the neck in Mongolian style, for example, nicely combined something deemed Chinese with international, modern dance language. After 1976, these developments were not reversed, but built upon.

We have seen in the preceding chapters the interconnectedness and ambition of cultural production in the 1960s and 1970s. A model opera, its heroes, and episodes reappeared in a full range of cultural forms, from the performing to the plastic arts. The formulas and style of these operas also animated a great deal of practice in other genres, from films to story-telling, even acrobatics. This kind of intertextuality was not a new phenomenon in Chinese cultural history, but the ambition to create a new, coherent set of cultural principles and procedures was typical Cultural Revolution over-reach which ultimately doomed the attempt. It also aligned this period in China with fascist and other episodes of totalitarian excess elsewhere.[2]

The failings of Cultural Revolution cultural production are hardly surprising. As we have seen in their involvement in cultural production, the ambition of the cultural insurgents, including Jiang Qing, Yu Huiyong, and others, was breathtaking. Nothing short of the modern transformation of Chinese culture, from the popular to the most intellectual, was the collective project of these activists, even if their rhetoric spoke only of class struggle and proletarian liberation. It was a top-down project, propelled by political needs rather than an organic, mass response to changing circumstances, which was in marked contrast with the more natural, somewhat messier 'vernacular modernism' that had brought film, for example, into the heart of Chinese urban culture in the first half of the twentieth century.

One obvious failing of the Cultural Revolution years undermined the entire project. The inflation of rhetoric and language reached unprecedented heights (or depths) in the Cultural Revolution. Everything, from getting up in the morning to crossing the road, could be presented as part of some vast, all-encompassing, and life-or-death struggle between good and evil. On China's stages, on cinema screens, on gallery walls, and in publications, the idealized fighters in this never-ending conflict posed in inspired determination to succeed. Style took over from content, as the banality of much of this cultural production became obvious after years of unrelenting posturing. The repetition of images of characters like Yang Zirong, Fang Haizhen, Li Tiemei, and Wu Qinghua rendered them into kitsch icons. The images became empty of real substance and merely served as a kind of switch to turn on appropriate associations of idealistic sacrifice and heroism. They inhabited another universe, beyond reach and ineffably charming.

How most Chinese dealt with the inflation of public rhetoric and the hectoring delivered by public culture deserves further study. The heroic figures in several of the model works seem to have had real attraction for many viewers, at least initially. The novelty and invention of the modernized Peking operas, for example, were impressive for opera aficionados who were aware of earlier efforts to make opera more contemporary in content and style. The skills in lyric writing, musical composition, and staging brought to bear on the new opera stages produced dramatic images and, at the start, an emotional response from the viewing public. The skills of the professional actors in performing these new roles, always a major interest for the operagoer, were exemplary. The overall effect of these new works, sung and staged in new ways, was impressive.

A similar argument can be made for other kinds of new-style cultural production during these years. The innovation seen on the dance stage or heard in the concert hall offered pleasures to many audience members. Even in areas such as fiction, where official experimentation was relatively rare, readers could find small pleasures in the skills with dialogue and narrative of a writer like Hao Ran. Fiction and other writing could be enjoyed privately, which made it attractive for many when compared with the pleasures of a group as audience.

Another part of the pleasure of Cultural Revolution cultural production, at least for some consumers, was the capacity for many of these works to offer layered appreciation. What some viewers might see as a simple fight sequence, with thrilling acrobatic tumbling and flashing bayonets, other viewers might see parallels with, or references to, scenes from older-style operas. Some viewers could enjoy identifying the ways in which borrowings from other genres, films, and spoken drama, for example, had been incorporated into the modernized works.

We have observed, however, that the success of the model and other performances through repetition ultimately led to the failure of the works. Yang Zirong and his friends were everywhere, on stage, screen, poster, and billboard. As in the medieval church or in Buddhist worship, icons and images were keys to switching on automatic, internalized expressions of devotion. We should also note, however, that modernity is usually associated with the secular and the decline in religious affiliation and influence over society. Here again the modern aspirations of the Cultural Revolution were undermined by its devotional excesses. In a sense, Yang Zirong and his cohort became like brands of Coca-Cola and Nike were to become in another Chinese era and economic system. Like the modern brands, the Cultural Revolution figures induced unthinking recognition and acknowledgement, but the image became a simple signal, empty of much real meaning. Their significance lay merely in being and being seen. In this sense also the cultural products of the Cultural Revolution were decidedly modern. Like brands created and sold by major corporations, they were pushed with all the apparatus available to the modern Chinese state. Like portraits of Mao Zedong, they were everywhere, signifying not just a product but also a way of life and loyalty to a bigger brand.

But we could argue that the results, at least for the model operas and ballets, was distinctly anti-modern. The modernized Peking operas became so well-known and so predictable that they offered no surprises. This was precisely the predicament of traditional style opera by the middle of the twentieth century, a position to which old-style opera had returned by the end of the century: hackneyed, trying to include new stage effects, and enjoyed by a diminishing band of loyal fans, there not to see the new but for the familiar.

The broader insistence on a Manichean view of the world, which these Cultural Revolution icon-brands represented, rapidly become wearisome for most Chinese. Although nobody dared say so in public, among trusted schoolmates or family frustration with the empty rhetoric and meaning-less idealism was frequently expressed. A certain tone in singing an aria from one of the model operas, a certain flick of the head in exaggerated parody of one of the central heroes, a clever rewording of a well-known verse could provide an outlet for a largely unspoken but shared sense of the ridiculous. In more public settings, at the weekly political study ses-sion at work or when required to rally with other groups to denounce a centuries-old official or ancient philosopher, people went through the motions required of them. A sort of karaoke or empty speech became a common skill to allow Chinese to perform loyalty and group belonging. Those adept at reworking the phrases in the latest *People's Daily* editorial did well, whether or not they believed in what they regurgitated. Others tried to perform as appropriate.

The preceding chapters, though organized by genre or form, have tried to bring out the changes in these ten years and to differentiate the different phases of the cultural experience of producers and consumers. The opera, dance, and musical model performances represented an unprecedented degree of experimentation, even as they were appropriated by the cul-tural leadership. Red Guard innovation in the late 1960s has been noted in new-style stage works, even if the purposes were pure agitprop. As con-trols eased and possibilities widened, starting in 1972, various attempts to combine the specialist and the amateur, the conventional and the new, and the international with the Chinese made the era similar to other periods of Chinese cultural development in the twentieth century. Throughout the century, Chinese artists and audiences responded creatively to the new possibilities thrown up by China's changing engagement with modernity.

Viewing the ten years in the context of their century as a whole reveals much about the legacies of Cultural Revolution cultural production and practice. Just as styles and themes from earlier in the century informed and shaped attitudes and works in the ten years after 1966, so the years after 1976 could not eschew powerful influences and connections with the preceding period. Artists, performers, writers, politicians, and audiences were all deeply influenced by their direct or indirect experience of the 1966–1976 era. Even those most determined to reject the Cultural Revo-lution's themes and aesthetics found it difficult to deny its hold on their cultural, social, or political practice. Despite the denunciations of persons and the renunciation of practices following the arrest of the Gang of Four in October 1976, much of what appeared fresh and new in the so-called New Era (*xin shiqi*) had roots in the ten years before that date.

A clear connection was the Cultural Revolution experience of many of the new writers and artists who emerged in the 1980s. Much of that decade's innovation in, say poetry or fiction had begun underground among salons of returned sent-down youth and older writers that gathered from the late 1960s in Beijing and elsewhere. The only difference was that the 'misty poetry' could now be published, circulated, and discussed openly. Many of the painters who emerged first with works depicting Cultural Revolution victims and then began to depict contemporary society and experiment with abstract works had first begun to paint during the Cultural Revolution. Skills that had been honed on hackneyed and directly political subjects were subsequently applied to more experimental art that often combined Chinese with international elements. Amateur experience in song-and-dance troupes and other performances gave skills and confidence to new performers of avant-garde theatre.

Other creators of the new culture of the 1980s and 1990s had a more indirect debt to their Cultural Revolution experiences. The so-called fifth-generation filmmakers who turned Chinese filmmaking on its head in the 1980s are a good example of a deeper influence from these ten years. Being sent to the countryside or military, without the benefit of completing a proper Chinese high school education, gave many of this generation an opportunity and inducement to think seriously about their own predicament and the state of their society and culture. Film school in the late 1970s gave these people the tools with which to express this new thinking, with unexpected results that marked a "New Wave" in Chinese cinema. The toughness and harsh beauty of the first two films that announced their arrival, *The One and the Eight* (*Yige he bage*) and *The Yellow Earth*, owed something to the aesthetic of the modernized Peking operas. The emphasis on the plain, folk, and noble in these films had Cultural Revolution roots, even as the films questioned heroism.

Above all the post–Cultural Revolution innovators in Chinese art, literature, and culture generally shared a common attitude with Cultural Revolution artists and their managers. This was the abiding conviction in the power of art and literature to transform lives. The heroes or anti-heroes of the New Era may appear different from Yang Zirong, Fang Haizhen, and their companions from the Cultural Revolution stage and screen. Certainly, many of the new works tried to recover the local, authentic version of the folk and find real roots in the diversity of Chinese historical and social experience, in contrast to the modernist obliteration of difference in the earlier works. But even the new figures in the new-style works share roots with their predecessors in the determination to serve a social function and reshape society. The unspoken ambition of the new films and other art works in the 1980s to enforce social and intellectual transformation belonged in the preceding era. A new generation of artists and writers made clear, starting in the 1990s, their rejection of this social burden on creative work. Even the rejection, however, was a social act.

The rise of the modern, Chinese consumerist world by the early twenty-first century perhaps marked a bigger break than the seemingly more startling changes immediately after 1976. As suggested in the Introduction, the ideological commodification of culture in the Cultural Revolution can be said to have laid the groundwork for the commercialization of culture in this century. However, in an era of iTunes, private cars, and the Internet, the kind of assumptions of homogeneity and unified social purpose that lay behind both Cultural Revolution and post-1976 cultural production seemed to belong to another world. A new modernity in the first decade of the new century took on new meaning and left the hopes, dreams, and despair of the old century in its all-consuming wake. Nonetheless the continued cultural pertinence of the earlier era was evident. In September 2007, one of the opening performances in the determinedly modernist and international, egg-shaped National Theatre just west of Tian'anmen Square was the ballet *The Red Detachment of Women*.

Notes

INTRODUCTION: A REVOLUTION IN CULTURE

1. Roderick MacFarquhar and Michael Schoenhals, *Mao's Last Revolution*, Cambridge: Belknap Press of Harvard University Press, 2006, p. 1.
2. Their one specific reference to a Cultural Revolution 'model performance' is in error, when they have President Nixon and his wife in February 1972 attending a performance of the opera *The Red Detachment of Women* (p. 348), when it was the ballet version which they watched in the company of Mao's wife, Jiang Qing. I use throughout this study the old term 'Peking opera' to differentiate the city of Beijing from the art: thus the 'Beijing Peking Opera Company'.
3. Jung Chang, *Wild Swans: Three Generations of Chinese Women*, London: Flamingo, 1993 (first published in 1991) became the biggest selling non-fiction, non-trade book ever.
4. Richard Curt Kraus, *The Party and the Arty in China: The New Politics of Culture*, Lanham, MD: Rowman & Littlefield Publishers, 2004.
5. Yan Fu, a translator of Western political thought in the late nineteenth century, exemplified this ambivalent approach to the West; see Benjamin I. Schwartz, *In Search of Wealth and Power: Yen Fu and the West*, New York: Harper & Row, 1964.
6. Bonnie S. McDougall and Kam Louie, *The Literature of China in the Twentieth Century*, New York: Columbia University Press, 1997.
7. Xiaobing Tang, *Chinese Modern: The Heroic and the Quotidien*, Durham, NC: Duke University Press, 2000, esp. pp. 341–348.
8. Mao Hui, ed., *Xin Zhongguo wudao shidian* (A chronology of New China's dance), Shanghai: Shanghai yinyue chubanshe, 2005.
9. Zhang Zhen, *An Amorous History of the Silver Screen: Shanghai Cinema, 1896–1937*, Chicago: University of Chicago Press, 2005.
10. Patrick Hanan, *The Invention of Li Yu*, Cambridge, MA: Harvard University Press, 1988. See also his *Chinese Fiction of the Nineteenth and Early Twentieth Centuries: Essays*, New York: Columbia University Press, 2004.
11. *Fictional Authors, Imaginary Audiences: Modern Chinese Literature in the Twentieth Century*, Hong Kong: Chinese University Press, 2003, esp. pp. 5–6 and 46–74.

ONE: MODELLING A NEW CULTURE

1. Details of Yu's life are from Dai Jiafang, *Zou xiang huimie: '-Wen-ge' Wenhuabu zhang Yu Huiyong chenfu lu* (Heading towards destruction: the rise and fall of the Cultural Revolution Minister of Culture Yu Huiyong), Beijing: Guangming ribao chubanshe, 1994.

2. On the historical origins of Peking opera, see Colin P. Mackerras, *The Rise of the Peking Opera, 1770–1870: Social Aspects of the Theatre in Manchu China*, Oxford: Clarendon Press, 1972.

3. See Jia Zhigang, *Maixiang xiandai de lao xiju* (Old drama striding toward modernity), Beijing: Zhongguo xiju chubanshe, 1996, p. 31.

4. By the end of the month, the committee had become the Opera Reformation Bureau (*xiqu gaijin ju*) and thus formally part of the government apparatus. Each region, province, and major city had a branch in a bureau network across the nation. In July 1950, the bureau's work was absorbed into the Ministry of Culture's Opera Reformation Committee (*xiqu gaijin weiyuanhui*): Jia Zhigang, p. 37. About one percent of plays were deemed bad (*huai*). 'Shi nian lai xiju gongye de juda fazhan' (Great advances in the drama industry over the last ten years), *Xiju bao* (Drama), 1959, 19 (October), 70–71, has tables and explanatory notes showing the situation in 1949 and 1959. The world of Chinese statistics is a murky one. Jia Zhigang (p. 41) puts troupe numbers in 1952 at more than 2,000 and opera workers at 150,000 persons.

5. The rise of specialist writers of reformed opera is noted by Wang Xinmin, *Zhongguo dangdai xiju shigang* (An outline history of modern Chinese drama), Beijing: Shehui kexue wenxian chubanshe, 1997, p. 174.

6. This is not to deny that some of the greatest works in the traditional repertoire, such as *Romance of the West Chamber*, were originally written by highly educated scholars.

7. For further discussion of this change in policy emphasis, see Paul Clark, *Chinese Cinema: Culture and Politics since 1949*, New York: Cambridge University Press, 1987, pp. 63–64.

8. The two October 1959 issues of *Xiju bao* (Theatre Journal) included coverage of the tenth anniversary performances; see *Xiju bao* 1959, 19 (October), esp. pp. 35–42 (photospread) and pp. 43–60 (articles by performers), and *Xiju bao* 1959, 20 (October), 4 (on a meeting of troupe managers).

9. This is noted, for example, in Jia Zhigang, p. 51. The slogan was also rendered as 'concentrate writing on the 13 years' (*da xie shisan nian*).

10. One immediate casualty of the new policy was a film biography of Lu Xun, the original and greatest May Fourth writer. Zhao Dan, China's leading film actor, and others were preparing to start shooting at the Shanghai Film Studio when the prestige production was abandoned in favour of more topical stories.

11. 'Guanyu shangyan 'guixi' youhai haishi wuhai de zhenglun' (Debate on whether presenting 'ghost plays' is harmful or not), *Xiju bao*, 1963, 9 (September), 59. Of the twenty-six operas banned outright by the Ministry of Culture between 1950 and 1952, more than half were ghost plays; Xu Xianglin, *Zhongguo guixi* (Chinese ghost plays), Tianjin: Tianjin jiaoyu chubanshe, 1997, p. 88.

12. Jia Zhigang, pp. 51–52. See discussion of ghost plays by the novelist Mao Dun, then Minister of Culture, and others in *Xiju bao*, 1963, 10 (October), 60. Later that spring Shanghai's main newspaper published a feature article, 'On the notion that "ghost plays are not harmful"' (*'you gui wuhai' lun*). The article argued that operas with ghosts encouraged superstition and diverted audiences' attention from the here and now. Liang Bihui cited the well-known opera *Fifteen Strings of Cash* (*Shiwu guan*), which had been adapted into a successful film made for the tenth anniversary in 1959 and starring Zhou Xinfang, the most famous of contemporary Peking opera actors. *Fifteen Strings of Cash* had originally included ghostly elements, but this new version had eliminated them. After the Cultural Revolution, credit for this article was assigned to a writing group of allies of Mao's wife, Jiang Qing. The article appeared in *Wenhui bao*, 6 May 1963, p. 4: see Wang Xinmin, p. 176. Revival of ghost plays came after 1978. I remember the distinct excitement among the audience at a revival performance of the Kun opera *Li Huiniang* at the Jixiang Theatre in Goldfish Lane, Beijing, in October 1980. As we shall see, ghost plays were not completely eliminated from opera stages, if Cultural Revolution attacks on them are a reliable indication of their continued, often underground, performance.

13. The debates are summarized in *Xiju bao*, 1963, 10 (October), 59–63. Wu Han's point was made in his article, '*Lishiju shi yishu, ye shi lishi*' (History plays are art and also history), *Xiju bao*, 1962, 6 (June), 38–42. He was responding to an article (in *Xiju bao*, 1962, 5 (May), 33–37) by Wang Ziye titled 'History plays are art, not history'.

14. The play script (identified as the seventh draft) was published in *Beijing wenyi* (Beijing literature and art), 1961, 1 (January), 14–30. The absence of contemporary coverage in *Xiju bao* suggests a lack of popular and critical success. See, however, Deng Yunjian, '*Ping "Hai Rui ba guan"*' (Review of *Hai Rui Dismissed from Office*), *Beijing wenyi*, 1961, 3 (March), 47–48, and Qu Liuyi, '*Xiu wei gancao ji, gan zuo Nan Baogong: du "Hai Rui ba guan"* sanji' (Embarrassed by a licorice root prescription, daring to create a noble official: notes on reading *Hai Rui Dismissed from Office*), *Beijing wenyi*, 1961, 3 (March), 49–51.

15. '*Guanyu xiqu 'tuichenchuxin' wenti de taolun* (Discussions on 'pushing aside the old and presenting the new' in opera), *Xiju bao*, 1963, 9 (September), 53–59.

16. *Xiju bao*, 1964, 5 (May), 7–8. The last paragraph of this report notes that in addition Peking opera troupes were also performing from the traditional repertoire and newly written history plays, in the spirit of 'a hundred flowers blooming, and push aside the old and present the new'.

17. Benbao ziliaoshi, '*Guanyu Jingju yan xiandaixi de taolun* (Discussions on Peking opera performing modern plays), *Xiju bao*, 1964, 5 (May), 9–13. For a contribution that untypically makes direct reference to audiences, see Fan Junhong, '*Xuanti: Jingju fanying xiandai shenghuo xiezuo san bi*' (Selected topic: random notes on Peking opera reflecting modern life), *Xiju bao*, 1962, 11 (November), 16–20.

18. Dai Bufan, '*Bixu cong shenghuo chufa: qiantan xiqu xiandaiju neirong he xingshi de maodun wenti*' (We must start from life: thoughts on the issue

of the contradiction between content and form in modern-style opera), *Xiju bao*, 1963, 7 (July), 11–15.

19. These figures and what follows are from a *Xiju bao* report, 'Mao Zedong sixiang de guanghui shengli, shehuizhuyi xin Jingju xuanzao dansheng: ji yijiuliusi nian Jingju xiandaixi yanchu dahui' (A glorious victory for Mao Zedong Thought: announcing the birth of new socialist Peking opera: Record of the 1964 convention of modern Peking operas), *Xiju bao*, 1964, 7 (July), 14–17. See also De Qian and Qing Yang, '*Jingju geming xiandaixi guanmo zhaji*' (Notes on the revolutionary modern Peking opera convention), *Beijing wenyi*, 1964, 8 (August), 62–63, which concentrates on artistic questions. The second June issue of *Red Flag* included an editorial on modernizing opera as its first item: *Hongqi*, 1964, 12 (June), 1–4. Only Mao Zedong is named in the editorial. A substantial report on the convention appeared in *Hongqi*, 1964, 16 (August), 44–53. *Hongqi*, 1964, 2–3 (February), 58–64 had earlier featured three articles on the importance of opera modernization.

20. *Xiju bao*, 1964, 7 (July), 14–17. Jiang Qing is mentioned on p. 15 and the study of her talk on p. 16. Peng Zhen's speech is in *Hongqi*, 1964, 14 (July), 18–24. For one of Jiang Qing's previously rare public appearances, see the 1963 photo of her accompanying Mao after a performance of the spoken play *Lei Feng*, about the late model soldier. Although Jiang Qing stands prominently beside her husband, her presence is not noted in the one-page report with the photo: *Xiju bao*, 1963, 8 (August), 1.

21. A bound collection of the programme notes for each performance is held in the National Library, Beijing: Wenhuabu Beijing bianzhe kan, *Jingju xiandaixi guanmo yanchu dahui jiemudan (hedingben)* (Modern Peking opera performance convention playbills (collected)), 1964, unpaged.

22. Ma Shaobo, gen. ed., *Zhongguo Jingju shi* (A history of China's Peking opera), Beijing: Zhongguo xiju chubanshe, 1999, pp. 1867–1872. This is a three-volume, four-part study, produced under the auspices of the Beijing Art Research Institute and the Shanghai Art Research Institute.

23. The attack on these films is discussed more fully in Chapter Three.

24. In 1959 Wu had published an article that might form the basis for a play, *Hai Rui Curses the Emperor* (*Hai Rui ma huangdi*), in *People's Daily* (21 September 1959), but anonymously under the pen name of Liu Mianzhi. Wu Han was not alone in his admiration for Hai Rui. The eminent Shanghai-based Peking opera actor Zhou Xinfang created *Hai Rui Memorializes the Emperor* (*Hai Rui shang shu*), with encouragement from Zhou Yang, deputy head of the Party Propaganda Department. He performed it in 1959: *Xiju bao*, 1959, 19 (October), 22–23. The script was published in *Shanghai Drama* (*Shanghai xiju*), in a 1962 issue commemorating sixty years of Zhou Xinfang's stage career: Li Taicheng and Yao Yu, *Lüeduo yu pohia: jielu 'Jiang Qing fangeming jituan' zai Shanghai wenhua xitong de zuixing* (Plunder and persecution: exposing the crimes of the 'Jiang Qing anti-revolutionary clique' in the Shanghai city cultural apparatus), Shanghai: Shanghaishi wenhua shizhi bangongshi, 1999, pp. 9–10. Other Hai Rui operas had been written in the 1950s, including *Hai Rui bei xian* (Hai Rui shoulders the rope) and *San nü qiang ban* (Three women vie for the board): Ma Shaobo, p. 1895. A summary of the 1965 criticism of the play mentions simply that 'a Peking opera troupe also

performed it', without offering detail of the name of the company, the length of the run, location of the performance, etc.: *Xiju bao*, 1965, 12 (December), 23. Ma Shaobo's assertion that the play was 'performed for more than four years' is equally vague (p. 1896). It is unclear how publicly known was Mao's distribution of the thirty-nine documents in 1964.

25. For the political background, see MacFarquhar and Schoenhals, pp. 15–19. The allies included Jiang Qing and Kang Sheng, Cultural Revolution activists.

26. Quoted in Li Taicheng and Yao Yu, p. 11, who points out that Zhou Yang had suggested Zhou Xinfang create a play about Hai Rui in April 1959, three months before Peng Dehuai came under fire.

27. Peng Dehuai died, still in disgrace, in 1974. For more on him and the Lushan plenum, see Roderick MacFarquhar, *The Origins of the Cultural Revolution, Volume 2: The Great Leap Forward*, New York: Columbia University Press, 1983, pp. 187–251.

28. Ma Shaobo, pp. 1898–1900.

29. *Xiju bao* bianjibu, '*Zhi duzhe*' (To our readers), *Xiju bao*, 1964, 10 (October), 46–47.

30. Benbao ziliaoshi, '*Yijiuliuwunian geming xiandaixi da fengshou*' (The great bumper harvest in revolutionary modern drama in 1965), *Xiju bao*, 1966, 1 (January), 39–40, offers a list of all titles performed.

31. Noted in Bao Shiyuan, '*1950 nian 2 yue – 1965 nian 5 yue Shanghai xiqu, quyi huiyan jiyao*' (Summary of opera and *quyi* [folk vocal art form] joint performances in Shanghai, February 1950 to May 1965), *Shanghai wenhua shizhi tongxun* (Bulletin of the Shanghai cultural history gazetteer), 23 (December 1992), 29.

32. Jasper Becker estimates around thirty million lives lost in the famine between 1959 and 1962: *Hungry Ghosts. Mao's Secret Famine*, New York: Free Press, 1996.

33. See, for example, Wang Xinmin, pp. 179–180. The minutes are outlined in Ma Shaobo, pp. 1901–1903. Factional disputes meant that the wider public only saw the Minutes in May 1967: *Hongqi*, 1967, 9 (May), 11–20.

34. Wang Xinmin, pp. 179–180.

35. Qu Bo himself reviewed the play when it was first performed in mid-1958, finding much to praise. But he was dissatisfied with the presentation of Yang Zirong, whose cleverness in entering the bandit cave was not shown, nor was his extraordinary bravery: Qu Bo, '*Guan "Zhiqu Weihushan"*' (On watching *Taking Tiger Mountain by Strategy*), *Xiju bao*, 1958, 12 (June), 43.

36. Gao Jinxiao, '*Cuanduo yu pohai: Jiang Qing chaoshou Jingju xiandai xi "Zhiqu Weihushan" de yinmou*' (Usurpation and persecution: Jiang Qing's schemes to meddle with the modern Peking opera *Taking Tiger Mountain by Strategy*), *Shanghai wenhua shizhi tongxun*, 46 (September 1997), 62–63. See also Xu Xinjie and Cai Shicheng, eds., *Shanghai Jingju zhi* (Shanghai Peking opera gazetteer), Shanghai: Shanghai wenhua chubanshe, 1999, pp. 32, 131–132.

37. This account of the origins of the opera is largely drawn from Ma Shaobo, pp. 1928–1932, and the more detailed outline by Gao Jinxiao, pp. 62–69. I have also checked this against Gao Yilong and Li Xiao, *Zhongguo xiqu xiandaixi shi* (History of modern Chinese opera), Shanghai: Shanghai wenhua

chubanshe, 1999, pp. 272–274. On the adaptation from the novel, see also Cheng Guangwei, *Wenxue xiangxiang yu wenxue guojia: Zhongguo dangdai wenxue yanjiu (1949–1976)* (Literary imagination and literary state: contemporary Chinese literature), Kaifeng: Henan daxue chubanshe, 2005, pp. 153–157. Having given the adaptation her endorsement, Jiang Qing watched new versions in December 1963 and April 1964, encouraged by her future ally Zhang Chunqiao, deputy head of the Party's Propaganda Department in the city.

38. Gao Jinxiao, pp. 64–65. The musical extracts were in Lu Wenqin, comp., *Jingju xiandaixi changpian qupu xuan* (Selected recorded scores of modern Peking operas), Shanghai: Shanghai wenhua chubanshe, 1965.

39. Tong Xiangling (recorded by Qian Youzhong), 'Wo shi zenyang zai biaoyan yishu shang chuangzao Yang Zirong yi jiao de' (How I created the Yang Zirong character with performing art), *Shanghai wenhua shizhii tongxun*, 25 (April 1993), 37–39. Opera actors often gave oral accounts, which were written down by others, as their formal educational levels frequently made writing a challenge. Tong Xiangling was the younger brother of Tong Zhiling, who created the central character of the female Party secretary Fang Haizhen in another model opera, *On the Docks*: see the account of the creation of that opera later in this section.

40. Tong Xiangling, p. 38.

41. Ma Shaobo, p. 1930.

42. To record this new version the Central Newsreel and Documentary Film Studio made what one later source calls a 'study film' (*jiaoxue yingpian*) of the performance, Ma Shaobo, p. 1930.

43. Ma Shaobo, writing in the 1990s, makes the usual vague reference to some artists being attacked (*chongji*) or persecuted (*pohai*): p. 1930.

44. A May issue of *Red Flag*, the Party's main theoretical journal, included the *Tiger Mountain* performance script, giving credit to the collective authorship of the Shanghai Peking Opera Theatre and eliminating reference to the story's origins in Qu Bo's novel. This was the second time that *Red Flag* had included a literary work like a play script, after February 1965's publication of *Red Lantern*: *Hongqi*, 1967, 8 (May), 75–97. As early as July 1964, during the national Peking opera convention, Jiang Qing reportedly had suggested a title change for the opera and name changes for the major characters, supposedly to avoid association with Qu Bo's *Tracks in the Snowy Forest*: Gao Jinxiao, pp. 68–69. *Red Lantern* appeared in *Hongqi*, 1965, 2 (January), 34–55. See also Ma Shaobo, pp. 1930–1931.

45. Gao Jinxiao, p. 69.

46. This account of the opera's origins is drawn from Gao Yilong and Li Xiao, p. 279 and from Ma Shaobo, pp. 1937–1939.

47. Ma Shaobo, p. 1937.

48. These changes are outlined in a one-page report in *Xiju bao*, 1966, 2 (February), 35. The Aunt Cui character's original surname had been Li. Changing it avoided using the surname of the South Korean president during the war, Syngman Rhee.

49. Ma Shaobo, p. 1938.

50. Information on the origin comes from '*Yehuo shaobujin, chunfeng chui you sheng: Huju "Ludang huozhong" zai "Wen-ge" qianhou*' (Wild fire is not extinguished, the spring breeze starts up again: the Shanghai opera *Sparks amid the Reeds* before and after the Cultural Revolution), *Shanghai wenhua shizhi tongxun*, 39 (December 1995), 47–48; and from Zhou Xishan, '*Jingju "Shajiabang" dui Huju "Ludang huozhong" de qinquan yu gaibian deshi*' (The infringement of the Peking opera *Shajiabang* on the Shanghai opera *Sparks amid the reeds* and the merits and faults of the adaptation), *Shanghai xiju* (Shanghai theatre), 1997, 2 (February), 17–19. This 1997 report was prompted by a copyright infringement case brought against the Beijing adapters by the family of Wen Mu, the chief writer of the original Shanghai opera: see in addition *Shanghai xiju*, 1997, 2 (February), 15–16.

51. *Shanghai wenhua shizhi tongxun*, 39 (December 1995), 48. This article notes the number of positive reviews in important national media in 1963–1964: pp. 48–49.

52. The Shanghai writers changed the gender of the tea shop owner from that in the original newspaper article that had inspired the opera.

53. This account of the fortunes of *Shajiabang* is drawn chiefly from Jiang Zhishui, '*Cong "Ludang huozhong" dao "Shajiabang"*' (From *Sparks amid the reeds* to *Shajiabang*), *Xiju bao*, 1965, 2 (February), 34–37, Ma Shaobo, pp. 1935–1937, and Gao Yilong and Li Xiao, pp. 277–278. The date of Jiang Qing's first viewing is from *Shanghai wenhua shizhi tongxun*, 39 (December 1995), p. 49.

54. Rightists were those thousands of intellectuals who had been condemned in 1957 for having the temerity to raise criticisms of the Communist Party during the Hundred Flowers liberalization moment in 1956. Lu Jianhua, *Wang Zengqi zhuan* (Biography of Wang Zengqi), Nanjing: Jiangsu wenyi chubanshe, 1998, pp. 172–174. See also Chen Tushou, '*Wang Zengqi de Wen-ge shinian*' (Wang Zengqi's Cultural Revolution ten years), *Zhongguo wenxue xuankan* (Selections on Chinese literature), 1999, 1 (January), 170–175 (originally published in *Dushu*).

55. Lu Jianhua, pp. 177–178.

56. Tan Yuanshou, '*Jiefang sixiang, dapo kuangkuang: jiagong xiugai Guo Jianguang xingxiang de yi dian ganshou*' (Liberate thinking, break out of the frame: some feelings on the work of revising the image of Guo Jianguang), *Xiju bao*, 1965, 2 (February), 36–37. Such accounts of work on the model operas became common after 1966, but were usually not as concrete and revealing as this pre–Cultural Revolution article.

57. These (sometimes multi-ethnic) Inner Mongolian troupes (*Wulanmuqi* in Chinese) became a model for the organization and performance practices of amateur theatrical groups throughout China during the Cultural Revolution, especially in the 1970s. For an earlier view, see Benbao pinglunyuan, '*Wulanmuqi shi xiju gongzuozhe de bangyang*' (Ulan Muchir are models for drama workers), *Xiju bao*, 1964, 11–12 (December), 37–39. For later coverage, see *Renmin ribao*, 12 February 1974, p. 4.

58. Tan Yuanshou, p. 37. See also Beijing Jingjutuan, '"*Shajiabang*" xiugai guocheng zhong yi xie tihui' (Some lessons from the process of revising

Shajiabang), *Xiju bao*, 1965, 7 (July), 31–35. This article is mostly about a further reworking of the opera.

59. This contrast was obvious to me during two years as an exchange student in Beijing, from October 1974 to July 1976. The second year was spent in a mixed class of foreign and Chinese students, who were also our dormitory roommates. Performance in class could contrast with franker expression in the dorms.

60. *Xiju bao*, 1965, 7, 33. 'Too far out in front' translates '*zou de tai yuan*' (go too far distant).

61. This theory will be discussed in section 4 below. The work on Guo Jianguang's stage presence is reported in *Xiju bao*, 1965, 7 (July), 34–35.

62. The Shanghai report, first published in *Liberation Daily* (*Jiefang ribao*), was reproduced as '*Qishi, jiaoyu, biance: kan "Shajiabang", xiang Beijing Jingjutuan xuexi*' (Inspiration, education, spurring on: on watching *Shajiabang*, learning from the Beijing Peking opera company), *Xiju bao*, 1965, 7 (July), 36–37.

63. See Lu Wenqin, comp., musical scores published in 1965.

64. The following account of the Shanghai opera version is drawn from '*Yi zhan hongdeng liang sifang: Huju "Hongdeng ji" de dansheng he jienan*' (A red lantern lights all sides: the birth and tribulations of the Shanghai opera *The Red Lantern*), *Shanghai wenhua shizhi tongxun*, 39 (December 1995), 43–46. The Changchun studio produced a feature film from the script in 1963. The film was criticized during the Cultural Revolution, perhaps to obliterate the possibility of any comparisons between it and the model opera: see *Chinese Literature*, 1973, 7 (July), 78–87.

65. *Juben*, 1964, 2 (February), 40–70. The adaptors (rather than authors) were identified as Ling Dake and Xia Jianqing.

66. Ma Shaobo, p. 1932.

67. The seven- or eight-month delay in passing the script on to adaptors is not noted in most sources. It comes from Huang Huaying, '*Huifu lishi de zhenxiang: A Jia tan Jingju "Hongdeng ji" chuangzuo jingguo*' (Restoring the true historical pcture: A Jia talks about the experience of creating the Peking opera *The Red Lantern*), *Guangming ribao* (Guangming Daily), 29 December 1987, p. 3.

68. On A Jia's background see Ren Guilin, '*A Jia de yishu daolu*' (A Jia's artistic road), *Xiqu yishu* (Opera art), 1986, 2 (February), 77–80, 85. See also '*A Jia de yishu gexin jingshen*' (A Jia's spirit of artistic innovation) in *Liu Housheng xiqu changduan wen* (Long and short writings on opera by Liu Housheng), Beijing: Zhongguo xiju chubanshe, 1996, pp. 448–451.

69. Huang Huaying, p. 3.

70. Weng Ouhong, *Weng Ouhong bianju shengya* (Weng Ouhong's career in script writing), Beijing: Zhongguo xiju chubanshe, 1986, pp. 569–570.

71. This August 1964 trip is described in *Shanghai wenhua shizhi tongxun*, 39 (December 1995), 45. The date does not match A Jia's recollection in *Guangming ribao* of receiving the script in September or October, though he does record being ordered by Lin Mohan to go south to learn from the Shanghai company: Huang Huaying, p. 3. The 1964 convention programme note acknowledged adaptation from the *Huju* version.

72. Ma Shaobo, p. 1934. See, for example, Guo Xiaochuan, '*"Hongdeng ji" yu wenhua geming*' (*The Red Lantern* and the revolution in culture), *Xiju bao*, 1965, 6 (June), 25–29.

73. The description on the new script was 'revised according to the Peking opera *The Red Lantern*' (*genju Jingju "Hongdeng ji" gaibian*): *Shanghai wenhua shizhi tongxun*, 39 (December 1995), 46.

74. *Shanghai wenhua shizhi tongxun*, 39 (December 1995), 46.

75. *Zhuangmei* is mentioned in Liu Naichong, '*Rang geming de hongdeng zai Jingju wutai shang fangchu guangmang: zai Jingju "Hongdeng ji" paiyan chang shang*' (Let the red light of revolution shine brightly on the Peking opera stage: at the rehearsals of the Peking opera *The Red Lantern*), *Xiju bao*, 1964, 6 (June), 46–50, esp. p. 47, and in Ma Shaobo, p. 1933. On *The Yellow Earth*, see Paul Clark, *Reinventing China: A Generation and Its Films*, Hong Kong: Chinese University Press, 2005, pp. 82–89.

76. See Ouyang Wenbin and Xu Jingxian, '*Wei wuchanjieji yingxiong lizhuan: tan Jingju "Hongdeng ji" de juben gaibian*' (To glorify proletarian heroes: on the script revisions of the Peking opera *The Red Lantern*), *Xiju bao*, 1965, 4 (April), 30–33, esp. pp. 31–32.

77. Liu Naichong, p. 49.

78. Weng Ouhong, p. 571.

79. Huang Weijun, '*A Jia tan "Hongdeng ji"*', *Zhongguo xiju* (Chinese drama), 1991, 3 (March), 12–51, 41, esp. p. 41; Liu Naichong, pp. 47–48.

80. Ren Guilin, pp. 79–80.

81. Qian Haoliang, '*Wei geming er yanxi*' (Performing for the revolution), *Xiju bao*, 1965, 1 (January), 23–24. See also Qian Haoliang, '*Suzao gaoda de wuchanjieji yingxiong xingxiang*' (Mold great proletarian hero figures), *Hongqi*, 1967, 8 (May), 66–70, and an article by Qian in *Renmin ribao*, 13 May 1967, p. 4.

82. Ren Guilin notes Qian's subsequent 'treachery', p. 79.

83. Liu Naichong, p. 50.

84. Ouyang Wenbin and Xu Jingxian, p. 32. This centering of the heroes was a further beginning of what became the aesthetic theory of the 'three prominences' (*san tuchu*), discussed in section 4 below.

85. Yu Huiyong, from *Wenhui Daily* (*Wenhui bao*), 28 March 1965, quoted in '*Xijujie xianqi xuexi Jingju "Hongdeng ji" de rechao*' (Opera circles launch a wave of studying the Peking opera *The Red Lantern*), *Xiju bao*, 1965, 3 (March), 43. Yu that month joined the team revising the new Peking opera that became *On the Docks*.

86. For another contemporary report on interest in the new opera, see Luo Pinchao and Wen Juefei, '*Xue shen xue tou "Hongdeng ji"; yanhao geming xiandaixi*' (Make a thoroughgoing study of *The Red Lantern*; perform well revolutionary modern plays), *Xiju bao*, 1965, 3 (March), 44–45.

87. His previous given names had meant 'great roof-beam'.

88. Ma Shaobo, pp. 1934–1935.

89. Weng Ouhong, p. 578.

90. Weng Ouhong, p. 583.

91. This account of the fortunes of *On the Docks* draws on He Man and Shen Hongxin, '*Jingju "Haigang" zai chuangzuo yanchu de qianqianhouhou*'

(Background to the repeated creation and performance of *On the Docks*), in Li Taicheng and Yao Yu, pp. 29–49. He Man was one of the people in charge of the adaption of the opera into Peking opera. Li Xiaomin's 1958 experience is reported on p. 30.

92. He Man and Shen Hongxin, p. 31.

93. Yu Lie, '*Fang Huaiju "Haigang de zaochen" de bianju*' (An interview with the writer of *Early Morning on the Harbor*), *Shanghai wenhua shizhi tongxun*, 11 (December 1990), 40.

94. He Man and Shen Hongxin, pp. 34–35.

95. He Man and Shen Hongxin, p. 37.

96. He Man and Shen Hongxin, pp. 40–41.

97. At this point, play director Yang Cunbin and the 'old man' role-type actor who had joined the cast to play the young dock worker, were assigned away from the team: He Man and Shen Hongxin, pp. 42–43.

98. *On the Docks* is in *Hongqi*, 1972, 2 (February), 22–48.

99. The following is drawn from Shanghai Jingjutuan 'Haigang' juzu, '*Fanying shehuizhuyi shidai gongren jieji de zhandou shenghuo: geming xiandai Jingju "Haigang" de chuangzuo tihui*' (Reflecting the fighting life of the working class in the socialist era: the creative experience of the revolutionary modern Peking opera *On the Docks*), *Hongqi*, 1972, 3 (March), 37–45.

100. See, for example, *Wudao*, 1965, 4 (August), 3–11.

101. For a discussion of how Chinese ethnic minority films served a similar purpose of providing exotic relief in the 1950s and 1960s, see Paul Clark, 'Ethnic minorities in Chinese films: Cinema and the exotic', *East-West Film Journal*, 1, 2 (1987), 15–31.

102. For a positive assessment, see Yang Jian, '*Cong "geming xiandai Jingju" kan chuantong xiju de zhuanxing*' (The transformation of tradition as seen in the 'revolutionary modern Peking operas'), *Xiju: Zhongyang xiju xueyuan xuebao* (Theatre: Journal of the Central Drama Academy), 2003, 3 (September), 38–55, and Yan Lifeng, '*"Jingju xing Jing" yu "xin chengshi": dui yangbanxi de shenceng jiedu*' ('Peking operas are from Peking' and 'new patterns': a deep deciphering of the model performances), *Xiju yishu: Shanghai xiju xueyuan xuebao* (Theatre Art: Journal of the Shanghai Drama Academy), 2004, 3 (June), 36–43.

103. Wang Renyuan, *Jingju 'yangbanxi' yinyue lungang* (An outline theory of the music of the 'model performance' Peking operas), Beijing: Renmin yinyue chubanshe, 1999, pp. 11–14. For a generally positive assessment of the art (but not the politics) of the model operas, see Yu Cong and Wang Ankui, *Zhongguo dangdai xiqu shi* (History of contemporary Chinese opera), Beijing: Xueyuan chubanshe, 2005, pp. 558–569, 576–628 (including on music, pp. 597–622).

104. Wang Renyuan, pp. 68–103.

105. Wang Renyuan, pp. 164–174.

106. Wang Renyuan, pp. 181–193, 194–204. Wang ends his book with a chapter on the musical failings of the model operas, noting the usual criticisms of formulism and politicization. It does little to undermine the overall positive thrust of his study. For an endorsement of the continued value of the 'model opera' music for contemporary composers, see Yin Xiaodong,

'*Guanyu "Jingju 'yanbanxi' yinyue lungang" de yifeng xin*' (A letter about *An outline theory of the music of the 'model performance' Peking operas*), *Zhongguo Jingju* (China's Peking opera), 2002, 4 (August), 50–52.

107. See the superb scholarly study by Zhu Keyi, *Yuyanxue shiye zhong de 'yangbanxi'* (The 'model performances' from a linguistics point of view), Kaifeng: Henan daxue chubanshe, 2004, pp. 54–80 (on music) and pp. 260–316 (on differences with traditional opera language). See also Zhu's earlier '*'Yangbanxi' huayu dui chuantong xiqu huayu de chuancheng yu pianli*' (The inheritance and divergence from traditional operas of the language of the 'model performances'), *Fudan xuebao (shehui kexue ban)* (Fudan University Journal: social sciences issue), 2003, 3 (June), pp. 123–133.

108. Ma Shaobo, p. 1967: see also Gao Yilong and Li Xiao, pp. 289–290.

109. Writing credit was to the *Tiger Mountain* group of the Shanghai Peking Opera Company, though reportedly the article came from the pen of Yu Huiyong himself: Gao Yilong and Li Xiao, pp. 289–291. Wang Yao notes how the theory was behind the film adaptation of a short story, *Sparkling Red Star* (discussed in Chapter Three below): Wang Yao, *Chidao de pipan* (Tardy criticism), Zhengzhou: Daxiang chubanshe, 2000, pp. 117–125.

110. *Xiju bao*, 1965, 7, p. 34.

111. Zhong Wenyu, '*"Zhiqu Weihushan" de yuyan yishu*' (The art of the language in *Taking Tiger Mountain by Strategy*), *Beijing daxue xuebao: zhexue, shehui kexue ban (shi kan)* (Peking University Journal: philosophy and social science volume (test issue)), 1973, 1 (July), 95–103. The references to the 1967 and 1968 versions of the opera are on pp. 97 and 102. The Peking University journal had recently been revived as an outlet for what passed for academic articles. Gao Yilong and Li Xiao also acknowledge the language skill in the model operas in their 1999 study: pp. 296–297.

112. Wang Wei, '*Geming yangbanxi shi shixian "liang jiehe" chuangzuo fangfa de dianfan*' (The revolutionary model performances are examples of the practice of 'double combination' in creative methods), *Tianjin wenyi* (Tianjin literature and art), 1974, 5 (October), 52–57; esp. pp. 55–56. The 'double combination' was that of revolutionary realism and revolutionary romanticism that Mao had coined as a principle in literature and art in 1958. For a post-1976 denunciation of the 'three prominences', see Lou Qi, '*"Santuchu chuangzuo yuanze" shi "Sirenbang" cuandangduoquan de wenyi gangling*' (The 'three prominences creative principle' is the guiding theory in the Gang of Four's usurping of the power of the Party), *Zhongshan daxue xuebao (zhexue shehui kexue ban)* (Zhongshan University Journal (philosophy and social sciences issue)), 1977, 2 (March), 51–55, and two subsequent articles in the same issue, pp. 56–63.

113. Jiang Qing, '*Tan Jingju geming*' (Talking about the revolution in Peking opera), *Hongqi*, 1967, 6 (June), 25. Her numbers did not include amateur groups, nor apparently politically suspect 'black troupes'.

114. Gao Yilong and Li Xiao, p. 299.

115. Ma Shaobo, pp. 1981–1982.

116. Gao Yilong and Li Xiao, p. 296.

117. Gao Yilong and Li Xiao, pp. 303–305. In early versions of the opera Yang's waistcoat was leopard skin, but the final version saw him in Siberian tiger skin.

118. Of course, traditional operas on martial subjects also only rarely included this feature in their stories.

119. See MacFarquhar and Schoenhals, pp. 239–252.

120. But the *Red Detachment of Women* and *The White-haired Girl* both featured army men as the single, central character, according to the 'three prominences' theory: see Chapter Four. On women in the operas, see Li Xianglin, '*Cong "yangbanxi" kan nüxing xingxiang de kongdanghua*' (Emptiness of the female characters in the model performances), *Zhongguo Jingju*, 2000, 4 (August), 10–13.

121. See, for example, the hero of Ethel Lillian Voynich's 1913 novel, *The Gadfly* (in Chinese *Niumeng*). The Soviet film version is effectively used as a framework to help explain Red Guard idealism and romanticism in Carma Hinton, Geremie Barmé, and Richard Gordon's 2003 documentary on the Cultural Revolution, *Morning Sun*. For more on foreign novels, see Chapter Five, section 2.

122. For a published example of sent-down youth keenness for the *yangbanxi* experience, see Liu Jialing, *Jiyi xianhong* (Memories bright red), Beijing: Zhongguo qingnian chubanshe, 2002, pp. 1–15 (on Yang Zirong) and pp. 72–76 (on *White-Tiger Regiment*). For an eclectic discussion of the politics of Chinese theatre and the theatrics of Chinese politics, see Xiaomei Chen, *Acting the Right Part: Political Theater and Popular Drama in Contemporary China*, Honolulu: University of Hawai'i Press, 2002.

TWO: SPREADING THE NEW MODELS

1. Interview with Li Guang (and his wife, Shen Jianjing, who had featured in *Raid on the White-Tiger Regiment*), Beijing, 12 July 2002.

2. *Renmin ribao*, 24 May 1967, p. 1. Three articles, by Yu Huiyong on the operas, Zhong Runliang on the ballets, and Chen Rutang on the symphony, filled p. 6.

3. For an excellent discussion of the continued uses of models in contemporary China, see Børge Bakken, *The Exemplary Society: Human Improvement, Social Control, and the Dangers of Modernity in China*, Oxford: Oxford University Press, 2000.

4. Tan Yuanshou, p. 37.

5. '*Xijujie xianqi xuexi Jingju "Hongdeng ji" de rechao*' (A surge in drama circles to take up the study of the Peking opera *The Red Lantern*), *Xiju bao*, 1965, 3 (March), 42. The same phrase '*chuse de yangban*' was used in the 16 March issue of the Shanghai newspaper *Liberation Daily* (*Jiefang ribao*), which accounts for why the *Xiju bao* put quotation marks around the phrase.

6. Cited in Gao Yilong and Li Xiao, p. 271.

7. Quoted by Dai Jiafang, *Yangbanxi de fengfengyuyu: Jiang Qing, yangbanxi ji neimu* (The trials and hardships of the model performances: Jiang Qing, the model performances and the inside story), Beijing: Zhishi chubanshe, 1995, p. 25.

8. Shanghaishi renmin Huju tuan, *Xiju bao*, 1965, 7 (July), 36.

9. The modern opera historians claim this is the earliest reference to 'model performances' (*yangbanxi*), although the coupling of 'performance' with model is not indicated by the quotation from Jiang which they cite: Gao Yilong and Li Xiao, pp. 270–271.

10. Gao Yilong and Li Xiao, p. 271.

11. Gao Yilong and Li Xiao, p. 271. The *Red Flag* report on the event does not cover any speech by Kang Sheng. Of the six speakers summarized, only Jiang Qing mentions the model works by title: '*Shoudu juxing wenyijie wuchanjieji wenhua dageming dahui*' (Capital holds a Proletarian Cultural Revolution meeting of literature and art circles), *Hongqi*, 1966, 15 (December), 5–13.

12. Jiang Qing, '*Tan Jingju geming*'. The editorial is '*Huanhu Jingju geming de weida shengli*' (Acclaim the great victory in the Peking opera revolution), *Hongqi*, 1967, 6 (June), 28–29. The first pages of the issue of *Hongqi* were taken by a two-page editorial attacking the Confucian idea of 'cultivation' (*xiuyang*) and coverage of the establishment of the Beijing Revolutionary Committee to replace the old municipal government, including a speech by Jiang Qing. We should acknowledge that Jiang Qing's 1964 speech on opera undoubtedly went through numerous revisions and editing before its 1967 publication. Much could have been added or deleted with the benefit of almost three years' hindsight and her immediate needs in 1967. For an assessment of Jiang Qing's involvement in the 'model performances', see Tan Jiewen, '*Sanshi nian lai shi yu fei: "yangbanxi" sanshizhou dianji*' (Thirty years of positive and negative: saluting the thirtieth anniversary of the 'model performances'), *Wenyi lilun yu piping* (Literature and art theory and criticism), 1999, 4 (July), 45–52. For an approach as early as 1986 that praise for artistic achievements of the model performances should be separated from condemnation of the Gang of Four, see Hua Jian and Guan Defu, *Guanyu jige xiqu lilun wenti de lunzheng* (Debates on several theoretical issues regarding opera), Beijing: Wenhua yishu chubanshe, 1986.

13. The film title was literally 'Living forever in the flames' (*Liehuo zhong yongsheng*), but its usual English title uses the original novel's title. For a brief discussion, see Clark, *Chinese Cinema*, p. 104. This account of the aborted Peking opera adaptation comes from Lu Jianhua, pp. 179–180. Later, during the Cultural Revolution, Jiang Qing encouraged Red Guard attacks on Zhao Dan, whom she had known well in Shanghai in the 1930s. See also Yang Yiyan, '*Jiang Qing chashou "Hongyan" zhizao yinmou shimo*' (The ins and outs of Jiang Qing's plot to meddle in the creation of *Red Crag*), *Wenshi chunqiu* (Literary and historical annals [Guangxi]), 1995, 6 (December), 35–39. A version of *Hongyan* was included in the 1964 modern-subject Peking opera convention, performed by the Urumqi City Peking Opera Troupe from Xinjiang.

14. Other abortive attempts at modern-subject operas from the mid-1960s include *Red Seeds* (*Hongse de zhongzi*), which started as a Wuxi opera (*Xiju*), *Beacons on the Grasslands* (*Caoyuan fenghuo*), based on a Mongolian novel, and *Scouting across the Yangzi* (*Dujiang jiancha ji*), based on the 1954 film: see Lu Jianhua, pp. 180–181 and Weng Ouhong, pp. 582–583.

15. Yang Jian provides a useful review in his '*Di-erpi yangbanxi de chansheng ji yishu chengjiu*' (Birth and artistic achievements of the second tranche of model performances), *Xiju* (Theatre), 2000, No. 3 (June), pp. 85–93.

16. This account of the making of *Song of the Dragon River* comes mostly from Zhang Yuanpei, '*Xinhua Jingjutuan bianxie de "Longjiang song" weihe bei esha*' (Why the Xinhua Peking Opera Company's *Song of the Dragon River* was killed off), *Shanghai wenhua shizhi tongxun*, 47 (December 1997), 47–50. It also draws on Ma Shaobo, pp. 1941–1943.

17. Ma Shaobo, p. 1942.

18. Li Bingshu, '*Mao zhuxi de geming wenyi luxian gei le wo xin de yishu shengming*' (Chairman Mao's revolutionary line in art has given me a new life in art) in *Geming xiandai Jingju 'Longjiang song' pinglun ji* (Collection of articles on the revolutionary modern Peking opera *Song of the Dragon River*), Beijing: Renmin wenxue chubanshe, 1975, pp. 178–185. Li Bingshu's report was first published in *Hongqi*, 1972, 12 (December), 55–59.

19. This is true of many of the essays by actors about creating model-opera roles. It contrasts with the generalities of other opera specialists in similar reports.

20. This account of the making of *Azalea Mountain* draws mostly on Ma Shaobo, pp. 1943–1945.

21. Guo Yongjiang, '*Suyuan weijing shen xian shi: Qiu Shengrong paiyan "Dujuanshan" shimo*' (Departed before achieving his wishes: the full story of Qiu Shengrong's acting in *Azalea Mountain*), in *Qiu Sengrong yishu pinglun ji* (Collected articles on the art of Qiu Shengrong), Beijing: Zhongguo xiju chubanshe, 1984, pp. 199–208, esp. p. 200.

22. Guo Yongjiang, p. 205.

23. Guo Yongjiang, pp. 205–206.

24. Wang Zengqi, '*Yidai cairen wei jin cai: huainian Qiu Shengrong tongzhi*' (A generation of talents without limit: in memory of comrade Qiu Shengrong), in *Qiu Shengrong yishu pinglun ji*, pp. 211–216, esp. p. 215.

25. Xing Shi, '*Tuichenchuxin, guang cai zhao ren: tan "Dujuanshan" zai wudao he wuda sheji shang de chuangxin*' (Pull out the old, bring in the new; splendour shines on people: a discussion of innovation in the dance and martial acrobatics design of *Azalea Mountain*), in *Dujuanshan pinglun ji* (Collection of articles on *Azalea Mountain*), Beijing: Renmin wenxue chubanshe, 1974, pp. 163–166. The article had first been published in *Liberation Army Daily*, 19 November 1973.

26. 10 October ('Double Ten') was the anniversary of the 1911 anti-dynastic mutiny that lead to the establishment in 1912 of the Republic of China. It was China's national day until 1949, and celebrated as such on Taiwan after that year.

27. Gao Yilong and Li Xiao, p. 310.

28. Interview with Li Guang, Beijing, 12 July 2002. See also Xu Yingjie and Cai Shicheng, pp. 32, 132.

29. Li Guang interview, 12 July 2002.

30. Gao Yilong and Li Xiao, p. 311. Cui Wei had earlier been subject to Red Guard attack: see Chapter Three. Chen Huai'ai was the father of fifth-generation film director Chen Kaige.

31. Weng Ouhong, p. 583.

32. Work on *The Red Lantern* was more advanced, so A Jia's association with it once he came under attack was less damaging for that opera. The 1999 publication of the *Guerrillas on the Plain* script includes amateur photographs from the dress rehearsals and informative essays by Lin Mohan, Ministry of Culture patron of the project, and Zhang Dongchuan, who helped complete the script: A Jia and others, *Pingyuan youjidui* (Guerrillas on the plain), Beijing: Zhongguo xiju chubanshe, 1999, esp. pp. 1–3 and 111–121. See also Xing Ye, '"*Pingyuan youjidui*" *xiugai ji*' (Record of revising *Guerrillas on the Plain*), *Wentan fengyu* (Literary circle hardships), 1999, 5 (May), 74–77.

33. The following account relies mainly on a long article by Zang Tian, '*Cong "Nanhai changcheng" dao "Panshiwan": Jingju gaibian youxiu huaju "Nanhai changcheng" zhong de fengfengyuyu*' (From *Great Wall in the Southern Seas* to *Boulder Bay*: The trials and tribulations of the Peking opera adaptation of the outstanding spoken play *Great Wall in the Southern Seas*), *Shanghai wenhua shizhi tongxun*, 42 (September 1996), 21–27.

34. Gao Yilong and Li Xiao, p. 312.

35. I watched the opera in the Tianqiao Theatre in Beijing in the spring of 1976 and judged audience reception as distinctly lukewarm. See also Gao Yilong and Li Xiao, pp. 312–313.

36. On *quyi* adaptation of scenes from model operas, see Qu Liangbing, '*Wanziqian hong chun manyuan: xikan woshi quyi diaoyan*' (Bursts of colour everywhere: delight in watching our city's *quyi* selections), *Tianjin wenyi*, 1976, 7 (July), 56–57.

37. Bakken, pp. 169–209. For an example, see Shi Xiangrong, '*Jingxin wangzao wuchanjieji gao da yingxiong xingxiang: xuexi geming yangbanxi "san tu chu" chuangzuo yuanze de tihui*' (Painstakingly create the form of the mighty proletarian hero: understanding from studying the 'three prominences' creative principle of the revolutionary model performances), *Tianjin wenyi*, 1973, 3 (June), 66–69. On page 67 Shi refers to the heroes 'becoming models for the worker, peasant and soldier masses to study'.

38. See *Renmin ribao*, 16 January 1971, p. 3, and 26 January 1971, p. 3.

39. Gao Yilong and Li Xiao, p. 313.

40. Mao Shaobo, p. 1949.

41. *Zhongguo xiqu zhi, Hebei juan* (China opera gazetteer, Hebei volume), Beijing: Zhongguo ISBN zhongxin, 1993, pp. 738–739.

42. This account is from *Zhongguo xiqu zhi, Xinjiang juan* (China opera gazetteer, Xinjiang volume), Beijing: Zhongguo ISBN zhongxin, 1995, pp. 676–677.

43. This is based on my observations of audience responses to Uighur and other non-Han singers in theatrical song performances in late 1974 and 1975 in Beijing. Whether the audience delight was a form of interest in 'singing and dancing natives' is an issue for another context. Transplanting of model operas into ethnic minority dramatic forms in the southwest is noted, without assessment of the results, in Yuan Bingchang and Feng Guangyu, *Zhongguo shaoshuminzu yinyue shi (shangce)* (Musical history of China's minorities, vol. 1), Beijing: Zhongyang minzu daxue chubanshe, 1998, pp. 556–557.

44. Xiao Luan, '*Difang xiqu yizhi geming yanbanxi dayoukewei*' (The transplanting of model performances into local opera is very promising), originally

published in *Renmin ribao*, 28 August 1974, reprinted in, for example, *Yunnan wenyi* (Yunnan literature and art), 1974, No. 5 (October), pp. 6–9. Note that the author's name is a homonym (if the original tones are ignored) for 'little chaos'.

45. Gao Yilong and Li Xiao, p. 313.

46. Most reports did not mention that only two complete model operas (*Shajiabang* and *Song of the Dragon River*) were presented. Almost incidentally mentioned in reports of the 1974 performance convention are the names of three Peking operas, which were given trial presentations (*shiyan yanchu*) at the August gathering. They were the newly completed *Boulder Bay*, *The Investigation of a Chair* (*Shen yizi*), and *Fighting the Waves* (*Zhan hailang*). *Chair* had been presented in Peking-opera form by the Shanghai Performance Troupe at the 1964 modern-opera convention in Beijing: see Wenhuabu Beijing bianzhe kan, *Jingju xiandaixi guanmo yanchu dahui jiemudan (hedingben)*. Other model operas were presented only as extracts: Jin Qiu, '*Wanziqianhong chun man tai: xikan si sheng, shi, zizhiqu wenyi diaoyan*' (A riot of spring colour fills the stage: enjoying the four province, city, and autonomous region artistic performances), *Beijing daxue xuebao (zhexue, shehui kexue ban)*, 1974, 5 (October), 46–48, esp. pp. 46 and 47. A similar gathering in Shanghai that same month focused on how opera forms popular there (Shaoxing, Shanghai, and Huai opera) could transplant the model Peking operas: Ma Shaobo, p. 1949.

47. Shi Xiangrong, p. 68. See a discussion of the technical challengers to singers of local opera forms in *Renmin ribao*, 18 July 1975, p. 3.

48. Bell Yung, 'Model Opera as Model: From *Shajiabang* to *Sagabong*', in Bonnie S. McDougall, ed., *Popular Chinese Literature and Performing Arts in the People's Republic of China, 1949–1979*, Berkeley: University of California Press, 1984, pp. 144–164.

49. Tang Zhengxu, '*Yizhi geming yangbanxi, shenru kaizhan Chuanju geming*' (Transplant the revolutionary model performances, deepen the development of the revolution in Sichuan opera), *Sichuan wenyi* (Sichuan literature and art), 1973, 1 trial issue (January), 89–91.

50. These are listed in Gao Yilong and Li Xiao, p. 313 and discussed on pp. 314–317. Fang Jin, '*Xiaoxi chuangzuo de kexi shouhuo: ping Yueju yingpian "Banlan huasheng"*' (A delightful harvest from the creation of short works: review of the film *Half a Basket of Peanuts*), *Hongqi*, 1974, 6 (June), 76–79.

51. Gao Yilong and Li Xiao, p. 314. A version had been presented at the 1964 Beijing modern-opera convention.

52. Gao Yilong and Li Xiao, p. 315.

53. Zhongguo dianying ziliaoguan, Zhongguo yishu yanjiuyuan dianying yanjiusuo, eds, *Zhongguo yishu yingpian bianmu, 1949–1979* (Catalogue of Chinese art films), Beijing, 1982, pp. 836–837. See the 1964 opera convention programme: Wenhuabu Beijing bianzhe kan, *Jingju xiandaixi guanmo yanchu dahui jiemudan (hedingben)*.

54. This account is from Gao Yilong and Li Xiao, pp. 314–315.

55. Gao Yilong and Li Xiao, pp. 315–316. See also *Zhongguo yishu yingpian bianmu*, p. 987. Another modern *pingju* (Northern opera) is lauded in *Renmin ribao*, 5 February 1974, p. 3.

56. Chang Chun, 'Geming yangbanxi daidong le wenyi geming puji, shenru di fazhan: si sheng, shi, zizhiqu wenyi daioyan xuexi zhaji' (The revolutionary model performances drive the dissemination and deepening development of the literary and artistic revolution: study notes from the four province, city, and autonomous region artistic performances), Beijing daxue xuebao, 1974, 5 (October), 37–40, esp. p. 38.

57. Jin Qiu, p. 48.

58. Xiaojinzhuang Brigade Party Branch, 'Women shi zenyang kaizhan qunzhongxing de xue chang geming yangbanxi huodong de' (How we launched a mass activity learning to sing revolutionary model performance songs), Tianjin wenyi, 1975, 1 (January), 4–6.

59. A Pei, ''Sirenbang' jiqi yudang zai qunzhong wenyi zhong zhizao de san da yuan'an' (Three big cases of injustice created in popular literature and art by the Gang of Four and their confederates), Shanghai wenhua shizhi tongxun, 49 (July 1998), 43–47. See also Qin Yan, 'Nuli fazhan gongnongbing yeyu wenyi chuangzuo' (Work hard on developing literary and artistic creations by workers, peasants and soldiers), Hongqi, 1976, 6 (June), 59–64.

60. 'Weida shehuizhuyi zuguo xinxin xiangrong' (The great socialist homeland is full of life and vigor), Geming jiebanren (Revolutionary successors), 1974, 10 (September), 2–5. These pages covered cultural achievements of the Cultural Revolution, as part of a fourteen-page story. The magazine was edited and published by the Tianjin People's Publishing House. Several such magazines directed at school-age children appeared across China in 1973–1974.

61. Fujian Yongdingxian xuanchuanzhan, ed., Wuchanjieji wenhua dageming yi lai qunzhong wenyi chuangzuo xuan: di-yi qi (Selected mass literary writings since the Great Proletarian Cultural Revolution, volume one), Yongding county printery, 1974, p. 30 (in a 164-page volume).

62. Gongnongbing yanchang (Worker, peasant, soldier performances), 1972, 1 (February), 33–40.

63. These three paragraphs rely on Benbao bianjishi, 'Yanzhe Mao zhuxi de geming wenyi luxian shengli qianjin: zhuhe wosheng yijiuqisinian chuangzuo jiemu diaoyan dahui shengli kaimu' (Victoriously advancing on Chairman Mao's revolutionary literature and art road: congratulating the victorious opening of our province's 1974 creative performance convention), Yunnan wenyi, 1974, 1 (February), 4–5. For equivalent events for amateurs in Tianjin, see 'Shengqi bobo, fengfuduocai: 1974 nian Tianjinshi zhigong yeyu wenyi huiyan jianxun' (Full of vitality, rich in variety: brief report on the 1974 employees amateur literary and art performance event in Tianjin city), Tianjin wenyi, 1974, 4 (August), 88. The 1976 event is reported in Tianjin wenyi, 1976, 2 (May), 56. The 1975 Liaoning provincial professional equivalent is reported in Liaoning wenyi (Liaoning literature and art), 1975, 10 (October), 29 and 12 (December), inside front-cover photos.

64. See Zhongguo xiqu zhi, Shaanxi juan (China opera gazetteer, Shaanxi volume), Beijing: Zhongguo ISBN zhongxin, 1995, pp. 907–910, for a summary of the Shaanxi delegation's experience in Beijing.

65. See the Xinhua news agency report on the plans for the commemoration published in Hebei ribao, 16 May 1975, p. 1.

66. *Hebei ribao*, 22 May 1975, p. 1. Note also the script for a 'Peking opera dance' (*Jingju wudao*, without singing) on *Fighting the Waves*, written by A Jian based on the Shanghai Peking Opera Troupe's opera: *Renmin xiju* (People's theatre), 1976, 1 (March), 44–47. See also Xu Xinjie and Cai Chicheng, pp. 135–136 on the opera.

67. Hong Xi, '*Huaju geming de xin chengjiu: ping huaju "Dujuan shan"*' (A new achievement in the spoken drama revolution: a review of the play *Azalea Mountain*), *Renmin xiju* (People's drama), 1976, 3 (July), 70–73. Hong Xi (probably a pseudonym) is identified as from the Central May Seventh Arts University Theatre Academy.

68. Shi Zhongping, '*Xue geming yangbanxi, kai yi dai xin shi feng: xidu "Xiaojinzhuang shige xuan"*' (Study the revolutionary model performances, open up a new storm in poetry writing: delight at reading *Selected Poems of Xiaojinzhuang*), *Beijing daxue xuebao (shehui kexue ban)*, 1975, 2 (March), 74–80. For a poem for performance about presenting *Red Lantern*, see Zhang Yuebing, '*Hongdeng gao ju*' (Mounting 'Red Lantern'), *Shandong wenyi* (Shandong literature and art), 1974, 6 (December), 55–57.

69. See Duan Jingli, *Huxian nongmin hua chenfulu* (Record of the changing fortunes of the Hu County peasant painting), Kaifeng: Henan daxue chubanshe, 2005, pp. 166–173. For more on painting, see Chapter Four.

70. Xinhua xinwenshe, '*Zai geming yangbanxi de guanghui zhaoyao xia: geming wenyi gongzuoshe changtan xuexi geming yangbanxi de tihui*' (Under the brilliant illumination of the revolutionary model performances: revolutionary workers in art and literature freely discuss their understanding of studying the revolutionary model performances), in *Jingju geming shinian* (Ten years of the revolution in Peking opera), Zhengzhou: Henan renmin chubanshe, 1974, pp. 46–47.

71. See *Wudao*, 1976, 3 (July), 44–48.

72. Ma Shaobo, pp. 1953–1954.

73. See, for example, Tian Wen and Xin Xiao, '*Zan Jingju geming shinian*' (In praise of the ten years of the revolution in Peking opera), *Tianjin wenyi*, 1974, 4 (August), 24–27: quote is on p. 27. Note the title's play on the title of Jiang Qing's 1964 speech '*Tan Jingju geming*'.

74. Tian Wen and Xin Xiao make these comparisons throughout their article, above.

75. This section is drawn from my fuller study of these issues in Richard King ed., *Art and the Artist in Cultural Revolution China*, Vancouver: University of British Columbia Press (forthcoming).

76. *Tianjin ribao*, 2 October 1966, p. 6.

77. The documentaries included one on the Rent-Collection Courtyard (*Shouzu yuan*) in Sichuan: see Chapter Four.

78. See, for example, Ma Shijun, '*Woguo dianying faxing fangying gongzuo de huigu yu zhanwang*' (A recollection and prospects on Chinese film distribution and screening), in Zhongguo dianyingjia xiehui dianyingshi yanjiubu, ed., *Zhonghua renmin gongheguo dianying shiye sanshiwu nian, 1949–1984* (Thirty-five years of the PRC film industry), Beijing: Zhongguo dianying chubanshe, 1985, p. 340, for a typical somewhat ambiguous statement about seventeen years of films not being in distribution.

79. But the same page offers evidence of the dominance of the Peking opera form. The schedule for Hebei Television includes at 2 p.m. Peking opera, a segment followed only at 7 p.m. by Country Club (*Nongcun julebu*). Tianjin Television on 2 October at 10:00 in the morning and 1:10 in the afternoon had unspecified Peking opera listed in the schedule. What these programs of Peking opera consisted of is unclear, though presumably it was confined to the new, modernized works at a time when no full-length television or film versions are known to have been recorded.

80. Yu Hong and Deng Zhengqiang, *Zhongguo dangdai guanggao shi* (A history of advertising in contemporary China), Changsha: Hunan kexue jishu chubanshe, 2000, p. 10, indicates vestiges of advertising enterprises survived through the Cultural Revolution.

81. The third page also includes classified-style listings of name changes of several factories in the city. For example, the Tianjin City Social Welfare (*shehui fuli*) Number Two Paper Product Factory was to be known after 1 October as the Tianjin City East Wind Printing and Paper Product Factory.

82. *Yunnan ribao* (Yunnan Daily), 14 May 1967, p. 4 (advertisements); *Renmin ribao*, 21 May 1967, p. 4 (a report on amateur performers in Beijing); *Renmin ribao*, 12 May 1967, p. 3 (on the Guizhou performance).

83. See the schedule printed in *Ningxia ribao* (Ningxia Daily), 27 May 1968, p. 3.

84. *Ningxia ribao*, 25 May 1969, p. 4.

85. See, for example, *Dongfang hong* (*The East Is Red*, published by the Beijing Industrial University), 27 May 1967 issue, where the anniversary of Mao's *Talks* is celebrated without mention of the model works: reprinted in *Xinbian Hongweibing ziliao* (A New Collection of Red Guard Publications), Oakton VA: Center for Chinese Research Materials, 1999, pp. 703–704. The *Dongfang hong* issue of 14 June 1968, p. 2, shows a similar unexpected absence: *Xinbian Hongweibing ziliao*, p. 1388.

86. *Hongqi*, 1969, 10 (September), 37–40, esp. p. 39. Liu Xiaowei, as an eighteen-year-old sent to a May Seventh Cadre School northwest of Shijiazhuang in the company of several eminent Beijing performers, recalled performing extracts from old-style operas for local peasants, who greatly appreciated the opportunity: interview with Liu Xiaowei, Beijing, 6 August 2000.

87. For an example of amateur, factory-based performance of *Shajiabang*, see *Shanghai wenhua shizhi tongxun*, 22 (October 1992), 11.

88. See, for example, *Ningxia ribao*, 23 May 1971, p. 4. The stills of *Shajiabang* and *The White-Haired Girl* are described as from a television film and a television documentary, respectively. The newly available model films meant commemorations in Ningxia did not include the showing of old, pre–Cultural Revolution films, as had been usual in the immediately preceding years.

89. *Ningxia ribao*, 1 May 1972, p. 1, 16 May 1972, pp. 1–3, and issues in May 1973 give full coverage to the *Talks*, but seem to ignore the model performances.

90. *Xiju bao*, 1959, 19 (October), 70–71. A note indicates that the numbers from the armed forces and the mining industry had not been received and were not included in these data.

91. Wang Zicheng, '*Xiqu jiaoyu bixu gaige*' (Opera education must be reformed), *Xiju bao*, 1964, 3 (March), 38–42. Originally published in *Guangming ribao*, 20 February 1964.

92. For a glowing report on three opera companies, seen as models of proletarian service, see Xu Tie, '*Xiqu jutuan de geminghua*' (The revolution in opera companies), *Xiju bao*, 1964, 3 (March), 28–29.

93. Quoted in Ma Shaobo, p. 1904.

94. Ma Shaobo, p. 1905.

95. Reprinted in Zhonggong zhongyang bangongting, Guowuyuan mishuting, Wenhua geming lianhe jiedaishi, *Wuchanjieji wenhua dageming youguan wenjian huiji* (Compilation relevant to the Proletarian Cultural Revolution), Vol. 1 (February 1967), pp. 172–176 (quote is from p. 175). This is part of a sixteen-volume collection of documents, published in Beijing from 1967.

96. Volume 1, p. 176. Note a 14 July 1967 draft opinion concerned with troupe wages: Volume 3 (September 1967), pp. 129–131.

97. Ma Shaobo, p. 1906.

98. The second purpose served by the promulgation of the myth of massive disruption during the whole of the Cultural Revolution ten years helped explain the weakened condition of Chinese opera forms in the late 1970s and 1980s. Being out of action, even with model, Peking operas for at least a half-decade earlier could provide a welcome excuse for present failings.

99. Figures from the 1989 China Statistical Yearbook are provided in an appendix to Xie Bailiang, '*Zhongguo xiju fazhan de diyuxing tezheng*' (The regional features of China's stage performance development), *Wenyi yanjiu* (Research in literature and art), 1993, 6 (November), 99.

100. Lu Qun, '"*Wenhua dageming*" *qijian de yanchu guanli*' (Performance management in the Cultural Revolution period), *Shanghai wenhua shizhi tongxun*, 40 (March 1996), 46. The report is carefully dated 28 November 1995.

101. Lu Qun's 1995 report ends by contrasting this situation with a post-1976 increase in performances and audience numbers, but this does not invalidate its revealing data about 1966–1976 activity.

102. Some or all of these documents may have been adjusted or revised with hindsight by the editorial committees that worked through the 1980s and 1990s on their publication. But even granting the possibility of post–Cultural Revolution censorship, these appended documents provide a provincial-level insight into how Cultural Revolution policy was promulgated.

103. *Zhongguo xiqu zhi, Zhejiang juan* (China opera gazetteer, Zhejiang), Beijing: Zhongguo ISBN zhongxin, 1997, pp. 883–884. The document is dated 26 May 1966.

104. Sorting out of performance troupes had started in the early 1960s, after the economic disaster of the Great Leap Forward and consequent famine, and as part of the Socialist Education Movement in the countryside: see, for example, documents reproduced in *Zhongguo xiqu zhi, Xinjiang juan*, pp. 674–675, *Zhongguo xiqu zhi, Sichuan juan* (China opera gazetteer, Sichuan), Beijing: Zhongguo ISBN zhongxin, 1995, pp. 678–680, and *Zhongguo xiqu*

zhi, Yunnan juan (China opera gazetteer, Yunnan), Beijing: Zhongguo ISBN zhongxin, 1994, pp. 728–739.

105. *Zhongguo xiqu zhi, Zhejiang juan*, pp. 884–887.
106. *Zhongguo xiqu zhi, Hebei juan*, pp. 774–778. The phrase used to describe such organizations was 'self-sufficient' or more literally 'assuming responsibility for profits and losses' (*zifu yingkui*). This essentially meant the troupes were privately owned, though usually by a collective group not a single owner.
107. *Zhongguo xiqu zhi, Yunnan juan*, pp. 739–742.
108. *Zhongguo xiqu zhi, Yunnan juan*, pp. 743–744.
109. See, for example, Wei Wenhua, '*Shandong Shecun yeyu jutuan ershinian lai jianchi yan geming xiandaixi*' (Shandong's She Village amateur performing troupe has persisted for twenty years in presenting revolutionary modern performances), *Xiju bao*, 1965, 3 (March), 18–19.
110. *Zhongguo xiqu zhi, Yunnan juan*, pp. 744–746.
111. *Zhongguo xiqu zhi, Hebei juan*, pp. 736–737.
112. *Hebei ribao*, 20 February 1972, p. 1.
113. *Hebei ribao*, 3 March 1972, p. 4. See Chapter Four on Red Guard performances.
114. *Zhongguo xiqu zhi, Sichuan juan*, pp. 680–681.
115. See the bottom half of a page of advertisements in *Hebei ribao*, 22 May 1975, p. 4. The top half features listings of performances of the standard modern Peking operas.
116. *Hebei ribao*, 25 May 1972, p. 1.
117. *Xinjiang ribao*, 6 August 1975, p. 4. See also *Xinjiang ribao*, 7 August 1975, p. 1.
118. See the television and film listings in *Xinjiang ribao*, 12 August 1975, p. 4. At this time, almost all television sets were communally owned and watched. Private ownership only grew widespread in the 1980s, as did extended broadcasting hours.
119. *Xinjiang ribao*, 27 August 1975, p. 3.
120. See *Xinjiang ribao*, 30 August 1975, p. 4.
121. *Xinjiang ribao*, 27 August 1975, p. 3. The generic name of the commune indicates its newness and the underdeveloped nature of much of Xinjiang.
122. *Xinjiang ribao*, 14 September 1975, p. 3.
123. Reported, along with the closing ceremony, in *Xinjiang ribao*, 27 August 1975, p. 1.
124. A front-page editorial in the same issue raised the problem of old-style, bourgeois tendencies of arrogance and selfishness on the part of artists, something the provincial leaders do not appear to have raised at the gathering of participants for the closing ceremony: *Xinjiang ribao*, 27 August 1975, pp. 1 and 4.
125. See the Xinhua News Agency report published in *Xinjiang ribao*, 26 September 1975, p. 3.
126. See the page of advertisements for the National Day shows in *Xinjiang ribao*, 1 October 1975, p. 7.
127. This is a characterization of classical Chinese poetry that can be applied to the 1960s and 1970s opera experience.

THREE: FIXING CULTURE ON FILM

1. Interview with Li Wenhua, Beijing, 3 July 2002.
2. 'From a certain point of view, the "Great Cultural Revolution" first started in the realm of film'. Liu Jianxun, Liu Jianfeng, and Lu Yuan, eds., *Zhongguo dangdai yingshi wenxue* (Literature of contemporary Chinese film and television), Nanning: Guangxi renmin chubanshe, 1986, p. 235.
3. See Clark, *Chinese Cinema*, pp. 48–52. One of Jiang Qing's first post-1949 forays into politics was as a member of the 'investigation team' that examined Wu Xun's life in his home district in 1951 as part of the campaign against the bio-pic (see Clark, *Chinese Cinema*, p. 51).
4. The film was released in 1964 in large and small cities as an object for criticism, according to Xie Tieli in a 1993 interview: *Dianying yishu* (Film art), 1994, 1 (February), 9. For criticisms of the film, see Clark, *Chinese Cinema*, pp. 112–113. A similar mix of romantic gush and earnest revolution, *Song of Youth* (*Qingchun zhi ge*), adapted from a popular 1956 novel in 1959, had better timing and directly presented revolutionary activism: see Clark, *Chinese Cinema*, pp. 103–105.
5. On *February*, see *Wenyi bao* (Literature and art gazette), 1964, 8–9 (September), 30; and on *Lin Family*, see *Wenyi bao*, 1965, 6 (June), 2–5, 14.
6. Cited in Tian Jingqing, *Beijing dianying ye shiji, 1949–1990* (Achievements of the Beijing film industry), Beijing: Zhongguo dianying chubanshe, 1999, pp. 153–154.
7. *Wenyi bao*, 1966, 3 (March), 3–17.
8. See, for example, *Renmin ribao*, 19 April 1966, p. 6. For later criticism, see *Jiefangjun wenyi* (Liberation Army literature and art), 1968, 10 (May), 17–23 and the English-language *Chinese Literature*, 1968, 6 (June), 95–100. For more detail on these pre–Cultural Revolution attacks, see Clark, *Chinese Cinema*, pp. 129–131.
9. *Dazhong dianying* (Popular film), 1965, 6 (June), 29. This speech is part of a five-page transcript of speeches in similar vein by Shanghai filmmakers (pp. 27–31). The film's title in Chinese meant a city with an active (bourgeois) night life.
10. See, for example, *Dazhong dianying*, 1966, 5 (May), 31–33 and *Renmin ribao*, 22 May 1966, p. 3.
11. For criticisms of the film, see *Renmin ribao*, 30 July 1964, p. 6; 6 September 1964, p. 7; and 8 September 1964, p. 6; *Wenyi bao* 1964, 8–9 (September), 31–35; *Dazhong dianying*, 1964, 6 (June), 12–13; *Dazhong dianying* 1964, 8–9 (September), 18–22. 28. At this stage, it was still possible to publish a dissenting, supportive view of the film: *Renmin ribao*, 24 August 1964, p. 6. Yang Hansheng recalls the criticism in a postscript to his *Yang Hansheng dianying juben xuanji* (Selected film scripts of Yang Hansheng), Beijing: Zhongguo dianying chubanshe, 1981, pp. 325–326.
12. The *Renmin ribao* editors acknowledged the problems of investigating the settings of fiction in their preface to the published report: 15 November 1964, p. 7. This kind of investigation had been used during the criticism of *The Life of Wu Xun* in 1951 to establish what the peasants for whom Wu Xun had established his school for the poor generations earlier really thought about him.

13. See the somewhat tabloid extract from his full-length biography of Zhao by Ni Tu, 'Zhao Dan yu Jiang Qing' (Zhao Dan and Jiang Qing), *Yinmu* (Screen), 1987, 2 (April), 48–51.

14. Cited in Tian Jingqing, p. 154. On *Five Golden Flowers*, see Clark, *Chinese Cinema*, pp. 99–100. 'Butterfly lovers' refers to the well-known opera story of Liang Shanbo and Zhu Yingtai. Their love having been thwarted in life, they become a pair of butterflies in death.

15. See, for example, *Wenyi bao*, 1966, 5 (May 1966), 57–58. This was the last issue of *Wenyi bao* before the Cultural Revolution. Criticism continued, even in an English-language periodical: *Chinese Literature*, 1969, 11–12, 142–153.

16. Zhai Jiannong, '"Yangbanxi dianying" de xingshuai: "Wen-ge dianying"': 20 *shiji teshu de wenhua xianxiang, yi*' (The ups and downs of 'model performance films': Cultural Revolution film; a special phenomenon of twentieth-century culture), *Dangdai dianying* (Contemporary film), 1995, 2 (April), 39. See also *Dazhong dianying*, 1966, 4 (April), 16–18 and *Dazhong dianying*, 1966, 5 (May), 33–34.

17. Li Qingyue, *Ningxia dianying shihua* (Historical narrative of film in Ningxia), Yinchuan: Ningxia renmin chubanshe, 1995, pp. 89–90.

18. For details *Zhongguo yishu yingpian bianmu*, pp. 807–808, 812–814, 817. Of the eight Changchun productions, *Girl Divers* (*Nü tiaoshui duiyuan*) was clearly intended to be the box-office winner, given the attractions of its subject matter, a female diving team which spends much of its time in swim suits.

19. *Zhongguo yishu yingpian bianmu*, pp. 866–873, 875–876, 880–886.

20. *Zhongguo yishu yingpian bianmu*, pp. 890–893, 899–901.

21. *Zhongguo yishu yingpian bianmu*, pp. 915–918, 920–926. Only fifteen features are listed for 1966, the lowest level since 1953, when the last of the privately owned studios had been nationalized: *Zhongguo yishu yingpian bianmu*, pp. 929–946. Several such films from the Pearl River studio were completed in 1966, but only passed censorship for distribution in 1977, according to tables in an internal statistical compilation from the studio: *Zhujiang dianying zhipianchang 1958–1980 tongji ziliao* (Statistical data on the Pearl River Film Studio, 1958–1980), Guangzhou: Pearl River Film Studio, 1981, pp. 80–83 (from the China Film Archives, Beijing).

22. Zhongguo dianyingjia xiehui dianyingshi yanjiubu, *Zhonghua renmin gongheguo dianying shiye sanshiwu nian, 1949–1984* [hereafter *Sanshiwu nian*] contains 33 chapters and a postscript in its 417 pages. Coverage of the Cultural Revolution decade totals about twenty-five of these pages.

23. *Sanshiwu nian*, p. 45.

24. Yu Deshui, *Zhuying ren yu Zhuying de lu* (Pearl River Film Studio people and pathways), Guangzhou: Guangdong lüyou chubanshe, 1999, p. 125.

25. Interview with Huang Jianzhong, Beijing, 6 July 2002.

26. *Sanshiwu nian*, p. 59. In a 1993 interview, the Beijing studio actor Yu Yang claimed that in 1970 one-third of the Beijing studio cadres were exposed as '16 May elements' (*Wu-yiliu fenzi*), amounting to more than 200 persons: *Dianying yishu*, 1993, 4 (August), 81.

27. See her numbingly orthodox autobiography: *Suiyue youqing: Zhang Ruifang huiyilu* (Years of friendship: the memoirs of Zhang Ruifang), Beijing: Zhongyang wenxian chubanshe, 2005, pp. 362–373. Another eminent film actress, Xie Fang, completely omits reference to her Cultural Revolution

experiences in her two reminiscences: *Wo de qishinian: Xie Fang huiyilu* (My seventy years: Xie Fang's memoirs), Beijing: Xinxing chubanshe, 2006, and *Wangshi congcong* (The past rushes by), Beijing: Zuojia chubanshe, 1998.

28. See *Sanshiwu nian*, p. 143, and Yu Deshui, pp. 116–117. *Dazhong dianying*, 1966, 6 (June), 32–33 contains typical criticism in what turned out to be the last issue of the magazine for nine years.

29. Some of the smaller studios, founded in the Great Leap Forward in 1958, by the mid-1960s had skeleton staffs and were engaged mostly in assisting larger studios in making documentaries or features in its region.

30. *Sanshiwu nian*, pp. 167–168.

31. *Sanshiwu nian*, p. 124. A film of the opera was eventually completed in 1972 at the Changchun studio: *Zhongguo yishu yingpian bianmu*, p. 965.

32. Su Yun interview, Di Di, 'Shoupi Wen-ge gushipian shezhi shimo' (The ins and outs of the production of the first group of Cultural Revolution feature films), *Dianying yishu*, 1995, 3 (June), 87.

33. Yu Deshui, pp. 125–129. Pearl River's first film to be shown at an international film festival was one such news documentary, participating in September 1974 in a cultural film festival in Japan.

34. The titles and further viewing figures are given in Yu Li, ed., *Zhongguo dianying zhuanye shi yanjiu: dianying zhipian, faxing, fangying juan* (Research on Chinese film specialist history: film production, distribution and screening), Beijing: Zhongguo dianying chubanshe, 2006, pp. 110–111. See also Shan Wanli, *Zhongguo jilu dianying shi* (History of Chinese documentary film), Beijing: Zhongguo dianying chubanshe, 2005, pp. 234–235, and Fang Fang, *Zhongguo jilupian fazhan shi* (History of the development of Chinese documentary films), Beijing: Zhongguo xiju chubanshe, 2003, pp. 272–275. See an advertisement for the documentaries on Mao's fifth and sixth inspections in *Yunnan ribao*, 20 May 1967, p. 4.

35. On such events at Pearl River, see *Sanshiwu nian*, pp. 124–125.

36. The following figures are from Chen Huangmei, gen. ed., *Dangdai Zhongguo dianying* (Contemporary Chinese film), Beijing: Zhongguo shehui kexue chubanshe, 1989, Volume 1, pp. 325–326.

37. *Sanshiwu nian*, p. 111. A notable recent exception, with a lengthy account of events during the Cultural Revolution, is Deqinge'erma and Zhai Jiannong, *Zai dahai li hangxing: Yu Yang zhuan* (Sailing on the seas: A biography of Yu Yang), Beijing: Zhongguo dianying chubanshe, 2007, pp. 149–257.

38. Zhou Xiaobang, ed., *Beiying sishinian, 1949–1989* (Forty years of the Beijing Film Studio), Beijing: Wenhua yishu chubanshe, 1997, pp. 193–250. The following outline of events in 1966–1968 is drawn from the chronology in this volume, pp. 459–462.

39. Zhou Xiaobang, pp. 457–459.

40. Zhou Xiaobang, p. 459.

41. See *Hai Mo dianying juben xuanji* (Selected film scripts of Hai Mo), Beijing: Zhongguo dianying chubanshe, 1979, pp. 1–5.

42. See, for example, *Dianying yishu*, 1994, 3 (June), 62.

43. Based on an interview with Li Jun, in *Dianying yishu*, 1994, 6 (November), 86–87.

44. Li Jun interview, *Dianying yihsu*, 1994, 6 (November), 88.

45. Hu Chang, *Xin Zhongguo dianying de yaolan* (The cradle of new China's film), Changchun: Jilin wenshi chubanshe, 1986, p. 338.
46. Zhai Jiannong, *Dangdai dianying*, 1995, 2 (April), 39.
47. Tian Jingqing, p. 161.
48. These and other meetings are recorded in Tian Jingqing, pp. 161–162.
49. Tian Jingqing, p. 168.
50. The meeting and its resolutions are fully reported in Tian Jingqing, pp. 162–166.
51. Cited by Yu Yang in Di Di, '"*Huohong de niandai*": "*Wen-ge*" *gushi yingpian de xiandao*' (Fiery years: forerunners of Cultural Revolution feature films), *Dianying yishu*, 1993, 4 (August), 83.
52. Zhai Jiannong, *Dangdai dianying*, 1995, 2 (April), 40–41. Zhai Jiannong's *Hongse wangshi: 1966–1976 nian de Zhongguo dianying* (A red past: 1966–1976 Chinese films), Beijing: Taihai chubanshe, 2001, pp. 64–184 offers lively descriptions of the filming of the model performances. See also Feng Min, *Zhongguo dianying yishu shigang (1896–1986)* (Survey of Chinese film art), Tianjin: Nankai daxue chubanshe, 1992, p. 391. The three-times filming claim is made in *Zhongguo dianying nianjian, 1981* (China film yearbook), Beijing: Zhongguo dianying chubanshe, 1982, p. 713.
53. Biographical details are from *Zhongguo xiju dianying cidian* (China theatre and film dictionary), Beijing: Beijing guangbo xueyuan chubanshe, 1993, p. 512. See also the Xie Tieli interview: Di Di, '*Shenghuo shi yishu de yuanquan*' (Life is the fountainhead of art), *Dianying yishu*, 1994, 1 (February), 7–8. The CCP membership date (1942) is from Zhou Xiaobang, p. 571.
54. Interview with Xie Tieli, Beijing, 9 July 2002. Jiang Qing's view was also reported by Li Wenhua, interview, 3 July 2002.
55. See biographical details in *Zhongguo xiju dianying cidian*, p. 454. Qian joined the CCP in 1945 in Yan'an: Zhou Xiaobang, p. 567.
56. Xie Tieli interview, *Dianying yishu*, 1994, 1 (February), 10.
57. Mentioned in *Dianying yishu*, 1994, 3 (June), 62.
58. Zhou Xiaobang, p. 462. The formal announcement of the new site came in early February 1970: Zhou Xiaobang, p. 463.
59. These details of the making of the film are from Zhou Xiaobang, pp. 210–212. See also Fu Xiaohong, *Liangbu kua shengping: Xie Tieli koushu shilu* (Two steps bestriding life: Oral history of Xie Tieli), Beijing: Zhongguo dianying chubanshe, 2005, pp. 113–124. On the length of the film, see Gao Jinxiao, p. 68.
60. Interview with Xie Tieli, Beijing, 9 July 2002.
61. Accounts of the making of the early film versions of the 'model performances' make no mention of the black-and-white versions of *Taking Tiger Mountain by Strategy* and *Shajiabang* released in 1970 by Beijing Television. They are described as 'television screen reproductions' *dianshi pingmu fuzhi* in the *Zhongguo yishu yingpian bianmu*, pp. 956–957. Whether the crews making these screen versions exchanged ideas with the crews working at the Beijing Film Studio is unclear. Also released in 1970 was a television version of the ballet *The White-Haired Girl*, made by a crew from Shanghai Television and something called the 'Shanghai City Filming Team' (*Shanghaishi dianying shezhizu*), presumably a temporary unit pending the re-opening of production

at the Shanghai Film Studio, which combined the pre–Cultural Revolution Tianma and Haiyan studios: *Zhongguo yishu yingpian bianmu*, p. 954.

62. Interview with Xie Tieli, 9 July 2002.

63. See, for example, Zhou Xiaobang, pp. 211–212, and (in more showy vein) Wu Di, '*Xushixue fenxi: "yangbanxi" dianying de jizhi/moshi/daihao yu gongneng*' (Narratilogical analysis: mechanisms, patterns, codes, and functions of the model performance films), *Dangdai dianying*, 2001, 4 (August), 69–73. A notable exception is Gao Xiaojian, *Zhongguo xiqu dianying shi* (History of Chinese opera films), Beijing: Wenhua yishu chubanshe, 2005, who shows considerable respect for the efforts to render the *yanbanxi* on film: pp. 201–240, esp. 236–238.

64. *Red Flag* added to the publicity: Beijing dianying zhipianchang 'Zhiqu Weihushan' shezhizu, '*Huanyuan wutai, gao yu wutai: women shi zenyang ba geming xiandai Jingju "Zhiqu Weihushan" banshang yinmu de*' (Better and higher than the stage: how we took the revolutionary modern Peking opera *Taking Tiger Mountain by Strategy* to the screen), *Hongqi*, 1971, 3 (March), 72–80.

65. Data from *Zhongguo yishu yingpian bianmu*, pp. 966–968, 991, and Zhou Xiaobang, p. 212.

66. Biographical details from *Zhongguo xiju dianying cidian*, p. 233; Party membership is noted in Zhou Xiaobang, p. 546.

67. Biographical details can be found in *Zhongguo xiju dianying cidian*, p. 510–511. For typical criticisms of *Stage Sisters*, see *Dazhong dianying*, 1966, 5 (May), 31–33, and of the *Li* film, see *Dazhong dianying*, 1966, 6 (June), 34–35.

68. Wang Lian, '*Dongluan niandai de yingshi manyi: ji wo yu Xie Jin de chuangzuo youyi*' (Pleased with filming during the era of chaos: my creative friendship with Xie Jin), *Dianying yishu*, 1994, 3 (June), 75–76. See also Fu Xiaohong, pp. 129–133.

69. Zhongguo dianyingjia xiehui, eds, '*Sirenbang' shi dianying shiye de sidi: Wenhuabu dianying xitong jiepi 'Sirenbang' zuixing dahui fayan huibian* (The Gang of Four is the deadly enemy of the film industry: Collection of speeches at a conference of the Ministry of Culture's film system exposing and criticizing the Gang of Four), Beijing: Zhongguo dianying chubanshe, 1978, p. 183. The story is also noted by Tian Jingqing, p. 180. Li Wenhua (in an interview in Beijing on 3 July 2002) suggested the reason Jiang Qing rejected the first version was that the Pearl River Studio projector lens and booth glass were dirty, giving a murky quality to the rough-cut Jiang Qing watched there. Li is quoted to this effect also in Zhai Jiannong, *Hongse wangshi*, p. 148. Li claimed that all the *yangbanxi* films were made on Eastman Kodak film stock. At this time, China was attempting to manufacture its own colour film stock: see Yang Haizhou, ed., *Zhongguo dianying wuzi chanye xitong lishi biannianji (1928–1994)* (Historical chronology of the Chinese film materials system), Beijing: Zhongguo dianying chubanshe, 1998, p. 298.

70. Zhai Jiannong, *Hongse wangshi*, pp. 145–156. Zhai notes that Xie Tieli was the main director, assisted by Xie Jin (pp. 148–149). On pp. 157–167 Zhai includes an un-sourced transcript of a January 1973 meeting of Jiang Qing, other radical leaders, and the film crew led by Xie Tieli before the third version was filmed. On this third version, see Zhai, pp. 168–171. See also

Zhou Xiaobang, p. 212; *Zhongguo yishu yingpian bianmu*, pp. 966–967 and 978.

71. See, for example, the announcement in *Gansu ribao* (Gansu Daily), 23 May 1972, p. 1. The new films included also sixteen documentaries, newsreels, and animated films, made at the Xi'an Film Studio, the Pearl River studio and the Agricultural Film Studio.

72. Wang Lian, pp. 76–77. In a 1994 interview Xie Tieli, director of the *Tiger Mountain* film, dismissed filming in real locations as unsuited to the unrealistic conventions of opera: *Dianying yishu*, 1994, 1 (February), 10.

73. *Sanshiwu nian*, p. 45. The hats are those labels given enemies, the braids stand for weak points exploited by opponents, and the little shoes are an idiom for making trouble for someone.

74. Su Yun interview, p. 88.

75. Biographical data from *Zhongguo xiju dianying cidian*, p. 385 and Hu Chang, pp. 150–151. This history of the Changchun studio makes no specific reference to these two opera films, only to two opera adaptations being made during the Cultural Revolution.

76. Biographical details from Hu Chang, pp. 149–150, and *Zhongguo xiju xingpian cidian*, p. 308. On *Third Sister Liu*, see Loh Wai-fong, 'From romantic love to class struggle: some reflections on the film *Liu Sanjie*', in Bonnie S. McDougall, ed., *Popular Chinese Literature*, pp. 165–176.

77. Li Wenhua interview, Beijing, 3 July 2002. See also Fu Xiaohong, pp. 124–126.

78. His 1956 adaptation of a story by China's greatest twentieth-century writer, Lu Xun's *New Year's Sacrifice* (*Zhufu*), enhanced his reputation as a director of significant projects: biographical details from *Zhongguo xiju yingpian cidian*, p. 470. The Shanghai studio in 1957 had been split into three studios. The third, the Jiangnan studio, had lasted only a few years. The other studios stopped production in 1966.

79. *Zhongguo xiju yingpian cidian*, p. 342.

80. The fact that the Shanghai Film Studio chapter on thirty-five years of film production covers the Cultural Revolution proper in four lines out of twenty-five pages (*Sanshiwu nian*, p. 111) suggests a complex picture of motivations and divisions could be drawn. There was no rush to draw such a picture: Alone among the major studios, Shanghai had not produced a detailed history of itself a quarter of a century after the Cultural Revolution.

81. *Zhongguo yishu yingpian bianmu*, pp. 970–971. Biographical details from *Zhongguo xiju yingpian cidian*, p. 346. Sha went on after 1980 to specialize in musical and opera films. For more on Yin and music, see Chapter Four.

82. Su Yun interview, p. 88. Zhai Jiannong says the conference lasted to March 1973: *Dangdai dianying*, 1995, 2 (April), 41–42. As a student in Beijing from October 1974 until July 1976, I observed directly many such political 'discussion' sessions.

83. Su Yun interview, p. 88.

84. The innovations of the *Azalea Mountain* film are discussed in Zhou Xiaobang, pp. 213–216. The 1975 film was *Haixia*: see Chapter Five.

85. For biographical details, see *Zhongguo xiju dianying cidian*, pp. 322 and 484–485.

86. Cui was put in protective custody by the Public Security Bureau in April 1968, the same month that all his personnel records were removed from the studio: Zhou Xiaobang, p. 200.
87. Zhai Jiannong, *Dangdai dianying*, 1995, 2 (April), 42. On *Yezhu lin*, see *Zhongguo yishu yingpian bianmu*, pp. 698–699.
88. Interview with Li Guang, Beijing, 12 July 2002.
89. For brief biographies of Yu Deshui and Hong Xiannü, see *Zhongguo xiju yingpian cidian*, pp. 164 and 275–276, respectively.
90. *Zhujiang dianying zhipianchang 1958–1980 nian tongji ziliao*, pp. 22–23, 36. Total cost of the shoot was comparable with other films, despite it being a soundstage-based project: p. 37.
91. The filming is covered in the studio history, edited by Yu Deshui himself, pp. 133–136.
92. Yu Deshui, p. 141.
93. *Zhongguo yishu yingpian bianmu*, p. 1029. On the Tianshan studio, established in 1956 and by the early 1960s mostly given over to film dubbing into Uighur and Kazak, see *Sanshiwu nian*, pp. 191–203.
94. See *Zhongguo yishu yingpian bianmu*, pp. 1100–1101. On *Shen yizi*, see *Zhongguo yishu yingpian bianmu*, p. 1092. *Red Cloud Ridge* told the same story as the dance drama *Ode to Yimeng*; see Chapter Four.
95. See *Zhongguo yishu yingpian bianmu*, pp. 1017–1918 and 1025. For the opera script, see *Tianjin wenyi*, 1973, 4 (August), 65–70.
96. See *Zhongguo yishu yingpian bianmu*, pp. 1025–1026 and 1108–1109.
97. *Zhongguo yishu yingpian bianmu*, pp. 980–981. The director was the veteran filmmaker Wang Weiyi.
98. Preparation had taken five months from June 1972. These dates are from *Zhujiang dianying zhipianchang 1958–1980 tongji ziliao*, p. 23.
99. See *Zhongguo yishu yingpian bianmu*, pp. 1034–1035.
100. Zhou Xiaobang, pp. 232, 463. For an early 'review' of the new films, see Jiang Tian, '*Rang gongnongbing xingxiang laogude zhanling gushipian zhendi*' (Let worker-peasant-soldier images firmly occupy the feature-film battleground), *Hongqi*, 1974, 3 (March), 72–76.
101. The weaknesses of the new feature films helps account for the rise of a new cohort of filmmakers who burst into Chinese filmmaking in the mid-1980s as the 'fifth generation'. A reaction against the interminable preaching of these mid-1970s features shaped the film aesthetic of a generation. This somewhat reverse outcome was perhaps the major achievement of the films of the late Cultural Revolution: see Clark, *Reinventing China*.
102. Statistics are based on a count from yearly lists in *Zhongguo yishu yingpian bianmu*, which gives eleven titles for Beiying. The number 12 is from Zhou Xiaobang, p. 219. In the 1949–1965 period annual production had sometimes sunk to these levels, see the table in Clark, *Chinese Cinema*, p. 185.
103. See the credit listing and synopsis in *Zhongguo yishu yingpian bianmu*, pp. 864 and 976. The actor Li Rentang had been a member of this Chengde troupe before becoming a film actor.
104. Su Yun interview, p. 91.
105. The actor was Fang Hua, who played Song Jing. The production details for the two films are in *Zhongguo yishu yingpian bianmu*, pp. 162–163 and 989.

106. Zhu Jing, '*Buxi de geming huoju: Changying jianguo yilai geming lishipian manping*' (The unceasing real-life story of revolution: comments on revolutionary history films made at Changchun since 1949), *Dangdai dianying*, 1992, 2 (April), 33–34.

107. The two films are listed in *Zhongguo yishu yingpian bianmu*, pp. 138–139 and 994–995.

108. The two films are listed in *Zhongguo yishu yingpian bianmu*, pp. 94–96 and 992–993. The information and assessment is from Zhou Xiaobang, pp. 228–229. Zhang Ruifang, pp. 386–387. The other two pre–Cultural Revolution warfare films that had been shown in the late 1960s (*Mine Warfare* (*Dilei zhan*, 1962) and *Tunnel Warfare* (*Didao zhan*, 1965)) were not re-made in the mid-1970s. Presumably the pace of new productions made such rehashing of the old films unnecessary.

109. See *Zhongguo yishu yingpian bianmu*, pp. 895–896 and 1076–1077. Zhang Ruifang, p. 387. Shi Fangyu went on to head the Film Bureau of the Ministry of Culture in the early 1980s.

110. Pearl River Film Studio Script Department, '*Jinian lai juben chuangzuo he zugao qingkuang, yiji cunzai wenti*' (Conditions of the writing and commissioning of scripts in recent years, and existing issues), September 1974, 15 pp., in China Film Archive Library, Studio Files 00189. The wooden language of the new films provided a challenge: Xu Feng, '*Yuyan, yishi xingtai yu guanying jizhi: Wen-ge houqi dianying yuyan chutan*' (Language, ideology and film watching: preliminary exploration of the language of late Cultural Revolution films), *Xiju*, 2000, 2 (June), 135–142.

111. Zhou Xiaobang, pp. 219–220. The film is listed in *Zhongguo yishu yingpian bianmu*, p. 990.

112. Su Yun interview, p. 89. Hu Chang gives a 3 January 1973 completion date: p. 430.

113. The film is listed in *Zhongguo yishu yingpian bianmu*, pp. 975–976. Hao Ran's career and works are discussed in McDougall and Louie, pp. 257–260, 376–379, and in Chapter Five.

114. Reported in Hu Chang, p. 325.

115. Su Yun interview, p. 90. For a 1974 account by the filmmakers of how they applied the model-opera principals to enhance the heroism of the novel, see Xinhua xinwenshe, '*Zai geming yangbanxi de guanghui zhaoyao xia: geming wenyi gongzuoshe changtan xuexi geming yangbanxi de tihui*', in *Jingju geming shinian*, pp. 41–47. This book was published in provincial editions all over China in 1974.

116. Listed in *Zhongguo yishu yingpian bianmu*, pp. 1009–1010.

117. A film with this title had been half completed on the eve of the Cultural Revolution: Su Yun interview, p. 90. The film is listed in *Zhongguo yishu yingpian bianmu*, p. 977. The film was completed on 5 January 1973: Hu Chang, p. 430. The story became a new-style Peking opera in the mid-1970s.

118. The film was based on a short story by Xu Yingtong: *Zhongguo yishu yingpian bianmu*, p. 986.

119. The film was based on the novel *County Party Committee Secretary* (*Xianwei shuji*) by Yang Fengyue: *Zhongguo yishu yingpian bianmu*, pp. 1042–1043.

Chapter Five discusses several films associated with Communist Party factional conflict in these years.

120. The film was made at the Changchun studio from a collectively created script based on the story *Overture* (*Xuqu*) by Gu Yu: *Zhongguo yishu yingpian bianmu*, pp. 1043–1044. Filming was completed on 15 September 1976, shortly after Mao had died and three weeks before the arrest of his widow and some of her supporters: Hu Chang, p. 432.

121. Yu Yang interview, *Dianying yishu*, 1993, 4 (August), 84. Yu points out that Zhao Sihai, like the heroes of the model operas, lacks a family. His elderly mother is seen, but there is no wife or other family members: p. 82.

122. Chris Berry, 'Stereotypes and ambiguities: An examination of the feature films of the Chinese Cultural Revolution', *Journal of Asian Culture* (UCLA), Volume VI (1982), pp. 46–47.

123. Wang Tugen, '"*Wuchanjieji wenhua dageming*" *shi, xushi, yishi xingtai huayu*' (Discourse on the Great Proletarian Cultural Revolution history, narrative and ideology), *Dangdai dianying*, 1990, 3 (June), 34–45, especially pp. 38–41.

124. A 1997 history of the Beijing studio devotes several pages to explaining away the ideological and artistic shortcomings of *Breaking with Old Ideas*, which was criticized after October 1976 for being a 'Gang of Four' vehicle: Zhou Xiaobang, pp. 222–228. See also Di Di, '"*Juelie*" *jishi yu fenxi*' (Record and analysis of *Breaking with Old Ideas*), *Dianying yishu*, 1993, 2 (April), 76–84. Di and filmmakers interviewed by him make clear that the original September 1974 script was strictly about the educational revolution. The emphasis on 'capitalist roaders' in the party was a later addition, in some cases in post-production in dubbing dialogue: pp. 77–78. Mei Jiangping, '"*Juelie*" *gongying de yulun shuping*' (Public opinion and criticism of *Breaking with Old Ideas*), *Dianying yishu*, 1993, 2 (April), 85–88, 61, outlines the public response to the film on its release at New Years 1976.

125. See, for example, the critical collection of materials on '*zhongjian renwu*' in *Wenyi bao*, 1964, 8–9 (September), 15–20.

126. In order to avoid association with the discredited old term, in the Cultural Revolution these kinds of roles were identified with a new label, 'change characters' (*zhuanbian renwu*): see, for example, Feng Min, p. 403; *Dianying yishu*, 1994, 3 (June), 68.

127. Li Jun, translated in *Chinese Literature*, 1975, 2 (February), 94. According to a 1994 interview with director Li Jun, the film was shot between September 1973 and mid-1974. Such was the search for (political) perfection that crew even went a third time on location after the release of the film, mindful of thirty-four small points that Jiang Qing suggested changing. But, as the film had already be widely shown, including on television, film from that shooting was never incorporated into a revised version: *Dianying yishu*, 1994, 6 (November), 87, 88.

128. This analysis of audience response is based on my observations as a student in Beijing in the year the film was released. The makers presented their experience in Bayi dianying zhipianchang 'Shanshan de hongxing' chuangzuozu, sheyingzu, '*Zai yinmu shang wei wuchanjieji zhengguang: yingpian "Shanshan de hongxing" de yixie chuangzuo tihui*' (Win honor for the proletariat

on the screen: some creative understandings from the film *Sparkling Red Star*), *Hongqi*, 1974, 12 (June), 43–51.

129. Yu Yang interview, *Dianying yishu*, 1993, 4 (August), 82 and 84. Yu had made a lot of Chinese hearts beat faster in his role as a competitive swimmer, who spends much of the film clad in just a swim suit, in 1959's *Youth in Water* (*Shui shang chunqiu*).

130. *Zhongguo yishu yingpian bianmu*, pp. 1055–1056.

131. *Zhongguo yishu yingpian bianmu*, pp. 1054–1055. The script, started in 1965 and taken up again in the spring of 1972, went through twenty-six drafts before the film was completed in September 1976: Zhou Xiaobang, pp. 229–231.

132. See Clark, 'Ethnic minorities in Chinese films'.

133. *Zhongguo yishu yingpian bianmu*, pp. 1011–1012.

134. The three directors of the film included Shen Fu, who had made the much-criticized *Jiangnan in the North* in 1963: *Zhongguo yishu yingpian bianmu*, pp. 1077–1078.

135. Mao Tse-tung, *Selected Works, Volume III*, Beijing: Foreign Languages Press, 1965, p. 82. Compare with the slightly less emphatic original text in Bonnie S. McDougall, trans. and ed., *Mao Zedong's 'Talks at the Yan'an Conference on Literature and Art:' A translation of the 1943 text with commentary*, Ann Arbor: Center for Chinese Studies, University of Michigan, 1980, p. 70.

136. Wang Lian, pp. 77–78. Wang suggests Xie was attracted to the story because of his disabled son. Details are in *Zhongguo yishu yingpian bianmu*, pp. 1138–1139. The films stars Chen Chong (the later Joan Chen) in her first major screen role.

137. Yang Haizhou, pp. 244, 243. This 888-page chronology devotes 152 pages to the ten years of the Cultural Revolution, listing developments in the film materials industry in a matter-of-fact way, though noting major political documents and dates.

138. Yang Haizhou, pp. 245, 246–247.

139. Yang Haizhou, pp. 247–248.

140. Yang Haizhou, pp. 248–249, 253, 267.

141. Interviews with Zhang Jianya, Shanghai, 16 May 1986, 20 March 1987, and 2 July 1988. Jiang failed selection for the film-studio acting troupe, but found minor parts in two Shanghai productions through his father's connections: interview with Jiang Haiying, Shanghai, 15 May 1986. See Clark, *Reinventing China*, pp. 42–43.

142. Zhou Xiaobang, p. 219.

143. Yu Deshui, 141–142. Among the participants was Zhang Zeming, director of *Swansong* (*Juexiang*), who provided this information on how the classes were run: see Clark, *Reinventing China*, pp. 198–199.

144. *Zhuying chang juben chuangzuo zuotanhui jianbao* (Brief report on the script production conference at Pearl River Film Studio), No. 9 (20 April 1974), p. 2 (China Film Archive Library, Studio Files 00189). See also No. 1 (1 March 1974), p. 3, for a reference to 'the Central senior officer' at the opening of the conference. On the Lin Biao and Confucius campaign, see MacFarquhar and Schoenhals, pp. 366–373.

145. Report by Lu Yihao to the Studio Core Group, 30 August 1974, China Film Archives Library, Studio Files 00178.

146. Pearl River Film Studio Script Department, '*Guanyu bianjishi jinhou bianji gongzuo de yijian*' (Views on present and future editorial work by the editorial section), July 1975, 6 pp., in China Film Archive Library, Studio Files 00189.

147. Wang Junzheng, '*Wo de dianyingyuan*' (My cinema), *Dangdai dianying*, 1995, 5 (October), 72–75. On *Counterattack*, see Chapter Five. On the fourth generation, see Clark, *Reinventing China*, pp. 187–192.

148. This information comes from an interview with Zheng Guo'en, cinematography professor at the Beijing Film Academy, 9 June 1988, and in interviews at the Beijing Film Academy (then still in rural Zhuxinzhuang) and at the Film Research Institute of the Literature and Art Research Academy in Beijing, October 1980.

149. *Sirenbang shi dianying shiye de sidi*, p. 179.

150. These details are from Tian Jingqing, pp. 157–158. See also Yu Li, pp. 110–111.

151. *Renmin ribao*, 1 April 1967, pp. 1–3. See a second article in *Renmin ribao*, 6 April 1967, p. 4.

152. Zhai Jiannong, *Dangdai dianying*, 1995, 2 (April), 39.

153. *Dianying nianjian 1981*, pp. 713–714; Feng Min, pp. 394–395.

154. Hu Xingliang and Zhang Ruilin, *Zhongguo dianying shi* (History of Chinese film), Beijing: Zhongyang guangbo dianshi daxue chubanshe, 1995, p. 287. *Lao san zhan* was a play on the standard reference to three widely studied articles by Mao (1939, 1944, and 1945) as *lao san bian* (old three articles).

155. Zhang Ruifang, pp. 386–387.

156. Tian Jingqing, p. 181.

157. Tian Jingqing, pp. 184–185.

158. *Sanshiwu nian*, p. 340.

159. These figures and other details are from Tian Jingqing, p. 184. Sent-down youth interest in Albanian films is recalled by Liu Jialing, pp. 192–204. The only other Communist Party to support the Chinese party in its ideological split with Moscow was that of New Zealand. The secretary-general of the latter party, leader of a few dozen members and virtually unknown at home, was granted front-page audiences with Mao Zedong: see, for example, *Renmin ribao*, 13 March 1967, p. 1.

160. Liu Xinsheng, *Ershi shiji Zhongguo dianying yishu liubian* (Developments in twentieth-century Chinese film art), Beijing: Xinhua chunbanshe, 1999, p. 192.

161. Hu Chang, pp. 336–337. See also *Sanshiwu nian*, p. 325. In May 1976 Zhang Chunqiao approved a plan to import 505 foreign and Hong Kong films for apparently private viewing as reference material, a case cited to illustrate 'Gang of Four' hypocrisy: *Sirenbang shi dianying shiye de sidi*, p. 195. Foreign 'reference films' (*ziliao pian*) are mentioned in *Dianying yishu*, 1994, 3 (June), 69, in Wang Lian, p. 76, and by Zhang Ruifang, who dubbed a role in one, p. 388.

162. On these Cultural Revolution spoken dramas, including Red Guard plays, see Chapter Four. The Lenin films' impact on sent-down youth is recalled in Liu Jialing, pp. 178–191. There was even an uncompleted effort to make a modern-opera version of *Lenin in October*: Xu Chongdong, '*Guanyu xiandaixi "Liening zai shiyue"*' (On the modern opera *Lenin in October*), *Zhongguo Jingju*, 2001, 4 (August), 60.

163. Tian Jingqing, pp. 185–186.

164. These pessimistic reports are from the anti-Gang collection: *Sirenbang shi dianying shiye de sidi*, pp. 173–175.

165. Zhong Ying, '*Jinyibu fazhan nongmin dianying fangying wang*' (Further develop the film projection network in the countryside), *Hongqi*, 1975, 6 (June), 50–53. See also *Guangming ribao*, 23 July 1971, p. 2; *Renmin ribao*, 24 October 1973, p. 4; *Renmin ribao*, 30 June 1974, p. 3, and *Guangming ribao*, 13 May 1976, p. 2. Audiences numbers for *Tiger Mountain* in Clark, *Chinese Cinema*, p. 145, are in error by a factor of ten.

166. Tian Jingqing, p. 190.

167. On Ningxia, Li Qingyue, p. 93; on Fujian, *Guangming ribao*, 31 January 1974, p. 2; nationwide, Yu Li, p. 116.

168. *Sanshiwu nian*, p. 340. *Renmin ribao* on 1 October 1976 proudly announced forty-seven new films, ten of which were colour features (p. 5).

169. Quoted in *Dianying yishu*, 1994, 4 (August), 83.

FOUR: ELABORATING CULTURE: DANCE, MUSIC, STAGE, AND FINE ARTS

1. Liang Lun, '*Yao suqing "Sirenbang" zai wudao meixue shang de liudu*' (We should cleanse the baneful influence of the Gang of Four on dance aesthetics), *Wudao* (Dance), 1979, 1 (January), 13. For biographical background on Liang Lun, see Wang Kefen and Long Yinpei, *Zhongguo jin xiandai dangdai wudao fazhan shi* (History of modern and contemporary development of Chinese dance), Beijing: Renmin yinyue chubanshe, 1999, pp. 164–166. This is the most comprehensive history of dance in modern China.

2. Wang Kefen and Long Yinpei present a somewhat misleading picture of the genre, in line with similar sweeping statements about culture during the Cultural Revolution applied to other arts (pp. 314–315):

> On the dance stage, there were only the ballets *The Red Detachment of Women* and *The White-Haired Girl*, treated as 'model performances' and widely circulated and popularized. National and folk dance (*minzu minjian wudao*) and dances from everyday life without exception (*yigai*) were treated as 'feudal, bourgeois or revisionist' poisonous weeds requiring rooting out.

Typical also for such broad-brushed accounts of Cultural Revolution arts, the chapter at the start of which the above quotation appears goes on to present accounts of a fuller range of dance in these years than suggested by these words.

3. This historical account is based on Meng Changyong, '*Huashuo "Dongfang hong"*' (All about *The East Is Red*), *Cikan* (*Words*), 1987, 6 (November),

39–40. Wang Kefen and Long Yinpei, pp. 275–278, gives a listing of the songs and dances and an account of the musical.

4. Jin Ming, 'Cong "Dongfang hong" da gewu tan qi' (Talking from the dances of *The East Is Red*), *Wudao*, 1997, 1 (January), 54–55. Jin Ming acknowledges a debt to minority dances and an urge to further progress such dance adaptation.

5. Dai Ailian, a Caribbean-born Chinese, was most associated with the promulgating of ballet in China. In September 1950 she produced China's first full-length ballet, *Dove of Peace (Heping ge)*, at the start of the Korean War. It reportedly struck many viewers as a distinctly foreign form. One response was a statement: 'Legs all over the place; workers, peasants, soldiers can't stand the pace' (*Datui manchang pao, gongnongbing shoubuliao*). The *Dove of Peace* fell to earth after just a few performances. See Li Jieming, '*Zhongguo balei bainian ji*'(Commemorating one hundred years of Chinese ballet), *Dongfang yishu* (Eastern art), 1996, 3 (March), 11–15 reprinted in *Yinyue, wudao yanjiu* (Music and dance research: Renmin daxue reprints), 1996, 4 (April), 88–89.

6. This account of the making of the ballet is largely based on Jiang Zuhui, '*Xinwei de huiyi: wuju 'Hongse niangzijun' de chuangzuo licheng*' (A bitter memory: the creative process of *The Red Detachment of Women*), *Wudao*, 1987, 11 (November), 22–23. For an early account, see Li Chengxiang, '*Pojiuchuangxin, wei fazhan geming de balei wuju er fendou*' (Destroy the old, create the new: struggle to develop revolutionary ballet dance-dramas), *Wudao*, 1965, 2 (April), 16–20. Mao and other leaders watched the ballet in Spring 1965. See also Zhongguo wujutuan, '*Mao Zedong sixiang zhaoyaozhe wuju geming de shengli qiancheng: paiyan geming xiandai wuju 'Hongse niangzijun de yixie tihui*' (Mao Zedong Thought is illuminating the prospects for victory in the dance-drama revolution: some understandings from rehearsing the revolutionary modern dance-drama *The Red Detachment of Women*), *Hongqi*, 1970, 7 (July), 66–77, reproduced in *Hongqi*, 1972, 2 (February), 32–43.

7. Qinghua ('outstanding and beautiful') was named Qionghua (a flower said to convey immortality) in the original film. The film's guarded suggestion of romantic feelings between the young woman and her Party instructor is obliterated in the ballet version, though ballet audiences familiar with the 1961 film version could still imagine things. For a critical assessment of the politics of the music of the ballet, see Hong Yun, '*Wuju "Hongse niangzijun" wudao yinyue yanjiu*' (Research on the dance music of the dance-drama *Red Detachment of Women*), *Zhongguo yinyuexue* (Musicology of China), 2004, 3 (September), 78–85.

8. Jiang Zuhui, p. 23.

9. A standard history, Wu Xiaobang, gen. ed., *Dangdai Zhongguo wudao* (Contemporary Chinese dance), Beijing: Dangdai Zhongguo chubanshe, 1993, p. 248, claims the first performance was on 1 June 1964. The September date is from Jiang Zuhui, pp. 22 and 23.

10. One dance source claims that the new ballet was filmed in 1965, though it is not listed in the standard filmography of feature films made between 1949 and 1979. It may be a television recording, though the source uses the term

film: Wu Xiaobang, p. 248. In 1966 Jiang Zuhui was invited to direct the new ballet in Albania. It also played in Romania and Yugoslavia. The choice of Eastern European countries was an obvious snub to classical Russian ballet.

11. The Changchun studio history omits mention of the foreign crew members: Hu Chang, pp. 92–97. See also Onozawa Wataru, 'Wo zai Huabei dianying-dui de rizi' (My days in the North China Film Group), Dianying chuangzuo, 1996, 5 (October), 68–73.

12. This account of the birth of the ballet is based on Qian Zhenhua, 'Huiyi balei wuju "Baimaonü" de dansheng' (Recalling the birth of the ballet The White-Haired Girl), Shanghai wenhua shizhi tongxun, 15 (August 1991), 41–43. See also Shanghaishi wudao xuexiao, 'Balei wuju "Baimaonü" de chuangzuo, yanchu' (The creation and performance of the ballet dance-drama The White-Haired Girl), Shanghai wenhua shizhi tongxun, 40 (March 1996), 30–34, and Yu Luyuan, 'Biao shehuizhuyi zhi xin, li wuchanjieji zhi yi: daxing geming balei wuju "Baimaonü" de dansheng' (Express socialist newness, stand up for the proletariat: the birth of the full-length ballet dance-drama The White-Haired Girl), Wudao, 1966, 3 (June), 37–42 (reprinted from Renmin ribao). This was the last issue of Wudao for ten years.

13. Wenxue yishu yanjiuyuan yinyue wudao bu wudaozu, 'Jiang Qing shi pohuai wuju "Baimaonü" de zuiku huoshou: geming xiandai wuju "Baimaonü" diaocha baogao' (Jiang Qing is the cruellest hand behind the attacks on the dance-drama The White-Haired Girl: a report on an investigation of the revolutionary modern dance-drama The White-Haired Girl), Wudao, 1977, 2 (March), 7. This 1977 source (pp. 7–10 and 21) is one of the few that acknowledges the Japanese example. By the 1990s most accounts had erased this Japanese connection. The Matsuyama company had presented a solo based on Xi'er, the heroine of the musical The White-Haired Girl in 1958 in China: Chinese Literature, 1965, 1 (January), 113.

14. Shanghaishi wudao xuexiao, pp. 30–31.

15. Shanghaishi wudao xuexiao, pp. 30–31. The musical score proved so successful it took on a life of its own, being played on radio and performed live, with choruses, in the decades since its creation.

16. An earlier, shorter version had been presented at the same Shanghai festival a year earlier. See Wudao, 1965, 3 (June), 32. For a review, see Ding Xuelei, 'Baleiwu geming de xinhua: ping balei wuju "Baimaonü"' (A new flower in the ballet revolution: critique of the ballet dance-drama The White-Haired Girl), Wudao, 1965, 4 (August), 15–16.

17. Shanghaishi wudao xuexiao, p. 32. These had been standard themes in dance creation in the first half of the 1960s: Li Wei and Ren Fang, Zhongguo xiandai, dangdai wudao fazhan gailun (Outline of the development of modern and contemporary Chinese dance), Chengdu: Sichuan daxue chubanshe, 2006, pp. 61–66.

18. Qian Zhenhua, for example, makes this point: p. 42.

19. Shanghaishi wudao xuexiao, p. 33; Qian Zhenhua, p. 42.

20. Shanghaishi wudao xuexiao, p. 32.

21. An immediate post–Cultural Revolution account asserts that Jiang Qing was instead occupied 'watching obscene films and engaged in ballroom dancing': Wenxue yishu yanjiuyuan, p. 8.

22. Wenxue yishu yanjiuyuan, pp. 8–9. Also reported, more briefly, in Shanghaishi wudao xuexiao, p. 34.

23. Shanghaishi wudao xuexiao, p. 34; Wenxue yishu yanjiuyuan, p. 10. Soon after the fall of the Gang of Four, accusations flew that Jiang Qing allies had retrospectively invented a history of her consistent support for the ballet from its beginnings as a short work. Instead suggestions were made in 1977 that she had consistently expressed skepticism about the work.

24. 'Baleiwu geming de zhilu mingdeng' (The beacon guide to the revolution in ballet), Renmin ribao, 24 May 1967, p. 6.

25. Zhongguo wujutuan, p. 77. An anti-Gang of Four denunciation contends that the ballet achieved artistic success despite Jiang Qing's interference: Zhongguo wujutuan dou pipanzu, 'Bao xia "qishou" de huapi: cong wuju "Hongse niangzijun" de chuangzuo kan Jiang Qing de zhen mianmu"' (Peel back the flagman's mask: Jiang Qing's true face revealed in the creation of the dance-drama The Red Detachment of Women), Wudao, 1976, 5 (November), 14–16.

26. See Li Xifan, 'Zai liang tiao luxian jianrui douzheng zhong dansheng de yishu mingzhu: cong balei wuju "Baimaonü" de zai chuangzuo kan Zhou Yang wenyi heixian ji qi zong houtai de "xie zhenshi" miulun de pochan' (A pearl born from the sharp conflict between the two lines: evidence from the creation of The White-Haired Girl of the bankruptcy of the 'write about real life' fallacy of Zhou Yang and those backstage), Guangming ribao, 19 May 1967, pp. 5–6. For a similar, full-page comparison between the Yan'an opera and the ballet from the same time, see Gong Dun, 'Mao zhuxi geming wenyi luxian de weida shengli: tan balei wuju "Baimaonü" de gaibian' (A great victory of Chairman Mao's revolutionary line on literature and art: a discussion of the adaptation of the ballet dance-drama The White-Haired Girl), Renmin ribao, 11 June 1967, p. 6. Gong Dun was a pseudonym used by Yao Wenyuan and his writing group.

27. In addition, several key members of the creative team that had produced The White-Haired Girl in the 1960s had been labelled as 'capitalist roaders' or 'anti-model performance'. They were only rehabilitated after the fall of the Gang of Four. Even as late as April 1976, in the midst of the mass criticism of Vice-Premier Deng Xiaoping prompted by the 5 April Qingming festival demonstrations in Tian'anmen Square, Jiang Qing is reported to have asked that The White-Haired Girl be brought to Beijing to be inspected again in the light of recent political developments in case it might be seen secretly to express support for the 'rightist deviationist wind to reverse the correct verdicts' that the demonstrations supposedly represented: Shanghaishi wudao xuexiao, p. 34; Wenxue yishu yanjiuyuan, pp. 10, 21.

28. See the article on alleged resistance to this broadcast in the Red Guard broadsheet Tianjin xin wenyi (New Tianjin literature and art), July 1968, p. 4, reprinted in Xinbian Hongweibing ziliao, p. 6252.

29. Qian Zhenhua writes of two filmings in 1970: the first for television, the second as filming in colour: p. 42. This may be wrong, as the first colour-film version, according to the standard listing of films from 1949–1979, came in 1972: see below.

30. *Zhongguo yishu yingpian bianmu 1949–1979*, p. 968. The 1970 version is listed on p. 954.

31. Qian Zhenhua offers some details, including the revival of a 1965 version of the ballet after December 1976, to put some distance between it and the Gang of Four: p. 42.

32. Shanghaishi wudao xuexiao, p. 33.

33. Li Xifan (p. 5) echoes Mao's Yan'an *Talks* with this phrase.

34. This paragraph is based on observations made while visiting China in the summer of 1973 and while living as a student in Beijing and travelling widely between late 1974 and mid-1976.

35. See Zhang Fengshou, ed., *Zhongguo dianshi wenyixue* (Chinese television art), Beijing: Beijing guangbo xueyuan chubanshe, 1999, pp. 24–25.

36. These are listed in Zhai Zixia ed., *Zhongguo wuju* (Chinese dance-drama), Beijing: Zhongguo Shijieyu chubanshe, 1996, pp. 478–483.

37. Unusually, the dance is named after the late soldier. One of the three chore-ographers listed is Zhai Zixia, chief editor of the 1996 volume above: p. 478.

38. Zhai Zixia, pp. 478 and 479.

39. A chronology in the official history of contemporary dance in China notes its establishment in 1972 without providing any other information: Wu Xiaobang, p. 476. The same source dates the ballet in 1973, rather than 1974: p. 253. Wang Kefen and Long Yinpei provide the original name of the company, but do not give a date for its establishment: p. 319.

40. See the half-page of stills in, for example, *Hebei ribao* (Hebei Daily), 24 May 1975, p. 4.

41. Wang Kefen and Long Yinpei, pp. 319–321. Wu Xiaobang also dates this ballet's first performance in 1973, p. 478. A Peking-opera version of *Hongsao* was presented by a combined Zibo and Qingdao cities opera troupe from Shandong at the 1964 modern-subject opera convention in Beijing: Wen-huabu Beijing bianzhe kan, *Jingju xiandaixi guanmo yanchu dahui jiemudan (hedingben)*. For a dance version of *Hongsao*, see *Wudao*, 1965, 5 (May), pp. 28–29.

42. *Zhongguo yishu yingpian bianmu, 1949–1979*, pp. 1028–1029. These two ballets are also discussed in Wang Kefen, Long Yinpei, and Zhang Shiling, *20 shiji Zhongguo wudao* (Twentieth-century Chinese dance), Qingdao: Qing-dao chubanshe, 1992, pp. 195–199.

43. Wang Kefen and Long Yinpei, pp. 323–324.

44. Quite how new the work was is unclear, as the pre–Cultural Revolution national minorities art festival in Beijing in late 1964 had included a similarly titled *Happily Giving Spare-Time Grain* (*Xi song gongyu liang*), listed as a dance from the Yi people who inhabited a broad band of southwestern China. The 1964 dance is listed in Wang Kefen and Long Yinpei, p. 285. The title seems to refer to food (not strictly speaking grain) raised by the characters in their spare time.

45. Wang Kefen and Long Yinpei, pp. 324–325. See also Wang Kefen, Long Yinpei, and Zhang Shiling, pp. 199–201. A similar dance from 1973, *The Good 'Menba' on the Snowy Peaks* (*Xueshan shang de hao 'Menba'* (Menba are traditional healers in Tibetan society), was set in Tibet: see Wang Kefen and Long Yinpei, pp. 325–326. See also Zhai Zixia, p. 479, which renders

the title *Xueshan 'menba'*, and Wang Kefen, Long Yinpei, and Zhang Shiling, pp. 201–202.

46. This claim and the details on the dance are from Wang Kefen and Long Yinpei, pp. 326–328. For a stage photo, see *Wudao*, 1976, 3 (July), inside front-cover.

47. For a typical account of a provincial music and dance festival, featuring young creators and performers, see *Anhui wenyi* (Anhui literature and art), June 1973, pp. 76–78. The dance activities of the Daxing county amateur art propaganda team outside Beijing are presented by Xin Wentong, '*Laizi qunzhong douzheng de yishu: tan Daxingxian yeyu wenyi xuanchuandui de wudao chuangzuo*' (Art from the masses' struggles: discussion of the dance creation of the Daxing county literature and art propaganda team), *Hongqi*, 1974, 6 (June), 80–84. Efforts to incorporate everyday movements and tools into dances are outlined.

48. Wang Kefen and Long Yinpei, p. 328. *Journey with a Storm Lantern* (*Zou madeng*) was a masked children's dance first presented in 1958 but revived in 1974: Liang Lun, p. 12.

49. Information on the 1976 festival is from '*Quanguo wudao (duwu, shuangren wu, sanren wu) diaoyan shengli jieshu*' (Report on the victory of the nation-wide solo, duet and trio dance exhibition), *Wudao*, 1976, 1 (March), 44–45 and from Wang Kefen and Long Yinpei, pp. 328–333.

50. The 1999 source (Wang and Long) that provides these statistics implies that the rest of the performances (about one-third) could be considered apolitical: presumably celebrations of ethnic-minority dance culture and of youthful vigor in general.

51. *Wudao*, 1976, 1 (March), 44–45. *Wudao*, like other such magazines, had ceased publication in spring 1966. *Wudao*, 1976, 2 (May), 3 (July) and 4 (September) all feature photos of dances from this festival of small-scale dances, in centre photo spreads or on inside front and back-covers.

52. Yu Ping, *Zhongguo xiandangdai wudao fazhan shi* (History of modern and contemporary dance development in China), Beijing: Renmin yinyue chuban-she, 2004, pp. 101–102. One prize-winner at the 1976 festival was the trio *Golden Seeds* (*Jinse zhongzi*), for which the full choreography of the dance was published in book form in 1977 by the People's Music Press, after the fall of the Gang of Four: Zhai Zixia, p. 480. The dance was the work of the Jilin City Song and Dance Company.

53. Mao Hui, pp. 5–8.

54. Zhai Zixia, p. 481.

55. Zhai Zixia, p. 481. Summaries of the dances suggest simplification of the opera plots to allow for dance mime in the place of opera lyrics.

56. Liu Enbo, pp. 10–13.

57. Qinghua daxue yeyu wenyidui, '*Fan'an buderenxin*', *Wudao*, 1976, 3 (July), 28–29. Liu Enbo (page 13) suggests this was prominent coverage given to a Gang of Four work, but the article covers the top two-thirds of a double-page spread only, in a section entitled 'Introducing New Works'. The half-page is followed, however, by an article by the same amateur group on pp. 30–32. Qinghua University since the late 1970s has preferred to style itself Tsinghua University in English, after the fashion of Peking University.

58. For a listing of the so-called 'second group' of 'model performances', see, for example, Wang Xinmin, p. 220. For a review of the piano work, see Ding Xuelei, *'Renmin zhanzheng de zhuangli songge: ping gangqin xiezouqu "Huanghe"'* (A magnificent ode to people's war: critique of the piano concerto *The Yellow River*), *Hongqi*, 1970, 5 (May), 63–70.

59. One extreme example of assessments of the Cultural Revolution's musical significance is a two-part article on forty years of Chinese musical aesthetics, after 1949, which jumps from 1963 to 1979, with just a few lines on the Cultural Revolution: Wang Ningyi, *'Mengsheng, shiluo, fusu, fazhan: xin Zhongguo yinyue meixue sishi nian (1949–1989)'* (Conception, loss, recovery and development: forty years of new China's musical aesthetics) in two parts, *Yuefu xinsheng* (Journal of the Shenyang Conservatory), 1993, 1 (March), 24–26, 32 and 2 (June), 13–17.

60. Details from Wang Yuhe, chief editor, *Zhongguo xiandai yinyue shigang 1949–1986* (Survey of Chinese modern music), Beijing: Huawen chubanshe, 1991, p. 18.

61. Wang Yuhe, pp. 59–60.

62. The instruments used in Chinese music making were re-assessed, and a new bobbin device for stringed instruments invented that made playing easier by keeping strings tauter for longer: Wang Yuhe, p. 69.

63. For Red Guard accounts of the making of this work, see *Hongse pipanzhe* (Red critic), 24 May 1967, p. 2 (reprinted in *Xinbian Hongweibing ziliao*, p. 2501) and *Tianjin xin wenyi*, February 1968, p. 4 (reprinted in *Xinbian Hongweibing ziliao*, p. 6042).

64. Wang Yuhe, pp. 130, 184. In 1959 Luo produced a symphonic poem (*jiaoxiang shi*) titled 'Mu Guiying assumes command' (*Mu Guiying guashuai*), based on the Henan opera of the same name that had been rewritten in 1954. On the Henan opera, see *Zhongguo da baike quanshu: xiqu, quyi* (China encyclopaedia: opera and *quyi*), Beijing, Zhongguo da baike quanshu chubanshe, 1983, p. 261. The opera was 'transplanted' into Peking-opera form in 1959, when the legendary actor Mei Lanfang performed the title role.

65. Shanghai yinyuetuan, *'Wei chuangzao wuchanjieji de jiaoxiang yinyue nuli zuozhan: chuangzuo yanchu geming jiaoxiang yinyue 'Zhiqu Weihushan' de yixie tihui'* (Fight hard to create proletarian symphonic music: some understanding of the creation and performance of the symphonic *Taking Tiger Mountain by Strategy*), *Renmin yinyue* (People's music), 1976, 2 (May), 14–19. For an earlier, Red Guard account, see *Beijing gongshe* (Beijing commune), 18 May 1967, p. 3 (reprinted in *Xinbian Hongweibing ziliao*, p. 359).

66. Shanghai yuetuan pipan zu, *'Yi pian wei "Sirenbang" zaofan geming yulun de duwen: ping "Wei chuangzao wuchanjieji de jiaoxiang yinyue nuli zuozhan"'* (A poisonous article supporting the Gang of Four's rebel revolutionary rumours: a criticism of 'Fight hard to create proletarian symphonic music') *Renmin yinyue*, 1978, 4 (April), 33–37.

67. Wang Yuhe, pp. 132–133. The most famous composer who turned his hand to this august task was Zheng Lücheng, writer of the 'Song of the Eighth Route Army' and the 'Eighth Route Army March'. In the Cultural Revolution Zheng put five of Mao's poems to music and combined them with songs

about the Long March which he had written to produce *On the Long March* (*Changzheng lu shang*), a mixed-voice cantata. Zheng's *On the Long March* was never publicly performed during the Cultural Revolution.

68. As a student in the History Department of Peking University at the time, I learned to sing the songs with my Chinese worker-peasant-soldier classmates, who were also our roommates.

69. Wang Yuhe, pp. 216–217. A comprehensive 1988 collection of plot summaries of musicals includes none from the Cultural Revolution: Li Gang, ed., *Zhongguo geju gushi ji* (Collected Chinese musical drama stories), Beijing: Renmin yishu chubanshe, 1988. In 1975 Jiang Qing reportedly ordered Shanghai composers and lyricists to start work on a modern musical version of *The White-Haired Girl*, the 'model performance' ballet. The musical version was to be based on the Hebei clapper-opera rendition of the Yan'an 'rice-sprouts song'. In this new version, the central character was to have been Wang Dachun, the heroine's Red Army fiancé. Xi'er, the white-haired young woman and a female friend, would flee into the mountains to conduct armed struggle. But this rumored plan for a version somewhat different from the familiar ballet was never effected before the arrest of the Gang of Four. *Liu Sanjie* was denounced in the pages of *Guangxi ribao* as a 'poisonous weed' in 1970, a rather late date perhaps reflecting local affection for the musical: see Zheng Ming, '"*Liu Sanjie*" *fan yapo, shi geming de: ping minjian gewuju* "*Liu Sanjie*" *de zhengzhi qingxiang*' (*Liu Sanjie* opposes oppression and is revolutionary: a critical discussion of the political tendencies of the folk musical *Liu Sanjie*), *Guangxi ribao* (Guangxi Daily), 27 November 1978, p. 2.

70. In 1979 He Lüting published a withering response to Yao Wenyuan: '*Yao Wenpi yu Debiaoxi*' (Yao Wen-fart and Debussy), *Xueshu yuekan* (Academic monthly), 1979, 1 (January), 47–54. This came after his political rehabilitation at the Shanghai Conservatory in mid-December 1978: *Wenhui bao* (Wenhui Daily), 27 December 1978, p. 3.

71. '*Yinggutou yinyuejia He Lüting*' (A dauntless musician: He Lüting), *Jiefang ribao* (Liberation Daily), 13 January 1979, p. 2.

72. One estimate counted more than 100 articles on the subject in national media, starting in December 1973, after a roundtable discussion on the issue in Shanghai in November and a Beijing meeting called by Yu Huiyong on 7 December. See Ju Qihong, *20 shiji Zhongguo yinyue* (Twentieth-century Chinese music), Qingdao: Qingdao chubanshe, 1992, pp. 103–105.

73. For other articles, see Chao Hua, '*Wubiaoti yinyue meiyou jiejixing ma?*' (Does non-programatic music not have a class character?) and an article by the music department of the Central May Seventh Art University in *Beijing ribao* (Beijing Daily), 6 January 1974, p. 3, and a similar article in *Guangming ribao*, 24 January 1974, p. 3.

74. Wang Yuhe, pp. 246–247. See also Liu Shikun, '"*Sirenbang*" *gao* "*biaoti, wubiaoti yinyue de taolun*" *shi weile shenme?*' (What was the purpose of the Gang of Four's discussion of programatic and non-programatic music?) in *Wenyijie baluan fanzheng de yici shenghui: Zhongguo wenxue yishu jie lianhehui di-sanjie quanguo weiyuanhui di-sanci kuoda huiyi wenjian fayan ji* (A grand meeting to restore order in the literary and art world:

collected documents and speeches from the fourth enlarged plenum of the third national committee of the Chinese association of literary and art circles), Beijing: Renmin wenxue chubanshe, 1979, pp. 511–519. This view is confirmed by Richard Curt Kraus in his excellent *Pianos and Politics in China: Middle-Class Ambitions and the Struggle over Western Music*, New York: Oxford University Press, 1989, pp. 170–173.

75. Planning for the NZNYO tour is documented in Ministry of Foreign Affairs files in Archives New Zealand, Wellington: BEI26/5/2/2 Part 1. The Chinese sponsors were the Chinese People's Association for Friendship with Foreign Countries (*You-Xie*). Audience response is from personal observations at the concerts in Beijing.

76. '*Geming gequ xuan*' (Selected revolutionary songs), *Hongqi*, 1965, 3 (March), 31–49.

77. I remember the highlight for the Chinese audience at a concert at the Central Minorities Institute in Beijing in late 1974 being a Uighur female soloist 'duelling' in song with her male, hand-drum accompanist. There was even a hint of sexual excitement in the delivery of the song, something usually absent from mainstream Chinese performances.

78. For a po-faced analysis of whether such songs could be sung in the 1990s (arguing that they should not be), see Gong Fu, '*Guanyu 'Hong taiyang ge chao' de sikao*' (Thoughts on the 'Red Sun song craze'), *Neibu wengao* (Internal manuscripts), 1992, 11 (June), 12–14. But the continuing power of the well-written songs, Gong Fu acknowledges, was a challenge to present-day song writers.

79. Sun Huanying, '*Ping suowei "yulu ge"*' (Assessing so-called 'quotation songs'), *Wenhui bao*, 8 February 1979, p. 4.

80. Ju Qihong, pp. 89–91. Ju compares the 'rebel songs' with the songs of early humans in ancient times. On Red Guard songs, see Yang Jian, '*Wenhua dageming shiqi de Hongweibing yinyue*' (Red Guard music in the Great Proletarian Cultural Revolution period), *Zhongguo qingnian yanjiu* (China youth research), 1997, 2 (March), 25–28. On later, 'educated youth' songs, see Dai Jiafang, '*Wutuobang li de aige: 'Wen-ge' qijian zhiqing gequ de yanjiu*' (Mournful songs in Utopia: research on 'educated youth' songs in the Cultural Revolution), *Zhongguo yinyuexue*, 2002, 3 (September), 5–25.

81. See section 3 of this chapter.

82. Stephen Jones, *Plucking the Wind: Lives of Village Musicians in Old and New China*, Leiden: CHIME Foundation, 2004, pp. 165–168.

83. See McDougall and Louie, pp. 194–196.

84. Ju Qihong, pp. 84–85.

85. Ju Qihong, pp. 96–97.

86. See the detailed account of Yin's career in Kraus, pp. 128–160.

87. Bian Meng, *Zhongguo gangqin wenhua zhi xingcheng yu fazhan* (The formation and development of piano culture in China), Beijing: Huayue chubanshe, 1996, pp. 67–68.

88. The *Red Lantern* adaptation was a collaboration between Yin Chengzong and the Peking-opera actors Qian Haoliang and Liu Changyu and had been first performed publicly in July 1968: Chu Wanghua, '*"Huanghe" gangqin xiezouqu shi zenmeyang dansheng de?*' (How did the 'Yellow River' piano

concerto come into being?), *Renmin yinyue*, 1995, 5 (May), 5. See also the account by Kraus, pp. 144–146.

89. Bian Meng, p. 69. Details on A Bing and the piece are from *Zhongguo yinyue cidian* (Chinese musical dictionary), Beijing: Renmin yinyue chubanshe, 1985, pp. 1, 97. The piece has also been adapted for a Chinese-instrument orchestra and for a Western-instrument quartet.

90. Bian Meng analyzes the piece in detail: pp. 75–79. On the original *pipa* music, see *Zhongguo yinyue cidian*, p. 418.

91. Bian Meng, p. 69. Bian praises the musical achievements of these compositions: p. 79. During the Cultural Revolution Yin Chengzong ('support the clan') had adopted Chengzhong ('respect the masses') as his given names: Kraus, p. 147.

92. See Chu Wanghua, pp. 4–8 and Kraus, pp. 148–150 for the background to the *Yellow River Concerto*.

93. Details on the film are in *Zhongguo yishu yingpian bianmu*, pp. 970–971. The film is praised for its rhythmic editing of shots in Xin Jing, '*Xin de tansuo, xin de shouhuo*' (New explorations, new results), first published in *Renmin ribao*, 2 March 1973, reprinted in *Huanyuan wutai, gaoyu wutai: geming yangbanxi yingpian pinglunji, di-yi qi* (Even better than the stage: collected critiques of model performance films, part one), Beijing: Renmin wenxue chubanshe, 1976, pp. 70–77. On the concerto, see Bian Meng, p. 68. Li Delun's friendship with Jiang Qing is noted by Kraus, p. 145.

94. *Guangming ribao*, 20 January 1974, p. 1.

95. Ju Qihong, p. 98. See also Ding Xuelei, *Renmin zhanzheng*, 63–70, esp. pp. 64–65.

96. Zhongyang Wu-qi yishu daxue yinyue xueyuan chuangzuo yanjiushi, '*Fangeming wenhua weijiao de pochan: baolu "Siren bang" dui Nie Er, Xian Xinghai de gongji*' (The bankruptcy of the anti-revolutionary encirclement and suppression of culture: exposing the attacks by the Gang of Four on Nie Er and Xian Xinghai), *Renmin yinyue*, 1977, 2 (March), 6–8, on page 7 asserted that Jiang Qing had ordered the writing of the concerto in 1970.

97. The concert also indicated the cultural leadership's increasing weakness in competition with pragmatists grouped around Vice-Premier Deng Xiaoping.

98. Details of the performers' units are from Zu Zhensheng, *Zhongguo yinyue zhihuijia shengya* (Careers of Chinese music conductors), Beijing: Zhishi chubanshe, 1999, p. 272. Also included in the program were Chinese folk musical works by Nie Er and Xian Xinghai, played by a ninety-five-person orchestra made up of members of several Beijing companies.

99. Guang Weiran (words), Xian Xinghai (music), *Huanghe dahechang: jinian Xian Xinghai shishi sanshi zhou nian* (*Yellow River Cantata*: commemorating thirty years since the passing of Xian Xinghai), Beijing: Renmin yinyue chubanshe, 1975, 43 pp. and *Nie Er Xian Xinghai gequ xuan: jinian Nie Er shishi sishi zhou nian, Xian Xinghai shishi sanshi zhou nian* (Selected songs by Nie Er and Xian Xinghai: commemorating forty years since the passing of Nie Er and thirty years since Xian Xinghai's passing), Beijing: Renmin yinyue chubanshe, 1975, 30 pp. A massed choral performance in Spring 1976, pictured in the centrespread of *Wudao*, 1976, 3 (July), features a massive choir in the Capital Gymnasium performing new songs against the 'reversal of verdicts'.

100. Wang Yuhe, '*Zhongguo xiandai hechang yinyue (1946–1976)*' (Modern Chinese choral music), *Yinyue yanjiu* (Music research, Renmin daxue reprints), 1989, 2 (June), 52–54.

101. Shi Yuemeng, '*"Sirenbang" pohuai geming qunzhong gequ zuixing bixu qingsuan*' (We must expose and criticize the crimes of the Gang of Four in damaging revolutionary popular songs), *Renmin yinyue*, 1978, 4 (July), 18–19.

102. Jiang Boyan, '*Shanghai yinyue chuangzuo ziliao zhaiji, er*' (Notes on materials on musical creation in Shanghai, 2), *Shanghai wenhua shizhi tongxun*, 42 (September 1996), 48. Jin Yueling's age is calculated from Kraus, p. 178.

103. Ju Qihong, p. 100.

104. *Yunnan wenyi*, 1973, No. 1 (inaugural issue: August), pp. 12–14. The minority asssociated with the last of these songs is no loner listed among the official fifty-five minorities. Four of the seven songs identified an individual as having 'sorted out' (*zhengli*) the song. Two were collective creations. The reference to *New Songs from the Battlefields* is from Ju Qihong, p. 101.

105. See Wang Yuhe, '*50 nian Zhongguo yinyue huigu zhi san: "Wen-ge" shiqi he "Wen-ge" hou de boluanfanzheng*' (Review of 50 years of Chinese music, part three: Cultural Revolution period music and the bringing of order after the Cultural Revolution), *Zhongguo yinyue*, 2000, No. 3 (June), pp. 1–3.

106. Jiang Boyan, p. 48.

107. Jiang Boyan, pp. 48–49. See the overview in Miao Jianhua and Hong Yun, *Zhongguo yinyue chubu* (Introduction to Chinese music), Guangzhou: Guangdong renmin chubanshe, 2000, pp. 448–454.

108. Kraus, p. 157.

109. Bian Meng, pp. 68–69. *Shang, guan, gai* is explained in Li Gucheng, *Zhongguo dalu zhengzhi shuyu* (Chinese mainland political terminology), Hong Kong: Zhongwen daxue chubanshe, 2nd edition, 1992, p. 107. See also Ma Da, '*Ershi shiji Zhongguo xuexiao yinyue jiaoyu fazhan gaikuang: 16: "Wenhua dageming" shiqi de zhongxiaoxue yinyue jiaoyu (1966–1976)*' (Survey of the development of twentieth-century Chinese school music education: part 16: High school and primary school music education in the Great Cultural Revolution period), *Zhongguo yinyue jiaoyu* (Chinese music education), 2001, 4 (April), 39–40, and part 17, '*"Wenhua dageming" shiqi de shifan yinyue jiaoyu*' (Music teacher training in the Great Cultural Revolution period), *Zhongguo yinyue jiaoyu*, 2001, 5 (May), 34–36. Preparatory work on the Central May Seventh Arts University had symbolically begun on 1 January 1970: Su Jinan, ed., *Zhongguo jin, xiandai (1840–1989) yinyue jiaoyu shi jinian* (Chronology of the history of modern musical education in China), Jinan: Shandong youyi chubanshe, 2000, p. 198. Su notes that the Arts University was formally established only in August 1973: p. 237.

110. Li Huanzhi, '*Fennu pipan "Sirenbang" esha minzu yinyue de zuixing*' (Indignantly criticize the crimes of the Gang of Four in throttling folk music), *Renmin yinyue*, 1978, 4 (July), 15–17, 32. An article in similar vein is Wen Ping, '*Zai douzheng zhong huifu he fanrong minzu shengyue yishu*' (In the midst of struggle restoring and making prosperous folk vocal music), *Guangming ribao*, 13 October 1978, p. 3. For *sanfan fenzi*, see Li Gucheng, pp. 69–70.

111. Liang Maochun, '*Dangdai minzu qiyue hezou chuangzuo sishi nian (1949–1989)*' (Forty years of contemporary instrumental ensemble composition),

Yinyue tansuo (Music explorations: Journal of the Sichuan Conservatory), 1992, 2 (June), 14–15, reprinted in *Yinyue, wudao yanjiu* (Renmin daxue reprints), 1992, 9 (September), 62–72, esp. pp. 65–66.

112. Zu Zhensheng, p. 41.

113. Zu Zhensheng, p. 62.

114. Zu Zhensheng, p. 74.

115. Zu Zhensheng, pp. 85–86.

116. Zu Zhensheng, pp. 114–116. See also the similar experience of Huang Feili, in Zu Zhensheng, pp. 96–97.

117. Zu Zhensheng, p. 162.

118. Zu Zhensheng, pp. 228–229. I remember attending a live performance of the suite in early 1976 and being struck by the unusual, and highly effective, part-singing.

119. Zu Zhensheng, p. 196. His Cultural Revolution experience, and that of his daughter Hu Mei, the future fifth-generation film director, is outlined in Clark, *Reinventing China*, pp. 22–23, 36.

120. Zu Zhensheng, p. 401.

121. Zu Zhensheng, pp. 330–331.

122. Zu Zhensheng, p. 263. See Yang Hongnian's similar experience in Yunnan (Zu Zhensheng, pp. 353–354) and Xia Feiyun's role conducting the operas *Tiger Mountain* and *Boulder Bay*: Zu Zhensheng, pp. 390–391.

123. See, for example, Gao Wensheng's assertion that 'during the Cultural Revolution, as a matter of fact, there was no drama (*xiju*)': Gao Wensheng, ed., *Zhongguo dangdai xiju wenxue shi* (History of contemporary Chinese drama writing), Nanning: Guangxi renmin chubanshe, 1990, p. 201. This does not prevent Gao from mentioning several Cultural Revolution spoken dramas elsewhere in the 442-page book. He manages to devote over five pages to the Cultural Revolution in the historical overview at the start of the book. He quotes Jiang Qing declaring, among other things, that 'spoken drama is already dead' (*huaju yijing si le*): see pp. 32–37, esp. p. 34.

124. Wang Xinmin, p. 208. Wang also has a section on the Cultural Revolution in his *Zhongguo dangdai huaju yishu yanbian shi* (Evolution of contemporary Chinese play art), Hangzhou: Zhejiang daxue chubanshe, 2000, pp. 144–152.

125. This account is based on a pioneering article by Yang Jian (born 1952), a teacher at the Central Drama Academy in Beijing: '*Wenhua dageming de Hongweibing xiju*' (Great Cultural Revolution Red Guard drama), *Xiju* (Drama), 1995, 3 (September), 51–64. For the script of a typical short play, 'Pig Farm Story' (*Zhuchang gushi*), by an army propaganda team, see *Wenyi cailiao* (Literature and Art Materials), 15 June 1967, p. 4 (reprinted in *Xinbian Hongweibing ziliao*, p. 9253). See also Yang Jian, '*Wenhua dageming zhong de Hongweibing huaju*' (Red Guard spoken drama in the Great Cultural Revolution), *Zhongguo qingnian yanjiu*, 1995, 1 (January), 34–73 (Part One) and 1995, 2 (March), 25–28 (Part Two).

126. These examples are among many recorded by Yang Jian, *Xiju*, p. 54. For photographs of such performances, see for example, *Fuhu zhanbao* (Lurking tiger battlefield report), 21 July 1967, p. 4; *Hongse zaofanzhe* (Red rebel), 8 October 1966, p. 7; and a later performance in *Wenyi geming* (Literature and

art revolution), 28 January 1970, p. 4 (reprinted in *Xinbian Hongweibing zilao*, pp. 1814, 8971, and 6715, respectively). For 1965 versions of such political tableaux, see *Wudao*, 1965, 2 (April), inside front-cover. The arrest of the Gang of Four in October 1976 was marked with identical types of stage and street tableaux: see photos in *Wudao*, 1976, 5 (November), inside back-cover.

127. Yang Jian, *Xiju*, p. 55. The summer of 1967 also saw professional song-and-dance troupes, including army performers, presenting new works.

128. Yang Jian, *Xiju*, p. 55. Jinggangshan was the region in southern Jiangxi in which the Communist Party established a Soviet government in the early 1930s prior to the Long March (1934–1935).

129. Yang Jian, *Xiju*, pp. 55–56. See also Wang Xinmin (1997), pp. 208–209, who seems less clear about the details of these dramas. The January Storm established a new city leadership in Shanghai: MacFarquhar and Schoenhals, pp. 163–169.

130. Yang Jian reprints a production script for part of the play, showing professional sound, music, and lighting cues: Yang Jian, *Xiju*, pp. 57–60.

131. Yang Jian, *Xiju*, pp. 60–62.

132. Yang Jian, *Xiju*, pp. 60, 61. These details on television are from Wu Suling, *Zhongguo dianshiju fazhan shigang* (Survey of the development of Chinese television drama), Beijing: Beijing guangbo xueyuan chubanshe, 1997, pp. 57–58.

133. *Renmin ribao*, 12 May 1967, p. 3, and 31 May 1967, p. 8. The May Ninth name of the troupe referred to one of several dates on which the now discredited provincial leadership had attempted to suppress Red Guard rebels. The People's Liberation Army's drama troupes also contributed in 1966–1967 to this flurry of new style agitprop dramas: Zheng Bangyu, ed., *Jiefangjun xiju shi* (History of Liberation Army drama), Beijing: Zhongguo xiju chubanshe, 2004, pp. 312–313, 600–601.

134. Yang Jian, *Xiju*, p. 63.

135. Yang Jian, *Xiju*, p. 63.

136. See, for example, the article on a 'little theatre group' (*xiao jutuan*) in Da'an county in the Northeast, *Jilin ribao* (Jilin Daily), 16 May 1969, p. 3. Such activities could draw on similar efforts in the Socialist Education Movement prior to 1966: see Wen Zhixuan, '*Nongmin huanying geming xiaoxi*' (Peasants welcome revolutionary short plays), *Hongqi*, 1965, 12 (November), 35–36.

137. For an example, see Zheng Yanfu, '*Gan, gan, gan*' (Work, work, work) and Xi Shuke, '*Dazhai lu shang chang xin'ge*' (Singing new songs on the Dazhai road), *Sichuan wenyi*, 1976, 2 (February), 46–48. See also Yang Jian, '*Lishi goule: Neimeng yu Dongbei de zhiqing wenyi*' (Outline history: educated youth literature and art in Inner Mongolia and the Northeast), *Zhongguo qingnian yanjiu*, 1998, 5 (September), 33–35.

138. Ge Yihong, ed., *Zhongguo huaju tongshi* (General history of Chinese spoken drama), Beijing: Wenhua yishu chubanshe, 1990, pp. 446–447.

139. Hu Ke, '*Jianguo wushinian huaju licheng de huigu*' (Review of the fifty-year course of spoken drama since 1949), *Wenyi lilun yu piping* (Literature and art theory and criticism), 1999, 4 (July), 38. On army plays after 1972, see

Zheng Bangyu, pp. 315–326. The Stanislavsky acting system was attacked as bourgeois: see, for example, Shanghai geming dapipan xiezuo xiaozu, '*Ping Sidannisilafusiji 'tixi'*' (Critique of the Stanislavsky 'system'), *Hongqi*, 1969, 6–7 (July), 36–46.

140. Liang Bingkun, *Beijing Renyi de gushi* (Story of Beijing People's Art Theatre), Beijing: Shiyue wenyi chubanshe, 1992, pp. 264–267.

141. Liang Bingkun, p. 301. The definition of *san ming san gao*, used in the 1950s and 1960s, is from Li Gucheng, p. 77.

142. Liang Bingkun, pp. 301, 302, and 304.

143. These details on the Shanghai People's Art Theatre are from Xiao Wu, '*Fangyan huaju tuan*' (Local-dialect spoken-drama troupes), *Shanghai wenhua shizhi tongxun*, 27 (August 1993), 38–41.

144. Xiao Wu, p. 40. The usual phrase was 'seize revolution and promote production' (*zhua geming, cu shengchan*). Assignment to the summer work apparently provided an excuse for the Shanghai theatre to sever its ties with the Shanghai dialect drama company.

145. Xia Liang, *Jutan manhua* (Theatre chat), Beijing: Zhongguo wenlian chubanshe, 1985, pp. 210–211.

146. From Shen Xiaoyu and Gao Yan, '*Wo bu wanmei, dan zhuiqiu wanmei: ji dianying yanyuan Tang Guoqiang*' (I'm not perfect, but I strive for perfection: on film actor Tang Guoqiang), *Renwu* (People), 1990, 1 (January), 36–40 (whole article 36–48). Tang was cast in *Drama on the Southern Ocean (Nanhai fengyun)*, filmed on Hainan Island, and went on to achieve film stardom in the 1980s.

147. Wu Suling, p. 61.

148. Details are from Ma Wei, '*Nuli suzao tong zouzipai douzheng de yingxiong dianxing: tan woshi jinnian lai chuangzao de bufen xiju zuopin*' (Work hard to portray heroic models to struggle against capitalist roaders: a discussion of some Tianjin drama works created in the last few years), *Tianjin wenyi*, 1976, 8 (August), 19–23, 48. For more on *Red Pine Fort*, see Chapter Five.

149. The future Gang of Four reportedly were bitterly against the revival of the play and the subsequent work on turning it into a Peking opera: see Tianjinshi Jingju santuan, '*Wei hanwei Mao zhuxi geming luxian er zhandou: yizhi huaju 'Wanshui qianshan' de yidian tihui*' (Fight to defend Chairman Mao's revolutionary line: some understanding from transplanting the spoken drama *Ten Thousand Rivers and a Thousand Mountains*), *Tianjin yanchang* (Tianjin performance), 1977, 1 (January), 58–59.

150. See, for example, *Renmin ribao*, 5 August 1975, p. 3.

151. See, for example, *Renmin ribao*, 7 September 1976, p. 4; *Renmin xiju*, 1976, 4 (August), 73–74.

152. See *Tianjin wenyi*, 1974, 1 (January), 38–40; *Tianjin yanchang*, 1976, 3 (July), 42–43; *Renmin xiju*, 1976, 4 (August), 75–76.

153. This was cited after 1976 as evidence of Jiang Qing's inconsistency: see Tian Hai, '*Jiang Qing he "chufang fengbo"*' (Jiang Qing and the 'kitchen storm'), *Tianjin wenyi*, 1977, 3 (March), 34–35.

154. *Tianjin wenyi*, 1974, 1 (January), 34–37. On radio, see *Renmin xiju*, 1976, 4 (August), 77. For an example of an established *kuaiban* performer's

experience, see Gao Hongshun, '"Wen-ge" zhong de Gao Yuanjun' (Gao Yuanjun in the Cultural Revolution), *Quyi*, 2000, 1 (January), 31.

155. See *Shanghai wenhua shizhi tongxun*, 27 (August 1993), 35 and 31 (April 1994), 61.

156. Zhao Kezhong, '*Shanghai "gushihui" de xingcheng jiqi licheng*' (Shape and course of Shanghai's 'story-telling sessions'), *Shanghai wenhua shizhi tongxun*, 23 (December 1992), 30–34, esp. pp. 33–34.

157. The standard history presents a gloomy account of the 1966–1976 period: Wang Jue, Wang Jingshou, and Teng Tianxiang [Fujita Kaoru], *Zhongguo xiangsheng shi* (History of Chinese comic dialogues), Beijing: Beijing yanshan chubanshe, 1995, pp. 264–267. See also Wang Ruolin, '*Jiankang de xiao: tan "Wa bao"*' (Healthy laughter: on *Baby Precious*), *Tianjin wenyi*, 1973, 1 (January), 41–42. For examples of *xiangsheng*, see He Kuang and Lu Guangbo, '*"Longjiang" hua kai chun manyuan*' (*Longjiang* flowers fill the world with spring), *Wenyi zuopin* (Literary and art works [Anhui]), 1973, 9 (September), 56–57, and Shanghai Jiangnan zaochuangchang chuangzuo zu, Shanghai gejuyuan wenyi jingqidui, '*Jinjunhao*' (Bugle call), *Chaoxia*, 1974, 10 (March), pp. 68–73.

158. *Shanghai wenhua shizhi tongxun*, 4 (June 1989), 44.

159. *Shanghai wenhua shizhi tongxun*, 6 (December 1989), 5. On Beijing troupes, see Ying Shu, '*"Wen-ge" zhong Zhongguo zajituan yu Zhongguo mu'ou yishu jutuan de "po si jiu"*' ('Smashing the four olds' at the China Acrobatic Troupe and the China Puppet Theatre in the Cultural Revolution), *Beijing dangshi yanjiu* (Beijing Party history research), 1996, 2 (April), 42.

160. Tian Peize, '*Jianguo 45 nian lai de Shanghai qunzhong geyong huodong*' (Shanghai mass singing activities in the 45 years after 1949), *Shanghai wenhua shizhi tongxun*, 34 (October 1994), 53–57, esp. pp. 54–55.

161. Julia F. Andrews makes this point briefly in her excellent *Painters and Politics in the People's Republic of China, 1949–1979*, Berkeley: University of California Press, 1994, p. 316.

162. From the text of Jiang Qing's remarks to Red Guards reprinted in *Jinggangshan zhanbao* (Jinggangshan battlefield report), 9 December 1967, p. 1, a newspaper jointly published by Red Guards of the Central Art Academy and the Central Academy of Arts and Crafts (*Zhongyang gongyi meishu xueyuan*), reprinted in *Xinbian Hongweibing ziliao*, p. 4428.

163. See Melissa Schrift, *The Biography of a Chairman Mao Badge: The Creation and Mass Consumption of a Personality Cult*, New Brunswick: Rutgers University Press, 2001 and Wang Anting, ed., *Mao Zedong xiangzhang tupu* (Illustrated catalogue of Mao badges), Beijing: Zhongguo shudian chubanshe, 1993 for a 350-page collection of Mao badges.

164. Maria Galikowski notes that these paintings often re-invented historical episodes, giving Mao more importance than he deserved: see her *Art and Politics in China, 1949–1984*, Hong Kong: The Chinese University Press, 1998, pp. 149–152.

165. For examples, among many in the volume, see the pioneering history by Wang Mingxian and Yan Shanchun, *Xin Zhongguo meishu tushi, 1966–1976* (Illustrated history of New China's fine art), Beijing: Zhongguo qingnian chubanshe, 2000, pp. 41, 129.

166. See Wang Mingxian and Yan Shanchun, pp. 54–69, and Galikowski, pp. 148–149.

167. These silk versions were the product of the Hangzhou East is Red Silk Weaving Factory.

168. Galikowski, p. 148; see, for example, Wang Mingxian and Yan Shanchun, pp. 64–65.

169. Wang Mingxian and Yan Shanchun, pp. 42–44.

170. On a visit to Shaoshan in February 1975, I was told the statue was raised to measure 12.26 meters from the ground. Mao was born on 26 December 1893. The branch railroad to the village of Shaoshan was opened in December 1967 to help facilitate Red Guard and others' pilgrimages.

171. For a Red Guard account of the suite's making, emphasizing the obstacles put up by pre-1966 cultural authorities at the Sichuan Art Academy, see *Tiyu zhanxian* (Sports battlefront), 4 February 1967, p. 3 and 9 February 1967, p. 5, reproduced in *Xinbian Hongweibing ziliao*, pp. 5842 and 5848, respectively.

172. *Tianjin ribao*, 2 October 1966, p. 6. A rather breathless account of the statues can be found in Wang Zhi'an, *Hongtian juechang: 'Shouzu yuan' nisu qiguan* (Sensational perfection: the wonder of the *Rent-Collection Courtyard* clay sculptures), Chengdu: Tiandi chubanshe, 2001. Wang notes the Beijing exhibition on pp. 289–291. The Party's chief organ also publicized the statues: see the illustrated article on them by Cai Ruohong, '*Mao Zedong wenyi sixiang de shengli: ping "Shouzu yuan" nisu qunxiang*' (Victory of Mao Zedong's line in literature and art: critique of the clay sculpture ensemble *Rent Collection Courtyard*), *Hongqi*, 1966, 3 (March), 26–33.

173. The group was called *Wrath of the Serfs* (*Nongnu fen*) and was housed at the Tibetan Revolutionary Museum in Lhasa. It was the work of a mixed group of ten professionals from the May Seventh Art University, an art teacher from the Lu Xun Art Academy in Shenyang, and three members of staff of the museum: *Meishu*, 1976, 1 (March), 26–28.

174. I visited Shenyang in July 1973. The statue remained there in 2007. For illustrations and discussion, see Wang Mingxian and Yan Shanchun, pp. 160–169.

175. Wang Mingxian and Yan Shanchun discuss Red Guard art on pp. 6–23. Julia F. Andrews covers this and the attacks on established artists on pp. 319–342.

176. See *Wenyi zhanbao* (Literature and art battlefield report), 14 July 1967, p. 6, with a Cheng Shifa portrait printed with crossed lines through it, reproduced in *Xinbian Hongweibing ziliao*, p. 6771. Julia F. Andrews mentions Cheng's difficulties, p. 343. By 1973 Cheng Shifa's works were back in the public eye: see, for example, the coloured plate 'Practising acupuncture' in *Chinese Literature*, 1973, 5 (May), after page 56. On the fortunes of one aspect of traditional art, the artists' materials suppliers of Liulichang district in Beijing, see Wang Xuetai, '*Wen-ge zhong de Liulichang*' (Liulichang in the Cultural Revolution), *Shiyue* (October), 1999, 5 (October), 211–219.

177. Reproduced in Wang Mingxian and Yan Shanchun, p. 189.

178. Wang Mingxian and Yan Shanchun reproduce many works from the 1972–1975 period on pp. 180–213. See also Harriet Evans and Stephanie Donald,

eds, *Picturing Power in the People's Republic of China: Posters of the Cultural Revolution*, Lanham: Rowman & Littlefield, 1999.

179. For illustrations, see Wang Mingxian and Yan Shanchun, pp. 111–116. See also a review of Hu county painting in *Renmin ribao*, 5 December 1972, p. 4. On National Day 1973 a Beijing exhibition of paintings from Hu county opened in Beijing. For a review, written by Liu Chunhua, painter of 'Mao Goes to Anyuan', see *Guangming ribao*, 19 October 1973, p. 4. See also *Guangming ribao*, 10 October 1973, p. 4; *Guangming ribao*, 16 October 1973, p. 2 and *Renmin ribao*, 29 March 1974, p. 3.

180. I recall on a visit to Hu county in July 1975 the defensiveness of our hosts (and the consternation of our Beijing teachers) when this notion was raised by a couple of my French schoolmates.

181. This point is made in the valuable study of Huxian painting by Duan Jingli, pp. 70–82, 90–95.

182. Duan Jingli, pp. 133–152.

183. On 'The Old Party Secretary', see Duan Jingli, pp. 166–173. On amateur painters and exhibitions, see the article in the second issue of the newly revived (after ten years) magazine *Meishu*, 1976, 2 (May), 44–45. See an article by five Hu county artists: Zhou Wende and others, '*Jinwo huabi, huiji meishu zhanxian de daotui niliu*' (Grasp the brush tightly, fight back against the falling back countercurrent on the fine art battlefront), *Shaanxi wenyi* (Shaanxi literature and art), 1974, 3 (May), 69–73.

184. Galikowski, p. 143. Julia F. Andrews claims the first students of the new art department entered in March 1974 (p. 367), but other students had been there for some time.

185. Julia F. Andrews, p. 348. For a fine example, see Cheng Mian's 'A good doctor for the poor and lower-middle peasants', in *Beijing xin wenyi* (New Beijing literature and art), test issue 4 (October 1972), inside back-cover. This is reproduced in Wang Mingxian and Yan Shanchun, p. 88.

186. Wang Mingxian and Yan Shanchun provide a two-page listing of art publications in 1967 from Beijing–Tianjin area Red Guard groups: pp. 22–23.

187. Julia F. Andrews, p. 134. For examples of *lianhuanhua*, see Wang Mingxian and Yan Shanchun, pp. 190 and 193.

188. These exhibits are listed in An Shiming, ed., *Beijing meishu huodong dashiji, 1949–1989* (Record of major events in Beijing art activities), Beijing: Beijingshi meishujia xiehui, 1992 (internal circulation), p. 17. Beijing-based exhibitions in this latter part of the Cultural Revolution through until 1978 were the responsibility of a 'Beijing City Art and Photography Exhibition Office' (*Beijingshi meishu sheying zhanlan bangongshi*), under the Beijing City Cultural Bureau (*Beijingshi wenhuaju*): An Shiming, p. 17.

189. See a 'review' and article on Chinese painting, arguing works must reflect the era, in *Renmin ribao*, 14 October 1973, p. 3, and another review in *Renmin ribao*, 15 November 1973, p. 4.

190. Julia Andrews (pp. 359–360) notes that professional painters were asked to repaint parts of some works. Gao was selected by Wang Mantian, the woman who had been put in charge of fine arts in 1970 (pp. 349–350).

191. Chen Changqian, ed., *Dangdai Zhongguo sheying yishu shi (1949–1989)* (History of contemporary Chinese photographic art), Beijing: Zhongguo

sheying chubanshe, 1995, pp. 22, 60. There were four such exhibitions in Beijing before October 1976. The 1972 exhibition had been preceded by an October–November 1970 Beijing meeting on photographic work in the armed forces: p. 230.

192. Chen Changqian writes of 'model' (*yangban*) people and work units and the use of the 'three prominences', though he notes a new group of younger photographers emerging in the mid-1970s (pp. 22–23, 61–62, 115–116). For a relatively subtle, yet highly political, photograph featuring an older and younger soldier in an indistinct, though apparently private setting, see 'Tanxin' (A heart-to-heart talk) by Lu Zhenhai, reprinted in *Shandong wenyi* (Shandong literature and art), 1974, No. 4 (August), inside front-cover.

193. In 1974 eleven provinces, Shanghai and Tianjin conducted colour-photography classes and other training classes: Chen Changqian, p. 231.

194. For an entertaining analysis, see Roderick MacFarquhar, 'On Photographs', *The China Quarterly*, 46 (June 1971), 289–307.

195. See, for example, the cover and illustrations in the October 1976 issues of *China Pictorial* or *China Reconstructs*.

196. Jiang Qing was apparently attacking Zhou Enlai, who had encouraged new work by seasoned professionals for visitors' enjoyment: Julia F. Andrews, pp. 368–376. See also Galikowski, pp. 158–163. Elaine Johnston Laing, *The Winking Owl: Art in the People's Republic of China*, Berkeley: University of California Press, 1988 is another source on this exhibition, at which the book-title painting was displayed as an example of allegorical dissidence. This exhibition had parallels with the Nazi exhibition of 'degenerate art' in 1937: see Richard Overy, *The Dictators: Hitler's Germany and Stalin's Russia*, London: Allen Lane, 2004, pp. 359–360.

197. The latter exhibitions included 320 art works and 175 photographs: An Shiming, p. 17.

198. An Shiming, p. 18.

199. Quoted in Lü Peng and Yi Dan, *Zhongguo xiandai yishu shi, 1979–1989* (History of modern Chinese art), Changsha: Hunan meishu chubanshe, 1992, p. 11.

200. Noted in Lü Peng and Yi Dan, p. 385.

201. *Meishu*, 1976, 1 (March), 19, reproduced in Lü Peng and Yi Dan, p. 13.

202. Lü Peng and Yi Dan, p. 13. The reference to theatricality is on p. 12.

203. For an example of blackboard art, see Wang Mingxian and Yan Shanchun, p. 120.

204. *Meishu*, 1977, 1 (January), 29; see Figure 4.4.

205. *Meishu*, 1976, 1 (March), inside front-cover; reproduced in Lü Peng and Yi Dan, p. 13.

206. Julia Andrews discusses the experience of Tang Muli: pp. 353–359. Wang Mingxian and Yan Shanchun offer a chapter on such artists: pp. 80–97.

207. For further discussion, see Chapter Five.

208. The Zhengzhou building is reproduced in Wang Mingxian and Yan Shanchun, p. 178. Datong, in northern Shanxi province, featured a mini-Great Hall of the People by July 1975, when I visited.

209. Listed in the chronology at the back of Wang Mingxian and Yan Shanchun, p. 224.

210. These buildings are illustrated in the chapter on the 1965–1979 period titled 'Political nature, types and regionalism' (*zhengzhixing, leixingxing he diyuxing*) in Zou Deyi, *Zhongguo jianzhushi tushuo: xiandai juan* (Illustrated history of Chinese architecture: modern volume), Beijing: Zhongguo jianzhu gongye chubanshe, 2001, pp. 163–206. The Guangzhou and Guilin buildings are on pp. 171–172 and 180–182.

211. See Zou Deyi, pp. 183–184 and 192, respectively. I passed through the latter building briefly in July 1973. A similar field of experimentation were the various residences for Mao Zedong's use around the country built after the 1950s.

FIVE: WRITING WRONGS: PUBLIC AND PRIVATE FICTIONS AND RESISTANCE

1. See Zhang Yang's lengthy account of the novel and his life in '*Di-er ci woshou*' *wenziyu* (The *Second Handshake* literary inquisition), Beijing: Zhongguo shehui chubanshe, 1999 and his reworking of this in *Wo yu 'Di-erci woshou*' (*The Second Handshake* and I), Beijing: Zhonggong dangshi chubanshe, 2007.

2. For a brief account of Ba Jin's troubles, see Wang Yao, *Zhongguo dangdai sanwen shi* (History of contemporary Chinese prose), Guiyang: Guizhou renmin chubanshe, 1994, pp. 112–113.

3. Wang Yao, '"*Wen-ge wenxue*" jishi' (Chronology of 'Cultural Revolution' literature), *Dangdai zuojia pinglun* (Contemporary writer reviews), 2000, 4 (April) [hereafter *Jishi*], 22.

4. Chen Qiguang, for example, makes the claim about *Jiefangjun wenyi* in his *Zhongguo dangdai wenxue shi* (History of contemporary Chinese literature), Guangzhou: Jinan daxue chubanshe, 1998, p. 321. The true picture is indicated by issue numbers in the Peking University Library holdings of these journals.

5. Wang Yao, *Jishi*, p. 19. There were sensitive, and ultimately abandoned, efforts to write an official biography of Lu Xun in these years: Gu Yuanqing, '*Yu Qiuyu yu "Shi Yige": "Wen-ge" niming xiezuo yanjiu zhiyi*' (Yu Qiuyu and 'Shi Yige': one piece of research on anonymous writings in the Cultural Revolution), *Lu Xun yanjiu yuekan* (Lu Xun research monthly), 2001, 1 (January), 53–55.

6. The poster is reproduced in Wang Mingxian and Yang Shanchun, p. 208.

7. For a biographical sketch, see '*Hao Ran jianjie*' (Brief introduction to Hao Ran), *Daxing'anling wenyi* (Daxing'anling literature and art), 1974, 2 (February), 75–77. See also Kai-yu Hsu, *The Chinese Literary Scene: A Writer's Visit to the People's Republic*, New York: Vintage Books, 1974, pp. 86–99. Parts 2 and 3 of *Bright Sunny Skies* were published in January 1973: *1973 quanguo zong shumu* (National book catalogue), Beijing: Zhonghua shuju, 1976, p. 117.

8. Michael Egan argues that the later novel was less successful as a literary achievement than the pre–Cultural Revolution *Bright Sunny Skies*: 'A Notable Sermon: The Subtext of Hao Ran's Fiction', in McDougall, *Popular Chinese Literature*, pp. 224–241. See also Richard King, 'Revisionism and

Transformation in the Cultural Revolution Novel', *Modern Chinese Literature*, 7, 1 (1993), 105–130.

9. Listeners were also drawn to Hao Ran's novels when they were broadcast in multiple parts on radio: Hong Zicheng, *Zhongguo dangdai wenxue shi* (History of contemporary Chinese literature), Beijing: Beijing daxue chubanshe, 1999, p. 205 n. 17. For a technical analysis of Hao Ran's language invention, among other novels, see Lan Yang, *Chinese Fiction of the Cultural Revolution*, Hong Kong: Hong Kong University Press, 1998. See also Tan Jiewen, '*Guanyu "Jinguang dadao" de jidian sikao*' (Thoughts on *The Golden Road*), *Wenyi lilun yu piping*, 2002, 1 (January), 68–73.

10. This expression could cover a range of combinations, depending on its application: Chao Feng, '*Wenhua dageming' cidian* (Dictionary of the Great Cultural Revolution), Hong Kong: Ganglong chubanshe, 1993, p. 6. In literary production it often meant leaders, writers, and the masses being jointly responsible for producing a work: Laifong Leung, *Morning Sun: Interviews with Chinese Writers of the Lost Generation*, Armonk: M. E. Sharpe, 1994, p. 233.

11. Chen Qiguang, pp. 328–329. On the Hao Ran novel's use of the 'three prominences' and other failings, see Michael Egan, pp. 240–242.

12. Hong Zicheng, pp. 209–210.

13. See *1973 quanguo zong shumu*, pp. 236–237.

14. On the continued effort to find appropriate poetic forms after 1949, see Kai-yu Hsu, 'Contemporary Chinese Poetry and Its Search for an Ideal Form', in McDougall, *Popular Chinese Literature*, pp. 244–265, esp. pp. 262–263.

15. Perry Link, *The Uses of Literature: Life in the Socialist Chinese Literary System*, Princeton, NJ: Princeton University Press, 2000, p. 114.

16. See the pioneering chronicle by Yang Jian, *Zhongguo zhiqing wenxue shi* (History of Chinese 'educated youth' literature), Beijing: Zhongguo gongren chubanshe, 2002 [hereafter *Zhiqing*], pp. 92–103. On Red Guard poetry, see Wang Jiaping, '*Hongweibing "xiaobao" jiqi shige de jiben xingtai*' (Red Guard newspapers and the basic features of their poetry), *Wenyi zhengming* (Literature and art debates), 2001, 5 (May), 4–9.

17. Gu Yuanqing, ed., '*Zhongguo (dalu) dangdai wenxue lilun piping dashiji (1976)*' (Chronology of main events in contemporary Chinese (mainland) literary theory criticism), *Dangdai wenxue yanjiu ziliao yu xinxi* (Contemporary literature research materials and information), 1998, 6 (December), 45. See also Bonnie S. McDougall, 'Poems, Poets and *Poetry* 1976: An Exercise in the Typology of Modern Chinese Literature', *Contemporary China*, 2, 4 (1978), 76–124.

18. Chen Qiguang, p. 329.

19. Hong Zicheng, pp. 206–207. Wang Jiaping characterizes Cultural Revolution poetry (public and private) as 'complex and rich': *Wenhua dageming shiqi shige yanjiu* (Research on Great Cultural Revolution poetry), Kaifeng: Henan daxue chubanshe, 2004, pp. 291–302. Wang provides a five-page bibliography of poetry volumes published between 1972 and 1976: pp. 308–312.

20. *Xiaojinzhuang shige xuan*, Tianjin: Tianjin renmin chubanshe, 1976. For an example of Xiaojinzhuang as a model for literary creation elsewhere, see Zhonggong Gejiu shiwa diaochazu, '*Yong shehuizhuyi zhanling nongcun*

sixiang wenhua chendi: Gejiushi Baohe gongshe xuexi Xiaojinzhuang jingyan de diaocha' (Use socialism to capture the old places of rural ideology and culture: investigation of the study of the Xiaojinzhuang experience at Baohe commune in Gejiu city), *Yunnan wenyi*, 1975, 2 (February), 59–62.

21. Liu Fuchun, *Zhongguo dangdai xinshi biannianshi (1966–1976)* (Annals of new poetry in contemporary China), Kaifeng: Henan daxue chubanshe, 2005.

22. See Wang Qingsheng and Fan Xing, '*Xin Zhongguo wenxue minzuxing de huigu yu sikao*' (Review and reflections on the national qualities of New China's literature), *Wenxue pinglun* (Literary criticism [Beijing]), 1999, 4, 27–35, esp. pp. 30–31.

23. Bonnie S. McDougall, 'Writers and Performers, Their Works, and Their Audiences in the First Three Decades', in McDougall, *Popular Chinese Literature*, pp. 295–296.

24. Song Yingli and others, *Zhongguo qikan fazhan shi* (History of the development of Chinese periodicals), Kaifeng: Henan daxue chubanshe, 2000, pp. 283 and 276.

25. Liu Gao and Shi Feng, eds, *Xin Zhongguo chuban wushi nian jishi* (Chronology of fifty years of New China's publishing), Beijing: Xinhua chubanshe, 1999, pp. 416–417. Book publications per head reached unprecedented levels after 1980 with economic growth.

26. Liu Gao and Shi Feng, pp. 122–124, 129, 128, 139–140.

27. See Richard King, 'Models and misfits: Rusticated youth in three novels of the 1970s', in William A. Joseph, Christine P. W. Wong, and David Zweig, eds, *New Perspectives on the Cultural Revolution*, Harvard Contemporary China Series: 8, Cambridge: Council on East Asian Studies, 1991, pp. 245–248. For an example of educated youth amateur writing and performance, see Cheng Dichao, '*Laizi guangkuo tiandi de zhandou yishu: xikan woshong nongken xitong qingnian yeyu chuangzuo jiemu diaoyan*' (Fighting art that's come from a vast universe: delight at watching selected performances created by the amateur young people of our province's land reclamation system), *Yunnan wenyi*, 1975, 2 (February), 69–71.

28. Laifong Leung, pp. 180, 190 n. 1. For examples of collections of short stories, poems, and dramatic performances by sent-down youths published in Shanghai, Tianjin, Guangdong, Jiangsu, and Shanxi in 1973, see Liu Gao and Shi Feng, p. 147, and *1973 quanguo zong shumu*, pp. 121, 123, 137, 138, 156, 654.

29. Laifong Leung, p. 274. McDougall and Louie note the Cultural Revolution experience of these younger writers in their *The Literature of China in the Twentieth Century*, pp. 418–419.

30. Laifong Leung, pp. 116–117. For another instance of a sent-down youth newspaper, see p. 140.

31. Laifong Leung, pp. 233–234, 229. Leung appears incorrect in saying *Deng* appeared in *Shanghai ribao*. The novel is discussed in Richard King, pp. 248–251.

32. Wang Yao, *Jishi*, pp. 25, 27. Jiang Zilong even had a story appear in the first new issue of the prestigious *People's Literature* (*Renmin wenxue*) in January 1976: Chen Sihe, ed., *Zhongguo dangdai wenxue shi jiaocheng* (Lectures on contemporary Chinese literary history), Shanghai: Fudan daxue chubanshe, 1999, p. 167.

33. The editors called for submissions to the monthly and the book series that 'purposefully reflect the life of struggle in the Cultural Revolution': *Chaoxia*, 1974, 1 (January), last page.

34. These qualities are praised by the Zhongwenxi ernianji erban shupingzu, '*Wenhua dageming de zan'ge: ping "Chaoxia congshu" "Yuqu"*' (Song of praise for the Great Cultural Revolution: critique of *Prelude* in the Chaoxia book series), *Beijing shifan daxue xuebao (shehui kexue ban)* (Beijing Normal University Journal: social science issue), 1976, No. 3 (May), pp. 72–76. Qing Ming, ed., *Xuqu: 'nuli fanying Wenhua dageming de douzheng shenghuo' zhengwen xuan* (*Prelude*: selection of solicited articles purposefully reflecting the life of struggle in the Great Cultural Revolution), Shanghai: Shanghai renmin chubanshe, 1975. See also Wang Yao, *Jishi*, p. 24. For other Wang Yao writings on Cultural Revolution literature, see the Bibliography. On 'plot literature' see Yang Jian, *Zhiqing*, pp. 258–260, 264–274, 281–282.

35. Wen Rumin and others, '*Guanyu "Zhonghua 'Wen-ge' shiqi wenxue" de duihua*' (Dialogue about 'Hurtful remarks on Cultural Revolution-period literature'), *Dangdai wenxue yanjiu ziliao yu xinxi*, 1998, 5 (October), 23.

36. Hand-copied poetry was already circulating among sent-down youths in the summer of 1969: Zhang Ming and Liao Yiwu, eds, *Chenlun de shengdian: Zhongguo ershi shiji 70 niandai dixia shige yizhao* (Sinking holy place: death pictures of underground poetry in China's 1970s), Urumqi: Xinjiang qingshaonian chubanshe, 1994, p. 260.

37. Hong Zicheng's modern literary history devotes a short section to handcopied stories (*shouchaoben xiaoshuo*): pp. 215–218. See also Yang Jian, '*Wen-ge shiqi de minjian wenxue*' (Folk literature of the Cultural Revolution period), *Shanghai wenxue* (Shanghai literature), 2001, 7 (July), 61–64.

38. Chen Qiguang, p. 327. The attribution to a Beijing factory worker is by Song Yaolang, '*Yijiuqiliu nian, wenxue xinchao de faduan*' (Start of new literature in 1976), *Dangdai wenxue sichao* (Contemporary literary trends), 1986, 4 (July), 28.

39. Wang Yao, *Jishi*, p. 21. The latter was the work of Zhao Zhenkai, a.k.a. the poet Bei Dao. For a translation, see Zhao Zhenkai (Bei Dao), *Waves*, translated by Bonnie S. McDougall, Hong Kong: Chinese University Press, 1985. *Waves* is discussed in Yang Jian's detailed account, *Wenhua dageming zhong de dixia wenxue*, Beijing: Chaohua chubanshe, 1993 [hereafter *Dixia wenxue*], pp. 166–174. See also Yang Jian, *Zhiqing*, pp. 293–294.

40. Wang Qingsheng and Fan Xing, p. 31.

41. Song Yaolang, pp. 28–29. Already in June 1971 the central authorities expressed concern at 'illegal' (*feifa*) publishing at the local level: Liu Gao and Shi Feng, p. 132. On story-telling, see Yang Jian, *Dixia wenxue*, pp. 347–349.

42. From an interview by Laifong Leung, p. 94.

43. Interview with fifth-generation film director Peng Xiaolian, Beijing, 3 June 1988.

44. Wang Yao, *Jishi*, p. 22. The poet Duo Duo recalls these translations in Zhang Ming and Liao Yiwu, p. 195. I am grateful to Ian Lilly for the title of the Aksenov story.

45. The influence of these translations on young writers is discussed in the collection of literary memoirs of the Cultural Revolution and late-1970s

Democracy Wall movement: Zhang Ming and Liao Yiwu, pp. 2–3, 4–16. See also Yang Jian, *Dixia wenxue*, p. 86. 'Internal' (*neibu*) publications had different levels of restriction, but most seem to have been accessed by readerships wider than intended throughout the period since 1949.

46. See Shuyu Kong, 'For Reference Only: Restricted Publications and Distribution of Foreign Literature during the Cultural Revolution', *Yishu: Journal of Contemporary Chinese Art*, 1, 2 (Fall 2002), 76–85. For a sidelight on 'white-cover' books, see Wang Yao, *Chidao de pipan*, pp. 126–133.

47. Yang Jian, '*Lishi goule*', pp. 33–35. See also his fuller account in Yang Jian, *Zhiqing*, pp. 173–188.

48. Laifong Leung, pp. 98–99.

49. 'Salons' had first appeared in 1959 and found further impetus in 1964 among children of high-level cadres in Beijing. Maghiel van Crevel outlines the rise of underground writing in *Language Shattered: Contemporary Chinese Poetry and Duoduo*, Leiden: Research School CNWS, 1996, pp. 25–27, 42–61.

50. Yang Jian, *Dixia wenxue*, pp. 73–79 (on Li Li), 83–86. See also Yang Jian, *Zhiqing*, pp. 130–136, 192–204, 220–250. The police broke up Zhao's group in January 1974 during a sweep against 'underground literature': Yang Jian, *Dixia wenxue*, pp. 295, 296–297. See also Yang Jian, *Zhiqing*, pp. 283–291 and van Crevel, pp. 55–57.

51. Zhang Ming and Liao Yiwu, pp. 197–198. Many salon members shared the experience of being sent down to Baiyangdian Lake in Hebei, which, though dirt-poor, was relatively accessible to Beijing: van Crevel, pp. 47–50. Salons and poetry societies (*shishe*) are briefly discussed in Chen Sihe, pp. 170–174. See also Yang Jian, *Zhiqing*, pp. 238–247.

52. Yang Jian, *Dixia wenxue*, pp. 141–147.

53. Yang Jian, *Dixia wenxue*, pp. 201–238.

54. Chen Sihe, pp. 175–182. See also Li Runxia, '*Bei yanmo de huihuang: lun "Wen-ge dixia wenxue"*' (Brilliance snuffed out: on *Cultural Revolution Underground Literature*), *Jianghan luntan* (Hubei forum), 2001, 6 (June), 73–78.

55. Kai-yu Hsu touches on these in McDougall, *Popular Chinese Literature*, p. 260. Qingming was traditionally a time to honor dead ancestors and sweep their graves.

56. Chen Qiguang, pp. 332–338. The drumbeats were literal, as three days after the demonstration, I watched as worker-peasant-soldier students at Peking University were organized to celebrate spontaneously the decision of the Politburo that the demonstration was counter-revolutionary. Large drums on the backs of trucks were beaten wildly by appropriately joyful students. The poetry from the Qingming demonstrations was published in collections in 1977, once the event had been officially determined to have been directed against the 'Gang of Four': see, for example, Dong Huaizhou, ed., *Tian'anmen geming shiwen xuan* (Selected revolutionary poems and prose from Tian'anmen), Beijing: Beijing di'er waiguoyu xueyuan, 1977, and Dong Huaizhou, ed., *Tian'anmen shiwen xuan* (Selected poems and prose from Tian'anmen), Beijing: Beijing chubanshe, 1979, two volumes. For an assessment, see van Crevel, pp. 59–60.

57. As early as 1969 there were public indications that even the 'model performances' needed defending. *Red Flag* (*Hongqi*), 1969, 10 (September), 37–40

included an article headed 'Study the revolutionary model performances, defend the revolutionary model performances' (*Xuexi geming yangbanxi, baowei geming yangbanxi*) by Zhe Ping. While the rhetoric of these years constantly spoke of enemies attacking, this headline and the article indirectly referenced popular discontent with a diet of model operas and ballets.

58. Information from the chronology in Gao Wensheng, p. 401. The play's alternate title, *Case 302* (*San dong er anjian*), captured the thriller attraction of the work for audiences deprived of much such excitement in art.

59. Gao Wensheng, p. 401. The 'restoring the rites' (*fu li*) of the headline echoed the current campaign against Lin Biao and Confucius, who advocated such restoration.

60. Shen Youxin, '*Gonggu wuchanjieji zhuanzheng, pipan "Bu pingjing de haibin"*' (Consolidate the dictatorship of the proletariat, criticize *The Unquiet Seashore*), *Wenyi zuopin*, 1974, 5 (May), 56–59. See, for example, Liang Qiwu, '*Wuchanjieji zhuanzheng bu rong dihui: pipan da ducao "Bu pingjing haibin"*' (The dictatorship of the proletariat will not tolerate villification: criticizing the big poisonous weed *The Unquiet Seashore*), *Shaanxi wenyi*, 1974, 3 (May), 65–68.

61. The script is in both *Xiangjiang wenyi* (Hunan literature and art), 1973, 1 (January), 13–20 and in *Changsha wenyi* (Changsha literature and art), 1973, 1 (January), 59–74. Stills of the production are in *Xiangjiang wenyi*, 1973, 3 (May), inside front-cover and *Changsha wenyi*, 1973, 3 (June), inside front-cover.

62. Referred to in Di Di, *"Haixia" shijian benmo*, 65.

63. See, for example, Zhang Guilan, '*Xiuzhengzhuyi jiaoyu luxian de jiufan: ping Xiangju "Yuanding zhi ge"*' (Submission to the revisionist educational line: criticizing the Hunan opera *Song of the Teachers*), *Xiangjiang wenyi*, 1974, 3 (June), 13–14, 12 (an article by a worker-peasant-soldier student of the Chinese Department of the Hunan Normal Academy). More criticism, including reprint of an article by the Gang of Four writing group Chu Lan ('*Wei neitiao jiaoyu luxian chang zan'ge: ping Xiangju "Yuanding zhi ge"*' A song in favour of which educational line?: criticizing the Hunan opera *Song of the Teachers*) that had been published in *People's Daily* (4 August 1974), came in *Xiangjiang wenyi*, 1974, 4 (August), 4–19. The Gang of Four are reported to have watched the rough-cut of the filmed version as early as 28 July 1973. A Gang-allied cultural leader Liu Qingtang is alleged to have authorized distribution of the film in Beijing, Shanghai, Tianjin, and Hunan Province to be accompanied by criticism of the work. See also Sheng Li, '*Xiuzhengzhuyi jiaoyu luxian de zhaohunqu: pipan Xiangju "Yuanding zhi ge"*' (A siren song to the ghosts of the revisionist line in education: criticism of the Hunan opera *Song of the Teachers*), *Tianjin wenyi*, 1974, 5 (October), 86–88.

64. Hunansheng Xiangjutuan, '*Chedi baolu "Sirenbang" esha Xiangju "Yuanding zhi ge" de taotian zuixing*' (Thoroughly expose the Gang of Four's towering crimes in smothering the Hunan opera *Song of the Teachers*), *Xiangjiang wenyi*, 1976, 6 (December), 97–100. A similar point about the anti-intellectualism of the criticisms of the play is made in Chen Shuliang, ed., *Hunan wenxue shi: dangdai juan* (History of Hunan literature:

contemporary volume), Changsha: Hunan jiaoyu chubanshe, 1998, pp. 150–151, 152–156.

65. Recorded as December 1973 in a post–Cultural Revolution defence of the opera in Hunansheng Xiangjutuan dangzhibu, '*Yiqu Mao zhuxi geming jiaoyu luxian de songge: henpi "Sirenbang" esha "Yuanding zhi ge" de zuixing*' (An ode to Chairman Mao's revolutionary educational line: resolutely criticize the crimes of the Gang of Four in smothering *Song of the Teachers*), *Renmin yinyue*, 1976, 5 (November), 26.

66. The fact that the film adaptation was made at the newsreel studio, rather than at one of the regular film studios, may indicate that the latter steered clear of the opera or that some group in the cultural leadership gave special encouragement to its making. The post–Cultural Revolution sources are silent on this prospect. The three pages on the Cultural Revolution years, in the thirty-page chapter on the history of the newsreel studio in *Sanshiwu nian*, pp. 252–254, make no mention of the film.

67. Items criticized included *Li Yuehua*, a *quyi* story written a veteran performer: Geng Ying, *Quyi zongheng tan* (Comprehensive chat on *quyi*), Shenyang: Chunfeng chubanshe, 1993, p. 46.

68. Chu Lan, '*Ping Jinju "Sanshang Taofeng"*' (Critique of the Shanxi opera *Climbing Peach Peak Three Times*), *Renmin ribao*, 28 February 1974, p. 1, reproduced in *Hongqi*, 1974, 3 (March), 60–65. For a succinct summary of the episode, see Chao Feng, pp. 270–271. For an example of criticism of the opera, see Tong Youwei, '*"Shubei" de mimeng zhuding yao pochan: pipan Jinju "Sanshang Taofeng"* (The doomed pipe-dream of the scoundrels will be bankrupt: criticism of the Shanxi opera *Climbing Peach Peak Three Times*)', *Tianjin wenyi*, 1974, 3 (March), 72–73. See also Wen Yi, '*"Keji fuli" de hei biaoben: pi Jinju "Sanshang Taofeng"*' (An example of 'self-restraint and restoring the rites': criticism of the Shanxi opera *Climbing Peach Peak Three Times*), *Beijing daxue xuebao (zhexue shehui kexue ban)*, 1974, 2 (April), 71–78 and Guangzhou roulei jiagongchang tuzai chejian gongren, Zhongshan daxue Zhongwenxi gongnongbing xueyuan de pipanzu, '*"San shang Taofeng" shi dui wuchanjieji wenhua dageming de fandong*' (*Climbing Peach Peak Three Times* is a reaction against the Great Proletarian Cultural Revolution), *Zhongshan daxue xuebao (zhexue shehui kexue ban)*, 1974, 3 (July), 80–82. Note the combination of abattoir workers and university students in the authorship of this last article.

69. Xiao Lin, '*Shei wei zhen shanmei, shijian shi biaozhun: cong "Sirenbang" pohai "Putao jia xia" deng wudao jiemu tan qi*' (Who is for the true, the good and the beautiful, practice is the criterion?: discussion starting from the Gang of Four's damage to *Under the Grape Trellis* and other dances), *Wudao*, 1978, 5 (May), 3–5. Xiao Lin is vague about details. He includes *Red Plum Ode* (*Hongmei song*) and *Swan Goose* (*Hongyan*) as dances that also came under Gang attack.

70. Criticism began on 30 January 1974 with a *People's Daily* review (p. 2), reprinted in *Red Flag*: Renmin ribao pinglunyuan, '*Edu de yongxin, beilie de shoufa: pipan Andongniaoni paishe de tiwei "Zhongguo" de fan-Hua yingpian*' (Venomous motives, underhand means: criticism of the anti-China film by Antonioni called *China*), *Hongqi*, 1974, 2 (February), 76–82. See also

Renmin ribao, 5 March 1974, p. 3, *Renmin ribao*, 18 March 1974, p. 3, Hua Yan, '*Daodi shi shei jia de* '"*gongju*"*? ping Andongniaoni de "shenbian*"' (Whose "tool" is this really?: criticizing Antonioni's "defence"'), *Hongqi*, 1974, 3 (March), 55–59.

71. At about this time the Dutch communist filmmaker Joris Ivens revisited China and filmed a cinema-verité series on everyday life, *How Yu Kong Moved the Mountain* (Fang Fang, pp. 285–288. The Chinese documentarists who participated learned how to move beyond the didactic (and hectoring) style of the regular Chinese documentary. Synchronized sound-recording, for example, was a major innovation.

72. *Zhongguo xiqu zhi, Sichuan juan*, pp. 680–681.

73. This strong impression is presumably the reason why this particular 13 April 1975 document is among those published in the 1993 provincial opera gazetteer: *Zhongguo xiqu zhi, Hebei juan*, pp. 742–743.

74. *Zhongguo xiqu zhi, Shaanxi juan*, pp. 907–910.

75. *Zhongguo xiqu zhi, Shaanxi juan*, pp. 907–908.

76. See *Zhongguo xiqu zhi, Xinjiang juan*, pp. 677–679.

77. *Hebei ribao*, 31 May 1975, p. 1. A review of a book of poetry by brigade members, published in early 1975, praised the works as models for mass creativity: Shi Zhongping, 74–80.

78. Reported, along with the closing ceremony, in *Xinjiang ribao*, 27 August 1975, p. 1. For a similar reference to the dangers of cultural work in 1971 in Yunnan province, see Chapter Two, section 5.

79. A front-page editorial in the same issue raised the problem of old-style, bourgeois tendencies towards arrogance and selfishness on the part of artists, something the provincial leaders do not appear to have raised at the gathering of participants for the closing ceremony: *Xinjiang ribao*, 27 August 1975, pp. 1 and 4.

80. Details are from Ma Wei, pp. 19–23, 48.

81. This account of the making of *Red Pine Fort* is from Tian Huawen, '*Cong fandong huaju "Hongsong bao" chulong qianhou, kan "Sirenbang" de cuandang yexin*' (From the complete story of the emergence of the reactionary spoken drama *Red Pine Fort* we can see the Gang of Four's ambitions to seize leadership of the Party), *Tianjin wenyi*, 1977, 2 (February), 38–41. See also Zhang Shengkang, '*Yinmou wenyi de biaoben: ping ducao huaju "Hongsong bao*"' (An exemplar of plot literature and art: criticism of the poisonous weed spoken drama *Red Pine Fort*), *Tianjin wenyi*, 1977, 11 (November), 33–36. This latter article provides details of plot and characterization, as does Ma Wei, pp. 20–23.

82. Ma Wei, p. 22.

83. Twelve of these portrayed 'capitalist roaders' in Party organizations at the regional or county level, while eight placed such traitors at the provincial, deputy minister, and ministerial levels: Wang Xinmin (1997), p. 214.

84. Wang Xinmin (1997), pp. 222–225.

85. The background to the Xi'an performance, with something of a defence of it, is provided in Xiang Min, '*"Tian'anmen zhan'ge' xiang shei tiaozhan?*' (*Battlesong of Tian'anmen* was a challenge to whom?), *Renmin yinyue*, 1979, 1 (January), 38–40.

86. Zhai Zixia, p. 482. The other dance was *Chongqing Newspaper Boys* (*Shancheng baotong*). The same episode was the basis of a late 1970s play and a 1979 feature film. Zhou Enlai seems to have only appeared as a projected image in the dance version.

87. Four other films, all made at the Shanghai studio, were cited in the late 1970s as 'plot films' (*yinmou dianying*), including *Chunmiao* (literally, Spring shoots), which was released in 1975: see *Sirenbang shi dianying shiye de sidi*, pp. 70–84 and Hu Xingliang and Zhang Rulin, pp. 290, 294.

88. See annual production chart in Hu Chang, p. 430.

89. Details can be found in *Zhongguo yishu yingpian bianmu*, pp. 987–989.

90. These details on the production and its aftermath are from Hu Chang, pp. 333–336. The State Council's Culture Group (*Wenhuazu*), in operation since 1971, became the Ministry of Culture (*Wenhuabu*) in early 1975.

91. See, for example, Feng Min, pp. 398–399.

92. For a lengthy post-Gang rebuttal of each of the ten criticisms by script-writer Zhang Tianyi, see '*Beibi de jiliang, edu de feibang: dui Jiang Qing yi bang "shi tiao yijian" de huiji*' (Despicable tricks, vicious slanders: counter-attacking Jiang Qing and co's 'ten objections'), *Renmin dianying*, 1976, 6 (October), 21–26. Appended to several articles on the incident is a copy of Jiang Qing's ten points, which cover almost one and a half pages: pp. 32–33. The objections included such points as Zhou Tingshan being shown as a man of action but not as a thinker, the struggles of revolution being presented but not the joys, and that the guidance by Zhou of an engineer smacked of a 'tendency towards persuasion by human feelings' rather than by political truth.

93. This is quoted, among other places, in Hu Chang, p. 335. Liu X X was Liu Qingtang, from the Ministry of Culture: see, for example, Zhou Xiaobang, p. 235. *The Pioneers* features in a summary of 1975's cultural tensions in Xia Xingzhen, '*Dangdai Zhongguo wenyishi shang tanshu de yi ye: 1975 wenyi tiaozheng shulun*' (A peculiar page in contemporary Chinese literary and art history: discussion of 1975's readjustment of literature and art), *Xin wenxue shiliao* (Historical materials on the new literature), 1994, 4 (December), 34–56.

94. Zhou Xiaobang, pp. 232–233.

95. Wang Haowei had graduated from the Beijing Film Academy in 1962 at age twenty-two, when she was assigned to the Beijing studio. Qian Jiang also shared cinematography duties on the project: see credits and synopsis in *Zhongguo yishu yingpian bianmu*, pp. 1014–1015.

96. The quote is from *Renmin dianying*, 1978, 5 (May), 16.

97. Much of this account of the *Haixia* episode is drawn from a two-part account based on interviews with most of the major players by Di Di, *Haixia' shijian benmo*. See also Fu Xiaohong, pp. 136–150. The labor at the locomotive factory is from Part 1, p. 63.

98. Zhou Xiaobang, pp. 232–233. Xie Tieli's creative reworking of the 'three prominences' in his film of the new model opera *Azalea Mountain* in 1974 had also apparently upset Yu Huiyong, the Shanghai composer who had become a leader in the national cultural apparatus in Beijing: Zhou Xiaobang, p. 324.

99. Quoted by Di Di, Part 1, p. 63.

100. Xie Tieli claimed the film took twenty months to make, and confirmed many of these details, in an interview, Beijing, 9 July 2002.
101. This point is obliquely made in Di Di, Part 1, p. 67.
102. Zhou Xiaobang, pp. 235–236. At a 4 April 1975 meeting with film workers representatives, Jiang Qing allegedly complained about the Beijing studio and its 'directors at the center' thinking.
103. Zhou Xiaobang, pp. 237–238; Di Di, Part 2, pp. 79–80.
104. See Di Di, Part 2, especially pp. 79–84.
105. The long letter to Mao is reproduced in Di Di, Part 2, pp. 84–85. It is also quoted at length in Xia Xingzhen, *1975: Wentan fengbao jishi* (1975: Record of the storm in literary circles), Beijing: Zhonggongdang chubanshe, 1995, pp. 59–61.
106. On this episode, see also the lengthy coverage in Zhou Xiaobang, pp. 232–239, 244, and, among others, the chronology in *Dianying nianjian 1981*, pp. 713–714; Qian Jiang, 'Lishi de panjue, zhenli de shengli' (The judgement of history, the triumph of the truth), *Renmin dianying*, 1978, 1 (January), 12–15; Yang Zhijie and Liu Zaifu, 'Ping "Sirenbang" dui "Haixia" de weijiao' (Critique of the Gang of Four's suppression of *Haixia*), *Renmin dianying*, 1978, 2 (March), 2–3.
107. Zhou Xiaobang, p. 246. This Beijing studio history has a section on *Counterattack*: pp. 244–250. Five persons from Tsinghua, seven persons from Peking University, and six studio personnel formed the creative group.
108. Zhou Xiaobang, p. 247. In May 1976, before the final script was finished, the crew went to Zhongshan University in Guangzhou to scout for locations. They filmed outside shots in July on the campus, according to an article by Zhongwenxi da pipanzu, 'Wei "Sirenbang" cuandangduoquan mingluokaidao de da ducao: ping fandong dianying "Fanji"' (A great poisonous weed to prepare the way for the Gang of Four's seizure of Party power: criticizing the reactionary film *Counterattack*), *Zhongshan daxue xuebao (zhexue shehui kexue ban)*, 1977, 1 (January), 68. In an interview in 2002, Li Wenhua said the filming took about half a year and post-production another half year: Beijing, 3 July 2002.
109. See the chapter on *Fanji*, written by the Beijing studio's criticism group, 'Huozhenjiashi de yinmo dianying: dui yingpian "Fanji" de zai pipan' (Truly plot literature and art: further criticism of the film *Counterattack*) in *Sirenbang shi dianying shiye sidi*, pp. 55–69, especially pp. 56–57.
110. Zhou Xiaobang, p. 245.
111. For credits and synopsis, see *Zhongguo yishu yingpian bianmu*, pp. 1056–1057.
112. For somewhat defensive praise of *Chunmiao*, which remains unavailable in China on VCD or DVD, see Li Li, 'Weihe fuxiu er qu?' (Why shake one's sleeve in displeasure?), *Yunnan wenyi*, 1976, 4 (April), 77–78.
113. In the sixty anti-'capitalist roader' (*zouzi pai*) films apparently in production in 1976, twenty-one lower-level leaders, twelve county-level Party secretaries, nine heads of central ministries, and one vice-premier were presented as 'capitalist roaders' in the CCP. Among other places, the figures are given in Chen Huangmei, Vol. 1, p. 344.

114. Perry Link notes that Mao similarly would only listen to traditional *xiangsheng* (comic dialogues) at regular private performances, according to the *xiangsheng* master Hou Baolin: Perry Link, 'The Genie and the Lamp: Revolutionary *Xiangsheng*', in McDougall, *Popular Chinese Literature*, p. 109.

115. The actor-administrator Qi Yingcai gives a vivid account of this episode in '*Ji neibu paishe chuantongxi shimo*' (Remembering the ins and outs of the restricted filming of traditional operas), *Shanghai wenhua shizhi tongxun*, 19 (May 1992), 31–37.

116. *Zhongguo yishu yingpian bianmu*, pp. 1046–1050, 1060–1070, 1078–1090, 1109–1119, respectively. Four of the Shanghai total are listed as products of the 'Shanghai Worker-Peasant-Soldier Film Technical Factory': pp. 1087–1090. See also Hu Chang, p. 325.

117. Chen was assigned this task in February 1976 by Jiang Qing herself, according to Di Di, Part 2, p. 87.

118. Qi Yingcai, pp. 36–37. Jiang Qing showed American films to Qi and others, to contrast the clarity of the Hollywood with the local product. Eastman film-stock was then imported for some of the old operas.

119. This point is made in Zhou Xiaobang, pp. 216–217.

120. On the dance drama, see Wang Kefen and Long Yinpei, pp. 211–215. The 1959 film is listed in *Zhongguo yishu yingpian bianmu*, pp. 518–520.

121. The film is listed in *Zhongguo yishu yingpian bianmu*, pp. 1053–1054.

SIX: CONCLUSION: FORCING MODERNITY

1. This book has not included coverage of sport, conventionally grouped with literature and art in Chinese cultural discourse. The themes presented here apply to sports also. These include the emphasis on mass participation and the amateur, the use of sports to symbolize national strength and pride (with the breaking of world records and participation in international competitions), the updating of folk Chinese sports, and resources devoted to specialist athletes and their trainers using modern techniques. Two recent general histories are Li Xiubo, *Zhonghua renmin gongheguo tiyushi jianbian* (Outline history of PRC sport), Beijing: Beijing tiyu daxue chubanshe, 2001, and Wu Shaozu, ed., *Zhonghua renmin gongheguo tiyushi (1949–1998) zonghejuan* (PRC sports history: comprehensive volume), Beijing: Zhongguo shuji chubanshe, 1999. See also the substantial, seventy-page chapter on the Cultural Revolution period in Chen Zhenhua, Lu Enting, and Li Shiming, *Zhongguo ticao yundong shi* (History of the Chinese gymnastics movement), Wuhan: Wuhan chubanshe, 1990.

2. The chapter titled 'Cultural Revolutions' in Richard Overy, pp. 349–391 offers intriguing parallels and differences with Chinese experiences in very different temporal and cultural contexts.

Bibliography

For ease of using the footnotes, this bibliography includes all books, key articles, and items for which there is more than one reference. It also lists publications by two of the most prolific Chinese writers on Cultural Revolution culture: Wang Yao and Yang Jian.

1973 quanguo zong shumu (National book catalogue, 1973), Beijing: Zhonghua shuju, 1976.

A Jia and others, *Pingyuan youjidui (Guerrillas on the plain)*, Beijing: Zhongguo xiju chubanshe, 1999.

A Pei, '"Sirenbang" jiqi yudang zai qunzhong wenyi zhong zhizao de san da yuan'an' (Three big cases of injustice created in popular literature and art by the Gang of Four and their confederates), *Shanghai wenhua shizhi tongxun*, 49 (July 1998), 43–47.

An Shiming, ed., *Beijing meishu huodong dashiji, 1949–1989* (Record of major events in Beijing art activities), Beijing: Beijingshi meishujia xiehui, 1992 (internal circulation).

Andrews, Julia F., *Painters and Politics in the People's Republic of China, 1949–1979*, Berkeley: University of California Press, 1994.

Bai Shiyuan, '*1950 nian 2 yue – 1965 nian 5 yue Shanghai xiqu, quyi huiyan jiyao*' (Summary of opera and *quyi* joint performances in Shanghai, February 1950 to May 1965), *Shanghai wenhua shizhi tongxun*, 23 (December 1992), 29.

Bakken, Børge, *The Exemplary Society: Human Improvement, Social Control, and the Dangers of Modernity in China*, Oxford: Oxford University Press, 2000.

Becker, Jasper, *Hungry Ghosts: Mao's Secret Famine*, New York: Free Press, 1996.

Berry, Chris, 'Stereotypes and ambiguities: An examination of the feature films of the Chinese Cultural Revolution,' *Journal of Asian Culture (UCLA)*, 6 (1982), 46–47.

Bian Meng, *Zhongguo gangqin wenhua zhi xingcheng yu fazhan* (The formation and development of piano culture in China), Beijing: Huayue chubanshe, 1996.

Cai Xiang, Fei Zhen, and Wang Yao, 'Wen-ge yu xushi: guanyu Wen-ge yanjiu de duihua' (The Cultural Revolution and narrative: A dialogue on Cultural Revolution research), Dangdai zuojia pinglun, 2002, 4 (July), 56–65.

Chang, Jung, Wild Swans: Three Generations of Chinese Women, London: Flamingo, 1993.

Chao Feng, 'Wenhua dageming' cidian (Dictionary of the Great Cultural Revolution), Hong Kong: Ganglong chubanshe, 1993.

Chen Changqian, ed., Dangdai Zhongguo sheying yishu shi (1949–1989) (History of contemporary Chinese photographic art), Beijing: Zhongguo sheying chubanshe, 1995.

Chen Huangmei, gen. ed., Dangdai Zhongguo dianying (Contemporary Chinese film), Beijing: Zhongguo shehui kexue chubanshe, 1989, 2 vols.

Chen Qiguang, Zhongguo dangdai wenxue shi (History of contemporary Chinese literature), Guangzhou: Jinan daxue chubanshe, 1998.

Chen Shuliang, ed., Hunan wenxue shi: dangdai juan (History of Hunan literature: Contemporary volume), Changsha: Hunan jiaoyu chubanshe, 1998.

Chen Sihe, ed., Zhongguo dangdai wenxue shi jiaocheng (Lectures on contemporary Chinese literary history), Shanghai: Fudan daxue chubanshe, 1999.

Chen, Xiaomei, Acting the Right Part: Political Theater and Popular Drama in Contemporary China, Honolulu: University of Hawai'i Press, 2002.

Chen Zhenhua, Lu Enting, and Li Shiming, Zhongguo ticao yundong shi (History of the Chinese gymnastics movement), Wuhan: Wuhan chubanshe, 1990.

Cheng Guangwei, Wenxue xiangxiang yu wenxue guojia: Zhongguo dangdai wenxue yanjiu (1949–1976) (Literary imagination and literary state: contemporary Chinese literature), Kaifeng: Henan daxue chubanshe, 2005.

Clark, Paul, Chinese Cinema: Culture and Politics since 1949, New York: Cambridge University Press, 1987.

Clark, Paul, "Ethnic minorities in Chinese films: Cinema and the exotic," East-West Film Journal, 1, 2 (1987), 15–31.

Clark, Paul, Reinventing China: A Generation and Its Films, Hong Kong: Chinese University Press, 2005.

Dai Jiafang, 'Wutuobang li de aige: "Wen-ge" qijian zhiqing gequ de yanjiu' (Mournful songs in Utopia: research on "educated youth" songs in the Cultural Revolution), Zhongguo yinyuexue, 2002, 3 (September), 5–25.

Dai Jiafang, Yangbanxi de fengfengyuyu: Jiang Qing, yangbanxi ji neimu (The trials and hardships of the model performances: Jiang Qing, the model performances and the inside story), Beijing: Zhishi chubanshe, 1995.

Dai Jiafang, Zou xiang huimie: 'Wen-ge' Wenhuabu zhang Yu Huiyong chenfu lu (Heading towards destruction: The rise and fall of the Cultural Revolution Minister of Culture Yu Huiyong), Beijing: Guangming ribao chubanshe, 1994.

Deqinge'erma and Zhai Jiannong, Zai dahai li hangxing: Yu Yang zhuan (Sailing on the seas: A biography of Yu Yang), Beijing: Zhongguo dianying chubanshe, 2007.

Di Di, '"Haixia" shijian benmo' (Ins and outs of the 'Haixia' affair), Dianying yishu, 1994, 3 (June), 61–69 (Part 1), and 1994, 4 (August), 79–90 (Part 2).

Di Di, '"Huohong de niandai": "Wen-ge" gushi yingpian de xiandao' (Fiery years: forerunners of Cultural Revolution feature films), Dianying yishu, 1993, 4 (August), 81–86, 93.

Di Di, '"*Juelie*" *jishi yu fenxi*' (Record and analysis of *Breaking with Old Ideas*), *Dianying yishu*, 1993, 2 (April), 76–84.

Di Di, '*Shenghuo shi yishu de yuanquan*' (Life is the fountainhead of art: interview with Xie Tieli), *Dianying yishu*, 1994, 1 (February), 7–15, 73.

Di Di, '*Shoupi Wen-ge gushipian shezhi shimo*' (The ins and outs of the production of the first group of Cultural Revolution feature films: Su Yun interview), *Dianying yishu*, 1995, 3 (June), 87–91.

Ding Xuelei, '*Baleiwu geming de xinhua: ping balei wuju "Baimaonü"*' (A new flower in the ballet revolution: critique of the ballet dance-drama *White-Haired Girl*), *Wudao*, 1965, 4 (August), 15–16.

Ding Xuelei, '*Renmin zhanzheng de zhuangli songge: ping gangqin xiezouqu "Huanghe"*' (A magnificent ode to people's war: critique of the piano concerto *The Yellow River*), *Hongqi*, 1970, 5 (May), 63–70.

Dong Huaizhou, ed., *Tian'anmen geming shiwen xuan* (Selected revolutionary poems and prose from Tian'anmen), Beijing: Beijing di'er waiguoyu xueyuan, 1977.

Dong Huaizhou, ed., *Tian'anmen shiwen xuan* (Selected poems and prose from Tian'anmen), Beijing: Beijing chubanshe, 1979, 2 vols.

Duan Jingli, *Huxian nongmin hua chenfulu* (Record of the changing fortunes of the Hu County peasant painting), Kaifeng: Henan daxue chubanshe, 2005.

Egan, Michael, "A Notable Sermon: The Subtext of Hao Ran's Fiction," in McDougall, *Popular Chinese Literature*, 224–241.

Esherick, Joseph W., Paul G. Pickowicz, and Andrew G. Walder, eds., *The Chinese Cultural Revolution as History*, Stanford, CA: Stanford University Press, 2006.

Evans, Harriet, and Stephanie Donald, eds., *Picturing Power in the People's Republic of China: Posters of the Cultural Revolution*, Lanham, MD: Rowman & Littlefield, 1999.

Fang Fang, *Zhongguo jilupian fazhan shi* (History of the development of Chinese documentary films), Beijing: Zhongguo xiju chubanshe, 2003.

Feng Min, *Zhongguo dianying yishu shigang (1896–1986)* (Survey of Chinese film art), Tianjin: Nankai daxue chubanshe, 1992.

Fu Xiaohong, *Liangbu kua shengping: Xie Tieli koushu shilu* (Two steps bestriding life: Oral history of Xie Tieli), Beijing: Zhongguo dianying chubanshe, 2005.

Galikowski, Maria, *Art and Politics in China, 1949–1984*, Hong Kong: Chinese University Press, 1998.

Gao Jinxiao, '*Cuanduo yu pohai: Jiang Qing chaoshou Jingju xiandaixi "Zhiqu Weihushan" de yinmou*' (Usurpation and persecution: Jiang Qing's schemes to meddle with the modern Peking opera *Taking Tiger Mountain by Strategy*), *Shanghai wenhua shizhi tongxun*, 46 (September 1997), 62–63.

Gao Wensheng, ed., *Zhongguo dangdai xiju wenxue shi* (History of contemporary Chinese drama writing), Nanning: Guangxi renmin chubanshe, 1990.

Gao Xiaojian, *Zhongguo xiqu dianying shi* (History of Chinese opera films), Beijing: Wenhua yishu chubanshe, 2005.

Gao Yilong and Li Xiao, *Zhongguo xiqu xiandaixi shi* (History of modern Chinese operas), Shanghai: Shanghai wenhua chubanshe, 1999.

Ge Yihong, ed., *Zhongguo huaju tongshi* (General history of Chinese spoken drama), Beijing: Wenhua yishu chubanshe, 2000.

'*Geming gequ xuan*' (Selected revolutionary songs), *Hongqi*, 1965, 3 (March), 31–49.

Geng Ying, *Quyi zongheng tan* (Comprehensive chat on *quyi*), Shenyang: Chunfeng chubanshe, 1993.

Guang Weiran (words), Xian Xinghai (music), *Huanghe dahechang: jinian Xian Xinghai shishi sanshi zhou nian* (Yellow River Cantata: Commemorating thirty years since the passing of Xian Xinghai), Beijing: Renmin yinyue chubanshe, 1975.

Hai Mo dianying juben xuanji (Selected film scripts of Hai Mo), Beijing: Zhongguo dianying chubanshe, 1979.

Hanan, Patrick, *Chinese Fiction of the Nineteenth and Early Twentieth Centuries: Essays*, New York: Columbia University Press, 2004.

Hanan, Patrick, *The Invention of Li Yu*, Cambridge, MA: Harvard University Press, 1988.

He Lüting, '*Yao Wenpi yu Debiaoxi*' (Yao Wen-fart and Debussy), *Xueshu yuekan*, 1979, 1 (January), 47–54.

He Man and Shen Hongxin, '*Jingju "Haigang" zai chuangzuo yanchu de qianqianhouhou*' (Background to the repeated creation and performance of *On the Docks*), in Li Taicheng and Yao Yu, 29–49.

Hong Zicheng, *Zhongguo dangdai wenxue shi*, Beijing: Beijing daxue chubanshe, 1999.

Hsu, Kai-yu, *The Chinese Literary Scene: A Writer's Visit to the People's Republic*, New York: Vintage Books, 1974.

Hsu, Kai-yu, "Contemporary Chinese Poetry and Its Search for an Ideal Form," in McDougall, *Popular Chinese Literature*, 244–265.

Hu Chang, *Xin Zhongguo dianying de yaolan* (The cradle of new China's film), Changchun: Jilin wenshi chubanshe, 1986.

Hu Xingliang and Zhang Ruilin, *Zhongguo dianying shi* (History of Chinese film), Beijing: Zhongyang guangbo dianshi daxue chubanshe, 1995.

Hua Jian and Guan Defu, *Guanyu jige xiqu lilun wenti de lunzheng* (Debates on several theoretical issues regarding opera), Beijing: Wenhua yishu chubanshe, 1986.

Jia Zhigang, *Maixiang xiandai de lao xiju* (Old drama striding toward modernity), Beijing: Zhongguo xiju chubanshe, 1996.

Jiang Boyan, '*Shanghai yinyue chuangzuo ziliao zhaiji, er*' (Notes on materials on musical creation in Shanghai, 2), *Shanghai wenhua shizhi tongxun*, 42 (September 1996), 48.

Jiang Qing, '*Tan Jingju geming*' (Talking about the revolution in Peking opera), *Hongqi*, 1967, 6 (June), 25–27.

Jiang Zhishui, '*Cong "Ludang huozhong" dao "Shajiabang"*' (From 'Sparks in the reeds' to Shajiabang'), *Xiju bao*, 1965, 2 (February), 34–37.

Jiang Zuhui, '*Xinwei de huiyi: wuju "Hongse niangzijun" de chuangzuo licheng*' (A bitter memory: the creative process of *The Red Detachment of Women*), *Wudao*, 1987, 11 (November), 22–23.

Jones, Stephen, *Plucking the Wind: Lives of Village Musicians in Old and New China*, Leiden: CHIME Foundation, 2004.

Ju Qihong, *20 shiji Zhongguo yinyue* (Twentieth-century Chinese music), Qingdao: Qingdao chubanshe, 1992.

King, Richard, 'Models and Misfits: Rusticated Youth in Three Novels of the 1970s,' in William A. Joseph, Christine P. W. Wong, and David Zweig, eds., *New Perspectives on the Cultural Revolution*, Harvard Contemporary China Series: 8, Cambridge: Council on East Asian Studies, 1991, 243–264.

King, Richard, 'Revisionism and Transformation in the Cultural Revolution Novel,' *Modern Chinese Literature*, 7, 1 (1993), 105–130.

King, Richard, ed., *Art and the Artist in Cultural Revolution China*, Vancouver: University of British Columbia Press, forthcoming.

Kong, Shuyu, 'For Reference Only: Restricted Publications and Distribution of Foreign Literature during the Cultural Revolution,' *Yishu: Journal of Contemporary Chinese Art*, 1, 2 (Fall 2002), 76–85.

Kraus, Richard Curt, *The Party and the Art in China: The New Politics of Culture*, Lanham, MD: Rowman & Littlefield, 2004.

Kraus, Richard Curt, *Pianos and Politics in China: Middle-Class Ambitions and the Struggle over Western Music*, New York: Oxford University Press, 1989.

Laing, Elaine Johnston, *The Winking Owl: Art in the People's Republic of China*, Berkeley: University of California Press, 1988.

Leung, Laifong, *Morning Sun: Interviews with Chinese Writers of the Lost Generation*, Armonk: M. E. Sharpe, 1994.

Li Bingshu, '*Mao zhuxi de geming wenyi luxian gei le wo xin de yishu shengming*' (Chairman Mao's revolutionary line in art has given me a new life in art) in *Geming xiandai Jingju 'Longjiang song' pinglun ji* (Collection of articles on the revolutionary modern Peking opera *Song of the Dragon River*), Beijing: Renmin wenxue chubanshe, 1975, 178–185.

Li Gang, ed., *Zhongguo geju gushi ji* (Collected Chinese musical drama stories), Beijing: Renmin yishu chubanshe, 1988.

Li Gucheng, *Zhongguo dalu zhengzhi shuyu* (Chinese mainland political terminology), Hong Kong: Zhongwen daxue chubanshe, 2nd ed., 1992, 107.

Li Qingyue, *Ningxia dianying shihua* (Historical narrative of film in Ningxia), Yinchuan: Ningxia renmin chubanshe, 1995.

Li Taicheng and Yao Yu, *Lüeduo yu pohia: jielu 'Jiang Qing fangeming jituan' zai Shanghai wenhua xitong de zuixing* (Plunder and persecution: exposing the crimes of the 'Jiang Qing anti-revolutionary clique' in the Shanghai city cultural apparatus), Shanghai: Shanghaishi wenhua shizhi bangongshi, 1999.

Li Wei and Ren Fang, *Zhongguo xiandai, dangdai wudao fazhan gailun* (Outline of the development of modern and contemporary Chinese dance), Chengdu: Sichuan daxue chubanshe, 2006.

Li Xifan, '*Zai liang tiao luxian jianrui douzheng zhong dansheng de yishu mingzhu: cong balei wuju "Baimaonü" de zai chuangzuo kan Zhou Yang wenyi heixian ji qi zong houtai de "xie zhenshi" miulun de pochan*' (A pearl born from the sharp conflict between the two lines: evidence from the creation of *White-Haired Girl* of the bankruptcy of the 'write about real life' fallacy of Zhou Yang and those backstage), *Guangming ribao*, 19 May 1967, 5–6.

Li Xiubo, *Zhonghua renmin gongheguo tiyushi jianbian* (Outline history of PRC sport), Beijing: Beijing tiyu daxue chubanshe, 2001.

Liang Bingkun, *Beijing Renyi de gushi* (Story of Beijing People's Art Theatre), Beijing: Shiyue wenyi chubanshe, 1992.

Liang Lun, '*Yao suqing "Sirenbang" zai wudao meixue shang de liudu*' (We should cleanse the baneful influence of the Gang of Four on dance aesthetics), *Wudao* (Dance), 1979, 1 (January), 11–13.

Link, Perry, "The Genie and the Lamp: Revolutionary *Xiangsheng*," in McDougall, *Popular Chinese Literature*, 83–111.

Link, Perry, *The Uses of Literature: Life in the Socialist Chinese Literary System*, Princeton, NJ: Princeton University Press, 2000.

Liu Fuchun, *Zhongguo dangdai xinshi biannianshi (1966–1976)* (Annals of new poetry in contemporary China), Kaifeng: Henan daxue chubanshe, 2005.

Liu Gao and Shi Feng, eds., *Xin Zhongguo chuban wushinian jishi* (Chronology of fifty years of New China's publishing), Beijing: Xinhua chubanshe, 1999.

Liu Housheng xiqu changduan wen (Long and short writings on opera by Liu Housheng), Beijing: Zhongguo xiju chubanshe, 1996.

Liu Jialing, *Jiyi xianhong* (Memories bright red), Beijing: Zhongguo qingnian chubanshe, 2002.

Liu Jianxun, Liu Jianfeng, and Lu Yuan, eds., *Zhongguo dangdai yingshi wenxue* (Literature of contemporary Chinese film and television), Nanning: Guangxi renmin chubanshe, 1986.

Liu Xinsheng, *Ershi shiji Zhongguo dianying yishu liubian* (Developments in twentieth-century Chinese film art), Beijing: Xinhua chunbanshe, 1999.

Loh Wai-fong, 'From Romantic Love to Class Struggle: Some Reflections on the Film *Liu Sanjie*,' in Bonnie S. McDougall, ed., *Popular Chinese Literature*, 165–176.

Lu Jianhua, *Wang Zengqi zhuan* (Biography of Wang Zengqi), Nanjing: Jiangsu wenyi chubanshe, 1998.

Lü Peng and Yi Dan, *Zhongguo xiandai yishu shi, 1979–1989* (History of modern Chinese art), Changsha: Hunan meishu chubanshe, 1992.

Lu Qun, '"*Wenhua dageming*" qijian de yanchu guanli' (Performance management in the Cultural Revolution period), *Shanghai wenhua shizhi tongxun*, 40 (March 1996), 46.

Lu Wenqin, comp., *Jingju xiandaixi changpian qupu xuan* (Selected recorded scores of modern Peking operas), Shanghai: Shanghai wenhua chubanshe, 1965.

Ma Shaobo, gen. ed., *Zhongguo Jingju shi* (A history of China's Peking opera), Beijing: Zhongguo xiju chubanshe, 1999.

MacFarquhar, Roderick, "On Photographs," *The China Quarterly*, 46 (June 1971), 289–307.

MacFarquhar, Roderick, *The Origins of the Cultural Revolution, Volume 2: The Great Leap Forward*, New York: Columbia University Press, 1983.

MacFarquhar, Roderick, and Michael Schoenhals, *Mao's Last Revolution*, Cambridge, MA: Belknap Press of Harvard University Press, 2006.

Mackerras, Colin P., *The Rise of the Peking Opera, 1770–1870: Social Aspects of the Theatre in Manchu China*, Oxford: Clarendon Press, 1972.

Mao Hui, ed., *Xin Zhongguo wudao shidian* (A chronology of New China's dance), Shanghai: Shanghai yinyue chubanshe, 2005.

Mao Tse-tung, *Selected Works, Volume III*, Beijing: Foreign Languages Press, 1965.

McDougall, Bonnie S., *Fictional Authors, Imaginary Audiences: Modern Chinese Literature in the Twentieth Century*, Hong Kong: Chinese University Press, 2003.

McDougall, Bonnie S., trans. and ed., *Mao Zedong's 'Talks at the Yan'an Conference on Literature and Art': A translation of the 1943 text with commentary*, Ann Arbor: Center for Chinese Studies, University of Michigan, 1980.

McDougall, Bonnie S., "Poems, Poets and *Poetry* 1976: An Exercise in the Typology of Modern Chinese Literature," *Contemporary China*, 2, 4 (1978), 76–124.

McDougall, Bonnie S., ed., *Popular Chinese Literature and Performing Arts in the People's Republic of China, 1949–1979*, Berkeley: University of California Press, 1984.

McDougall, Bonnie S., and Kam Louie, *The Literature of China in the Twentieth Century*, New York, Columbia University Press, 1997.

Miao Jianhua and Hong Yun, *Zhongguo yinyue chubu* (Introduction to Chinese music), Guangzhou: Guangdong renmin chubanshe, 2000.

New Zealand Ministry of Foreign Affairs and Trade, files related to the 1975 visit to China of the New Zealand National Youth Orchestra, held in Archives New Zealand, Wellington.

Nie Er Xian Xinghai gequ xuan: jinian Nie Er shishi sishi zhou nian, Xian Xinghai shishi sanshi zhou nian (Selected songs by Nie Er and Xian Xinghai: commemorating forty years since the passing of Nie Er and thirty years since Xian Xinghai's passing), Beijing: Renmin yinyue chubanshe, 1975.

Ouyang Wenbin and Xu Jingxian, '*Wei wuchanjieji yingxiong lizhuan: tan Jingju "Hongdeng ji" de juben gaibian*' (To glorify proletarian heroes: on the script revisions of the Peking opera *The Red Lantern*), *Xiju bao*, 1965, 4 (April), 30–33.

Overy, Richard, *The Dictators: Hitler's Germany and Stalin's Russia*, London: Allen Lane, 2004

Qi Yingcai, '*Ji neibu paishe chuantongxi shimo*' (Remembering the ins and outs of the restricted filming of traditional operas), *Shanghai wenhua shizhi tongxun*, 19 (May 1992), 31–37.

Qian Haoliang, '*Suzao gaoda de wuchanjieji yingxiong xingxiang*' (Mold great proletarian hero figures), *Hongqi*, 1967, 8 (May), 66–70.

Qian Haoliang, '*Wei geming er yanxi*' (Performing for the revolution), *Xiju bao*, 1965, 1 (January), 23–24.

Qian Zhenhua, '*Huiyi balei wuju "Baimao nü" de dansheng*' (Recalling the birth of the ballet *The White-Haired Girl*), *Shanghai wenhua shizhi tongxun*, 15 (August 1991), 41–43.

Qing Ming, ed., *Xuqu: 'nuli fanying Wenhua dageming de douzheng shenghuo' zhengwen xuan* (Prelude: purposefully reflecting the life of struggle in the Great Cultural Revolution selection of solicited articles), Shanghai: Shanghai renmin chubanshe, 1975.

Qiu Sengrong yishu pinglun ji (Collected articles on the art of Qiu Shengrong), Beijing: Zhongguo xiju chubanshe, 1984.

Ren Guilin, '*A Jia de yishu daolu*' (A Jia's artistic road), *Xiqu yishu* (Opera art), 1986, 2 (February), 77–80, 85.

Renmin ribao pinglunyuan, '*Edu de yongxin, beilie de shoufa: pipan Andongniaoni paishe de tiwei "Zhongguo" de fan-Hua yingpian*' (Venomous motives, underhand means: criticism of the anti-China film by Antonioni called *China*), *Hongqi*, 1974, 2 (February), 76–82.

Sanshiwu nian, see Zhongguo dianyingjia xiehui dianyingshi yanjiubu.

Schrift, Melissa, *The Biography of a Chairman Mao Badge: The Creation and Mass Consumption of a Personality Cult*, New Brunswick, NJ: Rutgers University Press, 2001.

Schwartz, Benjamin I., *In Search of Wealth and Power: Yen Fu and the West*, New York: Harper & Row, 1964.

Shan Wanli, *Zhongguo jilu dianying shi* (History of Chinese documentary film), Beijing: Zhongguo dianying chubanshe, 2005.

Shanghai Jiangnan zaochuangchang chuangzuo zu, Shanghai gejuyuan wenyi jingqidui, '*Jinjunhao*' (Bugle call), *Chaoxia*, 1974, 10 (March), 68–73.

Shanghai Jingjutuan 'Haigang' juzu, '*Fanying shehuizhuyi shidai gongren jieji de zhandou shenghuo: geming xiandai Jingju "Haigang" de chuangzuo tihui*' (Reflecting the fighting life of the working class in the socialist era: the creative experience of the revolutionary modern Peking opera *On the Docks*), *Hongqi* (Red Flag), 1972, 3 (March), 37–45.

Shanghaishi wudao xuexiao, '*Balei wuju "Baimaonü" de chuangzuo, yanchu*' (The creation and performance of the ballet dance-drama *White-Haired Girl*), *Shanghai wenhua shizhi tongxun*, 40 (March 1996), 30–34.

Shanghai wenhua shizhi tongxun (Bulletin of the Shanghai cultural history gazetteer), Nos. 1–52 (1988–1999).

Sirenbang shi dianying shiye de sidi, see Zhongguo dianyingjia xiehui.

Song Yingli and others, *Zhongguo qikan fazhan shi* (History of the development of Chinese periodicals), Kaifeng: Henan daxue chubanshe, 2000.

Su Jinan, ed., *Zhongguo jin, xiandai (1840–1989) yinyue jiaoyu shi jinian* (Chronology of the history of modern musical education in China), Jinan: Shandong youyi chubanshe, 2000.

Tan Jiewen, '*Sanshinian lai shi yu fei: "yangbanxi" sanshizhou dianji*' (Thirty years of positive and negative: saluting the thirtieth anniversary of the 'model performances'), *Wenyi lilun yu piping* 1999, 4 (July), 45–52.

Tang, Xiaobing, *Chinese Modern: The Heroic and the Quotidien*, Durham, NC: Duke University Press, 2000.

Tian Jingqing, *Beijing dianying ye shiji, 1949–1990* (Achievements of the Beijing film industry), Beijing: Zhongguo dianying chubanshe, 1999.

Tian Peize, '*Jianguo 45 nian lai de Shanghai qunzhong geyong huodong*' (Shanghai mass singing activities in the 45 years after 1949), *Shanghai wenhua shizhi tongxun*, 34 (October 1994), 53–57.

Tong Xiangling (recorded by Qian Youzhong), '*Wo shi zenyang zai biaoyan yishu shang chuangzao Yang Zirong yi jiao de*' (How I created the Yang Zirong character with performing art), *Shanghai wenhua shi zhi tongxun*, 25 (April 1993), 37–39.

van Crevel, Maghiel, *Language Shattered: Contemporary Chinese Poetry and Duoduo*, Leiden: Research School CNWS, 1996.

Wang Anting, ed., *Mao Zedong xiangzhang tupu* (Illustrated catalogue of Mao badges), Beijing: Zhongguo shudian chubanshe, 1993.

Wang Jiaping, *Wenhua dageming shiqi shige yanjiu* (Research on Great Cultural Revolution poetry), Kaifeng: Henan daxue chubanshe, 2004.

Wang Jue, Wang Jingshou, and Teng Tianxiang [Fujita Kaoru], *Zhongguo xiang-sheng shi* (History of Chinese comic dialogues), Beijing: Beijing yanshan chubanshe, 1995.

Wang Kefen and Long Yinpei, *Zhongguo jin xiandai dangdai wudao fazhan shi* (History of modern and contemporary development of Chinese dance), Beijing: Renmin yinyue chubanshe, 1999.

Wang Kefen, Long Yinpei, and Zhang Shiling, *20 shiji Zhongguo wudao* (Twentieth-century Chinese dance), Qingdao: Qingdao chubanshe, 1992.

Wang Lian, '*Dongluan niandai de yingshi manyi: ji wo yu Xie Jin de chuangzuo youyi*' (Pleased with filming during the era of chaos: my creative friendship with Xie Jin), *Dianying yishu*, 1994, 3 (June), 75–78, 74.

Wang Mingxian and Yan Shanchun, *Xin Zhongguo meishu tushi, 1966–1976* (Illustrated history of New China's fine art), Beijing: Zhongguo qingnian chubanshe, 2000.

Wang Renyuan, *Jingju 'yangbanxi' yinyue lungang* (An outline theory of the music of the 'model performance' Peking operas), Beijing: Renmin yinyue chubanshe, 1999.

Wang Xinmin, *Zhongguo dangdai huaju yishu yanbian shi* (Evolution of contemporary Chinese play art), Hangzhou: Zhejiang daxue chubanshe, 2000

Wang Xinmin, *Zhongguo dangdai xiju shigang* (An outline history of modern Chinese drama), Beijing: Shehui kexue wenxian chubanshe, 1997.

Wang Yao, *Chidao de pipan* (Tardy criticism), Zhengzhou: Daxiang chubanshe, 2000.

Wang Yao, '*Fei zhishifenzi xiezuo: "Wen-ge wenxue" de yizhong chaoliu yu ying-xiang*' (Writing by non-intellectuals: a current and deviation in 'Cultural Revolution literature'), *Suzhou daxue xuebao (zhexue shehuikexue ban)* (Suzhou University journal. philosophy and social science issue), 2000, 2 (April), 88–96.

Wang Yao, '*Guanyu "Wen-ge wenxue" de shiyi yu yanjiu*' (On the interpretation of and research on 'Cultural Revolution literature'), *Wenyi lilun yanjiu* (Literature and art theory research), 1999, 5 (October), 57–64.

Wang Yao, '*Maodu zhongzhong de "guodu zhuangtai": guanyu xin shiqi wenxue "yuantou" kaocha zhi yi*' (Numerous contradictions of 'hyper conditions': one investigation of the 'fountainhead' of New Period literature), *Dangdai zuojia pinglun* (Review of contemporary writers), 2000, 5 (October), 22–32.

Wang Yao, '*Sixiang licheng de zhuanhuan yu zhuliu huayu de shengchan: guanyu "Wen-ge wenxue" de yige cemian yanjiu*' (The process of ideological transformation and the birth of mainstream discourse: sideways research on 'Cultural Revolution literature'), *Dangdai zuojia pinglun*, 2001, 4 (August), 19–27.

Wang Yao, '*"Wen-ge" dui "Wu-si" ji "xiandai wenyi" de xushu yu chanshi*' (A Cultural Revolution description and interpretation of May Fourth and modern literature), *Dangdai zuojia pinglun*, 2002, 1 (January), 61–102.

Wang Yao, '*"Wen-ge wenxue" jishi*' (Chronology of 'Cultural Revolution' literature), *Dangdai zuojia pinglun* (Contemporary writer reviews), 2000, 4 (April), 18–28.

Wang Yao, '*Wen-ge zhuliu yishi xingtai yu Hao Ran chuangzuo de yanbian*' (Cultural Revolution mainstream thought and the evolution of Hao Ran's writing), *Suzhou daxue xuebao (zhexue shehuikexue ban)*, 1999, 3 (May), 48–54.

Wang Yao, '*Wen-ge zhuliu wenyi sixiang de goucheng yu yunzuo*' (Cultural Revolution mainstream ideology's form and functioning), *Huaqiao daxue xuebao (zhesheban)* (Huaqiao University journal: philosophy and social science issue), 1999, 2 (June) 56–62.

Wang Yao, *Zhongguo dangdai sanwen shi* (History of contemporary Chinese prose), Guiyang: Guizhou renmin chubanshe, 1994.

Wang Yuhe, '*Zhongguo xiandai hechang yinyue (1946–1976)*' (Modern Chinese choral music), *Yinyue yanjiu* (Music research), 1989, 2 (June), 52–54.

Wang Yuhe, chief ed., *Zhongguo xiandai yinyue shigang 1949–1986* (Survey of Chinese modern music), Beijing: Huawen chubanshe, 1991.

Wang Zhi'an, *Hongtian juechang: 'Shouzu yuan' nisu qiguan* (Sensational perfection: the wonder of the Rent-Collection Courtyard clay sculptures), Chengdu: Tiandi chubanshe, 2001.

Wenhuabu Beijing bianzhe kan, *Jingju xiandaixi guanmo yanchu dahui jiemudan (hedingben)* (Modern Peking opera performance convention playbills (collected)), 1964, unpaged.

Wenxue yishu yanjiuyuan yinyue wudao bu wudaozu, '*Jiang Qing shi pohuai wuju "Baimaonü" de zuiku huoshou: geming xiandai wuju "Baimaonü" diaocha baogao*' (Jiang Qing is the cruellest hand behind the attacks on the dance-drama *The White-Haired Girl*: a report on an investigation of the revolutionary modern dance-drama *The White-Haired Girl*), *Wudao*, 1977, 2 (March), 7–10, 21.

Weng Ouhong, *Weng Ouhong bianju shengya* (Weng Ouhong's career in script writing), Beijing: Zhongguo xiju chubanshe, 1986.

Wu Ganbo, *Guoyue suibi* (Notes on Chinese music), Hong Kong: Wenhua jiaoyu chubanshe, 1996.

Wu Han, '*Hai Rui ba guan*' (Hai Rui dismissed from office), *Beijing wenyi*, 1961, 1 (January), 14–30.

Wu Shaozu, ed., *Zhonghua renmin gongheguo tiyushi (1949–1998) zonghejuan* (PRC sports history: comprehensive volume), Beijing: Zhongguo shuji chubanshe, 1999.

Wu Suling, *Zhongguo dianshiju fazhan shigang* (Survey of the development of Chinese television drama), Beijing: Beijing guangbo xueyuan chubanshe, 1997.

Wu Xiaobang, gen. ed., *Dangdai Zhongguo wudao* (Contemporary Chinese dance), Beijing: Dangdai Zhongguo chubanshe, 1993.

Xia Liang, *Jutan manhua* (Theatre chat), Beijing: Zhongguo wenlian chubanshe, 1985.

Xia Xingzhen, *1975: Wentan fengbao jishi* (1975: Record of the storm in literary circles), Beijing: Zhonggongdang chubanshe, 1995.

Xiaojinzhuang shige xuan (Selected poems from Xiaojinzhuang), Tianjin: Tianjin renmin chubanshe, 1976.

Xiao Wu, '*Fangyan huaju tuan*' (Local-dialect spoken-drama troupes), *Shanghai wenhua shizhi tongxun*, 27 (August 1993), 38–41.

Xinbian Hongweibing ziliao (A New Collection of Red Guard Publications), Oakton VA: Center for Chinese Research Materials), 1999, 20 vols.

Xinhua xinwenshe, '*Zai geming yangbanxi de guanghui zhaoyao xia: geming wenyi gongzuoshe changtan xuexi geming yangbanxi de tihui*' (Under the brilliant illumination of the revolutionary model performances: revolutionary workers in art and literature freely discuss their understanding of studying the revolutionary model performances), in *Jingju geming shinian* (Ten years of the revolution in Peking opera), Zhengzhou: Henan renmin chubanshe, 1974, 41–47.

Xu Xianglin, *Zhongguo guixi* (Chinese ghost plays), Tianjin: Tianjin jiaoyu chubanshe, 1997.

Xu Xinjie and Cai Shicheng, eds., *Shanghai Jingju zhi* (Shanghai Peking opera gazetteer), Shanghai: Shanghai wenhua chubanshe, 1999.

Yang Haizhou, *Zhongguo dianying wuzi chanye xitong lishi biannianji (1928–1994)* (Historical chronology of the Chinese film materials system), Beijing: Zhongguo dianying chubanshe, 1998.

Yang Hansheng dianying juben xuanji (Selected film scripts of Yang Hansheng), Beijing: Zhongguo dianying chubanshe, 1981.

Yang Jian, '*Cong "geming xiandai Jingju" kan chuantong xiju de zhuanxing*' (The transformation of tradition as seen in the 'revolutionary modern Peking operas'), *Xiju: Zhongyang xiju xueyuan xuebao* (Theatre: Journal of the Central Drama Academy), 2003, 3 (September), 38–55.

Yang Jian, '*Di-erpi yangbanxi de chansheng ji yishu chengjiu*' (Birth and artistic achievements of the second tranche of model performances), *Xiju* (Theatre), 2000, 3 (June), 85–93.

Yang Jian, '*Lishi goule: Neimeng yu Dongbei de zhiqing wenyi*' (Outline history: educated youth literature and art in Inner Mongolia and the Northeast), *Zhongguo qingnian yanjiu* (China youth research), 1998, 5 (September), 33–35.

Yang Jian, '*Wen-ge shiqi de minjian wenxue*' (Folk literature of the Cultural Revolution period), *Shanghai wenxue* (Shanghai literature), 2001, 7 (July), 61–64.

Yang Jian, '*Wenhua dageming de Hongweibing xiju*' (Great Cultural Revolution Red Guard drama), *Xiju* (Drama), 1995, 3 (September), 51–64.

Yang Jian, '*Wenhua dageming shiqi de Hongweibing yinyue*' (Red Guard music in the Great Proletarian Cultural Revolution period), *Zhongguo qingnian yanjiu*, 1997, 2 (March), 25–28.

Yang Jian, *Wenhua dageming zhong de dixia wenxue*, Beijing: Chaohua chubanshe, 1993.

Yang Jian, '*Wenhua dageming zhong de Hongweibing huaju*' (Red Guard spoken drama in the Great Cultural Revolution), *Zhongguo qingnian yanjiu*, 1995, 1 (January), 34–73 (Part 1), and 1995, 2 (March), 25–28 (Part 2).

Yang Jian, *Zhongguo zhiqing wenxue shi* (History of Chinese 'educated youth' literature), Beijing: Zhongguo gongren chubanshe, 2002.

Yang, Lan, *Chinese Fiction of the Cultural Revolution*, Hong Kong: Hong Kong University Press, 1998.

Yang Zhijie and Liu Zaifu, *Hengmei ji* (Scowling collection), Tianjin: Baihua wenxue chubanshe, 1978.

'*Ye huo shao bu jin, chun feng chui you sheng: hu ju "Ludang huozhong" zai "Wen-ge" qianhou*' (Wild fire is not extinguished, the spring breeze starts up again: the Shanghai opera *Sparks amid the Reeds* before and after the Cultural Revolution), *Shanghai wenhua shizhi tongxun*, 39 (December 1995), 47–48.

'*Yi zhan hongdeng liang sifang: Huju 'Hong deng ji' de dansheng he jienan*' (A red lantern lights all sides: the birth and tribulations of the Shanghai opera *The Red Lantern*), *Shanghai wenhua shizhi tongxun*, 39 (December 1995), 43–46.

Ying Shu, '"Wen-ge" zhong Zhongguo zajituan yu Zhongguo mu'ou yishu jutuan de "po sijiu"' ('Smashing the four olds' at the China Acrobatic Troupe and the China Puppet Theatre in the Cultural Revolution), *Beijing dangshi yanjiu* (Beijing Party history research), 1996, 2 (April), 42.

Yu Cong and Wang Ankui, *Zhongguo dangdai xiqu shi* (History of contemporary Chinese opera), Beijing: Xueyuan chubanshe, 2005.

Yu Deshui, *Zhuying ren yu Zhuying de lu* (Pearl River Film Studio people and pathways), Guangzhou: Guangdong lüyou chubanshe, 1999.

Yu Hong and Deng Zhengqiang, *Zhongguo dangdai guanggao shi* (A history of advertising in contemporary China), Changsha: Hunan kexue jishu chubanshe, 2000.

Yu Li, ed., *Zhongguo dianying zhuanye shi yanjiu: dianying zhipian, faxing, fangying juan* (Research on Chinese film specialist history: film production, distribution and screening), Beijing: Zhongguo dianying chubanshe, 2006.

Yu Lie, '*Fang Huaiju "Haigang de zaochen" de bianju*' (An interview with the writer of *Early Morning on the Harbor*), *Shanghai wenhua shizhi tongxun*, 11 (December 1990), 39–42.

Yu Ping, *Zhongguo xiandangdai wudao fazhan shi* (History of modern and contemporary dance development in China), Beijing: Renmin yinyue chubanshe, 2004.

Yuan Bingchang and Feng Guangyu, *Zhongguo shaoshuminzu yinyue shi (shangce)* (Musical history of China's minorities, vol. 1), Beijing: Zhongyang minzu daxue chubanshe, 1998.

Yung, Bell, 'Model Opera as Model: From *Shajiabang* to *Sagabong*,' in McDougall, *Popular Chinese Literature*, 144–164.

Zang Tian, '*Cong "Nanhai changcheng" dao "Panshi wan": Jingju gaibian youxiu huaju "Nanhai changcheng" zhong de fengfeng yuyu*' (From *Great Wall in the Southern Seas* to *Boulder Bay*: the trials and tribulations of the Peking opera adaptation of the outstanding spoken play *Great Wall in the Southern Seas*), *Shanghai wenhua shizhi tongxun*, 42 (September 1996), 21–27.

Zhai Jiannong, *Hongse wangshi: 1966–1976 nian de Zhongguo dianying* (A red past: 1966–1976 Chinese films), Beijing: Taihai chubanshe, 2001.

Zhai Jiannong, '"Yangbanxi dianying" de xingshuai: "Wen-ge dianying": 20 shiji teshu de wenhua xianxiang, yi' (The ups and downs of 'model performance films': 'Cultural Revolution' film; a special phenomenon of twentieth-century culture), *Dangdai dianying* (Contemporary film), 1995, 2 (April), 39, 37–43.

Zhai Zixia ed., *Zhongguo wuju* (Chinese dance-drama), Beijing: Zhongguo Shijieyu chubanshe, 1996.

Zhang Fengshou, ed., *Zhongguo dianshi wenyixue* (Chinese television art), Beijing: Beijing guangbo xueyuan chubanshe, 1999.

Zhang Guangmang, '*Zhishifenzi de chaoyue zhi jing: tan Wang Yao de wenxue yanjiu daolu yu xueshu gexing*' (Limits to the surpassing of intellectuals: on the scholarly characteristics of Wang Yao's literary research), *Dangdai zuojia pinglun*, 2003, 4 (July), 38–47.

Zhang Ming and Liao Yiwu, eds., *Chenlun de shengdian: Zhongguo ershi shiji 70 niandai dixia shige yizhao* (Sinking holy place: death pictures of underground poetry in China's 1970s), Urumqi: Xinjiang qingshaonian chubanshe, 1994.

Zhang Ruifang, *Suiyue youqing: Zhang Ruifang huiyilu* (Years of friendship: the memoirs of Zhang Ruifang), Beijing: Zhongyang wenxian chubanshe, 2005.

Zhang Yang, '*Di-er ci woshou*' *wenziyu* (The *Second Handshake* literary inquisition), Beijing: Zhongguo shehui chubanshe, 1999.

Zhou Yang, *Wo yu 'Di-erci woshou'* (*The Second Handshake* and I), Beijing: Zhonggong dangshi chubanshe, 2007.

Zhang Yuanpei, '*Xinhua Jingju tuan bianxie de "Longjiang song" wei he bei esha*' (Why the Xinhua Peking Opera Company's *Song of the Dragon River* was killed off), *Shanghai wenhua shizhi tongxun*, 47 (December 1997), 47–50.

Zhang, Zhen, *An Amorous History of the Silver Screen: Shanghai Cinema, 1896–1937*, Chicago: Chicago University Press, 2005.

Zhao Kezhong, '*Shanghai "gushihui" de xingcheng jiqi licheng*' (Shape and course of Shanghai's 'story-telling sessions'), *Shanghai wenhua shizhi tongxun*, 23 (December 1992), 30–34.

Zhao Zhenkai (Bei Dao), *Waves*, translated by Bonnie S. McDougall, Hong Kong: Chinese University Press, 1985.

Zheng Bangyu, ed., *Jiefangjun xiju shi* (History of Liberation Army drama), Beijing: Zhongguo xiju chubanshe, 2004.

Zhong Ying, '*Jinyibu fazhan nongmin dianying fangying wang*' (Further develop the film projection network in the countryside), *Hongqi*, 1975, 6 (June), 50–53.

Zhonggong zhongyang hangongting, Guowuyuan mishuting, Wenhua geming lianhe jiedaishi, *Wuchanjieji wenhua dageming youguan wenjian huiji* (Compilation relevant to the Proletarian Cultural Revolution), Beijing, 1967–1976, 16 vols.

Zhongguo dianyingjia xiehui, eds., '*Sirenbang*' *shi dianying shiye de sidi: Wenhuabu dianying xitong jiepi 'Sirenbang' zuixing dahui fayan huibian* (The Gang of Four is the deadly enemy of the film industry: Collection of speeches at a conference of the Ministry of Culture's film system exposing and criticizing the Gang of Four), Beijing: Zhongguo dianying chubanshe, 1978.

Zhongguo dianyingjia xiehui dianyingshi yanjiubu, ed., *Zhonghua renmin gongheguo dianying shiye sanshiwu nian, 1949–1984* (Thirty-five years of the PRC film industry), Beijing: Zhongguo dianying chubanshe, 1985 [*Sanshiwu nian*].

Zhongguo dianying nianjian, 1981 (China film yearbook), Beijing: Zhongguo dianying chubanshe, 1982.

Zhongguo dianying ziliaoguan, Zhongguo yishu yanjiuyuan dianying yanjiusuo, eds., *Zhongguo yishu yingpian bianmu, 1949–1979* (Catalogue of Chinese art films), Beijing, 1982, 2 vols.

Zhongguo wujutuan, '*Mao Zedong sixiang zhaoyaozhe wuju geming de shengli qiancheng: paiyan geming xiandai wuju "Hongse niangzijun de yixie tihui"*' (Mao Zedong thought is illuminating the prospects for victory in the dance-drama revolution: some understandings from rehearsing the revolutionary modern dance-drama *The Red Detachment of Women*), *Hongqi*, 1970, 7 (July), 66–77, reproduced in *Hongqi*, 1972, 2 (February), 32–43.

Zhongguo xiju dianying cidian (China theatre and film dictionary), Beijing: Beijing guangbo xueyuan chubanshe, 1993.

Zhongguo xiqu zhi, Hebei juan (China opera gazetteer, Hebei volume), Beijing: Zhongguo ISBN zhongxin, 1993.

Zhongguo xiqu zhi, Shaanxi juan (China opera gazetteer, Shaanxi volume), Beijing: Zhongguo ISBN zhongxin, 1995.

Zhongguo xiqu zhi, Sichuan juan (China opera gazetteer, Sichuan), Beijing: Zhongguo ISBN zhongxin, 1995.

Zhongguo xiqu zhi, Xinjiang juan (China opera gazetteer, Xinjiang volume), Beijing: Zhongguo ISBN zhongxin, 1995.

Zhongguo xiqu zhi, Yunnan juan (China opera gazetteer, Yunnan), Beijing: Zhongguo ISBN zhongxin, 1994.

Zhongguo xiqu zhi, Zhejiang juan (China opera gazetteer, Zhejiang), Beijing: Zhongguo ISBN zhongxin, 1997.

Zhongguo yishu yingpian bianmu, see Zhonguo dianying ziliaoguan.

Zhongguo yinyue cidian (Chinese musical dictionary), Beijing: Renmin yinyue chubanshe, 1985.

Zhou Xiaobang, ed., *Beiying sishi nian, 1949–1989* (Forty years of the Beijing Film Studio), Beijing: Wenhua yishu chubanshe, 1997.

Zhujiang dianying zhipianchang 1958–1980 tongji ziliao (Statistical data on the Pearl River Film Studio, 1958–1980), Guangzhou: Pearl River Film Studio.

Zhujiang dianying zhipianchang bianjishi, '*Guanyu bianji shi jinhou bianji gongzuo de yijian*' (Views on present and future editorial work by the editorial section), July 1975, 6 pp., in China Film Archive Library, Studio Files 00189.

Zhujiang dianying zhipianchang bianjishi, '*Jinian lai juben chuangzuo he zugao qingkuang, yiji cunzai wenti*' (Conditions of the writing and commissioning of scripts in recent years, and existing issues), September 1974, 15.

'*Zhuying chang juben chuangzuo zuotanhui jianbao*' (Brief report on the conference on script production at Pearl River Film Studio), No. 1 (1 March 1974), 4 pp. and No. 9 (20 April 1974), 7 pp. in China Film Archives Library, Studio Files 00189.

Zhu Keyi, *Yuyanxue shiye zhong de 'yangbanxi'* (The 'model performances' from a linguistics point of view), Kaifeng: Henan daxue chubanshe, 2004.

Zou Deyi, *Zhongguo jianzhushi tushuo: xiandaijuan* (Illustrated history of Chinese architecture: modern volume), Beijing: Zhongguo jianzhu gongye chubanshe, 2001.

Zu Zhensheng, *Zhongguo yinyue zhihuijia shengya* (Careers of Chinese music conductors), Beijing: Zhishi chubanshe, 1999.

Index

1964 convention, *see* modern-subject Peking opera performance convention (1964)

A Bing, 184

A Jia, 36, 37, 38, 39, 70

A Jian, 73

A Kejian, 188

acrobatics: in model operas, 33–35, 38, 43, 49, 51, 73; in operas, 32, 66–67, 69, 70–71, 173; non-opera, 90, 97, 100–101, 202, 256

actors, 48–49, 143–144, 135, 136–137, 268n39

Adolescence in the Flames of War, 115

Aihua Shanghai Opera Company, 35–36, 36, 37

Aksenov, Vasilii, 228

Albania, 151

allegory, historical, 234; *see also Hai Rui Dismissed from Office*

amateur, 253–254, 255, 260; performers, 102–103, 108, 160–170, 173, 202, 203; opera performers, 81–82, 91, 123, 154; performing troupes, 100, 101–102, 105, 106; writers, 85–86, 221, 225

Andrews, Julia F., 211

animation, 80, 134, 150–151, 170

Ankang District Song and Dance Ensemble, 178

Anti-Japanese War, 10, 23, 36, 204, 239–240; films on, 150; setting of model operas, 31, 35, 69, 162

Antonioni, Michelangelo, 234–235

Anyuan, 204–205

architecture, 215–216

army: *see* People's Liberation Army

Army Comes Camping in the Mountains, The, 173

art, fine, 202–215

Ashma, 178

audiences, 3–4, 4, 8, 48, 74–75, 132–133, 249, 250; and traditional opera, 11, 100; and model operas, 37–38, 49, 52, 54, 55, 56, 67; and modern-subject operas, 12, 15; dance, 159, 162, 163, 169; film, 113, 140, 144, 150–156, 251; music, 183; discontents of, 61, 66, 74, 76, 84, 236, 317n57; *see also* pleasures, cultural

August First Film Studio, 116, 118, 121–122, 133, 146, 158, 191, 200; films model works, 69, 126, 130, 131, 133, 172

Australia, 188, 190

Azalea Mountain, 62, 66–68, 72, 82, 103, 190, 235; film version, 82, 126, 131; other versions, 84, 85, 174

Ba Jin, 150, 218

bad characters, 51, 61, 141

Bai minority, 83, 178

Bakken, Børge, 74

ballad opera (*quju*), 84, 101

ballet, 7, 52, 96; model ballets, 57, 59, 116, 129, 158, 159–168, 180

Balzac, 228

barefoot doctors, 139, 190, 222, 245

'Battlesong of the People's Volunteers Army', 30

Battlesong of Tian'anmen, 239

Beethoven, 177, 179–180

Bei Dao, 316n39

Beijing City Hebei *Bangzi* Troupe, 107

Beijing City Worker-Peasant-Soldier Art
and Photography Exhibition, 211
Beijing Conservatory, 176
Beijing Daily, 20
Beijing Dance School, 247
Beijing Film Academy, 121, 132, 147–148,
194
Beijing Film Studio, 109, 112, 116, 132,
147, 158, 246; Cultural Revolution at,
117, 119, 120–121, 131, 133, 134; films
model works, 123–125, 129, 133, 171,
243; other films, 135, 136, 137, 240, 243,
244, 244–245, 247
Beijing Literature and Art, 220
Beijing Northern Opera (pingju) *Troupe*,
107
Beijing Peking Opea Company, 15, 31, 57,
66, 67
Beijing Peking Opera No. 2 Company, 17
Beijing People's Art Theatre, 43, 195,
195–196, 197–198, 199
Beijing Symphony Orchestra, 180
Beiying, *see* Beijing Film Studio
big-character posters, 71, 120, 213, 214
Big Li, Little Li and Old Li, 126
'black line in literature and art', 23–24,
112–113, 121, 221, 233, 234, 235, 237
'black-painting exhibition', 212
'black performances', 60, 91, 100
Bonds on the Plateau, 83
Book of Songs, The, 228
Boulder Bay, 62, 70–73, 87, 128, 133, 174
Brahms, 177
brands, 258
Breaking with Old Ideas, 141, 148, 239,
245
Bright and Brave, 178
Bright Sunny Skies, 137–138, 220
Buddhism, 57
Butterfly Lovers, The, 129

caidiao opera, 77
Cantonese opera, 17, 78, 84, 132, 134
Capital Gymnasium, 215–216
capitalist roaders, 175, 189, 238, 239,
322n113
Catcher in the Rye, 228
Central Academy of Art, 203, 207, 209
Central Academy of Arts and Crafts, 204
Central Ballet Company, 159–160
Central Drama Academy, 133, 194–195
Central May Seventh Art University, 148,
175, 186, 188, 209

Central Musical Theatre Ballet School, 171
Central National Music Orchestra, 177,
190
Central Newsreel and Documentary Film
Studio, 118, 130, 146, 158, 184, 246
Central Radio Station, 191, 194
Central Symphony Orchestra, 88, 130,
177, 183, 185
centralization, 56, 101, 255–256
Chained Dragon Lake, 138
Chairman Mao's Red Guards, 194
Chang Zhenhua, 136
Changchun City Peking Opera Company,
15
Changchun City Song and Dance
Company, 170
Changchun Film Studio, 35, 80, 115, 116,
130, 132, 133, 151; Cultural Revolution
at, 117, 118, 119, 122; films model
works, 128–129; others films, 135–136,
137, 138, 144, 161, 240, 242, 246
Chaoxia, 225, 228–229
Chen Chong (Joan), 293n136
Chen Chuanxi, 190
Chen Fangqian, 246, 247
Chen Gang, 188
Chen Hong, 63
Chen Huai'ai, 69, 131–132, 243, 246,
247
Chen Mingzhi, 188
Chen Pixian, 71
Chen Qitong, 200
Chen Shu, 136
Chen Xieyang, 191
Cheng Guoying, 210
Cheng Jihua, 113
Cheng Shifa, 207
Cheng Yin, 126, 130, 133, 136
Chengde Regional Spoken Drama
Company, 135
*Cherished Memories of the Bridge
Workers*, 239
Chi Qun, 244
China Art Gallery, 211, 212, 215
China Dance Drama Company, 170–171
China Film Corporation, 152, 154
China Music Academy, 176
China Musical and Dance Theatre, 194
China Opera Artists Association, 15
China Opera Gazetteer, 97–104 passim
China Peking Opera Academy, 35, 36, 57,
58–59
China Peking Opera Company, 246

China Peking Opera Theatre, 68, 69, 70, 191
China Railroad Song and Dance Ensemble, 170, 239
China Theatre Artists Association, 21
China Youth Art Theatre, 194
Chinese Academy of Social Sciences, 226
Chinese painting: *see* painting, Chinese (*guohua*)
Chinese People's Volunteer Army, 29
choral music, 186–187
Chu Lan, 233–234
Chu Wanghua, 184, 185
chuanlian, *see* Red Guards: travel by
Chunmiao, 139, 245
Chung Kuo Cina, 234–235
Chronology of New China's Dance, A, 7, 174
City Besieged, 115, 149
City without Night, 113–114, 136, 149
clapper opera, 17, 75, 79, 104, 133, 162, 247
clapper recitation (*kuaishu*), 195
clapper songs, 107
clapper story-telling, 201
Climbing Peach Peak Three Times, 79, 233–234, 234
Collecting Coal Cinders, 79
collective creation, 28, 135
comic books, 211, 224
comic dialogues (*xiangsheng*), 74, 96, 202, 323n114
commodification, of culture, 3–4, 258, 261
Communist Party, Chinese, 93–94, 94, 106–107, 120, 151, 164, 203, 219; before Cultural Revolution, 5, 11, 22, 32, 192; factions in, 2, 25, 26, 138–139, 236–237, 238, 244; Politburo, 121, 123–124, 244; Propaganda Department, 36
conductors, orchestral, 190–191
Conference on Army Literature and Art Work, *see subhead in* People's Liberation Army
Confucianism, 25, 57, 196; *see also* Criticize Lin Biao and Confucius campaign
consumerism, 261
costumes, in modern opera, 49
Counterattack, 238, 240, 244–245
'cow sheds' (*niupeng*), 39, 117, 124, 152
Cowfield Sea, 221
Criticize Lin Biao and Confucius campaign, 47, 147, 173, 212, 214, 223

Cui Wei, 69, 131–132
Culture Group (of State Council), 103, 130, 137, 241–242
Cultural Revolution: assessments of, 2, 119–120, 249, 295n2; start of, 15, 18–26, 52; three phases of, 7, 250; suffering in, 9, 118–119; victimhood, 95, 119
Cultural Revolution Group, 59, 94, 115, 120, 123–124, 196

Da Shichang, 137
Dance (film), 134
Dance (journal), 87, 174, 175
dance, 7, 105, 158–175, 234, 251; Western, 159, 168–169; *see also* ballet
dance-drama (*wuju*), 162, 170
Daqing, 212, 240
Daughter of the Commune Party Secretary, 200
Dazhai, 143, 144, 189–190, 200, 212, 238
Dazhai's Red Flowers Bloom Everywhere, 189–190
Debussy, Claude, 179
Deng Tuo, 24, 67
Deng Xiaoping, 213, 231, 233, 237–238, 242–243, 304n97; in 1976, 175, 240, 298n27; in film, 245
dialogue, in opera, 72, 73
Diao Deyi, 33
'Diary of a Madman, The', 195–196, 219
Dickens, 228
directors, theatre, 16, 43, 48
Dividing Line, The, 225
documentary film, 116, 122–123, 130, 190, 206, 235–236; of leaders, 118, 146, 149, 156; of performances, 131, 185, 245–246, 246
'Down and Out', 227
Drama on the Wharves, 200
Dream of the Red Chamber, The, 201, 224
drum singing, 183, 201
Du Spring Mountain, 67, 68
Dumas, 228
Duo Duo, 228
Dynasty of Lords, A, 227

Early Morning Dockside, 41
Early Morning on the Docks, 40, 42
Early Spring in February, 19, 112–113, 248; artists of, 109, 120, 124, 137, 143–144, 243

East China Regional Modern-subject
  Opera Convention (1965), 63
East Is Red, The: dance-drama, 158–159,
  168, 169, 190, 191, 193, 194; film, 124;
  song, 29, 30, 186
educated youth: *see* sent-down youth
'educated-youth literature', 229
educational revolution, 173; *see also*
  open-door schooling
Ehrenberg, Ilya, 228
Eleven Polyphonous Pieces, 188
Emei Film Studio, 134
Emerald Water and Red Flags, 31
Evening Chats at Yanshan, 24
Every Red Flower Turns towards the Sun,
  116
exhibitions, 211, 212
experimentation, artistic, 56, 87, 203, 250,
  257–258, 259

families, in model operas, 50
famine, 22, 267n32
Fang Haizhen, 40–42 passim, 48, 49, 50–54
  passim, 82, 103, 126–127, 257, 260
Farewell to My Concubine, 52–53
fascism, 74, 256, 312n196
February Storm, The, 193
Feng Zikai, 230
Ferry, The, 133
Ferry Crossing, The, 79, 84; dance, 174
fiction, 15, 46, 74, 218–229 passim,
  257–258
Fiery Years, The, 140–141, 143
Fifteen Strings of Cash, 265n12
fifth-generation filmmakers, 37, 146–147,
  148, 260, 290n101
Fighting the Flood, 108, 137, 138
Fighting the Flood Peak, 36
Fighting North and South, 126, 136, 144,
  150, 199
Fighting on the Plain, 55, 62, 69, 70, 103,
  135, 235; film version, 82, 131–132
Fighting the Waves, 84
film, 5–6, 8, 14, 15, 18, 91, 131, 191;
  influences opera, 11–12, 17, 37; and
  spoken drama, 192; attacked, 19, 113; of
  model performances, 4, 39, 75, 76, 87,
  91–92, 125–126, 154–155, 240;
  pre-1966, 89, 115, 149–150; features
  after 1974, 52, 74, 75, 111–112, 131,
  134–145; power of, 109, 111, 138–139,
  239, 251, 256; foreign, 105, 150–152; *see
  also* Hollywood

film distribution, 148–154
film equipment, 122, 123, 136, 146, 212,
  288n69
film personnel, 48, 110, 111, 118–119, 144,
  146–148
film projection teams, 82–83, 153–154
Fine Art, 212–213
Fishing Song, 188
Five Golden Flowers, 115
'Fleeing from Home', 227
Flower Seller, The, 151
flower-drum opera (*huaguxi*), 77, 80–81,
  81, 100, 101, 102, 159
Flowers Are Fine and the Moon Is Round,
  115
*Flowers Bloom on the Thousand-Year-Old
  Iron Tree*, 188, 198
*Flowers of Philosophy Bloom Everywhere
  in the Mountain Village*, 80
Flute and Drum at Sunset, 184–185
folk art, 208
folk dance, 49, 158, 162, 165, 168
folk music, 45, 176, 177, 183
folk songs, 158
'four modernizations', 245
'four olds', 120
Four Shaanxi Folk Songs, 188
fourth-generation filmmakers, 148
frozen pose (*liangxiang*), 28, 34, 85, 140,
  166
Fu Chaowu, 127
Fudan University, 218
Furnace Fire Is Pure Red, The, 213

Gadfly, The, 228, 274n121
Gambia, 195
Gang of Four, 26, 65–66, 112, 179, 240,
  244, 245, 247; accusations against, 60,
  119, 128, 187, 189, 242; arrest of, 145,
  165, 212, 238, 239; associates of, 104,
  175, 237
Gao Jingde, 211
Gate No. 6, 17
ghost plays, 14, 53, 60–61, 265n12
Golden Road, The, 138, 220, 221
Golden Seeds, 300n52
gramaphone records, 35, 84
Grand Festival, A, 239
Grandma Li, 37–38, 184
Great Leap Forward, 20, 159, 184;
  consequences of, 22, 30, 198; culture in,
  86, 110, 138, 195, 222, 223, 286n29;
  opera and, 12–13, 95, 282n104

Great Wall in the Southern Seas, 70–71
Great World, 97
Green Pine Ridge, 135, 137
Gu Hua, 225
Guang Weiran, 186
Guangming Daily, 35, 58, 66, 179
Guangxi Zhuang Autonomous Region
  Film Study Class, 134
Guangzhou Trade Fair, 185
Guerrillas on the Plain, 62, 70, 128,
  135–136, 240
Guilin opera (*Guiju*), 77
Guizhou Provincial Spoken Drama Troupe,
  196
Guo Jianguang, 32, 34, 48, 49, 50, 52, 54,
  57, 132
Guo Moruo, 186, 219
Guo Xianhong, 224
Guomindang, 6, 27, 70, 112, 171

Hai Mo, 121
Hai Rui Dismissed from Office, 15, 20,
  111, 193, 207, 231
Hai Rui Memorializes the Emperor, 21
Haixia, 111–112, 221, 240, 243–244
Haiyan Film Studio, 129
Half a Basket of Peanuts, 79, 80
Han Ling, 245
Han Qixiang, 189
Han Shaogong, 225
Han Xiaoqiang, 40, 42, 53, 54
Hanan, Patrick, 8
hand-copied literature, 217, 226–227, 229,
  230, 316n36
Hansen, Miriam, 7–8
Hao Liang, 244; *see also* Qian Haoliang
Hao Ran, 138, 220–221, 221, 257–258
Happily Giving Grain, 172, 175, 234
Harbin City Peking Opera Company, 35
Haydn, 180
He Long, 29
He Lüting, 179
He Man, 41, 70
Hebei Clapper Opera Leap Forward
  Company, 247
Hebei Daily, 103, 104
Henan opera (*Yuju*), 75, 84, 104
heroes, of model operas, 53–54, 140,
  141, 260; *see also under characters'*
  names
Heroic Little Sisters of the Grassland, 80,
  170
Heroic Sons and Daughters, 149–150

Hetian District Song and Dance Ensemble,
  105
history plays, 14–15, 18–19, 19–20
Historical Records, 228
Hollywood, 12, 144, 144–145, 152
Hong Changqing, 68, 160, 166
Hong Kong, 132, 149, 190
Hong Weimin, 196
Hong Xiannü, 132–133
Hu county paintings, 208–209, 210, 211,
  254
Hu Daxin, 82
Hu Defeng, 191
Hua Guofeng, 244
Huai opera, 39, 40, 73–74, 77, 79, 97,
  107
Huang Jianzhong, 117
Huang Yijun, 190
Huang Zuolin, 162
Huangmeixi (Anhui opera), 21, 107,
  129
Hubei opera, 84
Hugo, 228
Huju, see Shanghai opera
Hulunbei'ermeng Nationalities Song and
  Dance Troupe, 178
Hunan opera (*Xiangju*), 77, 79, 107,
  232–233
'hundred flowers' slogan, 212
Huo Fengling, 82
hybridity, 159, 251–252

'I Love Tian'anmen in Beijing', 187
icons, 258
'In Battleground Order', 214
In Lenin's Hometown, 195
In One's Prime, 200, 239
Inner Mongolia Art Theatre, 80
innovation, 157, 175, 213, 251, 257, 259;
  in music, 176, 182, 183, 257
insurgents, cultural, 15, 23–24, 111–112,
  176, 197, 235, 236, 256–257
Internationale, The, 30, 184
intertextuality, 194, 256
Investigation of a Chair, 84, 133
Island Militia Women, 221, 243
Ivens, Joris, 134, 320n71

January Storm, 96, 195, 239
Japan, 5, 165, 188, 195; *see also*
  Anti-Japanese War
Jia Pingwa, 225
Jiang Haiyang, 146–147

Jiang Qing, 47, 50, 56, 59, 192, 256–257;
  before Cultural Revolution, 23, 52, 59,
  115, 131, 266n20, 284n3;
and culture: on modern opera (1964), 16,
  16–18, 48, 59–61, 104, 235, 275n12; and
  model operas, 28, 29, 31, 36, 39, 40, 41,
  42, 50, 56–57; and other model
  performances, 62, 76, 163, 164, 178,
  190; and model performance films,
  123–124, 124, 127–128, 129; and other
  modern operas, 55, 63–64, 65–66, 67,
  68, 70, 72; and films, 115, 118, 122, 124,
  136, 137, 138, 152; criticizes films,
  241–242, 243, 244, 244–245; and music,
  179, 185; and other arts, 203, 212, 225,
  236, 246, 306n123; and Central May
  Seventh Arts University, 147, 148, 175;
and politics: allies of, 21, 38, 121, 234, 238;
  as factional leader, 24, 25, 89, 96, 201,
  213; weakening position of, 104, 175,
  230–231, 233, 235; and Xiaojinzhuang,
  82, 104, 223, 237; arrest of, 112, 212,
  240, 247; see also Gang of Four
Jiang Shuiying, 62–66 passim
Jiang Tao, 245
Jiang Zilong, 225
Jiang Zuhui, 160–161
Jiangnan in the North, 19, 114–115
Jiangxi opera (*Ganju*), 107
Jiao Juyin, 199
Jin Guolin,187
Jin Yueling, 187
Jinggangshan, 66, 67
Jones, Stephen, 183
Journey, The, 224
Ju Qihong, 183–186
Juben, 28, 36

Kafka, 228
Kang Sheng, 16, 25, 59
Kazak language, 104, 108
Ke Ling, 114
Ke Qingshi, 14
Ke Xiang, 66, 67, 82
Kerouac, 228
Kirghiz language, 104, 105
Korean War, 20, 27, 29–30, 149–150; see
  also North Korea
Kraus, Richard C., 3–4, 188
Kunming City Commerce Bureau Amateur
  Culture and Art Propaganda Team, 83

'Lamp, The', 225

language standardization, 220–221
lao san zhan, 150
Lao She, 218
laodiao ('old tune'), 75
League of Left-Wing Writers, 113
'Legend of Yangtian Lake', 225
Lei Feng, 207
Lenin, 203
Lenin in 1918, 151–152
Lenin in October, 151–152
Leningrad Conservatory, 184
Li Bingshu, 64–65
Li Cunbao, 225
Li Delun, 130, 185, 190
Li Guang, 55, 69, 108
Li Guoquan, 190
Li Hangyu, 228
Li Huiniang, 21, 53, 265n12
Li Li, 230
Li Ling, 183
Li minority, 172
Li Ping, 229
Li Rentang, 135
Li Ronglong, 214
Li Ruqing, 221, 243
Li Shaoran, 133–134
Li Shuangshuang, 17
Li Taicheng, 41, 71
Li Tiemei, 35, 37–38, 49, 50, 53–54, 54; as
  model, 82, 184; in images, 58, 60, 207,
  219, 257
Li Wenhu, 133
Li Wenhua, 109, 110, 112, 129, 137, 156,
  244
Li Xiaomin, 40, 41, 42
Li Xintian, 221
Li Yinghai, 185
Li Yuhe, 35, 37, 48, 49, 50, 53, 54; as
  model, 103, 184
Li Zhitian, 62, 65
Liang Bingkun, 198
Liang Lun, 157, 192, 216
liangxiang (frozen pose), 23, 34, 85, 140,
  166
Liang Xiao, 244
Liao Mosha, 24
Liaoning Film Corporation, 152–153
Liaoning Song and Dance Troupe, 107
Liberation Army Daily, 23, 60
Liberation Army Literature and Art, 219
Liberation Army Songs, 219
Liberation Daily, 59, 68, 225
libraries, 87

Life of Wu Xun, The, 110–111, 149
Lin Biao, 7, 23, 52, 59, 173, 231; *see also* Criticize Lin Biao and Confucius campaign
Lin Ju, 153
Lin Family Shop, The, 19, 113, 120, 124
Lin Mohan, 23, 36
Lin Nong, 138
Link, Perry, 323n114
literary magazines, 76–77
literature, 6; foreign, 228–229; official, 218–226; traditional, 228
Literature and Art Group, 121
'Little Eighth Route Army Soldier', 202
Little Guards of the Railroad, 170
'Little Red Book', 195
Little Sentinels of the Southern Seas, 185
Little Sisters of the Grassland, 80, 188
Little Soldier Zhang Ga, 150
Liu Binkun, 162
Liu Chunhua, 204–205
Liu Guoquan, 135
Liu Shaoqi, 204, 233–234, 241
Liu Zhide, 86, 209
Liu Zhongfu, 232
localism, in tastes, 21–22, 77, 108, 133, 197, 255–256, 260
London Philharmonic Orchestra, 179
Long March, 200
Long March Suite, The, 191
Louie, Kam, 6–7
love stories, 50–51; *see also* hand-copied literature
loyalty, displays of, 25, 182, 195, 199, 219, 259
Lu Changhai, 73
Lu Dingyi, 16, 25
Lü Peng, 213
Lu Xun, 195–196, 210, 219, 228, 264n10
Lu Xun Art Academy, 36
Luo Ruiqing, 16
Luo Zhongrong, 177
lyrics, opera, 31, 39, 42, 47

Ma Depo, 147
MacFarquhar, Roderick, 1, 5
'*Madman*' of the New Age, 195–196
Main Subject, 133–134
Manchukuo Film Studio, 143
Mao badges, 203–204, 204
Mao Dun, 113
Mao Hui, 7, 174

Mao Zedong, 8, 14, 24, 151–152, 205, 231, 253, 313n211;
and culture: on film, 149, 242, 244; as poet, 178, 187, 195, 196, 222, 223; other writings, 32, 45, 198, 224, 241; and traditional opera, 30, 111, 218, 245–246; watches Cultural Revolution performances, 28, 29, 31–32, 65, 80, 163, 233; on paucity of art, 75, 134, 155–156, 171; *see also* Yan'an *Talks*
and politics: at Yan'an, 6, 61, 189; before Cultural Revolution, 12–13, 22, 110–111, 123; launches Cultural Revolution, 1, 20, 23, 25, 26, 52, 184, 252–253, 253; adulation of, 74, 138, 158–159, 164, 181, 182, 186, 203–205, 258; reviews Red Guards, 118, 149; death of, 2, 212, 244
Mao Zedong Thought, 23, 98–99, 189
Mao Zedong Thought Propaganda Teams, 95, 121, 175
Mao Zedong Thought University, 121
Mao Zedong-ism Commune, 120–121
'March of the Volunteers', 115
martial arts, 165, 190
Marxism, 5, 26, 221
Masses Daily, 232
Matsuyama Ballet Company, 162
May Fourth, 5–6, 11, 184, 192; literature, 6, 14, 18, 112–113, 196, 218
May Ninth Revolutionary Rebel Troupe, 196
May Seventh Cadre Schools, 52, 254; artists at, 117, 121, 134, 198, 199, 209; writing from, 221, 230, 229
'May Seventh Music Training Course', 188
May 16 Circular, 18, 89, 93, 120
McDougall, Bonnie S., 6–7, 8, 223
Mei Hu opera, 84
middling characters, 41, 78, 141–142, 218–219
militarization, cultural, 51–52, 252
Mine Warfare, 150
Ming dynasty, 14, 226
Ministry of Culture, 10, 14, 84, 120, 121, 238, 244; and model works, 31, 160
minorities, ethnic, 159, 181, 182, 191, 256; audience appeal of, 115, 133, 134, 144; dances of, 158–159, 165, 168–169, 170, 173, 256
Minutes of the Conference on Army Literature and Art Work, 23–24
'misty poetry', 230, 260
'model films', 139–142

model operas, 2–3, 56, 57, 104, 182, 201, 202; art of, 43–54, 190; first five, 26–43; *see also under individual titles*
model performances (*yangbanxi*), 10, 27, 29, 39–40, 59, 88, 250; films of, 117, 123–134, 150, 154–155, 240; influence on other arts, 174, 203, 222, 225; importance of, 89–92; promulgation of, 56–62; *see also under individual titles*
models, 17, 24, 35, 57, 59
modern musicals (*geju*), 17, 48, 63, 97, 178–179, 186
modern-subject Peking opera performance convention (1964), 16–18, 21, 24, 27–28, 30, 31, 41, 67, 70; Jiang Qing's speech at, 48, 59, 104; operas not included, 40, 63
modernity, 7, 157, 191–192, 192, 208, 251–252, 255–256, 258–261
Mongolians, 104, 144, 170, 171
Moonlight on Second Spring, 184
Morning Sun, 274n121
'Moscow Nights', 188
Mother of the Hydrogen Bomb, 227
Mountain Flower, 143–144
Mountain Lilies Are Blooming Bright Red, 186–187
Mozart, 177
music, 97, 162, 175–192; in films, 140, 142–143; of model operas, 17, 33, 38, 44–45; *see also* modern musicals *and* Western music

Nan Batian, 160
Nan Shao, 221
Nanchang City Peking Opera Company, 17
Nanjing Military District Front-line Spoken Drama Troupe, 199
Nanjing Film Machinery Factory, 146
National Minorities Mass National Art Festival (1964), 116
National Opera Reform Committee, 12
'negative examples', 149, 244
New Director, The, 141
New Era (*xin shiqi*), 3, 9, 225, 226, 259–260
New Fourth Army, 31, 33, 34
New Songs from the Battlefields, 187
New Year pictures, 181, 212
New Youth, 6, 112
New Zealand, 188, 190, 294n159
New Zealand National Youth Orchestra, 180

newspapers, 256
newsreels, *see* documentary film
Nie Er, 115, 130, 186
Nie Zongming, 191
Niu Han, 230
Nixon, Richard, 234, 263n2
North Korea, 104, 150–151, 165; *see also* Korean War
Northern opera (*pingju*), 75, 77, 81, 90, 101, 104
Notes from Three Villages, 24

Ode to the Yimeng Mountains, 133, 170, 171, 171–172
Old but Still Red, 79
Old Party Secretary, The, 86, 209, 210
'old three fights' (*lao san zhan*), 150
On Contradiction, 45
On the Docks, 27, 49, 52, 59, 70, 82, 246–247, 252; creation of, 39–43, 66; film of, 109, 117, 126–128, 243; music versions, 185, 188
On the Road, 228
One and the Eight, The, 260
'One Year', 229
'open-door schooling', 209, 245
'Open Love Letters', 227
opera, modern, 15, 60, 70, 256, 257; *see also* model operas; modern-subject Peking opera performance convention (1964); *and under individual titles*
opera, regional, 45, 73–88, 255; *see also under names of different forms*
opera, traditional, 13, 13–14, 18, 49–50, 52–53, 131–132; filmed for Mao, 111, 125, 245–247; still performed, 22–23, 83, 91, 93, 282n86; after 1976, 258, 265n12, 292n98; *see also* 'black performances'
opera companies, 48, 55, 56, 79–80, 92–108
Opera Reformation Committee, 264n4
oral literature, 227; *see also* story-telling
Ormandy, Eugene, 179
Others Will Follow Us, 89; *see also The Revolution Has Successors*
'Our hearts and the Central Cultural Revolution [Group] are joined as one', 194

painting, 46, 47, 74, 86, 207–208, 210, 260; Chinese (*guohua*), 206–207, 211, 213, 251; handbooks, 213

Pearl River Film Studio, 116, 117, 118, 132–133, 134, 137, 147
peasant painting, see Hu county paintings
Peking opera: as national genre, 14, 21–22, 35, 77; see also model operas
Peking University, 244, 273n111, 300n57
Peng Dehuai, 20
Peng Xiuwen, 190
Peng Zhen, 16, 25, 66–67
People of the Mountains Welcome the Liberation Army, The, 187
People's Culture Publishing House, 29
People's Daily, 57, 60, 75, 76–78, 123, 223; attacks on art, 19, 20, 110–111, 149, 233–234, 234; editorials parroted, 25, 245, 259; publishes opera scripts, 29, 68, 88, 89
People's Liberation Army, 49, 121, 162, 195, 230; Conference on Army Literature and Art Work, 23–24, 59, 104, 113, 115, 235; role in Cultural Revolution, 7, 26, 51–52, 120, 150, 173; performing troupes in, 172, 173, 178
People's Literature Publishing House, 87
People's Music, 177–178, 189
People's Music Press, 186
performers, 81, 88, 93–94; see also opera companies
Philadelphia Orchestra, 179, 234
photography, 211–212
piano, 184–185, 185, 189
Piano Accompanied 'Red Lantern', Piano Concerto 'Yellow River', Revolutionary Symphonic Music 'Shajiabang', 130
picture stories, 211, 224
pingdiao (Hebei opera), 75
pingtan (Suzhou story-telling), 97, 183, 201
ping pong, 32, 38
Pioneers, The, 111–112, 240–242
'Pitiful Fortune, A', 228
pleasures, cultural, 142–144, 154–155, 257–258; see also audiences
'plot films', 321n86
'plot literature and art', 225
poetry, 15, 82–83, 222–223, 253–254; classical style, 178, 230; and model works, 46, 47, 74, 85–86; Poetry journal, 222; underground, 230–231, 260
'poisonous weeds', 20, 115, 117
political control, 197, 249, 250–251
pornographic writing, 253

posters, 207–208
'praise dances', 169–170; see also tableaux
'praise songs', 169
Precious Lotus Lamp, The, 247
Prelude, 225
'Pressure', 225
program music, 179
'Proletarian Cultural Revolution Is Really Good, The', 187
propaganda teams, 198, 198–199; see also Mao Zedong Thought Propaganda Teams
prose (sanwen), 229
Public Security Bureau, 121, 232
publishing, 87, 210, 223–224
puppets, 202
Pushkin, 228

Qi Benyu, 149
Qian Haoliang, 38, 39, 244
Qian Jiang, 124, 126, 128, 243
Qian Shouwei, 40
Qin Pengzhang, 190
Qing dynasty, 5, 149
Qingdao Spoken Drama Troupe, 199–200
Qinghai opera, 107
Qingming demonstrations (1976), 175, 230–231, 238, 239, 245, 298n27
Qionghua, 36
Qiu Shengrong, 66, 67
Qu Bo, 27, 267n35
Qu Wei, 188
'quotation songs', 182
quyi, 74, 91, 99, 201–202

radio, 81, 191, 194, 254, 256; songs on, 140, 180, 181; story-telling on, 201, 314n9
rap, Chinese, 189
rectification, 32, 94
Raid on the White-Tiger Regiment, 27, 29–31, 59, 133; film of, 118, 128–129
Rainy Night House Call, 190
Red Cloud Ridge, 84, 133
Red Crag, 61–62, 144
Red Detachment of Women, The: 1961 film, 36, 126, 128, 188; ballet, 57, 59, 155, 159–160, 164, 190, 261, 263n2; ballet filmed, 109, 117, 122–123, 124, 128, 129, 137; opera version, 36, 62, 68, 84, 130, 174–175, 246–247; other versions, 75
red and expert, 139, 208, 225

Red Flag, 42–43, 46, 59, 61, 91, 164,
    180–181, 213; publishes opera scripts,
    29, 30–31, 35, 39, 42, 66, 68
Red Flag Red Guards, 195–196
Red Flowers of Tianshan, 108
'Red Furnace Goes to the Mountains, The',
    225
Red Guards, 52, 121, 139, 173, 230, 239,
    251, 259; attack artists, 29, 37, 70, 190,
    202, 218; attack filmmakers, 115, 119,
    120, 131; in cultural organs, 71, 88, 203,
    207; performances by, 103, 169, 182,
    191, 194, 201, 229; spoken drama by,
    152, 193–196, 239, 255; publications,
    91, 194, 207, 210, 219, 222, 223;
    respond to Mao, 3, 7, 25, 26, 118, 184,
    203–204, 252–253; travel by, 94 117,
    148–149, 203–204
Red Guards of Lake Hong, 17, 178
Red Hawk of the Grasslands, 178
Red Lantern, The, 28, 32, 35, 40, 42, 89;
    creation of, 35–39, 46, 51, 57, 58, 70;
    filmed, 126, 128; music versions, 130,
    176, 184, 191; other versions, 75, 78–79;
    Uighur version, 75–76, 84, 105–106,
    108, 133; as model, 27, 58, 59, 60, 76,
    82, 207
Red Lantern Shines, The, 193–194
Red Leaves on the Fragrant Hills, 227
Red Odd-job Man, 83
Red Pine Fort, 200, 238–239
Red Sister-in-Law, 171
'Red Star Song, The', 187
Red Star Sparkles Splendidly, The, 185
regional opera, 45, 73–88, 255–256; *see
    also under names of different forms*
Rent Collection Courtyard, 194, 205–206
reportage, 221–222
Return, The, 217, 227, 247
Return to the Homeland, 227
*Reversing Verdicts Does Not Enjoy
    Popular Support*, 175
revisionism, 1, 175
Revolution Has Successors, The, 35; *see
    also Others Will Follow Us*
revolutionary committees, 118, 122, 196
revolutionary romanticism, 24, 145, 155,
    234
Revolutionary Successors, 82–83
rice sprouts dances, 158, 159
rice sprouts songs, 159, 172
'Rightist deviationist wind', 202, 213,
    237–238, 239, 245

Rightists, 31, 114
River, The, 190
roles, in opera, 48, 80–81
Romm, Mikhail, 151–152
Ruo Shi, 112
Russian novels, 228

Sacred Duty, The, 200
Sagabong, 78; *see also Shajiabang*:
    Cantonese opera version
salons, literary, 229–230, 260
Sang Hu, 129
Sartre, 228
Scarlet and the Black, The, 228
Schoenhals, Michael, 1, 5
Scout, The, 137
Scouting across the Yangzi, 136
sculpture, 74, 194, 205–206; *see also Rent
    Collection Courtyard*
Sea-river Village, 200
Second Handshake, The, 217, 226, 227,
    247–248, 253
Secret of the Axia River, 144
*Selected Poems and Lyrics from
    Xiaojinzhuang*, 223
self-criticism, 20–21
sent-down youth, 225, 251, 254–255, 260;
    art by, 187–188, 197, 214–215, 224; in
    art, 133–134, 173, 200, 226–230
Serf's Halberd, The, 196
'Serve the People', 198
sex, in dance, 165–168, 172
Sha Dan, 130
Shaanxi opera (*Qin qiang*), 84, 108
Shajiabang, 27, 44, 46, 57, 59, 89; creation
    of, 31–35; Cantonese opera version, 78,
    132, 134; other versions, 59, 74, 75, 77,
    78–79, 81, 133; filmed, 117, 128
Shajiabang symphony, 66, 84–85, 176,
    177, 178, 184, 190, 252; film of, 130,
    chorus version, 186
Shan Jianbo, 61
Shan Lianxiao, 58
Shandong opera, 21
Shandong Provincial Peking Opera
    Company, 30
Shandong Provincial Spoken Drama
    Company, 232
Shang Kuo, 215
Shanghai Animation Film Studio, 80,
    150–151
Shanghai Ballet Company, 160, 161–162,
    191

Shanghai City Culture Bureau, 27–28
Shanghai City Culture System
　Revolutionary Committee, 46
Shanghai City Dance School, 174, 191
Shanghai City Film Production Unit, 165
Shanghai City People's Shanghai Opera
　Company, 31, 59
'Shanghai Commune', 239
Shanghai Conservatory, 10, 29, 39, 41,
　176, 179, 188, 191
Shanghai Culture Publishing House, 28
Shanghai Dance School, 163
Shanghai Dialect Drama Company, 198
Shanghai Drama Academy, 193–194
Shanghai Film Projection Equipment
　Factory, 146
Shanghai Film Studio, 119, 119–120, 246,
　289n78; films model works, 73, 117,
　126, 165; feature films, 132, 135, 136,
　136–137, 144; staff of, 28, 133, 146–147,
　147
Shanghai Modern Musical Theatre Rebels,
　193
Shanghai Music Press, 179
Shanghai News Publishing House, 228–229
Shanghai opera (Huju), 15, 31, 36, 73–74,
　77, 97
Shanghai Peking Opera Company, 42, 70,
　73, 87, 133, 246
Shanghai Peking Opera Party Committee,
　28
Shanghai Peking Opera Theatre No. 1
　Company, 27
Shanghai People's Art Theatre, 193–194,
　198–199
Shanghai People's Huai Opera Company,
　40
Shanghai People's Publishing House, 87,
　221, 224, 225, 228–229
Shanghai People's Shanghai Opera
　Company, 35
Shanghai Puppet Theatre, 202
Shanghai Spoken Drama Company, 85
'Shanghai Spring', 162–163
Shanghai Symphony Orchestra, 107,
　177–178, 180, 185, 188, 190
Shanghai Youth and Children's Publishing
　House, 224–225
Shanghai Youth Peking and Kun Opera
　Company, 70–71
Shaanxi opera (Qin qiang), 84, 108
Shanxi opera (Jinju), 75, 79, 103, 233–234
Shaoshan, 205

Shaoxing opera, 17, 21, 58, 76, 77, 79, 80,
　97; in Stage Sisters, 114
Shen Fu, 24, 115, 293n134
Shen Xilin, 129
Shen Ximeng, 136
Shenzhen, 36
Shi Fangyu, 136
Sibelius, 180
Sichuan Academy of Fine Arts, 206
Sichuan Culture Bureau, 103
Sichuan opera (Chuanju), 17, 74, 78–79
Sihanouk, Norodom, 156, 190
Sima Qian, 228
singing, in operas, 44, 65; see also songs
Sister Aqing, 31, 32, 33, 46, 52, 54, 66, 132
Sisters of the Grassland, 213, 214
sixian opera, 75
Socialist Education Movement, 22, 23, 93,
　195, 233, 282n104
socialist realism, 13, 141–142; see also
　revolutionary romanticism
Song Jinxiu, 238
song and dance ensembles, 95, 101, 103;
　see also under troupe names
Song of the Dragon River, 42, 126, 128;
　making of, 62–66; transplanting of, 75,
　81, 105, 108
Song of the Mango, 139
Song of the Teachers, 79, 232–233, 234
Song of Youth, 284n4
songs, 176, 178, 180–182, 187–188; in
　ballets, 162; in films, 140, 142–143, 155;
　of model operas, 74, 81–82, 86–87
Sons and Daughters of the Grassland, 79,
　80, 170–171, 180
Sons and Daughters of Xisha, 221
Sorrows of the Forbidden City, 149
Soviet Union, 13, 107, 169, 170, 203, 221;
　and stage arts, 48, 85, 159, 195
Sparkling Red Star, 142–143, 174, 187,
　191, 202, 221
Sparks amid the Reeds, 15, 31, 32, 35, 40,
　51, 52, 59
specialists, 45, 123, 146–148, 169, 209,
　252; see also red and expert
Spindrift, 227, 247
spoken drama, 15, 17, 18, 85, 192–201,
　239, 306n123; influence on model
　operas, 11, 41, 48, 74; troupes, 91, 97,
　100, 102
sport, 332n1; see also ping pong
Spring in the Desert, 144
Spring in Dragon Bay, 200

Spring in Shanghai, 116
Spring on the State Farm, 224
Spring Thunder in the Southwest, 90, 196
stage design, 49–50
Stage Sisters, 19, 114, 126
State Council, 122, 238
State Council Culture Group, 65, 67
Stalin, 151–152, 203
Stanislavskian method, 85
Stendhal, 228
Storm over Gambia, 43
story-telling, 96, 201–202, 226; *see also*
    pingtan
street theatre, 74, 170, 195; *see also* Red
    Guards: performances by
Su Li, 128, 135–136
Su Yun, 118, 130
sung performance (*yanchang*), 103
Sunny Courtyard Story, 138
Super 8 film, 122, 153
Swan Lake, 161, 164

tableaux, 168, 194; *see also* Red Guards:
    performances by *and* street theatre
Taiwan, 70, 243
Taking the Road of 1917, 194
Taking Tiger Mountain by Strategy, 46, 47,
    59, 61, 66, 82; creation of, 27–29, 30,
    42, 45, 70, 72; film of, 117, 123–126,
    128, 154; music of, 38–39, 44, 63–64;
    transplanted, 74, 75, 78–79, 105–106;
    comic book, 224
Taking Tiger Mountain by Strategy
    symphony, 84–85, 177–178, 185, 188
Tan school, 32
Tan Yuanshou, 32, 32–33, 57
Tang Guoqiang, 199–200
Tang Jiang, 191
Tang Xiaobing, 7
Tang Xiaodan, 136
Tangju (Tangshan style opera), 75
Tao Lan, 112, 143–144
Tao Xiong, 72
Tchaikovsky, 177
television, 81, 179, 283n118; local stations,
    105, 200, 281n79; records new works,
    80, 84, 129, 164–165, 169, 287n61
Tempest on Miao Ridge, 79
Tempest Song, 178
*Ten Thousand Rivers and a Thousand
    Mountains*, 200
Theatre Journal (*Xiju bao*), 15–16, 21, 57,
    59

Theatre Script (*Juben*), 28, 36
Third Sister Liu, 128, 178
Third World, 40, 43, 150–151, 195
'three aims', 80
'three combinations', 118, 221
Three Kingdoms, The, 224
three prominences, 47, 54, 204, 220; in
    model operas, 34–35, 46–48, 125, 166; in
    feature films, 140–141, 241, 243
'three smashes', 80
Tian Han, 24, 193
Tian'anmen Square, 184, 230–231, 235,
    245, 261; *see also* Qingming
    demonstrations (1976)
Tianjin Acrobatic Troupe, 90
Tianjin City Peking Opera Company, 17
Tianjin City People's Art Theatre, 90
Tianjin City Third Peking Opera Troupe,
    201
Tianjin Daily, 89
Tianjin Hebei *Bangzi* Opera Company, 133
Tianjin Literature and Art, 225
Tianjin Northern Opera Company, 90
Tianjin *Quyi* Troupe, 201
Tianma Film Studio, 116, 129, 136, 247
Tianshan Film Studio, 133
Tibet, 75
Tibetan opera, 107
Ticket to the Stars, A, 228
Tong Xiangling, 28, 73
Tracks in the Snowy Forest, 27
transplanting, 55, 61, 105–106, 132–133,
    133–134, 254; across genres, 130, 174,
    174–175, 201; of model operas, 59,
    73–88, 89, 108
trail performance conventions, 12, 77; *see
    also* modern-subject Peking opera trial
    performance convention (1964)
Tsinghua University, 205, 244, 300n57
Tsinghua University Amateur Literature
    and Art Team, 175
Tumultuous Clouds Fly, 190
Tunnel Warfare, 150
Turkey, 179

Uighur minority, 104, 105, 234, 303n77;
    musical drama, 74, 75, 84, 108, 133
Ulan Muchir performance troupes, 32, 106
Under the Grape Trellis, 234
underground cultural production, 3,
    226–231, 253, 254–255
United States, 190, 195, 227; *see also*
    Nixon, Richard

Unquiet Seashore, The, 231–232
'Up to the Mountains, Down to the Villages Educated-Youth Writing Series', 224
Urgent Letter, 150

vernacular modernism, 7–8, 257
Vietnam, 151
Voynich, Ethel Lillian, 228

wages, 98, 99–100
Wang Dachun, 161, 162, 165, 166, 167–168
Wang Guangmei, 233
Wang Haowei, 243
Wang Hongwen, 239
Wang Jianzhong, 188
Wang Jinxi, 240
Wang Junzheng, 147–148
Wang Mantian, 311n190
Wang Ming, 62
Wang Renyuan, 44–45
Wang Shuyuan, 68
Wang Tugen, 141
Wang Xiaosheng, 225
Wang Yang, 120. 128, 136
Wang Zengqi, 31, 67
wanwanqiang opera, 84
War-horse Cries, 172–173
'Waves', 227
War of Resistance against Japan, *see* Anti-Japanese War
We Are All Sunflowers, 134
Weng Ouhong, 36, 39, 70
Wenhui bao, 20, 179
Western culture, 5–6, 7
Western music, 157, 175–176, 176–177, 177, 179–180, 188, 189, 190–191; influence in modern opera, 44, 45, 182; instruments, 30, 33, 44, 63–64, 130
White-Haired Girl, The: ballet, 57, 59, 116, 159–160, 161–164, 165–166, 171; film version, 129; opera, 174–175; other versions, 75, 180, 188
White-Haired Girl Suite, The, 185
White Snake, 52
Wild Boar Forest, 131–132
Wild Swans, 3
'willow plays', 107
women, 52–53, 208
Women of Nanjiang Village, 151
woodblock prints, 210–211, 213–214
worker, peasant, soldiers, 13, 15, 24, 43, 60
Worker, Peasant and Soldier Literature and Art, 82

Wrath of the Serfs, 310n173
'write about 13 years', 14
writers, of opera, 43
Writers Association, 219
Wu Han, 14–15, 19–20, 24, 25, 111, 193, 207
Wu opera, 80
Wu Qinghua, 68, 155, 160, 166–167, 257
Wu Xiaopei, 120
Wu Zetian, 21
Wu Zhaodi, 128, 135–136
Wuxi opera (*Xiju*), 21, 107

Xia Yan, 16, 23, 94, 113
Xi'an Conservatory, 176
Xi'an Film Studio, 116, 117–118, 146
Xian Xinghai, 130, 185–186
Xiang Kun, 144
Xiangjiang Literature and Art, 225, 232
Xiao Jianqiu, 112
Xiaojinzhuang, 81–82, 85–86, 104, 237
Xie Fang, 143–144, 247–248
Xie Jin, 114, 126–128, 139, 145
Xie Tian, 120
Xie Tieli, 112, 120, 124, 125, 126, 131, 243
Xie Yaohuan, 21
Xi'er, 161, 162, 167–168
Xiju bao, *see Theatre Journal*
Xing Ye, 136
Xinjiang Daily, 104
Xinjiang Song, Dance and Spoken Drama Company, 75–76
Xinhua Peking Opera Company, 63
Xu Yinsheng, 32, 38

Yan Fu, 263n5
Yan Liangkun, 190–191
Yan school, 33
Yan Weicai, 29–30, 50
Yan'an, 32, 117; art and literature at, 22, 36, 61, 189, 204, 222; artists' connections with, 23, 124, 126, 128, 129, 190–191, 218; and *The White-Haired Girl*, 159, 161, 163, 164
Yan'an *Talks* (1942), 6, 19, 61, 145, 159, 183; anniversaries of, 89: (22nd) 162–163, (24th) 89, (25th) 57, (26th) 164–165, (27th) 91, (28th) 185, (30th) 76, 92, 102, 128, 211, (31st) 92, (33rd) 84, 150, (34th) 202, 239; study of, 104, 235
Yang Cunbin, 41
Yang Hansheng, 114, 115

Yang Jian, 229, 230
Yang Lin, 170
Yang Zirong, 27, 37, 50, 53, 64, 260;
    creation of, 28–29, 47, 48, 49, 61; on
    film, 124, 126; images of, 29, 31, 106,
    207, 257, 258; popularity of, 29, 31, 106
yangbanxi, see model performances
Yangzhou opera (Yangju), 107
Yao Wenyuan, 21, 65–66, 179, 193, 202,
    233–234
Yellow Earth, The, 37, 214, 260
Yellow River, The (piano concerto), 84–85,
    130, 176
Yellow River Cantata, 130, 176, 184,
    185–186, 191
Yi Dan, 213
Yin Chengzong, 130, 184, 185, 251–252
Ying Yunei, 28
youth, 139; see also sent-down youth
Youth, 145
Youth in the Flames of Battle, 148
Youth Like Fire, 144
Youthful Generation, A, 136–137
Yu Deshui, 132
Yu Huiyong, 10, 12, 41, 244, 246,
    256–257; work on model operas, 29, 30,
    33, 63–64, 67, 72; on songs, 188, 189;
    comments on art, 38–39, 46, 127, 178
Yu Lan, 61
Yu Li'na, 185
Yu school, 33
Yu Shan, 136
Yu Yanfu, 241, 242
Yu Yang, 143
Yuan Binzhong, 37
Yuan Fang, 191
Yuan Xuefen, 58
Yun Song, 193
Yung, Bell, 78
Yunnan Literature and Art, 187
Yunnan opera (Dianju), 83, 100, 101, 102
Yunnan Song and Dance Company, 100

Zhang Chunqiao, 20–21, 30, 239, 244,
    294n161; and model operas, 36, 41, 64,
    65–66; and music, 179, 180

Zhang Dechun, 41
Zhang Geng, 44
Zhang Jianya, 146–147
Zhang Kangkang, 225
Zhang Lihui, 30
Zhang Ruifang, 117, 136, 137
Zhang Tianyi, 241, 242
Zhang Yang, 217, 218, 226, 227, 247
Zhang Yongmei, 39, 69
Zhang Zhen, 7–8
Zhang Zhenqi, 214
Zhang Zhongpeng, 135
Zhao Dan, 61, 115, 247, 264n10, 275n13
Zhao Ming, 136–137
Zhao Qing, 247
Zhao Shuli, 115, 218–219
Zhao Sihai, 140–141, 143
Zhao Yanxia, 66
Zhao Yifan, 230
Zhao Yonggang, 69
Zhe Ping
Zhejiang Academy of Arts, 207, 209, 211
Zhejiang Culture Bureau, 98
Zhejiang People's Publishing House, 80
Zheng Junli, 115
Zheng Lücheng, 301n67
Zhong Runliang, 164
Zhong Wenyu, 47
Zhongnanhai, 1
Zhou Enlai, 123, 179, 190–191, 235,
    239–240; death of, 230–231, 237–238;
    and film, 122–123, 131, 134, 146, 243,
    244; on literature and art, 75, 132, 171,
    224; watches model works, 16, 28, 163,
    199
Zhou Keqin, 225
Zhou Tingshan, 240–241
Zhou Xinfang, 265n12, 266n24
Zhou Yang, 23, 25, 94, 113, 164
Zhu De, 205
Zhu Lin, 224–225
Zhu Sujin, 225
Zhuang minority, 178
Zhuang opera (Zhuangju), 77
Zou Zhi'an, 225
Zunyi Conference, 191